HUME'S *ESSAYS*

David Hume's *Essays*, which were written and published at various junctures between 1741 and his death in 1776, offer his most accessible and often most profound statements on a range of subjects including politics, philosophy, aesthetics, and political economy. In Hume's lifetime, the readable and wide-ranging *Essays* acquired considerable fame throughout Europe and North America, influencing the writings of such diverse figures as James Madison and William Paley, yet they have not been given the same scholarly attention as his more famous philosophical works. This Critical Guide provides a series of in-depth studies of the *Essays*, as well as an account of the state of scholarship on the work. The thirteen chapters examine the *Essays* from historical, political, and philosophical perspectives, with the aim of restoring the work to its rightful place among Hume's works and in intellectual history more broadly.

MAX SKJÖNSBERG is Assistant Professor of Humanities in the Hamilton Center for Classical and Civic Education at the University of Florida. He is the author of *The Persistence of Party: Ideas of Harmonious Discord in Eighteenth-Century Britain* (Cambridge University Press, 2021) and the editor of Catharine Macaulay's *Political Writings* (Cambridge University Press, 2023).

FELIX WALDMANN is a Fellow of Corpus Christi College, Cambridge. He is editing the Clarendon Edition of David Hume's *Dialogues Concerning Natural Religion* and *Occasional Writings*.

CAMBRIDGE CRITICAL GUIDES

Titles published in this series:

(Continued after the Index)

HUME'S *ESSAYS*

A Critical Guide

EDITED BY

MAX SKJÖNSBERG

University of Florida

FELIX WALDMANN

University of Cambridge

CAMBRIDGE
UNIVERSITY PRESS

Shaftesbury Road, Cambridge CB2 8EA, United Kingdom

One Liberty Plaza, 20th Floor, New York, NY 10006, USA

477 Williamstown Road, Port Melbourne, VIC 3207, Australia

314–321, 3rd Floor, Plot 3, Splendor Forum, Jasola District Centre, New Delhi – 110025, India

103 Penang Road, #05-06/07, Visioncrest Commercial, Singapore 238467

Cambridge University Press is part of Cambridge University Press & Assessment, a department of the University of Cambridge.

We share the University's mission to contribute to society through the pursuit of education, learning and research at the highest international levels of excellence.

www.cambridge.org
Information on this title: www.cambridge.org/9781316517727

DOI: 10.1017/9781009047227

First published 2025

A catalogue record for this publication is available from the British Library.

Library of Congress Cataloging-in-Publication Data
NAMES: Skjönsberg, Max, 1987- editor. | Waldmann, Felix, editor.
TITLE: Hume's essays : a critical guide / edited by Max Skjönsberg, University of Florida; Felix Waldmann, University of Cambridge.
DESCRIPTION: Cambridge ; New York, NY : Cambridge University Press, 2024. | Includes bibliographical references and index.
IDENTIFIERS: LCCN 2024029171 (print) | LCCN 2024029172 (ebook) | ISBN 9781316517727 (hardback) | ISBN 9781009048361 (paperback) | ISBN 9781009047227 (epub)
CLASSIFICATION: LCC B1498 .H9295 2024 (print) | LCC B1498 (ebook) | DDC 192–DC23/eng/20240731
LC record available at https://lccn.loc.gov/2024029171
LC ebook record available at https://lccn.loc.gov/2024029172

ISBN 978-1-316-51772-7 Hardback

To James Harris

Contents

Figures

Contributors

ROSS CARROLL Dublin City University

DANIELLE CHARETTE University of North Carolina, Chapel Hill

TIMOTHY M. COSTELLOE College of William & Mary

TOM HOPKINS Selwyn College, University of Cambridge

R. J. W. MILLS University of St Andrews

LAURA NICOLÌ University of Turin and the Voltaire Foundation

MARGARET SCHABAS University of British Columbia

MAX SKJÖNSBERG Hamilton Center, University of Florida

MARK G. SPENCER Brock University

TIM STUART-BUTTLE University of York

MIKKO TOLONEN University of Helsinki

SYLVANA TOMASELLI St John's College, University of Cambridge

FELIX WALDMANN Corpus Christi College, University of Cambridge

MARGARET WATKINS Providence College

LINA WEBER Independent Scholar

Acknowledgements

The editors thank Hilary Gaskin for supporting this project, the anonymous readers of the proposal and manuscript, and the Press's production team. In addition to writing his own chapter, Robin Mills prepared the Index and assisted at various stages throughout the project, and we are deeply grateful to him. Pedro Faria and Elena Yi-Jia Zeng also played instrumental roles in producing this Guide and we renew our thanks to them for their learned assistance. Finally, we thank the contributors to this volume for their generosity and patience.

James Harris offered important advice at the start of the project. Hume scholars, present and future, are indebted to James for his contributions to Hume scholarship and much else. This volume is dedicated to him.

Abbreviations

The following abbreviations are used in the notes:

E (C)   David Hume, *Essays, Moral, Political, and Literary: A Critical Edition*, ed. Tom L. Beauchamp and Mark A. Box (2 vols., Oxford, 2021).

E (LF)   David Hume, *Essays, Moral, Political, and Literary*, ed. Eugene F. Miller, rev. ed. (Indianapolis, IN, 1987).

EHU   David Hume, *An Enquiry Concerning Human Understanding: A Critical Edition*, ed. Tom L. Beauchamp (Oxford, 2000).

EPM   David Hume, *An Enquiry Concerning the Principles of Morals: A Critical Edition*, ed. Tom L. Beauchamp (Oxford, 1998).

HE   David Hume, *The History of England: From the Invasion of Julius Caesar to the Revolution in 1688*, ed. William B. Todd (6 vols., Indianapolis, IN, 1983).

HL   David Hume, *The Letters of David Hume*, ed. J. Y. T. Greig (2 vols., Oxford, 1932).

NHL   David Hume, *New Letters of David Hume*, ed. Raymond Klibansky and Ernest Campbell Mossner (Oxford, 1954).

T   David Hume, *A Treatise of Human Nature: A Critical Edition*, ed. David Fate Norton and Mary J. Norton (2 vols., Oxford, 2007).

Hume never published a work with the one-word title 'Essays'. The work discussed in this Guide originated with Hume's *Essays, Moral and Political* (first edition, 1741), a title that was retained by Hume in two subsequent editions (1742) and (1748), before he adopted the title *Essays and Treatises on Several Subjects* (first edition, 1753). The latter constituted an amalgam of *Essays, Moral and Political* and Hume's *Political Discourses* (first edition, 1752). In 1760, Hume adopted the title *Essays, Moral, Political, and Literary* (first edition, London, 1760), which constituted a new amalgam of *Essays and Treatises on Several Subjects* with Hume's *Four Dissertations* (1757). An explanation of the bibliographical complexity involved in the commingling of these editions is beyond the scope of this Guide, but it is fortunately now the subject of careful study in *E* (C).

E (C) has superseded *E* (LF), which had served as the standard edition since its publication in 1987. The chapters here refer to both editions by their sigla to facilitate cross-referencing between existing scholarship – which has almost always used *E* (LF) – and any future scholarship – which ought now to prefer *E* (C). The transcriptions restrictedly favour the readings in *E* (C).

Introduction

Max Skjönsberg and Felix Waldmann

The objective of this Critical Guide is to provide a series of in-depth studies on the *Essays* of David Hume, as well as an account of the state of scholarship. In Hume's lifetime, the *Essays* acquired considerable *éclat* throughout Europe and North America; they influenced the writings of such diverse figures as James Madison and William Paley, and they have since become a staple of undergraduate and graduate curricula in history, politics, and philosophy. Yet the *Essays* have received comparatively modest attention in the scholarship of Hume's life and thought. The early tradition of Hume's intellectual biography, pioneered by J. Y. T. Greig and Ernest Campbell Mossner, subordinated the *Essays* to Hume's *Treatise* and *Enquiries* as monuments of Hume's contribution to the history of philosophy. This tendency diminished in the 1970s and 1980s, when Duncan Forbes, J. G. A. Pocock and Istvan Hont placed the *Essays* at the heart of their studies of Hume's political thought and political economy.[1] The significance of the *Essays* in James Harris's *Hume: An Intellectual Biography* (2015) bears witness to the importance that the work has since acquired in general reconstructions of Hume's intellectual commitments. However, there is no 'critical guide' to Hume's *Essays* in any language, with recent studies having focused more restrictively on Hume's political economy.[2] This book is intended to address this absence

---

[1] Duncan Forbes, *Hume's Philosophical Politics* (Cambridge, 1975); J. G. A. Pocock, 'Hume and the American Revolution: The Dying Thoughts of a North Britain', in J. G. A. Pocock, *Virtue, Commerce and History: Essays on Political Thought and History* (Cambridge, 1985), pp. 125–41; Istvan Hont, *Jealousy of Trade: International Competition and the Nation State in Historical Perspective* (Cambridge, MA, 2005).

[2] Carl Wennerlind and Margaret Schabas, eds., *David Hume's Political Economy* (New York, 2008); Angela Coventry and Andrew Walls, eds., *David Hume on Morals, Politics, and Society* (New Haven, CT, 2018). Hume's *History of England* has received comparatively greater attention: David Fate Norton and Richard H. Popkin, eds., *David Hume: Philosophical Historian* (Indianapolis, IN, 1965); Nicholas Capaldi and Donald Livingston, eds., *Liberty in Hume's History of England* (Dordrecht, 1990); Mark G. Spencer, ed., *David Hume: Historical Thinker, Historical Writer* (University Park, PA, 2013).

by providing scholars and students with a wide-ranging and accessible overview of the *Essays*. The recent publication of the Clarendon Edition of Hume's *Essays* (*E* (C)) is timed propitiously. The extraordinary editorial work of Professor Beauchamp and Professor Box has provided an unparalleled resource for the interpretation of the *Essays*, with a rich apparatus and a granular account of the complex history of the work's publication. This Critical Guide has benefitted enormously from their labours.

Hume wrote in the advertisement to the first two books of *A Treatise of Human Nature* (1739) that he intended to 'proceed to the examination of morals, politics, and criticism'.[3] His ambition was partly fulfilled by the third book of the *Treatise*, 'Of Morals', which he published in the following year.[4] Yet 'politics' and 'criticism', the latter comprising literature, aesthetics, and taste, were more substantively explored in the *Essays*, which he published in two volumes in 1741 (fifteen essays) and 1742 (twelve essays). In a succession of editions, Hume added new essays, revising the existing essays continuously, and withdrew others entirely. *E* (C) builds its 'critical text' of the *Essays* on the basis of twenty-two distinctive 'editions', although the term must be used carefully. One such edition was Hume's *Political Discourses* (1752), which introduced a series of new essays to the collection. According to Hume's own testimony in his autobiography, 'My Own Life' (1776), *Political Discourses* was the only publication in his lifetime that was successful on its first printing.[5] The *Essays* and the *Political Discourses* were published together as part of Hume's four-volume *Essays and Treatises on Several Subjects*, first appearing in 1753 and continuously republished with alterations from the 1750s through to the 1770s. For the 1772 edition of the *Essays*, Hume claimed to have carefully read the proofs five times over.[6] It is evident that he considered the work as a testament to his ingenuity; the posthumous edition of 1777 was to have included 'My Own Life', intimating the close association he had hoped to establish between the *Essays* and his accomplishments.

The Critical Guide begins by considering the eighteenth-century reception of the *Essays* (Part I), before examining their statements on philosophy and religion (Part II), politics (Part III), and political economy (Part IV). The richness of Hume's varied statements on philosophy, aesthetics,

---

[3] *T*, I, p. 2.
[4] Nicholas Phillipson, *David Hume* (Oxford, 2011), ch. 2; James A. Harris, *Hume: An Intellectual Biography* (Cambridge, 2015), pp. 154–66.
[5] *E* (LF), p. xxxvi.   [6] *HL*, II, p. 235.

politics, rhetoric, and political economy provoked a varied Anglophone and European reception. In Chapter 1, on Hume's British readers, Mark G. Spencer and Mikko Tolonen provide a synopsis of their wide-ranging investigation into textual reuse – a component of a wider programme of employing tools in digital humanities to study the reception of early modern texts. The frequent incidence of reuses of the *Essays* is more effectually recoverable by this process. Spencer and Tolonen have identified 1,050 cases of text reuse of Hume's essays in the eighteenth century, hundreds of which are 'hitherto unstudied'. These reuses ranged from plagiarism to paraphrase, where Hume's work was 'interpreted, even moulded' by authors to convey 'the gist of Hume's meanings or what they wanted it to be'. The duplicative processes of reuse often obscured Hume's authorship: *The Mitre and Crown* (1750) reprinted selections of 'no fewer than eight of Hume's essays' without attribution, except by reference to *The Craftsman*, where the essays had also appeared without attribution. Yet Hume's reception was not always silent. In primary-source compilations and popular 'readers', he found an extensive audience; these works, such as *The Beauties of English Prose* (1772), arguably 'served to bring Hume's essays, and usually his name, to many more readers than did any edition of his *Essays*'. The reuse of the essays in 'specialised compilations' on trade and commerce had the same dual character, sometimes in the space of one publication: the express attribution of the material to 'the ingenious Mr. Hume' in Malachy Postlethwayt's *The Universal Dictionary of Trade and Commerce* (1757) was coupled with the silent reuse of material elsewhere in the volume. Spencer and Tolonen trace the sentiment of the reception of the *Essays*, chronicling a distinctive shift from negative assessments prior to the 1760s to the laudatory appellations that attended Hume's 'canonization process' in the later eighteenth century.

In Chapter 2, on Hume's German reception, Lina Weber reveals the effects of this canonicity. By the later eighteenth century, pseudo-translations of works attributed to Hume revealed the 'significant reputation' that Hume enjoyed in German lands, 'such that publishers could expect to sell more copies of a travel guide if they presented it as a translation of a work by Hume'. Weber examines the publication history of Hume's *Vermischte Schriften*, a translation of Hume's *Essays and Treatises on Several Subjects* in four volumes that appeared between 1754 and 1756 in Hamburg and Leipzig. Hume's work was presented as 'markedly different and superior to German political and economic writings'. The reception of the collection was muted. German review journals had praised the English originals and French translations of the various essays as 'the most useful and innovative of Hume's publications'.[7] In contrast, *Vermischte Schriften* 'was almost entirely ignored'. Weber observes that this attenuated reception 'lies in the specifics of cameralism', whose adherents were warmer proponents of physiocracy. Isaak Iselin read Hume's *Essays* in the French translation twice in 1755, but had 'difficulties comprehending them' and 'discounted Hume's view on luxury as overly positive'. In the later eighteenth century, translators 'tried to integrate Hume's writings into German reform debates in the aftermath of the French Revolution'. Christian August Fischer's edition of Hume's essays, *David Hume's Geist*, which Fischer conjoined with a biographical sketch, presented Hume's work as the embodiment of a 'spirit of peace and moderation, of agreeableness and tolerance', which could countervail revolutionary fanaticism. In another guise, Garlieb Merkel's translation of 'Of the Original Contract' and Rousseau's *Du Contrat Social* (1762), published as *Hume's und Rousseau's Abhandlungen über den Urvertrag* (1797), utilised Hume in his 'effort to abolish the institution of serfdom in his native Livonia'.

In Chapter 3, Laura Nicolì extends this overview of Hume's reception to France. Hume's residence in Paris between 1763 and 1766 was foregrounded by his celebrity status and terminated with the regrettable apogee of his public life, his 'contestation' with Rousseau. As Nicolì notes, it is 'commonly acknowledged that Hume's intellectual relationship with French thinkers represents something of a paradox'. Although Hume was 'highly valued, the core of his philosophical thought remained basically uncomprehended in eighteenth-century France'. Moreover, Hume 'never felt comfortable with the militant ideological afflatus of the *philosophes*'. The Le Blanc, Mauvillon, and Mérian translations were the most prominent of those that appeared in French; others, such as the anonymous *Essais sur le commerce*, published in Amsterdam in 1766 and attributed tentatively to Turgot, diffused Hume's judgements to a Francophone readership by decoupling the essays on political economy from the remainder of his *Essays*. In addition to published books, the curiosity of French readers was satisfied by 'translations, summaries, excerpts, and reviews' that 'came out in periodicals almost without interruption'. These were not merely derivative of the published volumes. Nicolì conjectures that Nicolas-Claude Thieriot, with the collaboration of Voltaire, provided the first translation of 'Of National Characters'. The extent of interest commanded

[7] Günther Gawlick and Lothar Kreimendahl, *Hume in der Deutschen Aufklärung, Umrisse einer Rezeptionsgeschichte* (Stuttgart-Bad Cannstatt, 1987), pp. 68–70.

by Hume's writings was reflected by the translation in manuscript, evidently 'for her own amusement', by the young woman of letters Geneviève de Malboissière. France provided a separate venue for the publication of Hume's suppressed essays, 'Of Suicide' and 'Of the Immortality of the Soul', which found their way into print in 1770 through the offices of the Baron d'Holbach and his *coterie*. Nicolì shows that the process of translation was not free of interpolation; the addition of a 'heavy paratext' by Le Blanc typified the tendency of translators 'strategically' to direct their reader 'to a certain interpretation of the work'. In Nicolì's judgement, the *parti pris* conduct of reading and translation reflected a general inclination among Hume's French readers 'to find in Hume's words an exit from despotism and a path towards social happiness'. The chapter is keyed to three online open-access appendices: a chronology of eighteenth-century French translations of Hume's *Essays*; an inventory of publications and review of Hume's *Essays* in eighteenth-century French periodicals; and some other French reuses and responses to Hume's *Essays*.

In Chapter 4, Margaret Watkins returns to the subject of her recent monograph on the *Essays* as 'philosophy'.[8] Watkins contends that 'the form of the *Essays* implies an ongoing philosophical project with a significant sceptical difference from the systemic form of the *Treatise*'. In the latter, Hume conducts a search for general principles 'within a bounded domain': the human mind. In the *Essays*, Hume broadens his scope to an 'expanded set of questions'. A 'remarkable' difference in form distinguishes the works further. The *Treatise* has a 'unity of shape', which the *Essays* lack, with their frequent recourse to 'dichotomies or more complex divisions'. As Watkins observes, Hume often 'guides his readers through this process multiple times within a single essay. And the available branches at the end may not be at all what they appeared at the beginning'. If the *Treatise* portrays philosophy 'as a project one might complete', the *Essays* 'teach that philosophical thinking is never complete': 'a more profoundly sceptical pedagogy'.

In Chapter 5, this interest in form complements Tim Stuart-Buttle's exploration of Hume's 'essays on happiness', the term coined by John Immerwahr to describe 'The Epicurean', 'The Stoic', 'The Platonist' and 'The Sceptic', the four essays unified by a shared objective 'to explain accurately the sentiments of the ancient sects of philosophy'. As Stuart-Buttle writes, the essays 'disclose the extent of Hume's attentiveness to the relationship between literary form and philosophical content'. To interpret

---

[8] Margaret Watkins, *The Philosophical Progress of Hume's Essays* (Cambridge, 2019).

the essays, we must accept 'Hume's caution to his reader that each essay is an exercise in "personation" or philosophical ventriloquism'. Stuart-Buttle asks why Hume adopts the form of a monologue, in lieu of the more conventional use of dialogue. The answer lies with Hume's judgement of the dialogic form, as practised by Cicero, in which the interlocutors are guided to truth by the admonition and intercession of the wiser symposiast. Hume had identified the value of employing the ancient sects as analogues to the interlocutors in modern philosophical debate; as Stuart-Buttle notes, 'modern moral philosophers identified themselves – or, more commonly, their antagonists – with one or other of the ancient sects, by critiquing those sects an author could comment indirectly (but intelligibly) on the errors of their modern disciples'. Yet no one *porte-parole* of the sects speaks for Hume: 'the Stoic offers criticisms of the Epicurean, the Platonist of the Stoic and Epicurean, and the Sceptic of all three that there is good reason to think Hume shared'. No philosophy 'displaces the other'. Where the younger Hume had favoured Stoicism as his guide, with ruinous consequences, the Hume of the *Essays* enjoins his readers to 'sample the works of representatives of *all* the philosophical schools, because doing so will lead to self-knowledge'.

In Chapter 6, the purpose of philosophy recurs as the subject of Timothy Costelloe's discussion of aesthetics and the arts in the *Essays*. It is in connection with the discussion of 'the arts' and its synonyms that Hume contributed to 'aesthetics', although he never formulated a 'systematic presentation of his views'. Costelloe notes that the closest Hume came to this systematic exposition was in the series of essays devoted to 'pertinent topics', which Costelloe dubs the 'aesthetic essays': 'Of the Delicacy of Taste and Passion', 'Of Eloquence', 'Of Simplicity and Refinement in Writing', 'Of Tragedy', and 'Of the Standard of Taste'. The essays cannot be interpreted independently of the 'more general principles that Hume had framed already', which Costelloe illustrates with case studies of Hume on taste, literary style and artistic representation, tragedy, and the history and political economy of the arts. The application of these general principles is revealed by the parallel between the discovery of the general principles of morals, accessible by analysing 'that complication of moral qualities' that constitute 'PERSONAL MERIT', as Hume had noted in his *Enquiry Concerning the Principles of Morals* (1751), and the discovery of the 'principles of taste', which can be 'ascertained by analysing qualities of objects that constitute *aesthetic* merit, and this is achieved methodologically by cataloguing works that excite "durable admiration"', as Hume would note in 'Of the Standard of Taste'.

The *Essays* may seem to not have much to say about religion, with 'Of Superstition and Enthusiasm' (1741) being the exception. In Chapter 7, however, R. J. W. Mills shows that when the topic of religion arises in the *Essays*, we find Hume outlining the character and dangers of institutional religion on individual happiness and social stability and doing so in a analytical manner characteristic of his wider 'science of man'. Mills argues that Hume reduced religious belief and priestly power to the level of any other aspect of human life, susceptible of the 'scientific' observation that could lead to the identification of general principles. Piecing together Hume's various discussions of religion in the *Essays*, Mills finds Hume articulating a strong anticlericalism, in which religion is understood to be a natural propensity of human nature, exploited by priesthoods claiming power over others. In Hume's judgement, this exploitation required the subordination of church to state and our scepticism about clerical power.

In Chapter 8, Danielle Charette observes that Hume's concern with general principles is reaffirmed in the ostensibly 'speculative' 'Idea of a Perfect Commonwealth'. Charette clarifies that this essay is cogently interpretable as a response not only to Harrington's *Oceana* (1656) but also to Montesquieu's *Spirit of the Laws* (1748), particularly Montesquieu's criticism of *Oceana* in his chapter 'On the English Constitution', which might have 'prompted Hume to devise his alternative version of Harrington's commonwealth'. Hume attacked Harrington's definition of a commonwealth 'at both its "foundation" (i.e. the Agrarian law) and its "superstructure" (i.e. equal rotation)'. Hume's intention was to rebuild an *Oceana* according to 'different principles'. Though he was not inclined to hem this contemplated republic within narrow territorial bounds; we should resist 'the conventional assumption that Hume wrote "Perfect Commonwealth" with the aim of undermining Montesquieu's position that republican states must be small'. Moreover, Hume did not conceive of the Perfect Commonwealth as a utopia, a place of non-existence in the ambiguous sense conveyed by the term; the exercise was worth pursuing 'so that we may be able to bring any real constitution or form of government as near as possible' to the most perfect model, 'by such gentle alterations and innovations as may not give too great disturbance to society'.[9] In this, Hume was obedient to the observable restrictions of political society and the lessons of history. Hume accepted 'Harrington's basic thesis that an historical shift in the balance of property had empowered parliament and transformed England into a government of

---

[9] *E* (LF), pp. 513–14, *E* (C), p. 363.

laws', but 'he did not conclude that this shift necessitated a return to either the "equal agrarian" or "equal rotation" of offices on which Harrington founded Oceana'. Instead, Hume adapted Harrington's electoral framework to the spirit of commerce and competition that he and Montesquieu associated with modern England.

In Chapter 9, Max Skjönsberg illuminates another significant aspect of Hume's political thought: party. As Skjönsberg notes, 'Whig-Tory as well as Court-Country alignments' were 'integral' to British politics as Hume conceived of it, 'with the former dividing the political nation along religious and at least to an extent dynastic lines, and the latter reflecting parliamentary conflict and the workings of the mixed and balanced constitution'. Hume's historical inclinations are again present in 'Of Parties in General', with its recitation of the incidence of party in present and past polities. Party revealed the operation of a general tendency in human nature 'to dispute and seek to convert others'. 'Of the Parties of Great Britain' expressed a similar tendency to generalizable propositions about the conduct of politics; in Hume's judgement, 'party division was inevitable in mixed governments such as the British, delicately balanced between its monarchical and republican elements'. Hume returned to the contents of this essay in the ensuing years, revising it more than any other, as he sought to keep pace with the permutations of the political landscape, particularly in the form of Jacobitism in relation to the rising of 'Forty-five'. 'Of the Original Contract', 'Of Passive Obedience', and 'Of the Protestant Succession' each embodied Hume's critical engagement with the shibboleths of party in mid eighteenth-century England and Scotland. Each exemplified Hume's intention to 'sound a note of moderation amid division and pacify party animosity by revealing the strengths and weaknesses of the Tories' and Whigs' ideologies alike'.

As Ross Carroll observes in Chapter 10, this preparedness to contemplate the merits of legislation extended to Hume's discussion of political rhetoric. 'Of Eloquence' has confounded scholars on account of Hume's overt praise for 'ancient examples of political practice, particularly given his sensitivity to the historical gulf separating ancient and modern societies, and his unease with the demagoguery he considered characteristic of ancient polities'; the essay 'risks incoherence because Hume seems to backtrack in the essay's final paragraphs on his initial recommendation that English orators emulate the ancients'. In Carroll's judgement, the essay 'does possess an underlying coherence and offers a compelling account of both why English oratory had lagged behind that of other nations such as France and how it could yet be reformed'. Remedying this deficiency demanded the recognition that its cause was owed 'less to the unsuitability of pathetic speech to a modern commercial society, than to the peculiar place of Parliament in Britain's mixed constitutional order'. This conceit was criticised by Hugh Blair, who believed Hume 'had possibly overstated the similarity between the popular assemblies of Athens or Rome and the eighteenth-century House of Commons'. Moreover, it required a defence of a Parliament in its present form, where the crown could dispose of offices of state – the mark of corruption, according to Country sentiment. The reform of rhetoric envisioned by Hume necessitated his readers' concession that 'deliberative oratory had always to compete for the attention of listeners with the distant directives and inducements of the Court'. But to reform the latter – to the detriment of the crown's influence – would jeopardise 'England's peculiar constitutional order'.

This concern about the threats posed to political society in England suffuses several essays, but it acquires unusual prominence in Hume's treatment of political economy. The essays on political economy were not uniformly alarmist enjoinders to reform, although Hume's warning over the threat posed by public debt is perhaps his best known pronouncement in the work *en bloc*. Sylvana Tomaselli, in Chapter 11, locates Hume in the eighteenth-century debate on population. His essay 'Of the Populousness of Ancient Nations' engaged with Montesquieu's account of the same subject. Montesquieu's 'interest in the causal relations between mores, social practices and political institutions' necessitated Hume's occupation of the same ground, ensuring that the essay would contain 'several of Hume's interesting views on history, human nature, and politics'. Hume believed that the debate 'mattered' since it was 'indicative of peoples' "whole police, their manners, and the constitution of their government"'.[10] Tomaselli observes that Hume's concerns related to an epistemic restriction on discovering the present population of Europe. The matter 'seemed so uncertain to him that, in the absence of secure data, he would "intermingle the enquiry concerning *causes* with that concerning *facts*; which ought never to be admitted, where the facts can be ascertained with any tolerable assurance"'.[11] Yet Hume's concerns were not confined only to the determination of causes, since he believed that his inquiry could form the basis of a political remedy: 'Hume implicitly positioned himself as having a rather grander aim in endeavouring to identify the constraints on demographic growth and, presumably,

---

[10] *E* (LF), pp. 378–79, *E* (C), p. 281.   [11] *E* (LF), pp. 377–78, *E* (C), pp. 279–80.

encouraging their removal'. As Hume noted, 'it seems natural to expect, that, wherever there are more happiness and virtue, and the wisest institution, there will also be most people'.[12]

In Chapter 12 by Margaret Schabas, we find Hume engaged with the problem of economic inequality. On this subject, Hume was averse to egalitarianism: '[t]here will always be rich and poor, he believed, and property rights should trump compassion for the less well-off. As Schabas writes, property and rank were, in Hume's judgement, 'byproducts of our deeply-rooted passions for pride and envy, and essential for sustaining the upward trajectory of commercial prosperity and political stability that Hume celebrated in his own kingdom'. A 'perfect equality of possessions', Hume observed in the *Enquiry Concerning the Principles of Morals*, would 'soon degenerate into tyranny'.[13] This belief informed Hume's vision of preferable economic policy. Hume 'firmly believed that greater equality of *income* tends to increase aggregate happiness for the nation as a whole, and he broached various policies for taxes and trade to achieve these ends'. He wished to see 'ordinary labourers enjoy higher wages and lift themselves out of poverty through the acquisition of skills', while enlarging the membership of the 'middle station', increasing 'the number of tradesmen, merchants, and manufacturers'. In contrast with the received view, which holds that Adam Smith 'was the first major economist to acknowledge the plight of the lower orders', it is evident that Hume was 'of a similar mind'.

In Chapter 13 by Tom Hopkins, Hume turns to the compatibility of commercial change with the recalcitrant but remediable inclinations of human nature. According to Hume, 'the industry of individuals could be turned to the service of the public; the cultivation of reason would serve in the perfection of the laws and of the arts of government; and the diffusion of humane maxims of conduct and habits of civility would moderate the rigour of the magistrates and the zeal of partisans alike'. This implicated the history of commerce and the arts in the 'natural history of justice and property' that Hume had adumbrated in the *Treatise*, and it served as 'the basis for an extended critique of Locke's account of the origin of political society in contract'. This critique extended to Locke's monetary theory, which Hume's elaboration of the price-specie flow mechanism criticised to destructive effect. Yet the thrust of Hume's critique stemmed from a completely disparate vision of the relationship between the state and the economy. For Locke, the 'instability of money as a standard of value

---

[12] *E* (LF), p. 382, *E* (C), pp. 281–82.   [13] *EPM*, p. 21.

provoked an anxious search for means by which it could be confined to its proper function of giving circulation to wealth without subverting the established property order and with it, civil society'. In Hume's eyes, there 'was no need to entrust the fortunes of commercial society to regulative principles that were both artificial and arbitrary', as Locke had suggested; 'what was required for nations to flourish was the patient application of an ever-more refined prudential judgement on the part of statesmen'.

As these summaries testify, Hume's *Essays* alighted on an extraordinary array of topics. Yet these topics were not co-extensive with the boundaries of Hume's interests. Understanding the *Essays* is not a surrogate for understanding Hume's thought *simpliciter*, but the *Essays* are now indispensable to the exercise. We do not pretend that these chapters offer an exhaustive summary of the *Essays*. However, we hope that the Guide will shed light on many of the *Essays'* more important features, while also prompting fresh research into their composition, their arguments, and their reception. Hume's renown and notoriety were secured principally by his work as a historian and philosopher, but it is as an essayist – as an 'Ambassador from the Dominions of Learning to those of Conversation'[14] – where he is at his most engaging.

---

[14] *E* (LF), p. 535, *E* (C), p. 4.

PART I

Reception

CHAPTER I

The Reception of Hume's Essays in Eighteenth-Century Britain

Mark G. Spencer and Mikko Tolonen

In 1753, *A General Treatise of Naval Trade and Commerce* was published in a second edition in London.[1] It built upon the first edition of 1738–39, touting 'many considerable ADDITIONS, and a new PREFACE'.[2] That new preface was expanded from six to fifty-three pages, offering a substantial introductory essay for the two volumes of reprinted primary sources. Who the anonymous author of the Preface was, is not known. What also has gone unknown, until now, is that the Preface borrowed unabashedly from David Hume's essays, including several that had only recently been published. Entire paragraphs were lifted from Hume's texts and – with the works of select others such as Bristol's Josiah Tucker (1713–99) – woven into the Preface. Hume's 'Of Commerce', 'Of Luxury', 'Of Money', 'Of Interest', 'Of Taxes', 'Of Public Credit', and 'Of the Populousness of Ancient Nations' were all pillaged.[3]

While the extent of borrowing may be startling to modern eyes which see it as blatant plagiarism, it is much less surprising that Hume's essays

---

[1] Anon., *A General Treatise of Naval Trade and Commerce, As founded on the Laws and Statutes of this Realm, in which Those relating to his Majesty's Customs, Merchants, Masters of Ships, Mariners, Letters of Marque, Privateers, Prizes, Convoys, Cruizers, &c. are particularly considered and treated with due Care, under all the necessary Heads, from the earliest Time down to the present* (2 vols., London, 1753). Here and elsewhere, unless stated otherwise, in quotations we have maintained original spellings. For their work on this chapter, we thank members of the Helsinki Computational History group, and in particular Ville Vaara for optimizing the BLAST software for ECCO, developed at TurkuNLP group led by Filip Ginter; and Eetu Mäkelä for the development of the OCTAVO interface used in this study. The study has been supported by Academy of Finland (grant number 333716), Brock University, and the Social Sciences and Humanities Research Council of Canada.

[2] The first edition of *A General Treatise of Naval Trade and Commerce* (2 vols., London, 1738–39) is rare. English Short Title Catalogue (ESTC) id N7442 in ECCO lacks volume one. We are grateful to Special Collections, Osgood Hall Law School Library, York University, for providing us with photo reproductions of the Preface to the first edition held in their collection.

[3] See *General Treatise* (1753), Preface, pp. x–xii, xiv–xviii, xxi, xxviii, xxx, xxxvi–xxxviii, xliv. Borrowing of this nature was, of course, common in the eighteenth century when 'what constituted plagiarism was still in flux'; see Mark G. Spencer, 'Was David Hume, the Historian, a Plagiarist? A Submission from His *History of England*', *Clio*, 47 (2019), pp. 25–50, at p. 42.

would figure in a work of this sort. The *General Treatise*'s contents – exploring British trade, commerce, and laws in their historical and political settings – was right up Hume's alley. As this opening gambit hints, tracing the eighteenth-century reception of Hume's essays can at times be a complicated business. As we will see, much of it played out beyond authorised editions of the *Essays* and outside the works of the many prominent, contemporary writers who openly referenced them. This chapter sheds new light on the reception of David Hume's essays in eighteenth-century Britain. It does so by linking automated methods of text reuse detection with more traditional approaches to the history of ideas.

In the aftermath of what he considered to be the failure of his *Treatise of Human Nature*, Hume strove to reach a wider reading public by publishing short essays on topical moral, political-historical, literary, and economic subjects. As he explained in an advertisement attached to his first such collection of fifteen essays, the *Essays, Moral and Political* (1741): 'MOST of these ESSAYS were wrote with a View of being publish'd as WEEKLY-PAPERS, and were intended to comprehend the Designs both of the SPECTATORS and CRAFTSMEN'.[4] Additional collections of like matter followed. A second volume of *Essays, Moral and Political* – containing a dozen more pieces – was immediately published, in 1742, the same year the first volume saw its second edition, corrected. In 1748 came *Three Essays, Moral and Political* – adding to Hume's mix 'Of National Characters', 'Of the Original Contract', and 'Of Passive Obedience' – and yet another edition of *Essays, Moral and Political*, already the third, corrected and with additions, and the first of Hume's publications to display his name on its title page. More essays followed, such as the twelve published in 1752 as *Political Discourses* in octavo (March) and shortly thereafter duodecimo (May).

Many of these essays found their way into Hume's four-volume *Essays and Treatises on Several Subjects* of 1753, his post-*Treatise* collected works at the time. That collection was republished in various formats with known imprints dated 1756, 1758, 1760, 1764, 1767, 1768, 1770, 1772, and posthumously, but with authorial input, in 1777. As he was apt to do with all that he published, Hume fiddled continuously with the text of his essays. He revised and improved many, withdrew a handful, and

[4] *E* (C), p. 529. For a fuller publication history of Hume's essays, see *E* (C), pp. 401–45. See also Gregory Ernest Bouchard, 'The Philosophical Publishing Life of David Hume' (PhD dissertation, McGill University, 2013).

added twenty more, such as 'Of Tragedy' and 'Of the Standard of Taste' which debuted in Hume's *Four Dissertations* (1757). After his death, two additional essays were published, 'Of Suicide' and 'Of the Immortality of the Soul'. In total, Hume's corpus included forty-nine individual essays that concern us in this chapter.

Since the 1960s, particular attention in intellectual history has been placed on authorial intention. The aim of scholars when interpreting Hume's *Essays*, for example, has often been his intention when writing particular essays in a certain context.[5] While the negative reception of the *Treatise* is a point of departure for many interpretations of Hume, very little attention has been placed on the reception of Hume's *Essays* as a whole and how that might have impacted the development of his thought and publishing career.[6] This is manifested in the fact that no such systematic study that forms the backbone of our study has previously been conducted. If it had, we would not have been able to find hundreds of hitherto unstudied reuses of Hume's *Essays* in British eighteenth-century books. One of our main claims is that this kind of undertaking is by no means merely antiquarian in nature, but should inform our interpretations of Hume's thought and its relationship to his career.

Scholars often dream of chasing down every borrowing of a particular work or author. With the computational methods used in this chapter, it is possible to start thinking about the composition and the influence of Hume's *Essays* in new ways.[7] We use the concept of *text reuse* that refers to shared passages between two texts, regardless of whether they are quotations or reprints, full or partial, of printed texts.[8] There needs to be a concrete, shared passage between two works to qualify as text reuse; we are not aiming to detect allusions or indirect influence of books in other

---

[5] See James A. Harris, *Hume: An Intellectual Biography* (Cambridge, 2015), esp. pp. 143–87. For theoretical backing for this perspective, see Quentin Skinner, 'The Limits of Historical Explanations', *Philosophy*, 41 (1966), pp. 199–215; Quentin Skinner, 'Meaning and Understanding in the History of Ideas', *History and Theory*, 8 (1969), pp. 3–53; Hans Robert Jauss, 'Literary History as a Challenge to Literary Theory', *New Literary History*, 2 (1970), pp. 7–37; Martyn P. Thompson, 'Reception Theory and the Interpretation of Historical Meaning', *History and Theory*, 32 (1993), pp. 248–72.

[6] An important exception here is James Fieser's multivolume set *Early Responses to Hume*, 2nd ed. (Bristol, 2005). See also Peter Jones, ed., *The Reception of Hume in Europe* (London, 2005); Mark G. Spencer, ed., *Hume's Reception in Early America: Expanded Edition* (New York, 2017).

[7] For other similar studies, see e.g., Y. Ryan, A. Mahadevan, and M. Tolonen, 'A Comparative text similarity analysis of the works of Bernard Mandeville', *Digital Enlightenment Studies* 1(1) (2023), pp. 4, 28–58. doi: https://doi.org/10.61147/des.6.

[8] Text reuse often occurs between two works by the same author, although this chapter does not aim to look at the overlaps in Hume's works with respect to his essays.

ways. Text reuse, then, is an important aspect of reception studies but it does not tell the whole story of Hume's reception. We have used automated methods to detect all of the instances where texts included in Eighteenth Century Collections Online (ECCO) and Early English Books Online (EEBO-TCP phase II) are reused from an earlier work, or where a later work repeats a fragment.[9] What we end up with is a massive dataset of linked, text reuse fragments found in ECCO and EEBO-TCP (more than 250,000 works). Put together, this is the largest collection of printed data for British books from 1470 to 1800 available in machine-readable form.[10]

In this study, we have extracted a subset of this data that includes all the cases of text reuse between all the different editions of Hume's *Essays* and other works included in EEBO-TCP and ECCO.[11] Employing our OCTAVO Reader interface, we checked each text reuse case individually, deleting duplications and other instances that did not belong (such as when Hume and another eighteenth-century author quoted a common source) and also noted the context, sentiment, and attribution of each reuse. Through this process we confirmed some 1,050 cases of text reuse of Hume's essays in the eighteenth century. At the same time, we processed the initial 16,000 lines through automation, ending up with 1,400 cases

---

[9] We have then qualified, clustered, and compared those instances. In technical terms, the basic idea behind the computational method used was to create a dataset that identifies similar sequences of characters (from c. 150 to more than 2,000 characters each) instead of trying to match individual characters or tokens/words. This helped with the optical character recognition (OCR) problems that plague sources digitised from microfilm, such as ECCO. For technical information about the text reuse detection used in this study, see Aleksi Vesanto, 'Detecting and Analyzing Text Reuse with BLAST' (MA dissertation, University of Turku, 2019) and Aleksi Vesanto, Asko Nivala, Tapio Salakoski, Hannu Salmi and Filip Ginter, 'A System for Identifying and Exploring Text Repetition in Large Historical Document Corpora', *Proceedings of the 21st Nordic Conference of Computational Linguistics*, Gothenburg, Sweden, 23–24 May 2017. Linköping Electronic Conference Proceedings, pp. 330–33. About the content, bias and OCR issues in ECCO, see Mikko Tolonen, Eetu Mäkelä, and Leo Lahti, 'The Anatomy of Eighteenth Century Collections Online (ECCO)', *Eighteenth-Century Studies*, 56, (2022), pp. 95–123.

[10] This text reuse undertaking should be seen as one branch in a broad line of research carried out by the Helsinki Computational History Group led by Tolonen, resulting in several different kinds of studies combining digital humanities, book and intellectual history that use this data as a point of departure; see Leo Lahti, Jani Marjanen, Hege Roivainen and Mikko Tolonen, 'Bibliographic Data Science and the History of the Book (c. 1500–1800)', *Cataloging & Classification Quarterly*, 57 (2019), pp. 5–23.

[11] Next, we preprocessed this data by filtering out all clusters of text reuse that originate before the publication of different editions of Hume's *Essays* in order to focus on the reception of that work (and not, here, on the presence of other works in Hume's text). This gave us a dataset of text reuse of Hume's *Essays* consisting of approximately 16,000 lines. Because the method is still at the development stage – and there are also fragmented text reuses included in the data that cause some duplicates to be included in the data – we decided to annotate this large dataset by hand and, at the same time, to do further preprocessing independently, relying on computation.

out of which, when checked by hand, 250 cases turned out to be repetitions of different kinds but provided us with roughly 150 more instances. In total, we identified approximately 1,200 cases of text reuse of Hume's essays.[12]

Our approach, then, brings to light hundreds of instances of Hume's essays being reprinted, partially reprinted, quoted, closely paraphrased, or plagiarised, both at length and in brief in publications from 1741 to 1800.[13] Taken together, all of these reuses illuminate the reception of Hume's *Essays* in the eighteenth century. They offer a window on Hume's impact as an essayist and allow us to measure the reception of particular essays, comparatively, and in various genres and discourses, and in specific contexts that changed over time and with circumstances. Hume often turned up in what to Hume scholars may seem to be unexpected places. Our computers did not have preconceived ideas about where to look for Humean traces.

There were more full and partial reprintings of Hume's individual essays in the eighteenth century than has hitherto been appreciated. For instance, while several scholars have given attention to the contemporary reception of Hume's 'A Character of Sir Robert Walpole', none have yet discussed what we find to be one of the most interesting early reprintings of that essay in an eighteenth-century book.[14] In 1743, the bulk of Hume's sketch

---

[12] This number of 1,200 discovered cases of text reuses of Hume that is confirmed by checking each case by hand can be considered a significant number when at the same time we have excluded newspapers and magazines that were not collected into a printed volume for this study. The chapter's authors are working on a broader study that will include available newspapers and magazines, hence the scope here is only on works collected as books (i.e. a number of, say, *The Mitre and Crown* that was printed in the eighteenth century in a collection and included in ECCO is part of this study; a number of *The Craftsman* that was not printed in a collected work included in ECCO is not).

[13] While our study of Hume's reception is systematic, we are certain that there are cases that our method did not capture for one reason or another. Nevertheless, if we think about what we can do with respect to understanding the development and the use of Hume's *Essays* in the eighteenth-century public domain, this opens up whole new avenues for intellectual history, some of which we aim to demonstrate in this short chapter. At the same time, it is important to understand that this workflow is not limited to Hume, let alone the reception of his *Essays*. With the same kind of diligence we have used in combining algorithms at different stages of the study and annotating results by hand, it is possible to study the text reuse of *any* early modern text included in ECCO or EEBO-TCP, which is important for the future of reception studies in general. Towards this end, Helsinki Computational History Group has developed a public interface for the study of ECCO, see David Rosson, Eetu Mäkelä, Ville Vaara, Ananth Mahadevan, Yann Ryan, and Mikko Tolonen, 'Reception Reader: Exploring Text Reuse in Early Modern British Publications', *Journal of Open Humanities Data*, 9 (2023), pp. 1–11.

[14] See, recently, Marc Hanvelt and Mark G. Spencer, 'David Hume's "A Character of Sir Robert Walpole": Humean Faction Fears, the "Rage against the Scots", and Future Historians', *Scottish Historical Review*, 98 (2019), pp. 361–89.

of Walpole had a prominent place in Chevalier Dennis de Coetlogon's *Diogenes's Rambles: or, Humorous Characters of the most noted people at present in the World*. There, de Coetlogon – rightly identified on his title page as 'M.D. Knight of St. Lazare, and Member of the Royal Academy of Angiers' – gave '*The* Character of the late *Sir* R——— W——'.[15] It was his penultimate character sketch of fifteen. De Coetlogon's text was taken verbatim from Hume, except for the Chevalier's final paragraph, which appended this statement to Hume's account:

> Yet this very odd Composition [on Walpole, based on Hume's sketch] hath held us in worse than a slavish Subjection, for upwards of twenty Years, and has, at last brought over his Opposers to his Side.

> Nay, if that's the Case, cried I, let me be gone; for if this Wretch has been suffered to proceed so long with Impunity, it is impossible that there can be one left with the Spirit of a *Man* in the Kingdom; so farewell G-----t B----n. ------ *Hominem quaero*.[16]

Our research shows that Coetlogon was far from being alone in mining Hume's essays in this way for usable text.

The Craftsman's 10 October 1741 reprinting of Hume's 'Whether the British Government Inclines More to Absolute Monarchy, or to a Republic' has been widely noted, most recently being reproduced in the Clarendon Edition of Hume's *Essays*.[17] Our research – even before we incorporate periodical works more systematically – shows that *Craftsman* reprinting to be only the tip of an iceberg. In 1750, a two-volume printing of *The Mitre and Crown; or, Great Britain's True Interest* is characteristic of our findings.[18] Over a four-month period, from early October 1749 to early February 1750, substantive selections were reprinted as standalone pieces from no fewer than eight of Hume's essays: 'Of Avarice',[19] 'That

---

[15] Chevalier Dennis de Coetlogon, *Diogenes's Rambles: or, Humorous Characters of the most noted people at present in the world: In Allusion to the Story Of the Cynic's searching Athens at Noon-Day with a Candle and Lanthorn to find out a Man* (London, 1743), pp. 32–33. Coetlogon was a French physician who had moved to London about 1727. He was also the author of *An Universal History of Arts and Sciences* (1745), often considered a precursor of the *Encyclopaedia Britannica*. Little is known of his life, besides what he said about himself in the Preface to that work; see Jeff Loveland, *An Alternative Encyclopaedia? Dennis de Coetlogon's 'Universal History of Arts and Sciences' (1745)* (Oxford, 2010).

[16] Coetlogon, *Diogenes's Rambles*, pp. 32–33.

[17] See *E* (C), p. 709. See also Bouchard, 'Philosophical Publishing Life of David Hume', pp. 64, 205.

[18] This short-lived journal ran from October 1748 to February 1751. It was edited by George Osborne. On Osborne's citing Hume's *History* in an unpublished manuscript, see Max Skjönsberg, 'David Hume and the Jacobites', *The Scottish Historical Review*, 100 (2021), pp. 25–56, esp. p. 50.

[19] *Mitre and Crown*, 'Craftsman, Oct. 7, 1749', II, p. 28.

Politics May Be Reduced to a Science',[20] 'Of the Liberty of the Press',[21] 'Of the Independency of Parliament',[22] 'Whether the British Government Inclines More to Absolute Monarchy, or to a Republic',[23] 'Of the Original Contract',[24] 'The Sceptic',[25] and 'Of Liberty and Despotism'.[26] The source for each of these reprintings was given in *The Mitre and Crown* as a particular, dated issue of *The Craftsman*, where reportedly it had recently appeared.[27] Evidently, Hume's expressed design for his essays to be published in the weekly newspapers came about, in a fashion. However, neither his name nor the title of his essays was attached to any of these early reprintings of his words in *The Craftsman* or *The Mitre and Crown*.

Hume's words, we have found, were frequently reprinted for eighteenth-century readers in other types of venues too. An under-appreciated vehicle for spreading Hume's thought in the eighteenth century were primary-source compilations and popular readers of various sorts that also reached the general audience Hume sought. Such collections were crucial for canonising authors, and arguably they served to bring Hume's essays, and usually his name, to many more readers than did any edition of his *Essays*.[28] We might take *The Beauties of English Prose* (1772) as an example. That publication appropriated significant selections of nineteen of Hume's essays across its four volumes.[29] In several instances, the text of a single one of Hume's essays was distributed over several different headings, as when selections from 'Of the Rise and Progress of the Arts

---

[20] *Mitre and Crown*, 'Craftsman, Nov. 25, 1749', II, pp. 119–20; 'Craftsman, Jan. 6, 1750', II, p. 169.

[21] *Mitre and Crown,* 'Craftsman, Dec. 2, 1749', II, pp. 123–25.

[22] *Mitre and Crown*, 'Craftsman, Dec. 23, 1749', II, pp. 163–64.

[23] *Mitre and Crown*, 'Craftsman, Dec. 30, 1749', II, pp. 166–67 [166 misnumbered 196].

[24] *Mitre and Crown*, 'Craftsman, Jan. 13, 1750', II, p. 171.

[25] *Mitre and Crown*, 'Craftsman, Jan. 27, 1750', II, p. 211.

[26] *Mitre and Crown*, 'Craftsman, Feb. 10, 1750', II, p. 219.

[27] Survival of issues of *The Craftsman* for 1749 and 1750 is patchy. We have not been able to confirm all of *The Mitre and Crown*'s citations of the *Craftsman*. However, those issues that we have been able to locate confirm our findings (for instance, *Craftsman*, Saturday, 6 January 1750, reprinted on its front page a selection from 'That Politics May Be Reduced to a Science'; *Craftsman*, Saturday, 10 February 1750, reprinted on its front page a selection from 'Of Liberty and Despotism').

[28] For the use of a data-driven approach to understand the canon in the eighteenth century, see Mikko Tolonen, Mark Hill, Ali Ijaz, Ville Vaara and Leo Lahti, 'Examining the Early Modern Canon: The English Short Title Catalogue and Large-Scale Patterns of Cultural Production', in Ileana Baird, ed., *Data Visualization in Enlightenment Literature and Culture* (London, 2021), pp. 63–119.

[29] Anon., *The Beauties of English Prose: being a select collection of moral, critical, and entertaining passages, disposed in the manner of essays* (4 vols., London, 1772), I, pp. 90–92, 147–48, 148–49, 200–2, 203–4; II, pp. 12–13, 13–14, 44–46, 133–34, 150–52, 177–78, 181–82, 183–84, 187–91, 213–16, 216–17, 230–32, 250–53; III, pp. 24–27, 114–17, 117–19, 157–59, 197–99; IV, pp. 44–50, 75–78, 178–79. A typical reprinting was signed '*Hume's Essays*'.

and Sciences' were reprinted under headings entitled 'ANCIENT', 'GENIUS', 'POLITENESS', and 'POWER'.

Other collections of this sort also reprinted Humean selections during the author's lifetime. *The Beauties of the Magazines, and Other Periodical Works*, for instance, reprinted Hume's 'Of Impudence and Modesty', 'Of Love and Marriage', and 'Of Avarice', in 1775. The editor remarked: 'The Three following ESSAYS are written by DAVID HUME, Esq; but not inserted in the late Edition of his Works'.[30] In other words, essays that we consider 'withdrawn' from Hume's *Essays* continued to circulate widely in the eighteenth century, even while Hume lived.

Later, these sorts of publications similarly broadcast essays that Hume had left unpublished in his lifetime. In 1782, *The Beauties of Hume and Bolingbroke* added as a 'SUPPLEMENT', 'TWO Essays, one on Suicide, and the other on the Immortality of the Soul, being handed about as the production of Mr. HUME'. The anonymous editor explained, 'in a compilation of this kind it was thought they could not with propriety be wholly overlooked'. Yet, the editor added, they 'are accompanied with a few notes, which, we hope, will prevent their making any bad impressions on the young, the thoughtless, or the ignorant'.[31]

Our work shows this trend of appropriating Hume in multi-author collections expanded towards the end of the eighteenth century. In 1786, as an example, Franz Swediauer's *The Philosophical Dictionary* included nineteen selections from fourteen of Hume's essays.[32] The most popular of such late eighteenth-century publications themselves saw multiple editions. Vicesimus Knox's (1752–1821) *Elegant Extracts*, for instance, survives in imprints for 1785, 1789, 1790, and 1797. In each case, selections from nine of Hume's essays were made available to readers at the close of the eighteenth century. In these same years, Stanley Crowder's *Polite Preceptor* (1788 and 1795) reprinted selections from two of Hume's 'withdrawn' essays, 'Of Impudence and Modesty' and 'Of the Study of History'. The latter appeared under the descriptive title, 'The Study of History recommended to the Ladies', indicating its and Hume's polite readers included women.

---

[30] Anon., *The Beauties of the Magazines, and other Periodical Works, selected for a series of years: consisting of Essays, Moral Tales, Characters, and other Fugitive Pieces, in Prose* (2 vols., Altenburgh, 1775), I, p. 108. Hume's essays were reprinted back-to-back, I, pp. 108–26.

[31] Anon., *The Beauties of Hume and Bolingbroke* (London, 1782), p. 255.

[32] Franz Xaver Swediauer, *The Philosophical Dictionary: or, The Opinions of Modern Philosophers on Metaphysical, Moral and Political Subjects* (4 vols., London, 1786).

In 1800, Philadelphian Mathew Carey's *The School of Wisdom; Or, American Monitor*, took the trend across the Atlantic. It reprinted, under the heading 'LIBERTY of the PRESS', selections from the 'Constitution of NEW-HAMPSHIRE', the 'Constitution of VERMONT', John Trenchard and Thomas Gordon's *Cato's Letters*, and Hume's 'Of the Liberty of the Press'. Hume got the last word. He also got the final say on the topic of 'LIBERTY'. Carey reprinted a passage from 'Idea of a Perfect Commonwealth' in which Hume claimed, in part, 'Though it is more difficult to form a republican government in an extensive country than in a city; there is more facility, when once it is formed, of preserving it steady and uniform, without tumult and faction'.[33] Hume's vision had contributed to America's founding and it remained welcome advice in the politically fraught 1790s.[34] In these types of publications, Hume's text was also often reprinted as the lead section.

What all of this shows is that Hume's individual essays continued to set the parameters of discussion on their topics, offering a framework or agenda for the discussions long after the original context of Hume's *Essays* may have faded from view. Editors such as Knox, Swediauer, and Carey, in picking and choosing which selections of Hume to reprint and under what headings, all had a hand in directing Hume's reception. Subtly – and sometimes not-so-subtly – they interpreted, even moulded, for their audiences what they took to be the gist of Hume's meanings or what they wanted them to be. When Swediauer reprinted selections from 'Of Luxury', one of his favourite Humean titles, he did so under the headings 'Luxury and Refinement of Manners favourable to Liberty', 'The Effects of Luxury discoverable by a comparison of different contemporary nations', 'Luxurious Ages Most Happy', and 'Luxury and Refinement of Manners favourable to Government'.[35]

In a related way, eighteenth-century books sometimes drew upon Hume's *Essays* for their chapter's epigraphs. The anonymous author of *The Amicable Quixote; or, the Enthusiasm of Friendship* (1788) did so when he or she quoted from Hume's 'Of the Rise and Progress of the Arts and Sciences':

---

[33] Mathew Carey, *The School of Wisdom: or, American Monitor. Containing a Copious Collection of Sublime and Elegant Extracts, from the Most Eminent Writers, on Morals, Religion and Government* (Philadelphia, PA, 1800), pp. 211, 222–23.

[34] On this, and Hume's eighteenth-century American reception more generally, see Mark G. Spencer, *David Hume and Eighteenth-Century America* (Rochester, NY, 2005).

[35] Swediauer, *The Philosophical Dictionary*, pp. 122–33.

> Gallantry is not less compatible with *wisdom* and *prudence*, than with *nature* and generosity: and when under proper regulations, contributes more than any other invention to the *entertainment* and improvement of the youth of both sexes. Were we to rob the feast of all its garniture of reason, discourse, sympathy, friendship, and gaiety, what remains would scarcely be worth acceptance, in the judgement of the truly elegant and luxurious.[36]

For another anonymous author, that of *For All Ranks of People, Political Instructions*, it was Hume's 'Of the Populousness of Ancient Nations' that provided a chapter's epigraph.[37] Hume's essays provided chapter epigraphs for American political works too, as was the case for *The Security of the Rights of Citizens in the State of Connecticut Considered.*[38]

Passages from Hume's essays also provided books with their epigraphs. Glasgow printer Robert Urie quoted a passage from Hume's 'Of Simplicity and Refinement in Writing' on the title page of his 1752 edition of Thomas Parnell's (1679–1718) *Poems on Several Occasions.*[39] In 1758, for 'Stentor Tell-Truth, Esq.', pseudonymous author of *The Herald; or, Patriot Proclaimer*, it was Hume's 'Of Public Credit' that was placed on the title page: 'Effects will always correspond to causes; and wise regulations, in any common-wealth, are the most valuable legacy which can be left to future ages'.[40] Hume's 'That Politics May Be Reduced to a Science', provided an epigraph for *An Address to the Representatives in Parliament, upon the State of the Nation* (1779):

> For my part I shall always be more fond of promoting moderation than zeal, though perhaps the surest way of producing moderation in every party, is to encrease our zeal for the public.

Hume may have withdrawn 'Of the Study of History' from his *Essays*, but its lines continued to circulate widely in the eighteenth-century books of others. It even did so as an epigraph on the title page of a history of

---

[36] Anon., *The Amicable Quixote; or, The Enthusiasm of Friendship* (4 vols., London, 1788), II, p. 156.

[37] Anon., *For All Ranks of People, Political Instructions* (London, 1795), Part III, 'On Popular Discontent, the Mob; and the Destruction of the English Constitution', unpaginated headnote. This work also quoted from 'Whether the British Government Inclines More to Absolute Monarchy, or to a Republic', 'Of Parties in General', 'Of the Protestant Succession', and 'Of the Coalition of Parties'.

[38] Anon., *The Security of the Rights of the Citizens of the State of Connecticut Considered* (Hartford, 1792), p. 11, epigraph for Chapter IV: '*So great is the force of laws, and of particular forms of government, and so little dependence have they on the humours, and tempers of men, that consequences almost as general, and certain, may sometimes be deduced from them, as any which the mathematical sciences afford us.* HUME'.

[39] He reportedly quoted from "Mr. HOME'S [sic] ESSAYS, page 265. London Edition'.

[40] Anon., *The Herald; or, Patriot Proclaimer* (London, 1758), 'Number XI', p. 174.

England that competed with Hume's. The Dublin edition of Oliver Goldsmith's (1730–74) *A New Abridgement of the History of England* (1785) quoted Hume on its title page:

> A Man acquainted with History, may, in some Respects, be said to have lived from the Beginning of the World, and to have been making continual Additions to his Stock of Knowledge, in every Century.

Short excerpts from all of Hume's essays found their way into a myriad of eighteenth-century publications. That was so for several specialised compilations, especially ones related to trade and commerce. Thomas Mortimer (1730–1810) drew from 'the ingenious Mr. Hume' in his *A New and Complete Dictionary of Trade and Commerce* (1766) and later quoted from 'the justly celebrated DAVID HUME' in *The Elements of Commerce, Politics, and Finances* (1772).[41] Both reprinted selections from Hume's 'Of Public Credit'. Jacques Savary des Brulons's (1657–1716) work in its English translation by Malachy Postlethwayt (c. 1707–67), *The Universal Dictionary of Trade and Commerce* (1757), described Hume in similar terms ('the ingenious Mr. Hume' and 'the learned Mr. Hume') and similarly excerpted from Hume's 'Of Public Credit' and, also, 'Of Taxes'.[42] In the case of the latter, though, he – like others, as we shall see – excerpted Hume without attribution.

Other categories of books, grammars and style guides, for instance, did their share to rebroadcast selections from Hume's essays in smaller snippets and other settings. Some, such as John Wilson's *Principles of Elocution, and Suitable Exercises* (1798), a volume said to be by a 'teacher of elocution, Edinburgh', excerpted short passages from Hume's 'Of the Delicacy of Taste and Passion':

> Nothing is so improving to the temper as the study of the beauties either of poetry, eloquence, music, or painting; they give a certain elegance of sentiment, to which the rest of mankind are entire strangers. The emotions they excite are soft and tender. They draw the mind off from the hurry of business and interest, cherish reflection, dispose to tranquillity, and produce an agreeable melancholy, which, of all dispositions of the mind, is the best suited to love and friendship.[43]

---

[41] Thomas Mortimer, *A New and Complete Dictionary of Trade and Commerce* (London, 1766), unpaginated entry for 'Paper Credit'; Thomas Mortimer, *The Elements of Commerce, Politics, and Finances* (London, 1772), and editions of 1774 and 1780.

[42] Malachy Postlethwayt, *The Universal Dictionary of Trade and Commerce, translated from the French of the celebrated Monsieur Savary* (2 vols., London, 1757).

[43] John Wilson, *Principles of Elocution, and Suitable Exercises* (Edinburgh, 1798), p. xxv.

Intended as examples for rules of composition, they ensured Hume's passages reached an audience besides those who read Hume in his collections of *Essays*. Many, such as Joseph Priestley's *The Rudiments of English Grammar*, were printed in multiple editions. In Priestley's case, *The Rudiments* was reprinted in London and Dublin in 1761, 1768, 1771, 1772, 1784, 1786, 1789, and 1798. (Among its readers was David Hume. This we can surmise because Hume revised a passage in 'That Politics May Be Reduced to a Science', taking into account Priestley's quibble.[44]) Other guides, such as John Bascroft's *A Help to Elocution* (1770), reprinted Hume more substantially. Bancroft reprinted 'Of the Delicacy of Taste and Passion'[45] and 'Of Impudence and Modesty'[46] in their entireties, along with a selection from 'Of Superstition and Enthusiasm',[47] as 'Examples, selected from the Best Authors, for the Exercise of the Scholar in Reading and Declaiming'.[48] It is interesting to envision Hume's essays being read aloud in this way.

Grammars that followed Priestley's in drawing upon Hume's essays for writing examples, negative and positive, included Joshua Story's *An Introduction to English Grammar* (1783), Joseph Robertson's *An Essay on Punctuation* (1785), the Rev. James Milner's *A Collection of English Exercises, for the Use of Schools and Academies* (1792), and Lindley Murray's *English Grammar* (1795). Some repeated Priestley's Humean examples; others added their own. Murray's popular *Grammar*, which saw multiple editions, cited examples from Hume's 'Of Commerce', but also cribbed illustrative passages from 'Of the Protestant Succession', 'Of Liberty and Despotism', and 'Of the Dignity or Meanness of Human Nature'.

By the end of the century, we see that text and ideas from Hume's essays had become embedded in eighteenth-century British book culture. Additional evidence for this turns up in other places, as when books of humour drew from Hume's essays. Several did. Publications such as *The Jester's Magazine; or, The Monthly Merry-Maker* (1766), *Yorick's Jests* (1770), and *Fun for the Parlour: or, All Merry Above Stairs* (1771) drew fodder from Hume for their entertaining anecdotes and light historical stories. A favourite came from Hume's 'Of Polygamy and Divorces'.

---

[44] Priestley had argued in 1768 that in the sentence '*Notwithstanding of the numerous panegyrics on the antient English liberty*', Hume's 'of' was unnecessary (Joseph Priestley, *The Rudiments of English Grammar* (London, 1768), p. 160). The phrase was thereafter altered by Hume.
[45] Joseph Bascroft, *A Help to Elocution and Eloquence* (London, 1770), pp. 68–72.
[46] Ibid., pp. 72–75.   [47] Ibid., pp. 75–76.   [48] Ibid., p. 67.

In fact, our automated reuse method makes it possible to extract with some degree of certainty the most reused passages from all of Hume's essays across the entire eighteenth century. The top-three reused passages were these:

1. From 'Of Impudence and Modesty':

    Jupiter, in the beginning, joined Virtue, Wisdom and Confidence together, and Vice, Folly, and Diffidence; and in that society set them upon the earth ... Mankind, who saw these societies as Jupiter first joined them, and know nothing of these mutual desertions [that Hume had outlined], are apt to run into mistakes, and wherever they see impudence, make account of virtue and wisdom, and wherever they observe modesty, call her attendants vice and folly.[49]

2. From 'Whether the British Government Inclines More to Absolute Monarchy, or to a Republic':

    Upon a moderate Computation, there are near three millions a year at the disposal of the crown. The civil list amounts to near a million; the collection of the taxes to another; and the employments in the army and the navy, together with ecclesiastical preferments, to above a third million: An enormous sum, and what may fairly be computed to be more than a thirtieth part of the whole income and labour of the kingdom.[50]

3. From 'Of Liberty of the Press':

    It is apprehended, that arbitrary power would steal in upon us were we not careful to prevent its progress, and were there not an easy method of conveying the alarm from one end of the kingdom to the other. The spirit of the people must frequently be roused, in order to curb the ambition of the court; and the dread of rousing this spirit must be employed to prevent that ambition. Nothing is so effectual to this purpose as the liberty of the press, by which all the learning, wit, and genius of the nation, may be employed on the side of freedom, and every one be animated to its defence. As long, therefore, as the republican part of our government can maintain itself against the monarchical, it will naturally be careful to keep the press open, as of importance to its own preservation.[51]

Hume did not become famous because of his one-liners or highly quotable passages, but his one-liners and highly quotable passages sometimes became famous. As our top-three such passages show, some came from essays from Hume's first collection of *Essays* that continued to figure in the

---

[49] *E* (LF), pp. 554–55, *E* (C), pp. 19–22. [50] *E* (LF), p. 49, *E* (C), p. 62.
[51] *E* (LF), pp. 11–12, *E* (C), pp. 38–40.

contents of his *Essays and Treatises* throughout his lifetime, such as 'Of the Liberty of the Press'. But famous Humean passages were also from essays such as 'Of Impudence and Modesty', which, withdrawn from the *Essays*, continued to circulate widely nonetheless. In fact, all of the reuses of 'Of Impudence and Modesty' in our dataset date from after its removal from Hume's works in 1760. Also striking here is that the vast majority of those instances reused Hume's work without attributing it to him.

Eighteenth-century authors who reused Hume's essays without saying they were doing so included many more than those who cribbed silently from 'Of Impudence and Modesty' or writers such as Lindley Murray, Malachy Postlethwayt, and the anonymous author of *A General Treatise of Naval Trade and Commerce* with which this chapter began. Our research shows that almost all of Hume's essays were cribbed at one time or another in eighteenth-century British books. Perhaps in some cases Hume's catchy turns of phrase caught in authors' minds or maybe some could not resist borrowing from Hume a description cast in efficient prose. Wholesale plagiarism such as that in *A General Treatise* was also not uncommon.

For example, John Logan (1748–88) in *Elements of the Philosophy of History* plagiarised from Hume's 'Of Some Remarkable Customs'. 'In all party divisions, the interest of the Aristocracy was predominant in the first Legislature, that of the Democracy in the second', Logan copied without acknowledging his source.[52] The Reverend Logan also drew upon Hume without saying so when he delivered, during the American Revolution, a fast day sermon on Psalm cxxii. 6. Logan said of the British government, in a passage that was later published (1791) and then republished (1800) in Edinburgh:

> No action must be deemed a crime, but what the laws have plainly determined to be such; no crime must be imputed to a man, but from a legal proof before his judges; and these judges must be his fellow-subjects and his peers, who are obliged by their own interest, to have a watchful eye over encroachments and violence.[53]

The words were from Hume's 'Of the Liberty of the Press'.[54] In the same sermon, Logan, who was a private tutor to Sir John Sinclair

---

[52] John Logan, *Elements of the Philosophy of History, First Part* (Edinburgh, 1781), p. 146; *E* (LF), p. 372, *E* (C), p. 276.

[53] John Logan, *Sermons by the late Reverend John Logan* (Edinburgh, 1791), 'Sermon XIV', p. 299.

[54] Hume wrote: 'No Action must be deemed a Crime but what the Law has plainly determined to be such: No Crime must be imputed to a Man but from a legal Proof before his Judges: And even these Judges must be his Fellow-Subjects, who are obliged, by their own Interest, to have a watchful Eye over the Encroachments and Violence of the Ministers' (*E* (LF), p. 12, *E* (C)), pp. 38–40.

(1754–1835),[55] also silently borrowed from Hume's 'Of Commerce': 'Trade and industry are in reality nothing but a stock of labour, which, in time of peace and tranquillity, are employed for the ease and satisfaction of individuals; but in the exigencies of state, may in part be turned to public advantage.'[56] 'Philo-lerne' in *A Letter to a Member of the Irish Parliament* (1755); a letter writer 'To the NORTH BRITON' in 1769; compiler of *The Modern Monitor* (1771); 'The Clerk' in *The Edinburgh Eighth-Day Magazine* (1779); 'Hortensius' in *The Lounger* (1785); Lieutenant James Green in *A Historical Essay on Different Governments* (1793); Charles Hales in *The Bank Mirror; or, A guide to the funds* (1796); and dozens of other anonymous and obscure authors borrowed passages from Hume's *Essays* without saying they had done so.

A surprising number of better-known writers are also represented in this category of reuse. A chronological list of representative cases of unacknowledged borrowers would include these: John Ross, *A Discourse Delivered before the University of Cambridge* (1756); James Steuart, *An Inquiry into the Principles of Political Economy* (1767); Theophilus Parsons, *Result of the Convention of the Delegates holden at Ipswich* (1778); Jean Louis De Lolme, *Essay on Constitutional Liberty* (1780); Joseph Priestley, *Lectures on History, and General Policy* (1788); the Rev. John Adams, *The Flowers of Ancient History* (1789); William Nichelson, *A Treatise on Practical Navigation and Seamanship* (1792); William Godwin, *An Enquiry Concerning Political Justice* (1793). The vast majority of these instances that turned up in our study are new to Hume scholarship. There is no space to unpack their details here, but listing them provides a sense of the longer story that might be told.

Some of the most important findings of our study are illuminated by considering in aggregate the data about the reactions that Hume's *Essays* elicited in the eighteenth century.

If we first look at the different collections of Hume's essays, the *Political Discourses* stands out for the large number of times the individual essays in that collection were reused. Hume's earliest collection of essays, from 1741, also received a fair amount of reuse over the century, although only one of them placed in the overall top ten. As a group, the 1742 essays were

---

[55] Richard B. Sher, *The Enlightenment and the Book: Scottish Authors and Their Publishers in Eighteenth-Century Britain, Ireland, and America* (Chicago, 2006), p. 101.

[56] Logan, *Sermons*, p. 302. Hume wrote: 'Trade and industry are really nothing but a stock of labour, which, in time of peace and tranquillity, is employed for the ease and satisfaction of individuals; but in the exigencies of state, may, in part, be turned to public advantage' (*E* (LF), p. 262, *E* (C)), p. 205.

not as popular, although a handful of them were among Hume's most popular essays of all.

Drilling down to individual essays within those collections is also informative. For instance, it is interesting to note that no particular essay stands out from the 1741 collection. However, 'Of Impudence and Modesty' and 'Of the Study of History' – essays that were later withdrawn – do fairly well in their number of reuses, along with 'Of Liberty and Despotism', 'That Politics May Be Reduced to a Science', 'Of the Liberty of the Press', and 'Whether the British Government Inclines More to Absolute Monarchy, or to a Republic'. Most popular from the 1742 collection were 'The Sceptic' and 'Of the Rise and Progress of the Arts and Sciences', both of which placed in the top ten. Hume's 'Of National Characters', first published in 1748, was quite frequently reused too. Several essays within *Political Discourses* show up among Hume's most popular reuses. 'Of Public Credit', 'Of Commerce', 'Of Money', 'Of Luxury', 'Idea of a Perfect Commonwealth', 'Of the Protestant Succession', 'Of the Balance of Trade', and 'Of the Balance of Power', are all counted among the top twenty. 'Of the Populousness of Ancient Nations' stands out clearly as the most reused of all of Hume's essays.

There are other ways to approach this data too. For instance, an interesting comparative perspective derived from our data is that 'The Sceptic' and 'The Stoic' were reused frequently, whereas 'The Epicurean' and 'The Platonist' almost not at all. Also among Hume's least reused essays were 'Of Moral Prejudices', 'Of the Origin of Government', 'Of Essay-Writing', and 'Of the Middle Station of Life'. In the case of the latter, James Lackington accounts for almost all of its reuses when he quoted a line from it in his *Memoirs*.[57] Thus, some of Hume's 'withdrawn' essays really were withdrawn, inasmuch as their reception was muted. Following from this, if we roughly group Hume's essays to categories of their topics, we may note his political and literary essays, and those related to commerce and civil society more broadly, were often reused, whereas his essays with narrower religious and moral themes did not attract as much attention. All in all, when we try to understand the success of Hume's *Essays* in the eighteenth century through these reuse numbers, the role of the political/historical essays that he wrote needs to be underlined.

[57] James Lackington, *Memoirs of the Forty-Five First Years of the Life of James Lackington* (London, 1793), p. 413, and its reprintings.

We have also considered the reuses of the essays from several different statistical perspectives. For instance, we have registered if Hume was acknowledged or not; we have tabulated the ages (when known) of those who reused him, and we are working on illuminating the networks of publishers and others who figure in this story. Focusing on change over time brings other factors to the forefront.

For example, we studied overall sentiment ('positive', 'negative', 'neutral') with respect to the reuses and charted how that changed with time. The early essays received a more negative response up until the 1760s, after which a change commenced, as Hume's canonisation process developed towards the end of the century. However, at the same time, negative receptions also greeted some of Hume's later published essays, particularly 'Of Suicide' and 'Of the Immortality of the Soul'. The former, one commentator found 'horrible and shocking'. It was objectionable that Hume could hold:

> that man, and the life of an oyster, are of *equal* value: that it may be as criminal to act for the preservation of life, as for its destruction: that as life is so insignificant and vague, there can be no harm in disposing of it as we please: that there can be no more crime in turning a few ounces of blood out of their course (that is, in cutting one's throat) than in turning the waters of a river out of their channel.[58]

Negative reactions occasioned by the latter included an entire pamphlet against it.[59]

For *Political Discourses*, it is noticeable that there is a distinctly topical relevance with the essays in the collection immediately upon their first publication. Hume, it seems, had just cause to describe it as 'the only work of mine that was successful on the first publication'.[60] Nevertheless, many essays in *Political Discourses* remained popular throughout the century, contributing to 'Hume' becoming a household name. It is also interesting that 'Of Public Credit' and 'Of Commerce' provoked reactions across the eighteenth century, even gaining in popularity, while the impact for 'Of Balance of Power', 'Of Taxes', 'Of Interest', and 'Of Some Remarkable Customs' was immediate but not as lasting.

---

[58] William Jones, *Memoirs of the Life, Studies, and Writings of the Right Reverend George Horne, D.D.* (London, 1795), pp. 126–27.

[59] See Anon., *Dedicated to The Queen: An Essay on the Immortality of the Soul; Shewing the Fallacy and Malignity of a Sceptical One, Lately Published, Together with Another on Suicide; and Both Ascribed, by the Editor, to the late David Hume, Esq.* (London, 1784).

[60] *E* (LF), p. xxxvi.

Looking closer, we see that the reuse of particular essays changed with different eighteenth-century contexts. For instance, 'Idea of a Perfect Commonwealth' was first cited in the 1760s in the context of British politics. It then gained considerable traction, in both British and colonial publications as the American Revolution came into focus, with its reuses peaking in the 1770s. 'Many object to a republican government, as impracticable in a large state', declared 'Demophilus'. 'The contrary of this (says Hume) [*Per. Com.* 302.] seems evident. Though it is more difficult to form a republican government in any extensive country than in a city, there is more facility, when once it is formed, of preserving it steady and uniform, without tumult or faction, in the former than in the later'. Demophilus's remarks were made in 'The Propriety of Independency', an essay appended as 'ADDITIONS' to several editions of Thomas Paine's widely circulated *Common Sense*, published in Philadelphia and Boston. Later, in the changed context of the 1790s, writers in both the United States and Britain looked to Hume's essay for its remarks on filtering democracy.[61]

Other essays witnessed similarly changing life cycles. 'Of the Liberty of the Press' was reprinted several times in the 1750s and 1760s, quoted frequently in the 1770s – including in the context of the American Revolution – and then witnessed a dramatic ascendency as debate over a free press exploded in 1790s Britain. ''Tis sufficiently known ... That despotic power would steal in upon us, were there not an easy way of conveying the Alarm from one end of the Kingdome to the other', many quoted, making it one of Hume's most reused passages, as we have seen. Such was the popularity of 'Of the Liberty of the Press' that some even cited it mistakenly. In 1792, Thomas Erskine (1750–1823) could observe in a speech delivered to a jury at Guildhall and published as *The Celebrated Speech of the Hon. T. Erskine*: 'Hume himself expressly says, notwithstanding all we have heard of the antiquity of our constitution, that our monarchy was nearly absolute till the middle of the last century. I have his book in Court, and will read it to you. It is his Essay on the Liberty of the Press, vol. 1, page 15.' The passage Erskine quoted was actually from Hume's 'That Politics May Be Reduced to a Science'.

For some late eighteenth-century commentators, Hume's arguments had garnered additional strength with the passage of time. 'Such were the changes, that fifty years had produced at the time, when Hume wrote

---

[61] For a recent work on the Scottish context, see Danielle Charette, 'Hume's "Idea of a Perfect Commonwealth" and Scottish Political Thought of the 1790s', *History of European Ideas*, 48 (2022), pp. 78–96.

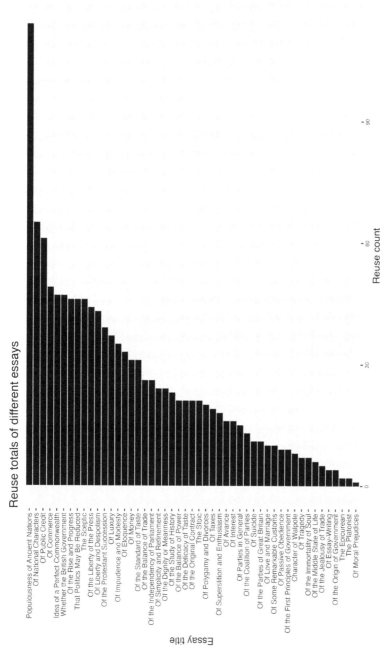

Figure 1.1   Reuse totals of Hume's Essays in the eighteenth century.

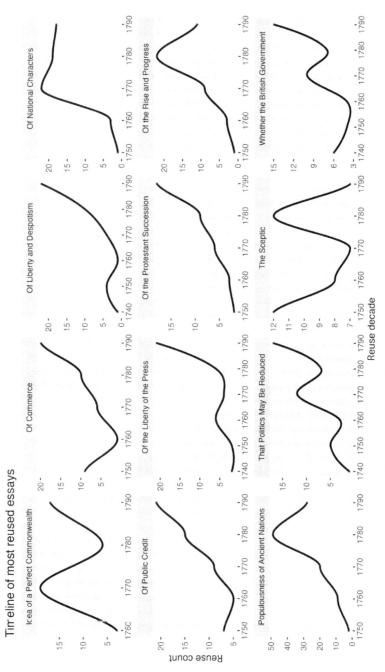

Figure 1.2 Most often reused essays: change over time.

his Essay', wrote Daniel Mitford Peacock in 1794 of 'Whether the British Government Inclines More to Absolute Monarchy, or to a Republic', 'and such the language, that might then have been held by those, who asserted, that the balance of the Constitution inclined towards democracy. Another term of fifty years has now elapsed; and how much more forcibly may the same argument be now urged!' For others, a new European era wrought by the French Revolution demanded that Hume's lessons could only be read with caution. 'Mr. Hume, with all his penetration', wrote one in 1795, 'could not foresee the revolution in France; and how much the establishment of liberty, in that extensive and enlightened country, would contribute to defeat the purpose of despots in all the nations of Europe.'[62]

The overwhelming number of reuse cases of 'Of the Populousness of Ancient Nations' stands out (Figure 1.1) also for the interesting pattern of reuses over time (Figure 1.2). These are robust observations that help us understand that Hume's contribution on this topic became entangled with the centre of Enlightenment discussion. Part of this was, of course, Hume's engagement with Montesquieu (1689–1755) and then the engagement of others, such as Robert Wallace (1697–1771), Chastellux (1734–88), and Thomas Robert Malthus (1766–1834), with Hume. However, Joseph Priestley's elaborate reuse (and frequent cribbing) of the essay is another part of the reactions that 'Of Populousness' produced. Connected to discussions of Hume's essay are a large pool of authors – more than fifty of them – underlining its centrality for eighteenth-century political debates in several contexts.

Indeed, taking Hume's essays as a whole, the range of topics and venues involved in the history of their eighteenth-century reuse is striking. It is a story that included not only the usual suspects of prominent political and economic thinkers, historians, philosophers, lawyers, and clergy but also scores of hack writers, anonymous authors, and a range of publishers, editors, and compilers; a motley crew from the notably famous to hopelessly obscure. A fuller understanding of the reception of Hume's *Essays* in eighteenth-century Britain finds a place for all of this, as our chapter has aimed to show.

---

[62] Vicesimus Knox, *The Spirit of Despotism* (London, 1795), p. 277.

CHAPTER 2

The Reception of Hume's Essays in Eighteenth-Century Germany

Lina Weber

In 1767 appeared *Abriß des Gegenwärtigen Natürlichen und Politischen Zustandes Großbritanniens: Ein Vollständiges Handbuch für Reisende*, or 'Outline of the current natural and political situation of Great Britain: A complete guide for travellers'. The imprint stated that the book was translated from an English original written by 'Mr Hume, author of the History of Great Britain'.[1] Almost four hundred pages long and in octavo, it was published by Johann Gottlob Rothe, the official bookseller of the Danish court and the University of Copenhagen. The *Abriß* started with a description of different parts of England and Wales, continued with some remarks on Scotland and Ireland, and then offered insights into various institutions, ranging from the courts in Lancaster to the personal guards of the king. It ended with an outline of Britain's interest in its colonies and of the country's national debt.

When the book was reviewed in the *Allgemeine Deutsche Bibliothek*, the most important review periodical in German, the judgement was harsh. Complaining about the recent upsurge in translations, the reviewer identified Hume's *Abriß* as 'surely the most miserable [translation] that this decade and maybe all earlier decades have seen'.[2] The reviewer blamed the translator's inability to understand either the English language or Hume's ideas. Johann Gottfried Herder came to a similar conclusion when he searched for an explanation of his unexpected dissatisfaction with Hume's most recent work. He wrote to Immanuel Kant, 'I am annoyed that his new *Abriß* of Great Britain has fallen into the hands of so half-witted a

---

[1] David Hume, *Abriß des Gegenwärtigen Natürlichen und Politischen Zustandes von Großbritannien: Ein Vollständiges Handbuch für Reisende, Nebst einer Umständlichen Nachricht von der Handlung, den Staatsverhältnissen und dem Interesse dieses Reiches, aus dem Englischen des Herrn Hume, Verfassers der Geschichte von Großbritannien* (Copenhagen, 1767). A second edition followed in 1771.

[2] Anon., 'Rev. of Hume, Abriß des Gegenwärtigen Natürlichen und Politischen Zustandes von Großbritannien', *Allgemeine Deutsche Bibliothek*, 7 (1768), pp. 64–67.

translator'.[3] To search for the English original of the *Abriß*, however, would be in vain. Hume never wrote a travel guide. The book might have been inspired by Hume's *History* and his *Essays and Treatises on Several Subjects*, but the *Abriß* does not resemble any of the texts that the Scottish philosopher published. This case of a pseudo-translation suggests that Hume enjoyed a significant reputation with eighteenth-century German readers such that publishers could expect to sell more copies of a travel guide if they presented it as a translation of a work by Hume.

It is by now well established that any translation entails transformation, both linguistically and culturally. Not only words but also their meaning need to be adapted to a different cultural context, political circumstances, and the taste of the audience. Translations make knowledge accessible, diffuse new ideas, and provoke reactions in the receiving culture. On the one hand, translations contribute to the standardisation and universalisation of concepts. On the other, through omissions, amendments, and modifications, translations reflect and confirm cultural specifications and discursive paradigms. Since the practice of translation entails conscious actions of interpreting the original text, translators play an important role in shaping the reception of a specific text in a new context.[4]

Translations and their great popularity in the eighteenth century have received extensive scholarly attention. After Latin retreated as a shared language of the learned and French became the language of the nobility and educated elites of Europe, the broadening of reading practices in the eighteenth century expanded the market for books in the vernacular. Translations started to serve as tools for modernisation. From a sense of cultural or economic backwardness, making knowledge available from those cultures that were perceived as more advanced was thought to bring about the much needed change for the better. In this way, translations were central to the Enlightenment.[5]

---

[3] Johann Gottfried Herder to Immanuel Kant, November 1767, in Rudolf Reicke, ed., *Kant's Briefwechsel, I, 1747–1788, Immanuel Kant: Gesammelte Schriften* (29 vols., Berlin, 1900–), X, p. 73.

[4] Stefanie Stockhorst, 'Introduction: Cultural Transfer through Translation: A Current Perspective in Enlightenment Studies', in Stefanie Stockhorst, ed., *Cultural Transfer through Translation: The Circulation of Enlightened Thought in Europe by Means of Translation* (Amsterdam, 2010), pp. 7–26.

[5] Fania Oz-Salzberger, 'The Enlightenment in Translation: Regional and European Aspects', *European Review of History-Revue européene d'Histoire* 13 (2006), pp. 385–409; Sophus A. Reinert, *Translating Empire: Emulation and the Origins of Political Economy* (Cambridge, MA, 2011); Antonella Alimento, 'Translation, Reception and Enlightened Reform: The Case of Forbonnais in Eighteenth-Century Political Economy', *History of European Ideas,* 40 (2014), pp. 1011–25; László Kontler, *Translations, Histories, Enlightenments: William Robertson in Germany, 1760–1795*

Research into the various processes of disseminating, translating, and receiving Hume's work has shown the central importance not only of his philosophical and historical writings but also of his *Essays*.[6] In France, the *Political Discourses* were translated three times in the 1750s and 1760s. Whereas the first translation from 1754 by Eléazar de Mauvillon (1712–79) was primarily driven by the prospect of making profit, the second French translation by the abbé Jean-Bernard Le Blanc (1707–81) was part of the Gournay group's attempt to encourage French emulation of British accomplishments in industry and political economy. The third French translation was published by an anonymous translator in 1767 and aimed to provide an alternative account of economic development to that of the *Économistes*.[7] Although the French translations of Hume's *Political Discourses* circulated widely in Europe, two Italian translations of selected essays were published to promote economic reforms in Venice and Sicily, while a Dutch translation served as a warning about the looming bankruptcy of Britain.[8]

For the reception of Hume in the German-speaking world, scholarly attention has hitherto focussed on the impact of his philosophy. Kant claimed that Hume's scepticism had 'interrupted his dogmatic slumber' and encouraged his formulation of critical philosophy.[9] Georg Wilhelm Friedrich Hegel afterwards reduced Hume's importance, arguing that he was merely a predecessor of Kant whose philosophy had become irrelevant.[10] Although bibliographical studies have shown the ready availability of Hume's essays for a German-speaking audience, very little is known

---

(New York, 2014), pp. 1–18; Silke Pasewalck and Matthias Weber, 'Einleitung', in Silke Pasewalck and Matthias Weber, eds., *Bildungspraktiken der Aufklärung/Education Practices of the Enlightenment* (Oldenbourg, 2020), pp. 1–8.

[6] For an overview on the European reception of Hume, see Peter Jones, ed., *The Reception of Hume in Europe* (London, 2005).

[7] Loïc Charles, 'French "New Politics" and the Dissemination of David Hume's *Political Discourses* on the Continent, 1750–70', in Carl Wennerlind and Margaret Schabas, eds., *David Hume's Political Economy* (London, 2008), pp. 181–202; Istvan Hont, 'The "Rich Country–Poor Country" Debate Revisited: The Irish Origins and French Reception of the Hume Paradox', in Wennerlind and Schabas, eds., *David Hume's Political Economy*, pp. 243–323, at pp. 267–74.

[8] Franco Venturi, 'Scottish Echoes in Eighteenth-Century Italy', in Istvan Hont and Michael Ignatieff, eds., *Wealth and Virtue: The Shaping of Political Economy in the Scottish Enlightenment* (Cambridge, 1986), pp. 345–62; Lina Weber, 'Predicting the Bankruptcy of England: David Hume's *Political Discourses* and the Dutch Debate on National Debt in the Eighteenth Century', *Early Modern Low Countries*, 1 (2017), pp. 135–55.

[9] Immanuel Kant, *Prolegomena zu einer Jeden Künftigen Metaphysik die als Wissenschaft Wird Auftreten Können* (Riga, 1783), p. 13.

[10] Manfred Kuehn, 'The Reception of Hume in Germany', in Jones, ed., *Reception of Hume*, pp. 98–138; Günther Gawlick and Lothar Kreimendahl, *Hume in der Deutschen Aufklärung. Umrisse einer Rezeptionsgeschichte* (Stuttgart-Bad Cannstatt, 1987), pp. 84–119.

about their context and their influence on the German Enlightenment.[11] To fill this gap, this chapter first outlines the impact of the Scottish Enlightenment on Germany more broadly and then investigates the publication and reception of the *Vermischte Schriften*, a translation of the *Essays and Treatises*, dating from 1754 to 1756. In its final section, the chapter analyses the retranslations of some of Hume's essays in the 1790s. Throughout the second half of the eighteenth century, as the pseudo-translated travel guide *Abriß* has already suggested, Hume was held in high esteem in the German-speaking world. The actual impact of his political and economic essays, by contrast, was relatively marginal.

2.1   The Scottish Enlightenment in Germany

Germany had previously shown very little interest in Britain. In the early eighteenth century, however, England became increasingly popular and gradually challenged the cultural dominance of France. This process started with the account of England in texts by Huguenot authors as the land of liberty and it was intensified by Voltaire's and Montesquieu's writings. Interpreted as factual descriptions of England, these French interpretations of England's constitution aroused curiosity in Germany about the country and its inhabitants. From the 1740s onwards, Germans increasingly travelled to London, Cambridge, and Oxford. Numerous travel accounts described the country, people, and customs of England to the German readership. Drinking tea and cultivating English gardens became widely practiced. English words were integrated into the German language. This broad cultural phenomenon in eighteenth-century Germany has been identified as 'Anglophilia' or even 'Anglomania', understood as an undifferentiated preference of anything English in all aspects of life. The emerging idea of England as the land of liberty, industry, and literary genius enabled German thinkers to criticise their own national circumstances. Although the view on England became more critical after the Seven Years' War, the English constitution continued to be greatly admired.[12]

---

[11] There are several bibliographies of German translations of the Scottish Enlightenment more broadly and Hume more specifically, see Norbert Waszek, 'Bibliography of the Scottish Enlightenment in Germany', *Studies on Voltaire and the Eighteenth Century*, 230 (1985), pp. 283–303.

[12] Michael Maurer, *Aufklärung und Anglophilie in Deutschland* (Göttingen, 1987); Jennifer Willenberg, *Distribution und Übersetzung Englischen Schrifttums im Deutschland des 18. Jahrhunderts* (Munich, 2008); Astrid Krake, '"Translating to the Moment" – Marketing and Anglomania: The First German Translation of Richardson's *Clarissa* (1747/1748)', in Stockhorst,

Following these growing cultural links between England and Germany, interest in English books increased considerably in the eighteenth century. A wide variety of theological, literary, political, and scientific books were either imported or reprinted. Although a growing number of Germans were able to read and speak English, particularly in the North, the overall number remained relatively small. Translations of English books became more frequent, reaching an unprecedented popularity and impact after 1740.[13] Most crucial for the dissemination of English books and for their translation were Leipzig, with its internationally renowned book fair, Hamburg, which had close commercial ties with Britain, and Hanoverian cities such as Göttingen.[14]

In Germany, as in Europe more broadly, translations were not always made from the English original. Depending on the availability of the original text and the linguistic skills of the translator, works were also translated via a third language, most often French. The author and publisher Friedrich Nicolai testified in 1773 that 'A translator from the English, for example, ranks higher than a translator from the French, as he is scarcer.'[15] While German translators may have aimed conscientiously to be true to the original, they commonly followed the practice of the time and translated relatively freely in order to produce a text that was accessible and pleasing to German readers.[16]

Whereas German interest in the first half of the eighteenth century focussed on England, Scotland became increasingly popular after the 1750s. German travellers started to visit Edinburgh. Most of the major and minor works of the Scottish Enlightenment were made accessible to a German-reading audience and were frequently republished or even retranslated. The books of Thomas Reid, Adam Smith, Adam Ferguson, and William Robertson were all translated into German and contributed to a modernisation of German philosophy. With their focus on sentiments and the sublime, translations of Francis Hutcheson, Lord Kames, and James

ed., *Cultural Transfer*, pp. 103–19, at p. 106. A nuanced overview on the changing German perception of England's constitution is provided by Hans-Christof Kraus, *Englische Verfassung und Politisches Denken im Ancien Régime. 1689 bis 1789* (Munich, 2006).
[13] An overview on the various ways in which English books entered the German market is provided by Willenberg, *Distribution und Übersetzung*, pp. 95–215.
[14] Maurer, *Aufklärung*, pp. 41–44.
[15] Friedrich Nicolai, *Das Leben und die Meinungen des Herrn Magister Sebaldus Nothanker* (3 vols., Berlin, 1773), I, p. 99. For German translators from the English, see Willenberg, *Distribution und Übersetzung*, pp. 215–69.
[16] Helmut Knufmann, 'Das Deutsche Übersetzungswesen des 18. Jahrhunderts im Spiegel von Übersetzer- und Herausgebervorreden', *Börsenblatt für den Deutschen Buchhandel – Frankfurter Ausgabe*, 91 (1967), pp. 2676–716, at pp. 2691–94.

Macpherson's *Ossian* informed the rise of the literary *Sturm und Drang* movement. Although Smith's *Wealth of Nations* was immediately translated by Friedrich Schiller, it was the two translations of James Steuart's *Inquiry into the Principles of Political Oeconomy* that had the most profound impact on German economic discourse.[17] Overall, Protestant and moderate works gained wide approval in the German Enlightenment.

Despite his critique of established religion and his philosophical scepticism, Hume too achieved considerable fame. Through the international book fairs in Leipzig and Frankfurt, the English originals and, more importantly, the French translations of his works were readily available for the learned in Germany. Le Blanc even claimed in a letter to Hume that Mauvillon's translation of the *Political Discourses* was specifically aimed at a German audience.[18] By the end of the eighteenth century, all of Hume's published works and some of his letters had been translated into German, enabling those unable to read foreign languages to access his writings. Hume's German translators came from a great variety of backgrounds, ranging from Lutheran pastors to young academics hoping to supplement their income. Despite their important role in transmitting and shaping the reception of Hume's ideas through selection, adjustments, and interpretations, very little is known about most of these translators. Their intentions were manifold. While some aimed to make useful knowledge widely accessible to a German audience or to satisfy a demand for Hume's writings, others attempted to control the way potentially dangerous ideas were received by framing their translations with annotations and introductions.[19]

2.2   Hume's *Vermischte Schriften*

The first publication in German of any of Hume's works was 'Of the Populousness of Ancient Nations' in the *Hamburgisches Magazin*, a popular journal for natural sciences, in 1753.[20] The text was identical to that in *Vermischte Schriften*, a translation of Hume's *Essays and Treatises on Several*

---

[17] See Keith Tribe, *Governing Economy: The Reformation of German Economic Discourse 1750–1840* (Cambridge, 1988), pp. 133–48; Fania Oz-Salzberger, *Translating the Enlightenment: Scottish Civic Discourse in Eighteenth-Century Germany* (Oxford, 1995); Kontler, *Translations, Histories, Enlightenments.*

[18] *HL*, I, 207.   [19] Gawlick and Kreimendahl, *Hume*, p. 37.

[20] David Hume, 'Von der Menge der Menschen bey den Alten Nationen', *Hamburgisches Magazin: Oder gesammelte Schriften, zum Unterricht und Vergnügen, aus der Naturforschung und den Angenehmen Wissenschaften Überhaupt*, 10 (Hamburg, 1753), pp. 451–502, 563–627.

Subjects in four volumes that appeared between 1754 and 1756 in Hamburg and Leipzig.[21] This German edition of Hume's essays was published with a privilege from the King of Poland and Elector of Saxony. Publishers could apply to the state authorities for such a privilege that gave them the sole right to print a certain work and intended to protect them from piracy. Illegal reprints were nonetheless common.[22] In the *Vermischte Schriften*, the original order of the four volumes had been changed and various editions of Hume's writings were used. The overall impression thus created is an uneven composition of miscellaneous versions of Hume's carefully curated essays. The translators' names were not revealed, suggesting that the translation had been made primarily for pecuniary purposes.[23] Scholarship has established that there were at least two translators and they have identified one of them. Hermann Andreas Pistorius (1730–98) was a recently graduated private scholar living in Hamburg who translated two volumes of the *Vermischte Schriften*. After he returned to his native island of Rügen to work as a Lutheran parish minister, Pistorius translated English theological works by David Hartley and Joseph Priestley, and wrote over one thousand reviews, including a critique of the works of Kant, for the *Allgemeine Deutsche Bibliothek*.[24] In all four volumes of *Vermischte Schriften*, the German translation is rather inelegant. The syntax is stiff and the choice of German equivalents often odd and inconsistent. 'Of the Independency of Parliament', for example, is translated as 'Von der Ununterwürfigkeit des Parlaments' in the table of contents of volume four, while the essay itself has the more common translation 'Von der Unabhängigkeit des Parlaments' as its title.[25]

Volume one of the *Vermischte Schriften* was entitled *Über die Handlung, die Manufacturen und die Andern Quellen des Reichthums und Macht eines Staats* (On commerce, manufactures, and the other sources of the richness and power of a state). This was Hume's *Political Discourses*, which

[21] For the background to the translation, see Gawlick and Kreimendahl, *Hume*, pp. 18–24.
[22] Willenberg, *Distribution und Übersetzung*, pp. 209–15.
[23] Kenneth E. Carpenter, *Dialogue in Political Economy: Translation from and into German in the 18th Century* (Boston, MA, 1977), p. 24.
[24] Little is known about Pistorius's life, see Hoxie N. Fairchild, 'Hartley, Pistorius, and Coleridge', *PMLA*, 62 (1947), pp. 1010–21, at pp. 1011–13; Bernward Gesang, *Kants Vergessener Rezensent: Die Kritik der Theoretischen und Praktischen Philosophie Kants in Fünf Rezensionen von Hermann Andreas Pistorius* (Hamburg, 2007), pp. XI–XII; Gesang, 'Pistorius, Herman Andreas (1730–98)', in Heiner F. Klemme and Manfred Kuehn, eds., *The Bloomsbury Dictionary of Eighteenth-Century German Philosophers* (London, 2010), pp. 589–91. These accounts rely on Pistorius's obituary published in *Intelligenzblatt der Neuen Allgemeinen Deutschen Bibliothek* (Kiel, 1799), pp. 198–200.
[25] David Hume, *Moralische und Politische Versuche, als Dessen Vermischter Schriften Vierter und Letzter Theil* (Hamburg, 1756), pp. [i], 72.

constituted the fourth volume of the original collection. The translator was Pistorius, who also added a preface. The second volume of the *Vermischte Schriften* was based on the second edition of the *Philosophical Essays Concerning Human Understanding*.[26] It was edited and annotated, but not translated, by Johann Georg Sulzer (1720–79), a theologian and Wolffian philosopher from Switzerland. The third volume of the *Vermischte Schriften* contained Hume's *An Enquiry Concerning the Principles of Morals*.[27] Translated by Pistorius from the first edition, it had neither a commentary nor a preface. Volume four, *Moralische und Politische Versuche*, was based on the third edition of the *Essays, Moral and Political*.[28] Hume, by contrast, had used the revised fourth edition of his moral and political essays as the first volume of the original *Essays and Treatises on Several Subjects*. The unknown translator refrained from adding any commentary.

The two volumes of the *Vermischte Schriften* that had prefaces told two different stories about the purpose of translating Hume's essays, showing a clear contrast between the view of his philosophical and his political and economic writings. Pistorius, in his preface to the first volume, claimed that there was a widespread desire to have access to the political philosophy of Hume, whom he ignorantly introduced as the secretary of the city of Edinburgh and a 'patriotic Englishman'.[29] Hume's work was presented as markedly different and superior to German political and economic writings. Pistorius explained that the high degree of liberty of expression and thought in Britain, which was unachievable in Germany, enabled Hume to gain deep insight into issues of statecraft and trade. These topics, although enormously important, were 'rather new in our language'. Since the principles laid out in Hume's essays were general and universally applicable, Pistorius argued that they were highly useful for nations other than England.[30] The case was different for philosophy. In the second volume of the *Vermischte Schriften*, Sulzer considered only Hume's

---

[26] David Hume, *Philosophische Versuche über die Menschliche Erkenntniß von David Hume, Ritter: Als Dessen Vermischter Schriften Zweyter Theil*, ed. Johann Georg Sulzer (Hamburg, 1755).

[27] David Hume, *Sittenlehre der Gesellschaft: Aus dessen Vermischter Schriften Dritter Theil* (Hamburg, 1756).

[28] David Hume, *Moralische und Politische Versuche, als Dessen Vermischter Schriften Vierter und Letzter Theil* (Hamburg, 1756).

[29] David Hume, *Vermischte Schriften über die Handlung, die Manufacturen und die Andern Quellen des Reichthums und der Macht eines Staats* (Hamburg, 1754), pp. [ii–iii]. The original publication of Hume's *Political Discourses* and their French translation had been reported in German periodicals in 1753, see Gawlick and Kreimendahl, *Hume*, p. 68.

[30] Hume, *Vermischte Schriften*, pp. [iii–v].

accessible writing style as a model worth imitating. The scepticism laid out
in the essays, by contrast, was presented as a tool to gain a better
understanding of the truth. According to Sulzer, German philosophers
had become too self-assured, indolent, and negligent. The need to rebut a
worthy enemy such as Hume would force them to sharpen their thinking
and increase their knowledge.[31]

Pistorius either exaggerated or misjudged the demand of German
readers for a collection of Hume's political and economic writings.
German review journals praised the English original and French translations of the various essays as the most useful and innovative of Hume's
publications.[32] Their German translation, by contrast, was almost entirely
ignored. In the review journal *Freye Urtheile und Nachrichten*, which
appeared tellingly with the same publisher as the *Vermischte Schriften*,
the publication of the German translation of the *Political Discourses* was
announced in 1754. The reviewer summarised Pistorius's view of Hume as
an unbiased and insightful Englishman, gave short accounts of the content
of each essay, and recommended the work to anyone interested in politics
since 'we have almost no or only very few publications on that matter in
German'.[33] An almost identical report appeared a year later in the journal
*Freymüthige Nachrichten von Neuen Büchern und Andern zur Gelehrtheit
Gehörigen Sachen*.[34] The publication of the fourth volume of the
Vermischte Schriften was announced in the short-lived *Altonaische
Gelehrte Anzeigen*. The article primarily summarised the content of the
essays and praised Hume as 'thorough, proper, penetrating, prolific, and
agreeable'.[35] No reviews of the philosophical volumes, that is to say, two
and three, seem to have been published. The appearance of a reprint of the
German translation of the *Political Discourses* in 1766 does not necessarily
mean that the work had been a great success and sold out fast.[36] Given that
the 1766 version is identical to the 1754 printing, only the flyleaf had been
changed, it seems likely that the widow of Adam Heinrich Holle, one of

---

[31] Johann Georg Sulzer, 'Vorrede', in Hume, *Philosophische Versuche*, pp. [i–xx].
[32] Gawlick and Kreimendahl, *Hume*, pp. 68–70.
[33] Anon., 'Rev. of Hume, Vermischte Schriften über die Handlung', *Freye Urtheile und Nachrichten
    zum Aufnehmen der Wissenschaften und Historie Überhaupt*, 11 (Hamburg, 1754), pp. 773–76.
[34] Anon., 'Rev. of Hume, Vermischte Schriften über die Handlung', *Freymühige Nachrichten von
    Neuen Büchern, und Andern zur Gelehrtheit Gehörigen Sachen*, 12 (Zurich, 1755), pp. 275–77.
[35] Anon., 'Rev. of Hume, Moralische und Politische Versuche', *Altonaische Gelehrte Anzeigen* (Altona,
    1759), pp. 85–87.
[36] As has been suggested by Gawlick and Kreimendahl, *Hume*, p. 23.

the original publishers, was trying to sell leftover stock by making it look like a new edition.[37]

The reason for the lukewarm response to Hume's political and economic essays lies in the specifics of cameralism. Due to a sense of missing out on the economic development of neighbouring countries, German universities were the first in Europe to establish chairs for local economic improvement in the early eighteenth century. The institutionalised science of cameralism aimed to train public administrators for the governing of economic processes. If Hume's essays had any impact on cameralistic thought, it was very limited. Scholars have suggested that Johann Heinrich Gottlob von Justi (1717–71), who was familiar with the English constitution and with the *Political Discourses*, might have been inspired by Hume's account of social cooperation, commercial progress, and money.[38] Evidence, however, remains circumstantial.

In the German-speaking political and economic debate more broadly, the engagement with Hume, like that with Smith before the 1790s, remained marginal. Although the *Essays* and the *Wealth of Nations* were readily available in French and German translations, rulers and thinkers outside the cameralistic universities rather appreciated the doctrines of the *Économistes*, a group of reformers who stressed the value of agriculture.[39] Isaak Iselin (1728–82), secretary of the republic of Basel and philosopher, for example, read Hume's *Essays* in the French translation twice in 1755. He had difficulty comprehending them, became 'almost a bit mad', and discounted Hume's view on luxury as overly positive.[40] It was François Quesnay and the *Économistes* who inspired Iselin's own writings on economic activity.[41] An exception was Philipp Peter Guden's (1722–94) *Polizey der Industrie*, which tellingly won a prize competition of the Royal Academy of Sciences in Göttingen in 1768. Guden, too, referred

---

[37] Tribe, *Governing Economy*, p. 134.

[38] Ulrich Adam, *The Political Economy of J. H. G. Justi* (Oxford, 2006), p. 54; Susan Richter, *Pflug und Steuerruder: Zur Verflechtung von Herrschaft und Landwirtschaft in der Aufklärung* (Cologne, 2015), pp. 247–49; Ere Nokkala, *From Natural Law to Political Economy: J. H. G. Justi on State, Commerce and International Order* (Zurich, 2019), p. 232. For Justi's view on the English constitution, see Kraus, *Englische Verfassung*, pp. 445–51.

[39] Tribe, *Governing Economy*.

[40] Isaak Iselin, Tagebuch 1755, Staatsarchiv Basel-Stadt: PA98a 5, p. 277. It seems that most of the German learned readers of Hume preferred the French translation of Hume's *Political Discourses*, see Tribe, *Governing Economy*, pp. 79 and 111.

[41] Isaak Iselin, *Schriften zur Ökonomie*, ed. Lina Weber in Isaak Iselin, *Gesammelte Schriften* (4 vols., Basel, 2016).

to the French translation of the *Political Discourses* and argued that Hume
had a wrong idea about money and its impact on industriousness.[42]

2.3   Retranslations of Hume's Essays

Despite the marginal impact that the *Vermischte Schriften* had on the
German-speaking world, several of Hume's essays were translated anew
and published in journals or in anthologies. A translation of 'Of the
Jealousy of Trade' appeared in 1761 in the short-lived *Hannoverische
Beyträge zum Nutzen und Vergnügen*.[43] A translation of 'Of Civil Liberty'
in *Kielisches Magazin vor die Geschichte, Staatsklugheit und Statenkunde* in
1784 was accompanied by extensive comments of the translator, the
professor and diplomat Johann Georg Wiggers (1748–1820). Wiggers
questioned, for example, the idea that commerce could flourish only in
free states.[44] *Beiträge zur Beförderung der Menschenkenntniß*, a moralistic
journal edited by the court counsellor and educationist Carl Friedrich
Pockels (1757–1814), published translations of 'Of National Characters'
in 1788 and of 'Of Superstition and Enthusiasm' in 1789.[45]

  In addition to these translations from the English original, the German
reading audience had access to Hume's writings via the French. *Das Genie
des Hrn. Hume* (1774) contained summaries of some of the moral, political, and economic essays as well as sketches of eminent men, such as
Luther and Henry VIII, and of historical periods, such as Europe in
1154 and Ireland under Elizabeth, that were taken from the *History*. The
translator, Johann Gottfried Bremer (fl. 1744), described Hume as the
most successful thinker on politics and morals and aimed at instructing the

---

[42] Philipp Peter Guden, *Polizey der Industrie, oder Abhandlung von den Mitteln, den Fleiß der
Einwohner zu Ermuntern* (Braunschweig, 1768), pp. 58, 63, 127. See also Gawlick and
Kreimendahl, *Hume*, p. 166.

[43] David Hume, 'Aus Humes Versuch über die Eifersucht in Ansehung der Handlung', *Hannoverische
Beyträge zum Nutzen und Vernügen, vom Jahre 1761*, 3 (Hannover, 1762), pp. 813–20.

[44] David Hume, 'Hume's Versuch Über die Bürgerliche Freiheit', trans. Johann Georg Wiggers, in
Valentin August Heinze, ed., *Kielisches Magazin vor die Geschichte, Statsklugheit und Statenkunde*, 2
(Kiel, 1784), pp. 59–110, at p. 92. The translation was made from the 1760 edition of the essay.

[45] David Hume, 'D. Hume's Versuch über die Nationalcharactere', trans. Carl Friedrich Pockels,
Beiträge zur Beförderung der Menschenkenntniss: Besonders in Rücksicht Unserer Moralischen Natur, 1
(Berlin, 1788), pp. 51–89. The translation was made on basis of the posthumous 1777 version of
the essay which included the revised controversial footnote on race. David Hume, 'D. Hume's
Versuch über Aberglauben und Schwärmerei', trans. Carl Friedrich Pockels, *Beiträge zur
Beförderung der Menschenkenntniss: Besonders in Rücksicht unserer Moralischen Natur*, 2 (Berlin,
1789), pp. 77–90.

youth in the most important principles of these sciences.[46] Nine of Hume's *Essays, Moral and Political* were included in the *Handbuch für den Staatsmann* (1791), an assembly of foreign works on politics, law, and economic life from authors ranging from Aristotle via Machiavelli to Condorcet.[47] In the case of Hume, the editor had omitted all topics that did not meet the purpose of the compilation to give the essays a 'more natural order' and to gain a more 'comprehensive understanding' of politics.[48] In these cases of double translation, the resulting German text was inelegant and relatively far removed from the English original. Yet they show that Hume's name enjoyed a high reputation and that his writings were considered to be instructive and valuable.

While the *Essays* started to lose prominence in Britain in the 1790s, translators tried to integrate Hume's writings into German reform debates in the aftermath of the French Revolution. They did this self-consciously, revealing their names on the translation's front page. The writer and historian Christian August Fischer (1771–1829) published a selection of Hume's political and economic essays together with a biographical sketch as *David Hume's Geist* in 1795. Aiming at a broad audience, Fischer wished that Hume's 'spirit of peace and moderation, of agreeableness and tolerance' would help overcome current fanaticism and revolutionary fervour.[49] The realisation of true liberty did not depend on the overthrowing of kings but on the improvement of the self. Fischer called on his readers to mount resistance to 'the despotism of your passions' and to fight the 'tyrannical power of your prejudices'.[50] In his translation, Fischer prioritised Hume's ideas over his style and took great liberty in finding German equivalents for original terms. The essay title 'Of Some Remarkable Customs', for example, was translated as 'Politische Anomalien'. Fischer added an essay on political prophesying without identifying his authorship, creating the impression that it was written by Hume. Set in 1787, the essay recounts a fictitious dialogue between James

---

[46] David Hume, *Das Genie des Hrn. Hume: Oder Sammlung der Vorzüglichen Grundsätze dieses Philosophen, Welche Zugleich einen Genauen Begriff der Sitten, Gebräuche, Gewohnheiten, Gesetze und der Regierungsform der Englischen Nation wie Auch Einige Hauptzüge ihrer Geschichte und Einige Kurze Anekdoten Berühmter Männer Enthält*, trans. Johann Gottfried Bremer (Leipzig, 1774), pp. [iii–iv].

[47] *Handbuch für den Staatsmann: Oder Analise der Vorzüglichsten Französischen und Ausländischen Werke Über Politik, Gesetzgebung, Finanzen, Polizei, Ackerbau, Handlung, Natur- und Staatsrecht* (2 vols., Zurich, 1791), I, pp. 128–241.

[48] Ibid., I, p. 129.

[49] David Hume, *David Hume's Geist: Erstes Bändchen Politik*, trans. Christian August Fischer (Leipzig, 1795), p. 3.

[50] Ibid., p. 6.

Mackintosh, Joseph Priestley, and Edward Gibbon about the horrors of the expected constitutional change.[51]

Instead of continuing and translating Hume's metaphysical treatise, as was originally intended, Fischer republished his collection with an added translation of 'Idea of a Perfect Commonwealth' under the title *David Hume's Politische Zweifel: Allen Partheien Gewidment* (David Hume's Political Scepticism: Dedicated to All Parties) in 1799. In a new preface, he repudiated a review of *David Hume's Geist* that was published in the *Neue Allgemeine Deutsche Bibliothek*. While the reviewer had praised Hume's achievement as philosopher and thinker, he blamed Fischer for failing to make a 'coherent whole' out of Hume's deep insights into issues that were of the utmost importance. As a result, the translation was neither instructive nor amusing.[52] Fischer responded by revealing his ethos. He explained that if the reviewer compared the translation with the original text, he would find that 'all essays (despite the last one) are a true imitation of the Humean, that not the words but the thoughts were reproduced carefully, [and] that they thus make a very coherent whole'.[53] Another reviewer in the *Allgemeine Literatur-Zeitung* agreed with Fischer and again emphasised the value of Hume's moderating, anti-revolutionary views.[54]

While Fischer used the translation of Hume's political and economic essays to protect the established order, the publicist Garlieb Merkel (1769–1850) utilised Hume's writings in his effort to abolish the institution of serfdom in his native Livonia. In 1796, Merkel transferred the critique of colonial enslavement in Guillaume Thomas Raynal's *Histoire des Deux Indes* to the case of Livonian serfs in his pamphlet *Die Letten* (1796).[55] A year later, he combined German translations of Hume's 'Of the Original Contract' and Rousseau's *Du Contrat Social*, publishing them as *Hume's und Rousseau's Abhandlungen über den*

---

[51] Ibid., pp. 225–32.
[52] Anon., 'Rev. of David Hume's Geist', *Neue Allgemeine Deutsche Bibliothek. Anhang zum Ersten bis Acht und Zwanzigsten Bande. Erste Abteilung* (Kiel, 1797), pp. 284–85.
[53] David Hume, *David Hume's Politische Zweifel: Allen Partheien Gewidmet*, trans. Christian August Fischer (Leipzig, 1799), p. vii.
[54] Anon., 'Rev. of David Hume's politische Zweifel', *Revision der Literatur für die Jahre 1785–1800 in Ergänzungsblätter zur Allg. Lit. Zeitung dieses Zeitraums. Zweyten Jahrgangs Erster Band* (Jena, 1802), cols. 140–42.
[55] For Merkel and his translation practices, see Julija Boguna, 'Nützt es dem Volke, Übersetzt zu Warden? Oder: Was Translation Über die (Livländische) Aufklärung Verraten Kann', in Pasewalck and Weber, eds., *Bildungspraktiken*, pp. 51–72.

Urvertrag (1797).[56] Merkel's aim was to 'correct many mistaken ideas that are currently dominating my fatherland'.[57] He expected that 'Rousseau's manly eloquence shall fill the breast of everyone who needs it with sparks of fire' and free Livonia from its 'self-inflicted mutilation'.[58] Hume's text, which is accompanied by highly critical comments by Merkel, served as a point of comparison for Rousseau's view on politics. Both are used as argumentative tools to strengthen Merkel's critique of the institution of serfdom, which he presented in an essay appended to the translation. Consequently, when Herder reviewed the translation, he had not much to say about Hume's essay but focussed on praising Merkel's analysis of the oppression of the Livonian peasants.[59]

2.4   Conclusion

It is remarkable that Hume's political and economic essays were translated yet another time and appeared under the rather literal title *David Hume's Politische Versuche* in 1800. The translator was Christian Jakob Kraus (1753–1807), professor of practical philosophy and cameralism at the University of Königsberg, who had been a student of Kant and Hamann. Having taught himself English, he translated Arthur Young's *Political Arithmetic* in 1776. His cameralistic teaching became increasingly influenced by Smith in the 1790s and he wrote a multivolume work entitled *Staatswirthschaft*, which was published posthumously and relied strongly on the *Wealth of Nations*.[60] For his German translation of Hume, Kraus selected those essays that were of general political interest and added a critical commentary at the end. A revised version was published in the posthumous collection of Kraus's works in 1813.[61]

[56] David Hume, Jean-Jaques Rousseau and Garlieb Merkel, *Hume's und Rousseau's Abhandlungen Über den Urvertrag: Nebst einem Versuch Über die Leibeigenschaft den Liefländischen Erbherren Gewidmet* (2 vols., Leipzig, 1797).

[57] Merkel, 'Vorbericht', in Hume et al., *Hume's und Rousseau's Abhandlungen*, I, pp. xi–xii.

[58] Merkel, 'Hochwohlgebohrne Herren!', in Hume et al, *Hume's und Rousseau's Abhandlungen*, I, pp. [iv–v].

[59] Anon., 'Rev. of Hume's und Rousseau's Abhandlungen über den Urvertrag', *Nachrichten von Gelehrten Sachen Herausgegeben von der Akademie der Nützlichen Wissenschaften zu Erfurt* 55 (1797), reprinted in Johann Gottfried Herder, *Sämtliche Werke*, ed. Bernhard Suphan (Hildesheim, 1880), XX, pp. 288–90.

[60] Kraus has received scant scholarly attention. The most comprehensive work on him is a dissertation: Erich Kühn, *Der Staatswirtschaftslehrer Christian Jakob Kraus und seine Beziehungen zu Adam Smith* (Königsberg, 1902). See also Manfred Kuehn, 'Kraus, Christian Jacob (1753–1826)', in Klemme and Kuehn, eds., *Bloomsbury Dictionary*, pp. 438–40.

[61] David Hume, *David Hume's Politische Versuche. Von Neuem aus dem Englischen Übersetzt Nebst einer Zugabe von Christian Jacob Kraus*, ed. Hans von Auerswald (Königsberg, 1813).

Kraus presented *Hume's Politische Versuche* as a much needed publication. Hume was 'one of the most original thinkers who has ever written'; his writing style was very clear; he knew how to address learned readers from all social classes.[62] Either oblivious of Fischer's adaptation or deliberately neglecting it, Kraus lamented that the last German rendition of Hume's work was outdated and out of stock.[63] He divided the selected essays into two groups. The 'staatswirthschaftliche Versuche' (state economic discourses) were particularly relevant for prospective businessmen studying cameralistic sciences. Although written in the 1750s, these essays still deserved to be read because they were classical contributions to the philosophic political economy tradition and because almost all later thinkers engaged with Hume. The second group of essays Kraus identified as 'staatsrechtlich' (concerning constitutional law). Like Fischer, Kraus considered them to be useful for a broader audience. After the French Revolution had given rise to wild political speculations, Hume's essays could help 'replace fantastical visions and airy theories with informed opinion and thorough investigation'.[64] Kraus added long comments to Hume's essays in which he engaged with certain themes such as the relationship between manufacturing and a state's power, the impact of wages on national wealth, and the disadvantages of a national debt.

It was Fischer who reviewed *Hume's Politische Versuche* in the *Neue Allgemeine Deutsche Bibliothek*. He wished that the translation had been 'a bit less timid' and was surprised that a 'very fervent admirer of David Hume' did not know the other translation of the essays from the 1790s.[65] A journalist suspected Fischer to be the reviewer and explained that *David Hume's Geist* or the reprinted *David Hume's Politische Zweifel* was not a translation but an unworthy 'mere extract, mixed with the nutrient of questions, exclamations, and apostrophes foreign to the original'.[66] A more detached reviewer in *Leipziger Jahrbuch der Neuesten Literatur* confirmed Kraus's claim that a new translation of Hume's 'instructive' essays had been desirable. Since 'the content of these political discourses and Hume's method of reasoning are well known', he concentrated on judging Kraus's

---

[62] Christian Jakob Kraus, 'Vorrede', in *David Hume's Politische Versuche. Von Neuem aus dem Englischen Übersetzt*, trans. Christian Jakob Kraus (Königsberg, 1800), p. vi. It seems that the work was translated in two versions, one with and one without the added commentary by Kraus.

[63] Ibid., pp. iv–v.   [64] Kraus, 'Vorrede', pp. vii–viii.

[65] Christian August Fischer, 'Rev of Hume, Hume's Politische Versuche', *Neue Allgemeine Deutsche Bibliothek. Anhang zum Neun und Zwanzigsten bis Acht und Sechzigsten Bande, Zweyte Abtheilung* (Berlin, 1803), p. 617.

[66] *Zeitung für die Elegante Welt*, 3 (Leipzig, 1803), cols. 675–77.

translation work, which he found overall satisfactory.[67] To the same conclusion came Georg Friedrich Sartorius (1765–1828), Professor of History at the University of Göttingen who published a textbook for teaching political economy based on Smith's *Wealth of Nations*, when he reviewed the posthumous edition of Kraus's translation of Hume's essays.[68] Although Hume's impact on German economic and political thought was overall marginal, he remained a well-known and highly valued authority on these subjects well into the nineteenth century.

---

[67] Anon., 'Rev. of Hume, Hume's Politische Versuche', *Leipziger Jahrbuch der Neuesten Literatur vom Jahre 1800. Zweyter Band Januar bis März 1801* (Leipzig, 1801), cols. 541–43.

[68] Georg Friedrich Sartorius, 'Rev. of Kraus, Vermischte Schriften vol. vii', *Göttingische Gelehrte Anzeigen* (Göttingen, 1814), pp. 1105–12.

CHAPTER 3

'Aussi hardi … qu'aucun philosophe en France':
The Eighteenth-Century French Reception of Hume's Essays [*]

Laura Nicolì

When David Hume arrived in Paris on 18 October 1763, he was already a celebrity. When he left the capital a little more than two years later, Friedrich Melchior Grimm could write with a touch of irony that

> Mr Hume ought to love France; he has received the most distinguished and flattering welcome there. Paris and the court competed with each other for the honour of surpassing themselves. Yet Mr Hume is as audacious in his philosophical writings as any philosopher in France.[1]

Courted by both Versailles and the Parisian society of men and women of letters, at least as much as he had always courted his French audience, *le bon David* had such a delightful time in Paris that he even 'thought once of settling there for life'.[2] All this – Hume's attraction for France ('a Place of the World which I have always admird the most'),[3] the warm reception he enjoyed in Paris, the adulation, the success, and his life-long French friendships (as well as enmities, in the infamous case of Rousseau) – is well known.[4] Likewise, it is also commonly acknowledged that Hume's

---

[*] Three Appendices supplement this chapter, respectively titled 'Chronology of Eighteenth-Century French Translations of Hume's *Essays*', 'Hume's *Essays* in Eighteenth-Century French Periodicals', and 'Some Other French Reuses and Responses to Hume's *Essays*'. The Appendices will not appear in the printed edition of the Guide. The Appendices will be available as an online resource, accessible on the permanent online research repository hosted by the University of Oxford. The Appendices are available at the following link: https://ora.ox.ac.uk/objects/uuid:2c7bf1c0-b3fe-4372-a013-a1186718090c. The digital object identifier is 10.5287/ora-8neaq8xzw. All translations in this chapter are my own. I am grateful to Giuseppe D'Ottavi and Emilio Mazza for their comments and suggestions.

[1] 'M. Hume doit aimer la France, il y a reçu l'accueil le plus distingué et le plus flatteur. Paris et la cour se sont disputé l'honneur de se surpasser. Cependant M. Hume est bien aussi hardi dans ses écrits philosophiques qu'aucun philosophe en France', *Correspondance littéraire, philosophique et critique*, 1 January 1766, ed. Maurice Tourneux (16 vols., Paris, 1877–82), VI, p. 458.

[2] *E* (LF), p. xxxix.   [3] *HL*, I, p. 398.

[4] James Seth, 'A Scottish Philosopher in France', *Transactions of the Franco-Scottish Society*, 5 (1910), pp. 208–18; Rudolph Mertz, 'Les amitiés françaises de Hume et le mouvement des idées', *Revue de littérature comparée*, 9 (1929), pp. 644–713; Antonio Santucci, 'Hume e i philosophes', *Rivista di filosofia*, 56 (1965), pp. 150–77; Ernest C. Mossner, 'Hume and the French Men of Letters', *Revue*

intellectual relationship with French thinkers represents something of a paradox. Although Hume was highly valued, the core of his philosophical thought remained basically uncomprehended in eighteenth-century France; and, despite a constant concern for his own French reputation and the circulation of his writings across the Channel, he never felt comfortable with the militant ideological afflatus of the *philosophes*. In the 1760s, Hume was at the peak of his success on the continent, so much so that one might say that, in Parisian circles, Anglomania took the form of Hume-mania. His reputation was not attributable to the *Treatise* (written in La Flèche, but translated into French only in 1878)[5] nor much to the *Enquiries* (despite their inclusion in the *Œuvres* translated by Jean Bernard Mérian), but mostly to his historical work and his writings on political, moral, esthetical, and religious matters. While the *History of England* established him as an outstanding historian, and the 'Natural History of Religion' and 'Of Miracles' an authoritative *esprit fort*, it was the *Political Discourses* first, and the complete *Essays* second, that confirmed him as a subtle political thinker and, what he cared about most, as a 'profound philosopher' in the eyes of the French.[6]

The point is not, as it has been suggested,[7] that Hume was seen in France as an historian or a political writer more than as a philosopher.

---

internationale de philosophie, 6 (1952), pp. 222–35; Mossner, *The Life of David Hume*, 2nd ed. (Oxford, 1980), esp. pp. 92–105, 409–556; Emilio Mazza, *La peste in fondo al pozzo: l'anatomia astrusa di David Hume* (Milan, 2012), pp. 109–18; Emilio Mazza and Edoardo Piccoli, '"La grande variété du goût": David Hume à Paris', in Cristophe Henry and Daniel Rabreau, eds., *Le Public et la politique des arts au siècle des Lumières* (Bordeaux, 2011), pp. 21–44.

[5] *E* (LF), p. xxxiv. On Hume at La Flèche see Dario Perinetti, 'Hume at La Flèche: Skepticism and the French Connection', *Journal of the History of Philosophy*, 56 (2018), pp. 45–74.

[6] For the most up-to-date account on the French reception of Hume's works, see Michel Malherbe, 'Hume's Reception in France', in Peter Jones, ed., *The Reception of David Hume in Europe* (London, 2005), pp. 43–97. Laurence Bongie's studies still remain a reference: see, in particular, 'Hume en France au dix-huitième siècle' (PhD dissertation, Sorbonne University, 1952); Laurence L. Bongie, 'Hume, Philosophe and Philosopher in Eighteenth-Century France', *French Studies*, 15 (1961), pp. 213–27, and Bongie, *David Hume: Prophet of the Counter-Revolution* (Oxford, 1965). See also Paul H. Meyer, 'Hume in Eighteenth-Century France' (PhD dissertation, Columbia University, 1954) and, for a synopsis, Alexander Lock, 'The Influence of the Published Works of David Hume in Eighteenth-Century France and Germany', *History Studies*, 10 (2009), pp. 45–61. On the 'little genuine intellectual affinity between Hume and the philosophes', see also James A. Harris, *Hume: An Intellectual Biography* (Cambridge, 2015), pp. 410–21; and Emilio Mazza and Gianluca Mori, 'How Many Atheists at D'Holbach's Table?', in Laura Nicolì, ed., *The Great Protector of Wits: Baron D'Holbach and His Time* (Leiden, 2022), pp. 173–201.

[7] See, for instance, Harvey Chisick, 'The Representation of Adam Smith and David Hume in the *Année Littéraire* and the *Journal Encyclopédique*', in Deidre Dawson and Pierre Morère, eds., *Scotland and France in the Enlightenment* (Lewisburg, 2004), pp. 240–63, who writes that 'Hume was known in France primarily as an historian, secondarily as an essayist concerned with economic, political, moral, and literary questions, and only incidentally as a philosopher' (p. 250).

Indeed, he was first and foremost seen as a philosopher; he was commonly
called a philosopher, and even a metaphysician. Regarding Hume, Grimm
declares that 'philosophers belong less to their homeland than to the
universe world',[8] and Voltaire, referring to the *Natural History of Religion*,
calls the author 'one of the most profound metaphysicians of our time'.[9]
The *History of England* is widely praised exactly for having been written '*en
philosophe*'. That philosophical character is stressed by the abbé Jean-
Bernard Le Blanc, among many others, in the introduction of his translation of *Political Discourses*: 'Mr Hume ... establishes his principles not as a
prejudiced Englishman, but as a political philosopher.'[10] Without a doubt,
Hume was considered 'one of the greatest philosophers of any age'.[11]

However, the question is what the French meant by that, what part of
Hume's philosophical thought reached a French audience, and to what
extent it had an influence on French debate. In this respect, the *Essays*
played a crucial role: it is by their means that a larger audience garnered an
awareness of Hume's philosophy. What is more, the *Essays* were Hume's
sole philosophical work that, in some way, was received according to the
author's (declared) intentions. While the *Treatise* essentially did not exist
for the French,[12] the meaning of the *Enquiries* was misunderstood, and the
writings on religion were appropriated for ideological purposes, the reading
of the *Essays* was largely consistent with Hume's introduction of them in
the Advertisement of the first edition in 1741 – an Advertisement that
never appeared in eighteenth-century French editions:

> Most of these essays were written with a view of being publish'd as Weekly-
> Papers ... But having dropt that Undertaking, partly from Laziness, partly
> from Want of Leisure, and being willing to make a Trial of my Talents for
> Writing, before I ventur'd upon any more serious Compositions, I was
> induced to commit these Trifles to the Judgment of the Public. Like most
> new Authors, I must confess, I feel some Anxiety concerning the Success of
> my Work: But one Thing makes me more secure, That the Reader may
> condemn my Abilities, but, I hope, will approve of my Moderation and

---

[8] 'les philosophes appartiennent moins à leur patrie qu'à l'univers', Grimm, *Correspondance littéraire*,
15 January 1759, eds. Ulla Kölving et al. (12 vols., Ferney-Voltaire, 2006–), VI, p. 19.
[9] 'un des plus profonds métaphysiciens de nos jours', Voltaire, 'Religion', in *Dictionnaire
philosophique*, ed. Christiane Mervaud (2 vols., Oxford, 1994 [1764]), II, p. 471.
[10] 'M. Hume ... établit ses Principes, non en Anglois prévenu, mais en Philosophe politique', 'Préface
du traducteur', in *Discours politiques de Monsieur Hume* (Amsterdam [Paris], 1754), I, p. xiii.
[11] Paul-Henri Thiry d'Holbach to Hume, 22 August 1763, in Paul-Henri Thiry d'Holbach, *Die
gesamte erhaltene Korrespondenz*, eds. Hermann Sauter and Erich Loos (Stuttgart, 1986), Letter 10,
p. 19.
[12] Despite a few accurate reviews of it appearing in French-language periodicals: Malherbe, 'Hume's
Reception', pp. 48–52.

> Impartiality in my Method of handling Political Subjects ... This Party-Rage I have endeavour'd to repress, as far as possible; and I hope this Design will be acceptable to the moderate of both Parties; at the same Time, that, perhaps, it may displease the Bigots of both.
>
> The Reader must not look for any Connexion among these Essays, but must consider each of them as a Work apart. This is an Indulgence that is given to all Essay-Writers; and, perhaps, such a desultory Method of Writing, is an equal Ease both to Author and Reader, by freeing them from any tiresome Stretch of Attention and Application.[13]

Nothing better than such 'trifles' to meet the taste of the Parisian society. Short, unconnected, and originally conceived for publication in periodicals, they fulfilled the *gazetiers'* wishes. Undemanding and brilliant in their ideas and enjoyable in their style, they provided excellent nourishment for the polite conversation of the *salons* and *cafés*. Their originality, coupled with their frequent treatment of subjects that were dear to the French public debate, made discussions passionate and spirited enough. As for being freed from 'Party-Rage', this clearly had, for foreign readers, a different meaning from that it had in the homeland. The French, in particular, would have appreciated Hume rising above the historical enmity between France and Great Britain, that is what they referred to when praising the *History* for being written *'en philosophe'*. Conversely, Hume was not as moderate when it came to religious matters, which certainly pleased a part of his French audience. Thus it was by means of such trifles that Hume's sceptical philosophy entered France.

3.1 Translating, Appropriating, Manipulating[14]

3.1.1 Books

The first of Hume's writings to be published in French was one of the essays, 'Of Polygamy and Divorces', which appeared in 1750 in the newly founded journal *Le Petit réservoir*.[15] The following year, the bookseller

---

[13] *E* (C), p. 529.

[14] A complete account of all translations and sources we refer to, as well as related secondary literature, is provided in the bibliographical Appendices to this chapter, which the reader should consult for detailed bibliographical information. See note * above.

[15] See 'Chronology of Eighteenth-Century French Translations of Hume's *Essays*', S1 (henceforth, the abbreviations we use to identify translations always refer to the first Appendix). 'Of Polygamy and Divorces' would go on to be a relatively fortunate essay, being translated again in *Mercure de France* in 1757 (S15), before entering the collective French editions of the *Essays*. It would also serve as one of the sources of the entry 'Mariage à temps' (1765) in the *Encyclopédie* and a critical reference of Baron d'Holbach in his *Morale universelle* (1776).

Michel Lambert failed to obtain the censorship administration's permission to publish a translation of what was known at the time as *Essays, Moral and Political*.[16] Thus Hume's first complete work to become available in French was, instead, *Political Discourses*. In 1754, two different translations appeared: one, which has been attributed to Eléazar de Mauvillon, was printed in Amsterdam by Schreuder;[17] the other, by the abbé Jean-Bernard Le Blanc, was printed in Paris by Lambert. The latter had finally obtained a *permission tacite*, and the following year, a second edition would be issued in Dresden, this time under the aegis of a *privilège royal*.[18] Both translations included all twelve essays contained in *Political Discourses*.[19] One of these essays, 'Of the Balance of Trade', was published in a third anonymous translation between September and November of the same year in the *Journal économique*.[20]

It would take ten years before the next French edition of the essays. In 1764, Jean Bernard Mérian's translation of *Essays, Moral and Political* was published as volume I of the second edition of Hume's works, titled *Œuvres de Mr. Hume*.[21] This first volume reproduced all the essays contained in the 1748 and 1753 English editions (which did not yet incorporate *Political Discourses*). Two years later, in 1766, a third partial translation of *Political Discourses* was released in Amsterdam. Consisting of the seven discourses on economics, it bore the title *Essais sur le commerce; le luxe; l'argent; les impôts; le crédit public, et la balance du commerce*. The identical volume was reissued the next year in Paris and Lyon.[22]

---

[16] C1.   [17] C2.   [18] C3(a) and C3(b).

[19] On the early French translations of *Political Discourses* see Loïc Charles, 'French "New Politics" and the Dissemination of David Hume's *Political Discourses* on the Continent', in Margaret Schabas and Carl Wennerlind, eds., *David Hume's Political Economy* (London, 2008), pp. 181–202; Michel Malherbe, 'Hume en France: la traduction des *Political discourses*', in Ann Thomson, Simon Burrows and Edmond Dziembowski, eds., *Cultural Transfers: France and Britain in the Long Eighteenth Century* (Oxford, 2010), pp. 243–56; and Gilles Robel, 'Hume's *Political Discourses* in France', in Stephen W. Brown and Warren McDougall, eds., *The Edinburgh History of the Book in Scotland. II: Enlightenment and Expansion 1707–1800* (Edinburgh, 2012), pp. 221–32. In general, the reception of *Political Discourses* has received much more attention in scholarship than that of the other *Essays*: see, for instance, T. V. Benn, 'Les *Political discourses* de David Hume et un conte de Diderot', in T. V. Benn et al., *Currents of Thought in French Literature: Essays in Memory of G. T. Clapton* (Oxford, 1965), pp. 253–76; Istvan Hont, 'The "Rich Country–Poor Country" Debate Revisited: The Irish Origins and French Reception of the Hume Paradox', in Schabas and Wennerlind, eds., *David Hume's Political Economy*, pp. 243–323; and Ryu Susato, 'Hume as an "Ami de la liberté": The Reception of His "Idea of a Perfect Commonwealth"', *Modern Intellectual History*, 13 (2016), pp. 569–96.

[20] S2. Could this be the work of the mysterious translator whom Grimm, in his review of Le Blanc's translation of the *Political Discourses*, claims is far better suited to the task? (*Correspondance littéraire*, 15 August 1754, eds. Kölving et al., I, pp. 249–50, at p. 250).

[21] C6(a).   [22] C7(a) and C7(b).

The anonymous translation had been attributed to Mlle de la Chaux, based on Diderot's short story 'Ceci n'est pas un conte', until Laurence Bongie showed her to be a fictional character; the question of the translator's identity remains open. Gilles Robel has suggested that 'the style may well point to Turgot, who translated two essays for the *Journal étranger* in 1760'.[23] The translator's critical remarks following some of the essays show a deep knowledge of economics and an acquaintance with the debate of the time, which would lend support to Robel's conjecture.

Throughout the eighteenth century, then, *Political Discourses* and *Essays, Moral and Political* remained two separate works for French readers, as they had been for the English until 1758 when Hume decided to blend them. A separate discussion is required for the fourfold series formed by 'The Epicurean', 'The Stoic', 'The Platonist' and 'The Sceptic', and 'Of Tragedy' and 'Of the Standard of Taste'. Their respective French histories took, from the beginning, a divergent direction from the other essays. The essays known as the 'four philosophers' are the only essays displaying a connection and dealing with a purely philosophical topic. It was not without reason that Mérian incorporated them in his first translation of Hume's works, the *Œuvres philosophiques de Mr. D. Hume*, along with the two *Enquiries*[24] and the writings composing *Four Dissertations* (among which were 'Of Tragedy' and 'Of the Standard of the Taste').[25] This first five-volume edition of Mérian's translation was issued in Amsterdam by Schneider in 1758–60. In 1764, the same publisher released a second edition, the aforementioned *Œuvres de Mr. Hume*. The title is more general, suppressing the adjective *'philosophiques'*, because this new edition, as we have seen, also featured the volume *Essais Moraux et Politiques*; this time, the 'four philosophers' took their place among the other essays as in the original work. In addition, in 1764, yet another bookseller, David Wilson from London, published a new edition of Mérian's translation, maintaining the title *Œuvres philosophiques*. In it, the texts are organised as they were in the first edition of 1758–60, with the 'four philosophers'

---

[23] Robel, 'Hume's *Political Discourses*', p. 226. For further details and references, see 'Chronology', note to C7(a).

[24] It is worth noting that, in Mérian's edition, the first *Enquiry* is called *Essais philosophiques sur l'entendement humain* (in accordance with the original title that Hume had changed in 1758), and the second *Enquiry* is titled *Essais de morale*. The French audience evidently appreciated the genre of the essay.

[25] The first two volumes, containing the *Essais philosophiques ... avec les quatre Philosophes*, were also issued as an independent two-volume set because of their evident coherence: see 'Chronology', note to C4(a).

annexed to the first *Enquiry*. The only difference is the addition of a new, sixth volume, including the *Essays* (except the 'four philosophers').[26]

Therefore, the 'four philosophers' followed in France two different paths: readers became familiar with them, on the one hand, as a sort of appendix to the first *Enquiry*, and, on the other hand, as 'trifles' among the others in the *Essays*. Conversely, they never read 'Of Tragedy' and 'Of the Standard of Taste' as part of the *Essays*: in all French editions of Hume's works, these two essays were published alongside 'Of the Passions' in a separate volume. Their exclusion from the *Essais* reflected Hume's original conception of them in *Four Dissertations* (although the first of these, the 'Natural History of Religion', was published in France as a separate work).

Finally, in 1788, in London, the Wilson edition was reissued with no changes save for the addition of a seventh volume containing the 1766 anonymous translation of the economics essays from *Political Discourses* mentioned previously.[27] Thus, for the first time, *Essays, Moral and Political* and (some of) *Political Discourses* were published in France as part of the same edition, although not as a single work. For eighteenth-century French readers, then, what we today call *Essays, Moral, Political, and Literary*, were at least three or four different works: *Discours politiques*, *Essais Moraux et Politiques*, *Dissertations sur les passions, sur la tragédie, sur la regle du goût*, and *Les quatres philosophes*.

3.1.2   Gazettes

The *gazettes* were the first and most effective vehicle for the reception of Hume's *Essays* in France.[28] Le Blanc's and Mauvillon's translations of 1754 were preceded not only by the early translation of 'Of Polygamy and Divorces' in *Le Petit réservoir* but also by notices of *Political Discourses* in *Journal britannique* and *Bibliothèque raisonnée* (in particular, 'Of Luxury',[29] 'Of the Populousness of Ancient Nations', and 'Of Commerce'). Moreover, 1754 also witnessed a third translation of 'Of the Balance of Trade', published in *Journal économique* (as we have seen), while reports with excerpts of 'Of Commerce', 'Of Luxury', and 'Of the Balance of Power' were provided by the *Journal étranger*.

---

[26] C4(b), C5(b), and C6(b).   [27] C4(c), C5(c), C6(c), and C7(c).
[28] Not much scholarship exists on this issue. For an initial step, see Chisick, 'Representation'.
[29] Although Hume retitled it 'Of Refinement in the Arts' in 1760, the original title is here adopted as it was used by the French.

In the years between the various translations in book format, French readers' curiosity about Hume's sentiments was nevertheless satisfied, as translations, summaries, excerpts, and reviews came out in periodicals almost without interruption. This is particularly true for the decade that separated Le Blanc's and Mauvillon's translations of *Political Discourses* in 1754 from Mérian's translation of *Essays, Moral and Political* in 1764. Many of the essays were translated or accounted for in journals. At least thirteen appeared in full translations, while others were summarised and sometimes commented on. Several reviews of the editions were also provided.

The role of the *Journal étranger* is particularly interesting. Besides the reports of three of the *Political Discourses*, nine of the *Essays, Moral and Political* appeared in French for the first time in it before they were included in Mérian's edition.[30] In addition, the translations of 'Of the Jealousy of Trade' and 'Of the Coalition of Parties' that were published in its issues of August and September 1760 remained the only French versions of those texts throughout the century,[31] because Hume added them only in 1760 and Mérian's translation did not take these additions into account. Incidentally, it is worth noting that in 1755–61, when all of these translations were published, the *Journal étranger* was printed by Michel Lambert,[32] the same bookseller who had failed to publish the *Essais de morale et de politique* in 1751 and later issued Le Blanc's *Discours politiques*. One might wonder whether the unknown 1751 translation was not dismembered for the individual pieces to be published in the journal.

The widespread *Mercure de France* was also very active in disseminating Hume's essays. It too provided the only known eighteenth-century French version of one of them, 'Of the Middle Station of Life',[33] which was excluded from Mérian's translation, when Hume suppressed it after the first 1742 edition. The ferment of the *gazetiers* around Hume's pieces is palpable. There are cases of the same essay simultaneously appearing in different journals, or issued twice in the same journal in different translations (for instance, 'Of the Study of History' in *Journal étranger*),[34] or of a compiler despising and suppressing the allegory of 'Of Impudence and Modesty' that had been already published in the same journal the year

---

[30] S3, S4, S8, S9(a), S10, S11, S12, S13, S18, S21, and S22.   [31] S19 and S20.
[32] See Marie-Rose de Labriolle, 'Journal étranger 1', in *Dictionnaire des journaux 1600–1789* (IHRIM / MSH-LES / Voltaire Foundation, 2015–2021), https://dictionnaire-journaux.gazettes18e.fr/journal/0732-journal-etranger-1.
[33] S17.   [34] S13 and S21.

before.[35] Otherwise, publishers were so eager to get Hume's work to press that certain translations of essays anticipated their publication in a volume – in particular, the translation of 'Of National Characters', which Mérian apparently communicated to the *Journal encyclopédique* in advance of its publication in a volume.[36] After Mérian's complete edition was issued in 1764, the translation activity of the periodicals slowed down, and the *gazetiers* preferred to focus on reviews of the edited volumes.

Although translations in periodicals were generally anonymous, we can reasonably conjecture the identity of some of their authors. We find among them some eminent names: it seems as though Nicolas-Claude Thieriot, with the collaboration of Voltaire, provided the first translation of 'Of National Characters',[37] Turgot those of 'Of the Jealousy of Trade' and 'Of the Coalition of Parties',[38] and Jean-Baptiste François de la Michodière a late translation of 'Of the Populousness of Ancient Nations'.[39] However, some translators rendered essays into French not with a view to publishing them, but rather for their own personal reasons or to circulate them among their acquaintances – after all, even Mérian's undertaking originated in this way.[40] For instance, in 1764, the young woman of letters Geneviève de Malboissière translated, for her own amusement, exercise and a desire to please her philosopher friend *M. Hume*, an attendee of her mother's *salon*, one of the most discussed essays of those years, 'Of the Rise and Progress of the Arts and Sciences'.[41] Hume-mania often affected young people: 'L'effervescence de nos jeunes têtes', Mme d'Épinay would observe, 's'est tournée de son côté'.[42]

---

[35] S3 and S10.

[36] S16. In 1757, the *Journal encyclopédique* also reviewed the 'four philosophers' in advance of their publication. It is likely that, in this case too, it was Mérian himself who provided the drafts.

[37] S5(a).   [38] S19 and S20.   [39] S26.

[40] See preface to *Œuvres philosophique de Mr. D. Hume* (Amsterdam, 1758): 'cette traduction n'étoit pas originairement destinée au Public: on y avoit travaillé uniquement pour faire connoître la Philosophie singulière de M. Hume à un Homme illustre, avec lequel on avoit souvent eu l'honneur de s'en entretenir'. The 'Homme illustre' was Pierre Louis Maupertuis, president of the Berlin Academy of Sciences.

[41] S23. On the translation, see Laura Nicolì, '"Mon Cool Warm Hearted Philosophe": Geneviève de Malboissière's Unpublished Translation of Hume's *Of The Rise and Progress of the Arts and Sciences*' (forthcoming). On Geneviève de Malboissière, see Albert de Luppé, ed., *Une jeune fille au XVIIIᵉ siècle. Lettres de Geneviève de Malboissière à Adélaïde Méliand (1761–1766)* (Paris, 1925), and Adeline Gargam, 'Geneviève-Françoise Randon de Malboissière', in *Dictionnaire de femmes de l'Ancienne France* (SIEFAR, 2014), http://siefar.org/dictionnaire/fr/Genevi%C3%A8ve-Fran%C3%A7oise_Randon_de_Malboissi%C3%A8re.

[42] Lucien Perey and Gaston Maugras, eds., *Une femme du monde au XVIIIᵉ siècle: dernières années de Mme d'Épinay* (Paris, 1883), p. 314 ('The effervescence of our young heads turned to his side'). The young Jean-Charles Trudaine de Montigny also dabbled in translating Hume's piece, the 'Natural History of Religion': see *HL*, I, p. 301, and II, App. C, p. 349.

3.1.3   Anthologies

The translation work of the 1750s and 1760s resulted in making available in French almost all of Hume's essays. They were usually translated in full, and their collections were organised in ways that reflect Hume's arrangement of them at one or another stage of their editorial history (with the exception of the 'four philosophers'). Thus, despite some translators' interventions to redirect, explain or moderate Hume's text, French readers had, after all, complete and relatively direct access to it. A second phase in the French reception came with the series of anthologies and collections of excerpts that followed one another in the years 1767–85. Selected essays of Hume's were integrated into collections of pieces by various authors, such as *Le Temple du bonheur* (1769), *Variétés angloises*, and Naigeon's *Recueil philosophique* (both of 1770).[43] There were also two anthologies entirely devoted to Hume, drawing extensively on the *Essays* and *Political Discourses*: the *Pensées philosophiques, morales, critiques, littéraires et politiques de M. Hume*, edited by Jean-Auguste Jullien de Boulmiers (1767), and *Le Génie de M. Hume* by Auguste-Pierre Damiens de Gomicourt (1770).[44] Both editors selected, cut and combined Hume's writings with complete nonchalance, resulting in a partial and distorted picture of his thought. However, although de Gomicourt seems to have done so out of a lack of care – the result rendering Hume 'incomprehensible by taking passages out of context and grouping maxims and reflections randomly'[45] – de Boulmiers did it programmatically, aiming to make Hume's views fully compatible with Christian orthodoxy. In his anthology, the original text was cut and interpolated, and many footnotes added containing critical remarks by the editor. These are announced in the preface: 'We have discarded all that could bring doubt into the minds, and trouble to the consciences ... we have adopted only what appeared to be in conformity with Christian morality.'[46] This havoc outraged Grimm:

> The service which our ruthless compilers have been doing for some time to all famous writers without consulting them has just been done to M. David Hume: that is to say, he has just been butchered, dissected, decomposed, and reduced in a volume entitled *Pensées philosophiques, morales, critiques,*

---

[43] Respectively, C4(c) and C4(d), S9(b) and S5(c), and S24(a) and S25(a).   [44] C8 and C9.

[45] Robel, 'Hume's *Political Discourses*', p. 226.

[46] 'Nous avons écarté tout ce qui pouvoit porter le doute dans les esprits, et le trouble dans les consciences ... nous n'avons adopté que ce qui a paru conforme à la Morale Chrétienne' (pp. iii–iv).

littéraires et politiques, de M. Hume … The compiler has taken care to remove from this extract everything that smacks of heresy, and he flatters himself with having succeeded in making the philosopher David Hume an edifying and orthodox writer.[47]

3.1.4   French-Born from the Press: 'Of Suicide' and 'Of the Immortality of the Soul'

'Of Suicide' and 'Of the Immortality of the Soul' are a chapter apart in Hume's reception across the Channel. They represent the strange case of writings originally written in English but first published in French rather than in English. They also offer a telling picture of the relationship between Hume and the *philosophes*.

Hume himself tells the first (British) part of the story in a letter to Strahan of 25 January 1772. He speaks about an alleged attempt by a London bookseller to publish the two essays, 'which were printed by Andrew Millar about seventeen Years ago, and which from my abundant Prudence I suppress'd and woud not now wish to have revivd'. In 1755, Hume had sent the two essays to Millar to be published in *Four Dissertations*:

> They were printed; but it was no sooner done than I repented; and Mr Millar and I agreed to suppress them at common Charges … Mr Millar assurd me very earnestly that all the Copies were suppress'd, except one which he sent to Sir Andrew Mitchell, in whose Custody I thought it safe. But I have since found that there either was some Infidelity or Negligence in the case; … there have other Copies got abroad.[48]

---

[47] 'On vient de rendre à M. David Hume le service que nos impitoyables compilateurs rendent depuis quelque temps à tous les écrivains célèbres sans les consulter: c'est-à-dire qu'on vient de le dépecer, disséquer, décomposer, et réduire à un volume intitulé *Pensées philosophiques, morales, critiques, littéraires et politiques, de M. Hume* … Le compilateur a eu soin de retrancher de cet extrait tout ce qui sent le fagot d'hérésie, et il se flatte d'avoir réussi à faire du philosophe David Hume un écrivain édifiant et orthodoxe', *Correspondance littéraire*, 15 February 1767, ed. Tourneux, VII, p. 247. Significantly, a similar judgement is expressed in the *Journal encyclopédique* (a periodical that, instead, appreciated *Le Génie de M. Hume*). The more conservative *Année littéraire* praised de Boulmiers' work.

[48] *HL*, II, pp. 252–53. On the complicated history of the two essays, see Ernest C. Mossner, 'Hume's *Four Dissertations*: An Essay in Biography and Bibliography', *Modern Philology*, 48 (1950), pp. 37–57, and Mossner, *Life*, pp. 319–35. On their circulation in France, see Laura Nicolì, 'The French Story of David Hume's Two Essays' (forthcoming). On the role of d'Holbach see Alain Sandrier, 'D'Holbach et Hume: scepticisme et propagande irréligieuse', in Geneviève Artigas-Menant et al., eds., *Les Relations franco-anglaises aux XVIIe et XVIIIe siècles: périodiques et manuscrits clandestins* (=*La Lettre clandestine*, 15 (2007)), pp. 221–39.

The second (French) part of the story, which Hume apparently ignored while writing to Strahan, involves the 'apostle of atheism', Baron d'Holbach and his circle. Two years before Hume's letter, in 1770, the two dissertations had appeared in French in a *Recueil philosophique* by various authors, anonymously edited by Jacques-André Naigeon.[49] Neither the author – Hume – nor the translator are indicated, but scholars generally agree in identifying the latter as d'Holbach.[50] At least one of the 'Copies' that 'got abroad' clearly reached the *coterie*.

In English, the two pieces would be published only after Hume's death: in 1777 as *Two Essays*, in an anonymous unauthorised version, and in 1783 in an as-yet unauthorised version that was the first to bear the author's name, alongside the mendacious statement 'Never before published.'[51] The latter edition was probably the basis for a new French translation of 'Of Suicide', issued in 1785, the introductory note of which repeats that 'this work had not yet been published'.[52] Finally, in 1792 Naigeon included the two pieces, in the same version as had appeared in 1770, in the entry 'David Hume' of his *Encyclopédie méthodique*, thus unmasking their authorship.

How and through whom d'Holbach managed to obtain the two essays, and whether this was done with Hume's consent, are open questions and perhaps destined to remain so. What is certain is that Hume's reputation in the eyes of the *philosophes* was mainly attributable to his anti-religious writings, primarily the 'Natural History of Religion' and 'Of Miracles'. The Baron and his friends would have liked Hume to write a militant history of the Church, which he never wrote.[53] In the *Essays*, little was militant in the sense that they would have liked. The juicy note on priests in 'Of National Characters' was suppressed in all French editions. The only essay specifically devoted to religion, 'Of Superstition and Enthusiasm', was far too subtle, concluding 'that superstition is an enemy to civil liberty, and enthusiasm a friend to it'.[54] Unsurprisingly, it was greeted with total indifference in France. 'The Sceptic' was decidedly too sceptical. The two suppressed dissertations eventually satisfied the

---

[49] S24(a) and S25(a).   [50] See 'Chronology', note to S24(a) and S25(a).
[51] In his will, Hume proposed an authorised posthumous edition of the two essays together with the *Dialogues*. This was not followed up: see *HL*, II, App. M, p. 453.
[52] S27. 'Cet ouvrage n'avoit point encore été publié' (non-numbered page).
[53] See Mertz, 'Les amitiés'; Mossner, *Life*, pp. 484–85; and Roger L. Emerson, 'Hume and Ecclesiastical History: Aims and Contexts', in Mark G. Spencer, ed., *David Hume: Historical Thinker, Historical Writer* (University Park, PA, 2012), pp. 13–36.
[54] *E* (LF), p. 78, *E* (C), p. 79.

philosophes' taste and expectations: getting straight to the point, Hume freed suicides 'from every imputation of guilt or blame'[55] by ridiculing the possibility of interference between human life and cosmic order, and freed the soul from any ties with immortality. While translating Hume, d'Holbach did not introduce the interpolations as he would when translating other authors. The two essays were sufficiently incendiary, and their author sufficiently influential, to make their simple printing and circulation an excellent weapon in the hands of freethinkers.

3.1.5   Translators and 'Gallicisers'

Owing to such intensive translation activity, a wide French audience could access the *Essays* by different means and, often, in more than one version. Of course, translators had a role in mediating Hume's thought. Some tried to stay as close as possible to Hume's text, intending simply to make it available to French readers. This is true of Mauvillon, Mérian and a number of translators of single essays. In these translations, interpolations are rare and are often a result of caution (for instance, the deletion of the note on priests), introductions are either scarce or merely informative, and editorial footnotes are mostly intended to provide French readers with some context they were unfamiliar with, or additional French references. Another type of translator is well exemplified by Le Blanc. On the whole, his rendering of the text respects the original. However, a heavy paratext is added, consisting of a long introduction, a rich apparatus of footnotes, and bibliographical annexes. Besides, Bolingbroke's *Réflexions politiques* are printed along with Hume's *Discours*. Through such editorial devices, the reader is strategically directed to a certain interpretation of the work, emphasising its affinity with the French circle of economists with which Le Blanc associated. Thus, the translation turns into adaptation and Hume's work is 'not just translated but "Gallicised"'.[56] Finally, a third approach is the outright manipulation that was operated by anthology compilers, who had the goal of making Hume's works more acceptable to orthodoxy, or simply more marketable.

3.2   French Mirror

The reception of the *Essays* followed many different routes in France, partly because of the history of their translation, and partly because of

---

[55] *E* (LF), p. 580.   [56] Robel, 'Hume's *Political Discourses*', p. 232.

the variety of intellectual concerns and attitudes Hume's work encountered and mobilised in that country. Although interest in the *Essays* was considerable, it was also very uneven: some essays attracted much more attention than others, and some attracted none at all. Generally, essays appealed to French audiences in two cases: when Hume directly or indirectly engaged in discussions with contemporary French thinkers, and when he expressed perspectives that could somehow be used to support causes dear to this or that intellectual group in France. The latter case plainly applies not only to 'Of Suicide' and 'Of the Immortality of the Soul' but also to other texts. In *Political Discourses*, especially those on political economy, Hume did both, which explains the work's positive reception in France. Clearly well-informed about the contemporary debate about political economy across the Channel, Hume cites and discusses theorists such as Jean-François Melon, Nicolas Dutot, Jean-Baptiste Dubos, Joseph Pâris-Duverney, Sébastien Le Prestre de Vauban, and, above all, Montesquieu, who is the implied interlocutor of the longest discourse, 'Of the Populousness of Ancient Nations'.[57] Thanks to this engagement with French thinkers and issues, and also to Le Blanc's promotional activity, the book aroused the interest of the influential group of economists and politicians of liberal inspiration who met in the salon of Mme Du Pré de Saint-Maur: this group included the Trudaine de Montigny father and son, Turgot, Morellet, Chastellux, and Helvétius, among others.[58] Such interest was not to be fleeting: many of these early admirers would later become Hume's associates during his stay in Paris almost ten years after Le Blanc's translation, and Turgot, as we have seen, would undertake his own translation of some of the essays.

In the *Essays* references to a French intellectual context, as well as history and public affairs, are prevalent. Among others, Hume discusses Fontenelle, Dubos, and, importantly again, Montesquieu.[59] Unsurprisingly, the essays containing such references attracted the most attention. Incidentally, even the curious early interest in 'Of Polygamy and Divorces' might be explained by a connection with Montesquieu (at least, in the compilers' eyes): *Le Petit réservoir* published it in his second issue, after having devoted a large section of the first issue to an apology of *De l'Esprit des lois*, including the chapters

---

[57] See M. A. Box and Michael Silverthorne, 'The "Most Curious & Important of All Questions of Erudition": Hume's Assessment of the Populousness of Ancient Nations', in Spencer, ed., *David Hume: Historical Thinker, Historical Writer*, pp. 225–54.
[58] We adopt here the conclusions of Charles, 'French "New Politics"'; Malherbe, 'Hume en France', and Robel, 'Hume's *Political Discourses*'.
[59] On the *Essays* and Montesquieu, see Chapter 11 by Sylvana Tomaselli in this volume.

on marriage.[60] There, Montesquieu is defended against the accusation of dealing with the subject without regard to revelation, which is exactly what Hume does as well. Thus, the publication of Hume's essay following the vindication of Montesquieu might have been a deliberate choice by the journal's editors. Be that as it may, there is no doubt that Hume's acquaintance with French sources, and his association with Montesquieu, was a crucial factor in the *Essays*' success in France.

However, Hume very rarely agreed with the French writers to whom he refers. Presumably, 'Of National Characters' is a critical response to Montesquieu's climate theory and emphasis on physical causes – a point that also enters in the discussion of 'Of the Populousness'.[61] In 'Of Tragedy', Hume distances himself from the aesthetic theories of both Dubos and Fontenelle. The discourses on political economy generally criticise the mercantilist and physiocratic views prevailing in Turgot's circle. In short, Hume seldom concurs with the opinions of his French interlocutors and especially the most celebrated among them, Montesquieu. Yet, this was the same Montesquieu who first recognised Hume's talents,[62] and with whom the latter entertained a flattering correspondence, and speaking of whom Le Blanc, expressing a common sentiment, wrote to Hume: 'You are the only one in Europe who could replace Mr President de Montesquieu.'[63] Hume was not invested by the French with such a prestigious legacy for the conclusions he reached, but rather for his methodological approach, for his regard 'to the general course of things'.[64] Turgot and the others wished to promote a science of commerce and, in this sense, Hume's approach was constructive. As for particular claims, Le Blanc and his associates adopted a peculiar strategy: rather than openly attacking Hume on their points of disagreement, they appropriated and adapted Hume's ideas, emphasising the priority of French sources from which Hume drew (in particular Melon) and redirecting his views by use of footnotes when needed.

---

[60] Montesquieu, *De l'Esprit des lois* in Montesquieu, *Œuvres complètes*, ed. Roger Caillois (2 vols., Paris, 1949–51), II, bk. XXIII, ch. 1–5, pp. 682–86.

[61] See, among others, Silvia Sebastiani, *The Scottish Enlightenment: Race, Gender, and the Limits of Progress* (New York, 2013), pp. 23–43; Emilio Mazza, 'Exposing the Children: Montesquieu, Hume and Something "Pretty Unusual"', *I Castelli di Yale*, 6 (2018), pp. 45–77; and Mazza, 'As "Men of sense": Godwin, Baroja, Bateson and Hume's "Of National Characters"', in Peter J. E. Kail, Angela Coventry, and Dejan Šimković, eds., *Hume's Legacy* (= *Belgrade Philosophical Annual*, 34 (2021)), pp. 159–82.

[62] John Hill Burton, *Life and Correspondence of David Hume* (2 vols., Edinburgh, 1846), I, p. 457.

[63] 'Vous êtes le seul dans l'Europe qui pouviés remplacer Mr le Président de Montesquieu', *HL*, I, p. 259n.

[64] *E* (LF), p. 254, *E* (C), p. 200.

As Michel Malherbe has observed, *Political Discourses* provoked a debate in which all participants belonged to the same philosophical space, and nationality mattered little.[65] This is true, for instance, of the reception of 'Of Luxury' – one of the most influential essays – and also of 'Of the Rise and Progress of the Arts and Sciences'. Both addressed long-standing issues that were at the core of the public debate in France and had important political implications. Generally speaking, they provoked a genuine unprejudiced discussion. Yet, the same cannot be said of essays where French authors were called into question. As a result of Hume's (alleged) attack on Montesquieu, 'Of National Characters' was probably the essay that provoked the most reaction, which was, with a few exceptions, defensive.[66] The same happened with 'Of the Populousness'. In this case, Montesquieu's vindication could even rely on the contribution of another Scot, Robert Wallace: his book in defence of the populousness of the ancient world was promptly reviewed in the *Journal britannique* a year after 'Of the Populousness'[67] and was later translated in a version that included a long critical examination of Hume's essay.[68] The French also did not particularly appreciate Hume's mistreatment of Corneille and Racine at the end of 'Of the Standard of Taste', as the passage in question is systematically reproached by all his commentators. Further examples are offered by the *Correspondance littéraire*. Grimm's attention was immediately caught by both 'Of Tragedy', which criticised Fontenelle and Dubos, and 'Of the Standard of Taste', where, despite no explicit reference on Hume's part, Grimm sees a possible comparison with Diderot's aesthetic theories. In both cases, Grimm sides with his fellow Frenchmen.[69] The historical rivalry between France and Britain was apparently not so easy to overcome, even when it came to *Saint David*.

3.3   Conclusion

Given that *Political Discourses* was the first of Hume's works to be translated into French, and given that this work begins with 'Of

[65] Malherbe, 'Hume en France'.
[66] Hélvetius was an exception: see Emilio Mazza and Michela Nacci, *Paese che vai: i caratteri nazionali fra teoria e senso comune* (Venice, 2021), pp. 77–141.
[67] For the review of 'Of Populousness' see *Journal britannique*, 7 (April 1752), pp. 387–411. The review of Wallace's *Dissertation* is in the same journal, 10 (March–April 1753), pp. 392–421.
[68] Robert Wallace, *Dissertation historique et politique sur la population des anciens tems, comparée avec celle du nôtre* (Amsterdam, 1769).
[69] Respectively: *Correspondance littéraire*, 1 January 1760, eds. Kölving et al., VII, pp. 3–7, and 1 and 15 August 1760, eds. Kölving et al., VII, pp. 185–187 and 207–9.

Commerce', it is via the initial pages of 'Of Commerce' that many French readers would have first encountered Hume. However, these pages do not speak about trade or politics, but about 'abstruse' philosophy:

> The greater part of mankind may be divided into two classes; that of *shallow* thinkers, who fall short of the truth; and that of *abstruse* thinkers, who go beyond it. The latter class are by far the most rare: and I may add, by far the most useful and valuable. They suggest hints, at least, and start difficulties, which they want, perhaps, skill to pursue; but which may produce fine discoveries, when handled by men who have a more just way of thinking. At worst, what they say is uncommon; and if it should cost some pains to comprehend it, one has, however, the pleasure of hearing something that is new. An author is little to be valued, who tells us nothing but what we can learn from every coffee-house conversation.[70]

The French had some trouble with Hume's abstruseness, and the first to experience these issues were his translators. For Mauvillon, the 'shallow thinkers' are '*Esprits superficiels*', while the 'abstruse' ones are '*Esprits solides*', who delve into truth ('approfondissent la vérité').[71] Le Blanc does worse, relying on a turn of phrase that gives the abstruse a negative connotation: the 'shallow thinkers' are 'hommes qui pour ne pas penser assez, n'arrivent pas jusqu'à la vérité'; the 'abstruse' ones are those 'qui pour penser trop, vont quelquefois au-délà'.[72] In any case, abstruseness is lost.

Everyone in Paris would have liked to have the eccentric Hume for dinner, and the public enjoyed his trifles because of 'the pleasure of hearing something that is new'. But when it came to the most philosophical or subtle essays, Hume's excessive 'taste for singularity' ('goût de la singularité')[73] and love for paradox[74] were disliked by both the conservatives and the radicals. And while de Boulmiers pounced on 'The Sceptic' with a barrage of critical remarks, the *philosophes* punished him with their indifference.

At the same time, it would be unfair to say that the success of the *Essays* in France was merely a matter of style. If it is true what Malherbe has stated, that the philosophical core of Hume's thought failed to have a

---

[70] *E* (LF), p. 253, *E* (C), p. 199. On Hume's abstruse philosophy, see Emilio Mazza, 'The Eloquent "Enquiry": Virtue or Merit in Its Proper Colours', in Jacqueline Taylor, ed., *Reading Hume on the Principles of Morals* (Oxford, 2020), pp. 300–23.

[71] Hume, *Discours politiques* (Amsterdam, 1754), p. 1.

[72] Hume, *Discours politiques* (2 vols., Amsterdam [Paris], 1754), I, pp. 1–2. The turn of phrase of the anonymous translator of the 1766 edition is similar.

[73] In Hume, *Pensées philosophiques* (Londres [Paris], 1767), p. iv.

[74] *Correspondance littéraire*, 15 August 1754, p. 250.

long-lasting impact on French culture, there are specific views and lines of reasoning expressed by Hume in some of his essays that not only animated the discussions of his time in France but also became a point of no return for the public debate in the years to come.

In the *Essays*, scepticism is in action. Hume silently conveys his sceptical philosophy by a sort of practical application to concrete matters: by 'starting some doubts, and scruples, and difficulties, sufficient to make us suspend our judgement on that head', as he put it concerning the ancient populousness.[75] He suggested hints and started difficulties, but he did not rule out the possibility that 'men with a more just way of thinking' might benefit from them to 'produce fine discoveries'. His French friends, fonder of discoveries than of the suspension of judgement, in trying to be those men, attempted to find in Hume's words an exit from despotism and a path towards social happiness.

---

[75] *HL*, I, p. 140. On the philosophical value of the *Essays* and their practical implications, see Margaret Watkins, *The Philosophical Progress of Hume's Essays* (Cambridge, 2019).

PART II

Philosophy

CHAPTER 4

Hume's Essays as Philosophy

Margaret Watkins

Is there philosophy in the *Essays*? Or real philosophy? Or philosophy worthy of the gaze of the contemporary professional philosopher? If one takes the practice of this species as normative, one would have had to answer in the negative for much of the twentieth century. Even those philosophers who read beyond the *Treatise* tended to dismiss these works, if they acknowledged them at all. I argue elsewhere that this was a mistake by showing the myriad ways in which the *Essays* address philosophical questions, as well as studying Hume's references to philosophy within the texts.[1] These references imply a broad conception of what philosophy is and an attitude towards philosophy that by no means despairs of its potential. Here, I take a different (though compatible) approach, arguing that the form of the *Essays* implies an ongoing philosophical project with a significant sceptical difference from the systemic form of the *Treatise*. But consideration of the *Essays'* form requires rejecting the assumption of our initial question. There is not philosophy *in* the *Essays*. The *Essays* are philosophy.

I begin by demonstrating that we find evidence in the *Essays* that Hume thought of himself as thinking philosophically, even narrowly conceived as the search for general principles often associated with the 'abstruse philosophy' of the *Treatise* and *Enquiries*. It may therefore seem plausible to see the *Essays* as merely continuing the project of the *Treatise*. I argue, however, that the distinction between the forms of the *Essays* and the *Treatise* complicates this reading of the relation between these texts. The pedagogy of the *Essays*, revealed in their form, indicates that philosophy is an ongoing project, a sceptical search that is sceptical even about its limits, rather than the system that the young Hume was confident could be completed within the boundaries of a treatise.

---

[1] Margaret Watkins, *The Philosophical Progress of Hume's Essays* (Cambridge, 2018). See especially pp. 2–4 and ch. 7.

4.1 Refining Science in the *Essays*

To query the presence or nature of 'philosophy in the *Essays*' suggests several assumptions, including (1) we know what 'philosophy' is, (2) it is something that can be found *in* a piece of writing, and (3) the *Essays* as a whole are not philosophy. They are chunks of writing into which philosophy may have been inserted, perhaps, or channels for philosophical content that Hume expressed more clearly and thoroughly in his 'philosophical' works. Each of these assumptions is problematic.

Many readers will have had the disconcerting experience of introducing students to the discipline of philosophy and being reduced to listing subfields of inquiry, questions philosophers ask, or dead white men. The desperate may resort to etymology, with vague allusions to love of wisdom. As Mark Jordan observes, 'there is no inductive agreement about the meaning of "philosophy" in the authors we habitually and sloppily call "philosophic"'.[2] Furthermore, we should distrust the notion that philosophy might be inserted into a text or extracted from it, perhaps with advanced techniques of exegetical chemistry. 'A word', Jordan notes, 'is not a container into which the distilled thought is poured, as if one were filling different glasses under a tap.'[3] Likewise, an essay is not a container into which we might pour a little philosophy, a little flattery of the public, and perhaps a little proto-social-science for ears that hear. It is a form of writing, and understanding forms of writing requires an appreciation of the significance of their shape and structure.

We might want to know whether Hume considered himself to be addressing philosophical questions in the *Essays*. This question is fair, although complicated by the possibility that his conception of philosophy may have changed over time and the truth that divisions among various disciplinary practices were not as pronounced then as at present. Hume refers to numerous activities and modes of thinking as philosophical in the *Essays*: philosophy is a practice of the ancients,[4] a character requiring the highest genius,[5] counsel to politicians and legislators,[6] a deceptive tool of

[2] Mark D. Jordan, 'The Terms of the Debate over "Christian Philosophy"', *Communio*, 12 (1985), pp. 293–311, at pp. 299–300.
[3] Mark D. Jordan, 'A Preface to the Study of Philosophic Genres', *Philosophy and Rhetoric*, 14 (1981), pp. 199–211, at p. 202.
[4] *E* (LF), p. 91, *E* (C), p. 88; *E* (LF), pp. 120–21, *E* (C), p. 107; *E* (LF), p. 414 n. 100, *E* (C), p. 301n92. The notes to this sentence are exemplary, not comprehensive.
[5] *E* (LF), p. 550, *E* (C), p. 14.
[6] For example, *E* (LF), p. 30, *E* (C), p. 50; *E* (LF), p. 507, *E* (C), p. 359.

politicians and legislators,[7] a therapy for the passions,[8] a Stoic fantasy of eliminating the passions,[9] an instigation to factionalism,[10] a cure for superstition,[11] and more.

That 'more' includes speculative science, akin to Hume's philosophical 'anatomy'. Some have classed the *Essays* as his painterly efforts — the logical sequel to the *Treatise*'s abstruse anatomy. 'First we had the anatomy, and now we have the painting', John Immerwahr says.[12] For those who think only the anatomy is real philosophy, this reading supports the narrative that Hume abandons philosophy after the *Treatise*. But there is evidence that he believes himself to be continuing 'anatomic' work in the *Essays*.

I cannot review here the substantial literature on the anatomist/painter distinction.[13] But three texts feed the discussion: (1) Hume's 1739 letter to Francis Hutcheson, in which he defends the *Treatise* against Hutcheson's charge that it lacks 'a certain Warmth in the Cause of Virtue';[14] (2) the last paragraph of the *Treatise*, which claims that his system allows us 'to form a just notion of the *happiness*, as well as of the *dignity* of virtue', although 'such reflections require a work apart', because 'the anatomist ought never to emulate the painter';[15] and (3) the opening section of the first *Enquiry*, where Hume uses the analogy to distinguish between two 'manners' of treating 'moral philosophy, or the science of human nature', and ends with the exclamation: 'Happy, if we can unite the boundaries of the different species of philosophy, by reconciling profound enquiry with clearness, and truth with novelty!'[16]

We find no reference to this distinction in the *Essays*, which might support Immerwahr's hypothesis: painters may strive to obscure anatomy's influence on their work, and the 'easy' writing style does not need defending as the 'abstruse' does.[17] But we do find a defensive passage that distinguishes between two ways of thinking, at the beginning of 'Of Commerce'. Does this distinction correspond to that between the anatomist and the painter?

---

[7] *E* (LF), p. 465, *E* (C), p. 332. 　　[8] *E* (LF), p.177n, *E* (C), p. 147n; *E* (LF), p. 244, *E* (C), p. 193.
[9] *E* (LF), p. 5, *E* (C), p. 36; *E* (LF), p. 539, *E* (C), p. 7.
[10] *E* (LF), p. 50, *E* (C), p. 63; *E* (LF), pp. 62–63, *E* (C), pp. 69–70.
[11] *E* (LF), p. 75, *E* (C), p. 78; *E* (LF), pp. 577–79.
[12] John Immerwahr, 'The Anatomist and the Painter: The Continuity of Hume's *Treatise* and *Essays*', *Hume Studies*, 17 (1991), pp. 1–14, at p. 7.
[13] For helpful reviews of this literature, see Kate Abramson, 'Happy to Unite, or Not?', *Philosophy Compass*, 1 (2006), pp. 290–302; and Abramson, 'Hume's Distinction between Philosophical Anatomy and Painting', *Philosophy Compass*, 2 (2007), pp. 680–98.
[14] *HL*, I, p. 32. 　　[15] *T*, p. 395. 　　[16] *EHU*, p. 12. 　　[17] Ibid.

Not on the face of things. Instead of being restricted to two manners of moral philosophy, this distinction encompasses 'the greater part of mankind' – not flatteringly. This greater part comprises, Hume writes, *'shallow* thinkers, who fall short of the truth' and *'abstruse* thinkers, who go beyond it'.[18] Most fall into the first category. The rare third type possesses *'solid* understanding'.[19] But Hume expresses fondness for the abstruse thinker, defending him as 'by far the most useful and valuable'. The shallow thinker 'tells us nothing but what we can learn from every coffee-house conversation'.[20] These thinkers do not seem to be the painters, whose successful efforts Hume praises. The painters' work 'enters more into common life; moulds the heart and affections; and, by touching those principles which actuate men, reforms their conduct, and brings them nearer to that model of perfection which it describes'; they therefore enjoy 'the most durable, as well as justest fame'.[21]

The abstruse thinkers in 'Of Commerce' and those of solid understanding, however, share a mode of thinking with the abstruse philosophers of the *Treatise* and *Enquiry*. The metaphor here is chemical, not anatomical. Shallow thinkers accuse the others of being 'refiners': abstruse thinking seeks 'to distinguish, in a great number of particulars, that common circumstance in which they all agree, ... to extract it, pure and unmixed, from the other superfluous circumstances'.[22] Compare this description to the effort to 'render all our principles as universal as possible, by tracing up our experiments to the utmost, and explaining all effects from the simplest and fewest causes' described as necessary in the introduction to the *Treatise*.[23] Both resemble the abstruse philosophers described in *EHU* 1, who, 'Proceeding from particular instances to general principles, ... still push on their enquiries to principles more general, and rest not satisfied till they arrive at those original principles, by which, in every science, all human curiosity must be bounded.'[24]

It is no surprise that the 'anatomist' seems to be a chemist here. Even in the *Treatise*, as Tamás Demeter argues, Hume's metaphorical anatomy depends on chemistry.[25] The chemistry metaphor clarifies that philosophical scientists' work requires ignoring elements that obscure relevant causal

---

[18] *E* (LF), p. 253, *E* (C), p. 199.   [19] *E* (LF), p. 254, *E* (C), p. 199.
[20] *E* (LF), p. 253, *E* (C), p. 199.   [21] *EHU*, p. 6.   [22] *E* (LF), p. 254, *E* (C), p. 199.
[23] *T*, p. 5.   [24] *EHU*, p. 5.
[25] 'In this sense Hume's anatomy of the mind is founded on its physiology, the study of its operations, which in turn is understood in terms of a chemical image of elective affinities and qualitative transformations' (Tamás Demeter, *David Hume and the Culture of Scottish Newtonianism: Methodology and Ideology in Enlightenment Inquiry* (Leiden, 2017), p. 145).

forces. An anatomist removes a protective, attractive covering, but every-thing underneath is of interest. The refining chemist removes impurities and extracts one substance of interest. In Hume's analogy, such substances are the 'general principles' that 'if just and sound, must always prevail in the general course of things, though they may fail in particular cases'.[26] This thought is also present in the *Treatise*: many of its intricate passages are paths Hume takes to explain why a general principle still applies despite an apparent exception.

As the introduction to 'Of Commerce' continues, Hume indicates that he is speaking in the voice of a philosopher. After the above remark about general principles prevailing, he adds, 'and it is the chief business of philosophers to regard the general course of things'.[27] The following paragraph makes it clear that this introduction is not to a single essay but to the whole of the *Political Discourses*: 'I thought this introduction necessary before the following discourses on *commerce, money, interest, balance of trade, &c.* where, perhaps, there will occur some principles which are uncommon, and which may seem too refined and subtile for such vulgar subjects.'[28] In these essays, at least, he writes as a philosopher, in accordance with a conception of philosophy articulated in his earliest published work.

Yet there is an important difference between the search for general principles in the *Political Discourses* and that in the *Treatise* and *Enquiries*. The latter search is within a bounded domain – the human mind. The introduction to the *Treatise* presents a foundationalist concep-tion of the 'science of MAN' – a warrior science, which, 'instead of taking now and then a castle or village on the frontier, [can] march up directly to the capital or center of [the other] sciences, to human nature itself; which being once masters of, we may every where else hope for an easy victory'.[29] The task of the *Treatise* is to discover the principles of the mind's 'powers and faculties', recognising that we cannot go beyond experience, but using 'careful and exact experiments, and the observation of those particular effects, which result from [the mind's] different circumstances and situ-ations'.[30] All the other sciences depend on this one, including 'Morals and criticism', which 'regard our tastes and sentiments' and 'politics', which 'consider men as united in society, and dependent on each other'.[31] Understanding the principles of human nature, and understanding the limits of our understanding, will allow us to build 'a compleat system of

---

[26] *E* (LF), p. 254, *E* (C), pp. 199–200.   [27] *E* (LF), p. 254, *E* (C), p. 200.
[28] *E* (LF), p. 255, *E* (C), p. 200.   [29] Ibid.   [30] *T*, p. 5.   [31] Ibid., p. 4.

the sciences, built on a foundation almost entirely new, and the only one upon which they can stand with any security'.[32]

The chastened opening of the first *Enquiry* evinces no such braggadocio about complete systems and easy victories over other sciences. And there is much disagreement over which, if any, of the manners of philosophy outlined in the first *Enquiry* Hume recommends. Its domain, however, is clear. The two manners of philosophy are both versions of 'moral philosophy,[33] or the science of human nature'.[34] What he is attempting is 'an accurate scrutiny into the powers and faculties of human nature'.[35]

Even if we limit ourselves to the essays in the first edition of *Political Discourses*, which 'Of Commerce' introduces, the range of topics they discuss is vast. Nonetheless, we can trust that Hume believes them to be about politics, in the broad sense that includes what we now call economics. We might think of these essays, therefore, as applications of the science of human nature to a 'dependent' science. This conception is not wholly wrong; Hume refers in the *Essays* to principles of human nature that he has identified in other works. And regardless of whether the principles of human nature appealed to in the *Essays* can be found in the *Treatise* or *Enquiries*, many of the arguments in the *Political Discourses* depend upon theses about how humans tend to behave and how various policies can be expected to influence that behavior.

There is something more going on here, however. Hume not only applies principles of human nature but he also continues to argue that there are such principles, that they operate as do natural causes with law-like regularity, and that this determinism holds even when events appear unaccountable or contrary to the general course of nature.

Hume prosecutes these theses at the beginning of 'Of Commerce' itself. These are the points missed by the shallow thinkers, for whom 'every judgment or conclusion ... is particular'.[36] Unable to see the general causes underlying particular events, they accuse the reasoning that uncovers these causes of being 'intricate and obscure'. (Note the common Latin root of 'intricate' and 'tricky'. The shallow thinkers believe that those of more profound understanding are playing tricks on them.) Hume's

[32] Ibid.
[33] Hume may not be using 'moral' here in the same way as he is in *EHU* 12.30 (p. 122): 'Moral reasonings are either concerning particular or general facts.' Here, 'moral' seems to mean only probable rather than demonstrative. The earlier references use moral in the sense of 'based on a knowledge of the general tendencies of human nature'. The *OED*, however, includes both these meanings in a single definition.
[34] *EHU*, p. 5.   [35] Ibid., p. 10.   [36] *E* (LF), p. 254, *E* (C), p. 199.

persuasion here is *ad hominem*. The vulgar have only particular judgments; only those of superior understandings recognise the general causes. But these paragraphs actually introduce a much longer argument for the existence of these causes, constituted by what he believes is the successful search for them in the succeeding essays. Here, he seeks to convince his readers rhetorically to take seriously the possibility of such causes, to persuade by asking them to join him among those of solid understanding.

This introduction also identifies an objection to such a science – the observation that in particular cases, general principles seem to fail. Hume recognises the veracity of this observation; hence his warning against using refined reasoning on particular matters: 'Something is sure to happen, that will disconcert his reasoning, and produce an event different from what he expected'.[37] Yet to infer from such experiences that no general principles are to be found is fallacious. Given the prevalence of hasty generalisation, it seems odd that Hume chooses to criticise 'every judgment' being particular. But he is recognising the converse fallacy of 'hasty counter-example', committed when people dismiss the general principle in light of a single or a few apparently contrary events. The vaccine is not efficacious, they reason, because there are breakthrough cases. Such reasoning leads to belief in libertarian free will: because apparently similar motives produce different effects, we posit actions with no causal motives whatsoever. It also generates belief in miracles: failing to understand the physics of freezing point depression, the shallow thinker believes a miracle has occurred when an impurity is added to water and it instantly becomes solid, since this is not how water generally behaves. In this case, the observer admits the existence of a cause, but it is one outside the natural order of things, beyond the reach of science. Both these beliefs Hume takes pains to undermine elsewhere.

The insistence on general principles, and the consequent value of the search for them that constitutes one kind of philosophical thinking, is not limited to the later essays. 'That Politics May Be Reduced to a Science', present in the *Essays* from the first edition of 1741, contends that 'so great is the force of laws, and of particular forms of government, and so little dependence have they on the humours and tempers of men, that consequences almost as general and certain may sometimes be deduced from them, as any which the mathematical sciences afford us'.[38] Hume details some 'universal axioms' that this science teaches, but the essay's title as well as his claim that he is presenting these axioms 'in order to prove more fully,

---

[37] Ibid.   [38] *E* (LF), p. 16, *E* (C), p. 42.

that politics admit of general truths, which are invariable by the humour or
education either of subject or sovereign', show that increasing confidence
in the possibility of general principles in politics is a significant aspect of
his aim.[39] 'Of Some Remarkable Customs' appears to cut the opposite
way, warning that 'that all general maxims in politics ought to be established with great caution'.[40] It details three exceptions to what any political
scientist would expect, thus calling into question the force of those
universal axioms.[41] Yet for each example, Hume explains the particular
causes that counteract the general principles in these cases. The essay,
therefore, does not undermine the relevant kind of scientific reasoning; it
reinforces its nature as probabilistic, while insisting that the exceptions are
explicable after the fact, if not predictable in advance.

Hume, in the *Essays*, therefore continues to make the case that we can,
as philosophical scientists, study human things — arguing that there are
general principles behind human behavior, adding to those identified in
other works, and applying the principles to an expanded set of questions.
'Of Superstition and Enthusiasm', for instance, seeks the causes of these
two modes of false religion in the principles of human nature. 'Of the
Dignity or Meanness of Human Nature' identifies the ability to engage in
such science as one of the aspects of humanity that elevates us above other
animals: the human 'traces causes and effects to a great length and
intricacy' and 'extracts general principles from particular appearances'.[42]
This language — referring to intricacy and extraction — is remarkably
consistent across the decade that separates the first publication of 'Dignity
or Meanness' and that of 'Of Commerce'.[43] And the Hume of the *Political
Discourses* does not think of himself as doing politics, economics, history,
or demography instead of philosophy. In 'Of the Populousness of Ancient
Nations', he indicates, as in 'Of Commerce', that the work he is doing is
philosophy: examining the records of history, 'philosophers ought to
abandon' any narratives prior to Thucydides, whose first page constitutes

[39] *E* (LF), p. 18, *E* (C), p. 43. See also Hume's discussion of the difficulty of distinguishing what arises
   from chance (or 'secret and unknown causes') from what arises from 'determinate and known
   causes' at the beginning of 'Of the Rise and Progress of the Arts and Sciences' (*E* (LF), pp. 111–12,
   E (C), p. 101).
[40] *E* (LF), p. 366, *E* (C), p. 273.
[41] The examples are the Athenian 'indictment of illegality', by which those who proposed a law could
   be punished by a common court after it had been passed by the assembly of the people; the system
   of two independent legislatures in the Roman republic; and the English custom of pressing seamen
   into service.
[42] *E* (LF), p. 82, *E* (C), p. 82.
[43] The former appeared in the first edition of *Essays, Moral and Political*, published in 1741 as 'Of the
   Dignity of Human Nature'; 'Of Commerce' appeared in 1752.

'the commencement of real history'.[44] This is direction offered to those engaged in the same inquiry Hume pursues in this essay. Even if we limit – contrary to his usage – philosophy to the search for general principles behind multiform phenomena, he continues to engage in philosophy in the *Essays*. But it is hard to see what would justify such a limit.

4.2 The Shape of The *Essays*

The presence of refining philosophical science does not distinguish the *Treatise* or *Enquiries* from the *Essays*. Clearly, however, there are remarkable differences in form. In 'On Philosophical Form: A Tear for Adonais', Louis Mackey uses the second *Enquiry*'s 'Of the Association of Ideas' as one of three examples to support his thesis that 'form and content are just as tightly bound to each other in a philosophical essay as they are in a poem or a novel or a drama'.[45] The others are Plato's *Euthyphro* and Thomas Aquinas's question on truth from the *Summa Theologica*. In each case, Mackey analyses the work's shape: Plato's is a circle; Thomas's, an arch; and Hume's, a flat plain. Mackey, along with Jordan's frequent references to 'shape' when discussing genres, inspires much of the following reflection on shape.

For Mackey, a work's shape reflects the thinker's metaphysics: the style tracks the writer's views about whether there is a sphere beyond nature or the visible world. Plato's circle points to the unity of the Form of the Good, Thomas's arch to the God who reaches down into a creation that always already points back to God. Hume's text shows that the method of analysis works as well 'on someone who is really prosaic, a philosopher who is thoroughly naturalistic or phenomenalistic in doctrine and in method'.[46] Mackey accordingly finds in Hume's essay a flat plain over which Hume skates somewhat randomly, moving stylistically by association as he claims that the mind itself moves. (Note that principles of association do not preclude some apparent randomness. The moss on the tree outside of my window resembles both seawater and mould; the principles of association do not alone determine which of these resemblances will happen to occur to me in any instance.)

Space precludes engaging this analysis of *EHU* 3 in depth, or considering in full the forms of the *Treatise, Enquiries,* and *Essays*. I will therefore

---

[44] *E* (LF), p. 422, *E* (C), p. 307.
[45] Louis H. Mackey, 'On Philosophical Form: A Tear for Adonais', *Thought*, 42 (1967), pp. 238–60, at p. 240.
[46] Ibid., p. 252.

consider in depth only the *Treatise* and the *Essays*.[47] In the *Treatise*, we do
not find a flat work, regardless of the relation between *EHU 3* and *Treatise*
1.1.4, 'Of the connexion or association of ideas'. Instead, the divisions
between book, part, and section numbers suggests a pyramid — a structure
we might expect to find in a work pointing towards something higher,
rather than the plain of a thoroughly naturalistic, prosaic philosopher. The
three books are at the top, the parts one level down, and the ninety
sections of the main body of the text stretched out below, at the foundation. But this pyramid is flattened at the top, with the three books on a
level and the one at the center ('Of the Passions') serving as bridge rather
than apex. It is more mesa than pyramid. Had Hume completed his
planned books on politics and criticism,[48] the top surface would be more
extended, augmenting the tabular effect.

What justifies thinking of this as a mesa rather than inverting it into a
bowl, with the sections at the wide top, or turning it on its side like on open
lily? Either one of these shapes seems to better suit the sceptical mind: they
suggest the possibility of further growth, development, or branching. At times
in the *Treatise*, Hume suggests such possibilities. He acknowledges that he
may have missed or overlooked something, invites his reader to fill in gaps,
and promises to revise his opinion accordingly. Yet a suspicious reader might
justly doubt the sincerity of such promises, since he often goes on to declare
his original reasoning certain or proved, perhaps even declaring the inad-
equacy of human faculties to come up with such alternatives.[49]

Regardless, the language with which Hume introduces the *Treatise* does
not suggest ongoing branching or openness. On the contrary, he promises
a 'compleat system of the sciences, built on a foundation almost entirely
new, and the only one upon which they can stand with any security'. The
'solid foundation' of this new science must be 'experience and observation', and we cannot expect any explanation of ultimate principles. But
once the work of experience and observation is finished, we can 'sit down
contented', satisfied by the gentle despair of being able to do no more.[50]
This is a stable structure whose base is wider than its summit, not a
precarious Chihuly macchia bowl.

---

[47] Although Hume titles the collection of his philosophical works *Essays and Treatises on Several Subjects*, he neither includes the *Treatise of Human Nature* nor uses the word 'treatise' in his titles within the collection. James Harris writes that in *ETSS*, 'The distinction between "essays" and "treatises" was the distinction, simply, between shorter and more extended pieces of writing' (James A. Harris, *Hume: An Intellectual Biography* (Cambridge, 2015), p. 303).
[48] See *T*, p. 2.   [49] See, for example, *T*, p. 141. But see also the qualification at *T*, p. 178.
[50] *T*, pp. 4–5.

There is no such unity of shape in the *Essays*. It is striking how many begin with dichotomies or more complex divisions. We find the distinction between that which is 'owing to *chance*' and that which 'proceeds from causes' ('Of the Rise and Progress of the Arts and Sciences'); between good and bad luxury ('Of Refinement in the Arts'); and between the ancient policy of saving for war during peace and the modern practice of contracting public debt in times of need ('Of Public Credit'). Sometimes the distinction is embedded in a question: for instance, the distinction between competing theses about governance at the beginning of 'That Politics May Be Reduced to a Science': 'whether there be any essential difference between one form of government and another' or 'whether every form may not become good or bad, according as it is well or ill administered'?[51] Some distinctions are implicit: the first sentence of 'Of the Original Contract' observes that 'no party, in the present age, can well support itself, without a philosophical or speculative system of principles, annexed to its political or practical one'.[52] Just offstage is another age in which no such dissimulation was required of those who banded together in parties just because of loyalty to a leader or mutual interest.[53] Sometimes an initial distinction branches into a complex tree: 'Of the First Principles of Government' opens with the claim that government is founded on opinion, not force: having chosen opinion from this dichotomy, Hume then distinguishes opinion of interest from opinion of right, and the latter into right to power and right to property. 'Of the Original Contract', again, presents several explicit distinctions in addition to the implicit one: speculative principles used to justify parties include contract theories and divine right theories; each has a theoretical component and a practical implication; each of these admits of an extreme and a just interpretation. Sometimes a distinction defines the entire essay: delicacy of taste or passion, an absolute monarchy or republic, superstition or enthusiasm, dignity or meanness.

Beginning with distinctions is not itself distinguishing: one need look no further than Hume's *Treatise* for precedent. Perceptions of the human mind are impressions or ideas; these are either reflective or secondary; part of the latter are passions. Nor is Hume unusual in this respect. This basic tool of analysis is to philosophy as a hammer is to carpentry.

The significance of these distinctions does not become apparent until we examine the end of the essays as well as their beginnings. We find the

---

[51] *E* (LF), p. 14, *E* (C), p. 41.   [52] *E* (LF), p. 465, *E* (C), p. 332.
[53] Compare 'Of Parties in General', *E* (LF), p. 56, *E* (C), p. 66; *E* (LF), p. 60, *E* (C), p. 68.

occasional tidy summation or attempt at *bons mots*, but remarkably often, the essays end with warnings. 'Of Refinement in the Arts' warns that government attempts to cure excessive luxury may encourage more harmful vices. 'Of the First Principles of Government' ends with a caution against 'encouraging a passion for . . . dangerous novelties'.[54] 'Of Simplicity and Refinement in Writing' advises that, given some signs of 'degeneracy of taste' into excess refinement, contemporary writers should err on the side of simplicity.[55]

A warning, as Hume knew well, is a persuasive device. At the beginning, he encourages the reader to see two (or more) possible directions for movement: the warnings suggest which one to take. These dichotomies are not the Vs of table legs, supporting a steady and enclosed structure. They are the rays of an angle, each of whose sides is a vector. The dichotomies of the *Essays* do not merely introduce Cartesian enumerations or Baconian tables. They instead introduce directions for actions or conclusions; the essay then demonstrates the consequences for proceeding in the various directions. Readers are not skating over a flat plain; they are clambering out on branches, only to sometimes find their extension cut off by Hume's arguments. Jumping to the next branch is rarely an option; one must retrace one's steps to the beginning and venture out again. Sometimes none of the branches seem very sturdy, and one has little choice but to linger near the trunk of the tree.

All of the above is oversimplified. Often Hume guides his readers through this process multiple times within a single essay. And the available branches at the end may not be at all what they appeared to be at the beginning.

Take, for instance, 'Of the Balance of Power' — best understood in relation to the previous two essays, 'Of the Balance of Trade' and 'Of the Jealousy of Trade'.[56] All three warn against policies rooted in jealousy rather than political wisdom. But 'Of the Balance of Power' begins with a question apparently of mere historical interest: 'whether the *idea* of the balance of power be owing entirely to modern policy, or whether the *phrase* only has been invented in these later ages?'[57] The presumption

---

[54] *E* (LF), p. 36, *E* (C), p. 53.   [55] *E* (LF), p. 196, *E* (C), p. 160.
[56] 'Of the Jealousy of Trade' was a later addition, first appearing in 1758. But it is clearly on the same theme as its flanking essays. A comprehensive study of the shape of the essays would need to consider that some of the essays are meant to be grouped together. For instance, the 'essays on happiness', 'Of the Original Contract' and 'Of Passive Obedience', and the essays initially published as *Political Discourses* contain internal references to the other members of their set.
[57] *E* (LF), p. 332, *E* (C), p. 252.

behind this question is that modern thinkers recognise that nations should strive to keep any one neighbour from gaining excessive power relative to the others. The essay thus begins by flattering modern readers who, it seems, are superior to their ancient counterparts. The flattery does not last long, however: the second sentence presents evidence to the contrary, noting Xenophon's awareness of the importance of the balance. The ensuing discussion hacks away at the remaining branches of modern pride on the subject: records of ancient practice show that Greek city-states acted in accordance with the principle, and the testimony of ancient historians and orators shows that its importance was recognised by contemporaries. In what turns out to be foreshadowing, Hume acknowledges the possibility that the Greeks acted from motives of '*jealous emulation*' rather than '*cautious politics*', but observes that 'the effects were alike'.[58] He admits that the surrounding principalities seemed oblivious to the encroaching threat of Rome, allowing the Romans to conquer enormous territory rapidly, ensuring their own enslavement and destruction. (It will be important to remember a point from the second *Political Discourse* – that Rome's destruction was ensured not by their reputed luxury but by 'an ill modelled government, and the unlimited extent of conquests'.[59] Rome's untrammeled expansion led to its eventual implosion.) Yet even in the Roman case, Hume cites an exception: Hiero of Syracuse aided Carthage to curtail Rome's power, and Polybius approves his 'great wisdom and prudence'.[60]

Thus where the essay began presenting an attractive branch of possibility – that the moderns are more politically wise than the ancients – that branch is severed by its twelfth paragraph. Attention to the balance of power had 'an influence on all the wiser and more experienced princes and politicians' of the ancient world. What's worse for modern prospects: 'even at present, however generally known and acknowledged among speculative reasoners, it has not, in practice, an authority much more extensive among those who govern the world'.[61]

At this point, it seems that an alternative branch is clear: rather than resting in a sense of superiority to the ancients, the moderns must pay more attention to the balance of power. And this seems to be where Hume is going. Who are the latter-day threats? He mentions the empire of Charles V, but it, like Rome, fell from power because of internal forces, including 'extensive but divided dominions' and wealth in gold and silver rather than labor and industry. We then arrive at the contemporary threat: France.

---

[58] *E* (LF), p. 334, *E* (C), p. 253.   [59] *E* (LF), p. 276, *E* (C), p. 214.
[60] *E* (LF), p. 337, *E* (C), p. 255.   [61] *E* (LF), p. 338, *E* (C), p. 255.

Here, he again begins with flattery: 'In the general wars, maintained against this ambitious power, GREAT BRITAIN has stood foremost; and she still maintains her station.'[62] Is the lesson then that Britons should feel proud of and continue their strategies to maintain the peace and freedom of Europe?

Hume quickly cuts off this branch also. Without denying some benefit from Britain's historical antagonism to France, he explains that the British have gone too far in the extent of their animosity and in ignoble motives. That 'spirit of jealous emulation' of which the Greeks were accused is no stranger to the British spirit: it has often led the British to extend violence beyond necessity 'from obstinacy and passion'.[63] It has also assured other European nations that they have a partner in any hostility towards France, multiplying and extending violent conflicts. Most dangerous of all from Hume's perspective, British hatred inspires the most dangerous of domestic policies — mortgaging 'our revenues at so deep a rate, in wars, where we were only accessories, . . . the most fatal delusion, that a nation, which had any pretension to politics and prudence, has ever yet been guilty of'.[64] The last paragraph of the essay indicates that, like earlier empires, French ambition contains the seeds of its own destruction. Without denying the evils of 'enormous monarchies', which are 'destructive to human nature . . . even in their downfal', Hume insists that this downfall 'never can be very distant from their establishment'.[65] He does not encourage complacency but warns that the eventual effect of intemperate hatred of France might be the opposite and also dangerous extreme of 'rendering us totally careless and supine with regard to the fate of EUROPE'.[66] But the present danger is immoderate hostility. This essay, then, carries the same message as its two predecessors: wise policy recommends a tempering of aggressions to Britain's neighbour across the Channel. The possible choices at the end are thus wide of what they appeared at the beginning, but only through the severing of the original branches do the true possibilities for growth become visible to the reader.

Consider an earlier essay on a different kind of topic, 'Of Eloquence', published in the second volume of *Essays: Moral and Political* in 1742.[67] Its opening distinction introduces another distinction. The first is between qualities of humanity with respect to their variation across periods of history. 'In *civil* history', Hume claims, there is 'a much greater uniformity than in the history of learning and science'; 'the wars, negotiations, and

---

[62] Ibid.   [63] *E* (LF), p. 339, *E* (C), p. 256.   [64] *E* (LF), p. 340, *E* (C), p. 256.
[65] *E* (LF), pp. 340–41, *E* (C), p. 257.   [66] *E* (LF), p. 340, *E* (C), p. 256.
[67] On this essay, see also Chapter 10 by Ross Carroll in the present volume.

politics of one age resemble more those of another, than the taste, wit, and speculative principles'.[68] The former depend on 'passions' stable in human nature; the latter on 'the sentiments and understanding, easily varied by education and example'.[69] The topic of this essay falls into the latter category, and Hume foreshadows here the significance of example and emulation in what follows. Note, however, the irony: this category of taste has great political significance: oratory is the aesthetic skill of legislature and judicial debate. Moreover, Hume's analysis concludes that modern oratory would better follow the ancient style — the 'sublime and *passionate*'.[70] He prepares us in this opening paragraph to have his initial distinction thoroughly undermined: with oratory, no appeal to expected variations in taste will suffice.

Here Hume offers little opening flattery, and only under a conditional: '*if* we be superior in philosophy, we are still, notwithstanding all our refinements, much inferior in eloquence'.[71] I do not doubt that he believes modern philosophy to be superior, but the conditional suggests a hesitation to assure readers of the same. He does not want them to get distracted by their superiority in one area when trying to persuade them to improve in another.

The structure of this essay is well-ordered; here Hume follows in writing the advice that he gives for speech at the end of the essay. He spends about a third of the essay amassing evidence for his claim of modern inferiority and then appears to begin a search for causes: 'One is somewhat at a loss to what cause we may ascribe so sensible a decline of eloquence in later ages.'[72] But this search turns out to be consummately practical. The first explanations he considers offer a very short branch indeed: they all imply that there is nothing for the insipid modern orator to do. Perhaps the ancient legal system's simplicity left more room and need for public debate, or its violence and disorder more need for vivid condemnation. Or perhaps modern audiences are just too rational to be susceptible to the wiles of the rhetorician. Hume objects to all these possibilities, but if any of them were cogent, those with discernment enough to perceive the decline would either have to accept that this form of beauty has been sacrificed to the age of reason or lament passively that contemporary circumstances are not fertile ground for brilliant speechmaking.

Having concluded that none of these explanations are satisfactory, Hume proffers another possibility — that no general explanation is

---

[68] *E* (LF), p. 97, *E* (C), p. 92.   [69] *E* (LF), pp. 97–98, *E* (C), p. 92.
[70] *E* (LF), p. 108, *E* (C), p. 98; italics mine.   [71] *E* (LF), p. 98, *E* (C), p. 92; italics mine.
[72] *E* (LF), p. 102, *E* (C), p. 94.

available; modern Britain suffers from an accidental want of rhetorical talent, with no inspiring models to 'rouze the genius of the nation, excite the emulation of the youth, and accustom our ears to a more sublime and more pathetic elocution'.[73] If the essay's goal were to discover a general explanation for its opening assessment, acceding to this hypothesis would constitute a failure. But if its aim is practical, the hypothesis provides another branch for action. If all we need are inspiring examples, any talented speaker bold enough to attempt sublime oratory might set a different course for the nation. The following paragraphs add encouragement, assuring that the public are the ultimate arbiters of oratory and will respond well to the effort, and that modern orators need not lose their grip on rational argument or extemporaneous locution to improve. The final paragraph then gives one specific piece of advice: that significant progress might be made by contemporary speakers emulating this well-structured essay (although Hume does not put it this way). They ought, without overwhelming their audiences with distinctions, 'to observe a method, and make that method conspicuous to the hearers, who will be infinitely pleased to see the arguments rise naturally from one another, and will retain a more thorough persuasion, than can arise from the strongest reasons which are thrown together in confusion'.[74]

These two very different essays take the reader on a journey that extends beyond the essays themselves. The journey within the essays is organised and methodical: these are not Montaignean streams of consciousness. And Hume offers clear advice for the course of action he believes ought to be pursued in each one. Yet the journeys are full of switchbacks, and in each he emphasises the influence of accidental causes beyond the deliberative control of any person or set of persons.

4.3   The Pedagogy of The *Essays'* Shape

What is the significance of these branching, shrinking, and lengthening vectors? Jordan insists that philosophical writing is always a form of pedagogy. There is, he observes, a 'root-connection between philosophy and teaching – that is, between philosophy and persuasion'.[75] What is the pedagogy of the *Essays'* shape, and how does that pedagogy differ from the *Treatise*'s?

The solid mesa of the *Treatise* portrays philosophy as a project one might complete. As we have seen, even in describing the sceptical limits of what follows in the *Treatise*'s Introduction, Hume expresses confidence in the consummate nature of the work: 'When we see, that we have arrived at the utmost extent of human reason, we sit down contented, tho' we be perfectly satisfy'd in the main of our ignorance . . . . And as this impossibility of making any farther progress is enough to satisfy the reader, so the writer may derive a more delicate satisfaction from the free confession of his ignorance, and from his prudence in avoiding that error, into which so many have fallen, of imposing their conjectures and hypotheses on the world for the most certain principles. When this mutual contentment and satisfaction can be obtain'd betwixt the master and scholar, I know not what more we can require of our philosophy.'[76]

This passage implicitly acknowledges the pedagogical relation between writer and reader: readers will be satisfied only if the writer has persuaded them that despair of 'more' is appropriate. Note also the ironic combination of certainty and scepticism: this certainty is born of despair rather than epistemic triumph, but Descartes himself could not be more confident in the completeness of his project. Hume speaks from the top of the mesa, looking down on apparently firm and balanced legs beneath him. The advertisement preceding this introduction does promise something more — the third volume on morals and the never-to-be-published volumes on politics and criticism. But these volumes would only further stabilise the shape: there is every indication that, once they are completed, philosophy will have no more to say.

The shape of the *Treatise*, in other words, teaches that philosophy is something to be pursued at a certain stage and then moved beyond, as Callicles claims in the *Gorgias*.[77] The rays and angles of the *Essays*, however, teach that philosophical thinking is never complete and appropriately ongoing. This is a more profoundly sceptical pedagogy, with no implication that one can rest assured that examination of the phenomena is complete or that one has done all that one philosophically can do. Again, Hume does not use 'philosophy' only to describe a particular epistemic or metaphysical project, but he does indicate in the *Essays* that he understands himself to be writing as a philosopher.

The search for principles of human nature remains germane, as does the broader search for causal principles. Without confidence that there are such principles, we invent other explanations — the explanations of

---

[76] *T*, p. 5.   [77] Plato, *Gorgias*, 485.

superstition that produce slaves and tyrants, and the explanations of free will that undermine our capacity for moral judgment and reform. By Hume's lights, these 'explanations' are no explanations at all. We can construct no political structures or moral policy on the basis of an arbitrary divine will or mysteriously undetermined free choice. Undermining the possibility of such constructions is only one of the evils attending these hypotheses. In the *Essays*, as elsewhere, Hume is eloquent on the harms — personal, social, and political — of the 'pestilent distemper' of superstition. His claim that philosophy is its only cure is high praise.[78] The ill effects of the free will hypothesis are related: ascribing human action to a mysterious undetermined principle rather than some aspect of a person 'that is durable and constant' subverts our ability to judge character, or it would if we were capable of believing it.[79] But superstition can warp our moral sentiments, including persuading us to believe in reprehensible doctrines of eternal punishment. 'To suppose measures of approbation and blame, different from the human, confounds everything', he writes in 'Of the Immortality of the Soul'.[80] One can imagine, of course, a religion whose measures of approbation and blame transcend the human in the direction of more love and acceptance, but this was not the religion with which Hume was best acquainted. And one must admit that it has never been the dominant religion of the West.

There is therefore a moral point to the search for underlying general principles, which means that philosophy — even if construed as this narrower project — always has a practical function. But Hume does not engage in this search only for 'practical' or 'normative' reasons in the *Essays*. The detail with which he probes for such principles, as well as the range of topics these probes engage, suggest a thinker who valued the search for its own sake. If so, then Hume the essayist belongs squarely in the tradition of scepticism that understood philosophy as a continual seeking that did not preclude action, either personal or political.[81]

Speaking of shapes, we have now come full circle. It is a mistake to search for philosophy *in* the *Essays*. The *Essays are* philosophical writing. Even on the narrow construal, Hume engages in philosophical thinking in the *Essays*. But there is no reason to accept that he conceives of philosophy narrowly: his use of the terms 'philosophy' and 'philosophical' throughout

---

[78] *E* (LF), p. 577.   [79] *EHU*, p. 74.   [80] *E* (LF), p. 595.
[81] On scepticism as seeking, see Robert C. Miner, 'Pascal on the Uses of Scepticism', *Logos*, 11 (2008), pp. 1–12, at pp. 3–4. On the possibility of combining scepticism with political action, see Watkins, *The Philosophical Progress of Hume's Essays*, pp. 240–41.

are broader than this conception allows. He conceives of himself as continuing to write as a philosopher in these sometimes orderly, sometimes disjointed texts. Moreover, the shape of the *Essays* indicates that philosophy ought to be an ongoing enterprise, not one to be concluded in contented despair. This change in manner thus implies a significant change of matter, insofar as Hume no longer presents scepticism as itself bounded by the knowledge of limits. Examining what further changes in matter follow from this architectonic one must be the work of another day.

CHAPTER 5

'The Sentiments of Sects'
Epicurean, Stoic, Platonist, Sceptic

Tim Stuart-Buttle

In the 'Advertisement' to volume 1 (1741) of the *Essays, Moral and Political*, Hume cautioned that his 'Reader must not look for any Connexion among these ESSAYS, but must consider each of them as a Work apart'.[1] Yet he also acknowledged, in the corresponding 'Advertisement' to volume 2 (1742), that the collection of four essays – 'The Epicurean', 'The Stoic', 'The Platonist', and 'The Sceptic' – represented an exception to this rule. He did so to offer a different caution: 'Tis proper to inform the READER, that, in those ESSAYS, intitled, *The Epicurean, Stoic*, &c. a certain Character is personated; and therefore, no Offence ought to be taken at any Sentiments contain'd in them.'[2] In the 1748 edition, Hume further qualified the purpose of these essays in a footnote at the start of 'The Epicurean':

> The intention of this and the three following essays is not so much to explain accurately the sentiments of the ancient sects of philosophy, as to deliver the sentiments of sects, that naturally form themselves in the world, and entertain different ideas of human life and of happiness. I have given each of them the name of the philosophical sect, to which it bears the greatest affinity.[3]

These pieces, which John Immerwahr aptly (and influentially) christened 'Hume's essays on happiness', reveal very considerable care, labour and artfulness on the part of their author.[4] If Hume was, until his dying day, committed to 'continually improving and correcting [his] Works in successive Editions', it is noteworthy that the only significant revision made to

---

[1] *E* (C), p. 529. [2] Ibid., p. 530. [3] *E* (LF), p. 138n1, *E* (C), p. 119n1.
[4] John Immerwahr, 'Hume's Essays on Happiness', *Hume Studies*, 15 (1989), pp. 307–24. This represented the first sustained treatment of the four essays; and all subsequent scholars who have worked on them quite properly acknowledge their debt to Immerwahr's path-breaking study.

the four essays was the addition of a footnote (revealingly, in Hume's own voice) to 'The Sceptic' in 1768.[5] The essays disclose the extent of Hume's attentiveness to the relationship between literary form and philosophical content; and, as Immerwahr was perhaps the first to recognise, their careful interpretation promises to illuminate fundamental aspects of Hume's philosophical project as a whole.[6] Yet here we recall Duncan Forbes's salutary warning to Hume scholars, that

> Hume is terrible campaign country, rugged, broken, cross-grained, complex, remorseless in its demands. One has to fight every inch of the way, and can never feel really secure. No interpretation ever seems to get going before it is pulled up almost immediately by some difficulty ... And this perhaps is the ultimate mystery of Hume's 'scepticism', which the devotees eventually attain to.[7]

In the case of the four essays, I will argue, a necessary point of departure is for the interpreter – initially, at least – to accept Hume's caution to his reader that each essay is an exercise in 'personation' or philosophical ventriloquism.[8] The 'mystery of Hume's "scepticism"' will not be demystified (if, indeed, it can be) simply by identifying Hume with 'The Sceptic', as various commentators have been inclined to do.[9] Rather than asking whether Hume's own 'sentiments' correspond 'naturally' to one or other of the sects, a better question to pose is why Hume's essays focus on 'sentiment' at all – rather than, for example, philosophical reasoning and argument. After all, it was axiomatic for Hume that 'all doctrines are to be suspected, which are favoured by our passions'.[10] It may be that my view

---

[5] *HL*, II, p. 239; this point is noted by T. H. Grose in *The Philosophical Works of David Hume*, eds. T. H. Green and T. H. Grose (4 vols., London, 1886), III, p. 45. On his deathbed, Hume 'diverted himself with inventing several jocular excuses, which he supposed he might make to Charon' so as to delay embarking on his boat to the underworld, notably that 'I have been correcting my works for a new edition': Adam Smith to William Strahan, 9 November 1776, in *E* (LF), pp. xliii–xliv.

[6] For particularly rich discussions of the four essays that probe the relationship between form and content, see Colin Heydt, 'Relations of Literary Form and Philosophical Purpose in Hume's Four Essays on Happiness', *Hume Studies*, 33 (2007), pp. 3–19; and Isabel Rivers, *Reason, Grace and Sentiment: A Study in the Language of Religion and Ethics in England, 1660–1780* (2 vols., Cambridge, 1991–2000), II, ch. 4.

[7] Duncan Forbes, *Hume's Philosophical Politics* (Cambridge, 1975), pp. viii–ix.

[8] For the popularity of such philosophical ventriloquism in the eighteenth century, further evidenced by Montesquieu's *Persian Letters* (1721), Voltaire's *Philosophical Dictionary* (1764), and the general popularity of the novel, see Genevieve Lloyd, *Enlightenment Shadows* (Oxford, 2013), esp. ch. 3.

[9] See particularly the comments by Grose in *Philosophical Works of Hume*, III, pp. 46–47; and Robert J. Fogelin, *Hume's Scepticism in the Treatise of Human Nature* (London, 1985), p. 119 (the Sceptic advances Hume's position 'under the thinnest possible disguise').

[10] Hume, 'Of the Immortality of the Soul', *E* (LF), p. 598.

of 'human life and of happiness' seems 'naturally' to correspond to that of the Stoic (for example), but this need not imply that the Stoics' attempt to *justify* such a view as inherently superior to all others by means of philosophical argument is a convincing (or even a legitimate) exercise.

A second, and related, question to ask is: why do Hume's essays take the form of philosophical *monologue*, rather than *dialogue*? Hume, like many contemporaries, saw the appropriateness and effectiveness of the dialogue form for certain kinds of philosophical inquiry.[11] The third Earl of Shaftesbury, whose 'rhapsodic style' Hume 'parodies' in 'The Stoic' and 'The Platonist', and Bernard Mandeville, whose critiques of Stoicism bear comparison to those offered by 'The Sceptic', had recently composed dialogues that focused squarely on the question of which ideas of 'human life and of happiness' (represented by different philosophical sects) were most philosophically compelling.[12] More pertinently still, commentators are agreed that Cicero's *De finibus bonorum et malorum* served as a model for Hume's four essays, and Hume's admiration for this work (and its author) is unquestionable.[13] But Cicero's work takes the dialogue form, as Hume's essays do not. If Hume was content to follow Cicero in employing the dialogue to interrogate the philosophical foundations of natural theology, the case was otherwise when it came to moral subjects.[14]

I turn to these two questions in Section 5.2. To broach them, however, a broader understanding of Hume's engagements with ancient philosophy – initially with a view to reforming himself (as a rather intense youth), and later to introducing a 'reformation' in 'the science of man' – is required.[15] This context is sketched, necessarily briefly, in Section 5.1.[16]

---

[11] Michael B. Prince, *Philosophical Dialogue in the British Enlightenment: Theology, Aesthetics and the Novel* (Cambridge, 1996).

[12] For Hume's parody of Shaftesbury's *Moralists*, see Rivers, *Reason, Grace and Sentiment*, II, p. 76.

[13] As evidenced by Hume's exchange with Hutcheson in 1739, discussed below. For Hume's admiration for Cicero, see Tim Stuart-Buttle, *From Moral Theology to Moral Philosophy: Cicero and Visions of Humanity from Locke to Hume* (Oxford, 2019), ch. 5.

[14] Hume's debt in the *Dialogues concerning Natural Religion* to the form, as well as content, of *De natura deorum* is universally acknowledged, but for an unusually penetrating analysis, see Christine Battersby, 'The *Dialogues* as Original Imitation: Cicero and the Nature of Hume's Skepticism', in Nicholas Capaldi et al., eds., *McGill Hume Studies* (San Diego, CA, 1976), pp. 239–52. Hume did, of course, write 'A Dialogue' on moral subjects, which concluded the second *Enquiry* (*EPM*, pp. 110–23), but this represents only a partial exception, as discussed below.

[15] *T*, p. 5.

[16] For a fuller account, see Tim Stuart-Buttle, '"An Authority from Which There Can Be No Appeal": The Place of Cicero in Hume's Science of Man', *Journal of Scottish Philosophy*, 18 (2020), pp. 289–309.

5.1 Ancient Moral Philosophy and the Science of Man

In the *Treatise*, Hume famously defended the need for a 'compleat system of the sciences, built on a foundation almost entirely new' on the basis that

> moral philosophy is in the same condition as natural, with regard to astronomy, before the time of *Copernicus*. The antients, tho' sensible of that maxim, *that nature does nothing in vain*, contriv'd such intricate systems of the heavens, as seem'd inconsistent with true philosophy, and gave place at last to something more simple and natural. To invent without scruple a new principle to every new phenomenon, instead of adapting it to the old; to overload our hypotheses with a variety of this kind; are certain proofs, that none of these principles is the just one, and that we only desire, by a number of falshoods, to cover our ignorance of the truth.[17]

The implication of this passage is clear. Hume conceded that 'some late philosophers in *England*' had 'begun to put the science of man on a new footing' ('Mr. *Locke*, my Lord *Shaftesbury*, Dr. *Mandeville*, Mr. *Hutcheson*, Dr. *Butler*, &c.'). Yet they had not fully emancipated moral philosophy – as Copernicus had astronomy, and Francis Bacon had natural philosophy – from the errors of the ancients, and thereby effected the 'total Alteration' for which Hume called.[18] With breathtaking (and perhaps ill-advised) audacity, Hume reprimanded one of those 'late philosophers' – Hutcheson, who was very much his senior and would later play a pivotal role in blocking Hume's candidacy for an academic post in Scotland – in precisely these terms.[19] Hutcheson, Hume declared, failed to grasp that a science of man based 'entirely upon experience' could 'never arrive at ultimate principles' in its treatment of morality.[20] Hutcheson's moral theory remained

> founded on final causes; which is a Consideration, that appears to me pretty uncertain & unphilosophical. For pray, what is the End of Man? Is he created for Happiness or for Virtue? For this Life or the next? For himself or his Maker? Your Definition of *Natural* depends upon solving these Questions, which are endless, & quite wide of my Purpose.[21]

---

[17] *T*, p. 4. [18] Ibid., p. 5 and n11.
[19] Roger Emerson, 'The "Affair" at Edinburgh and the "Project" at Glasgow: The Politics of Hume's Attempts to Become a Professor', in M. A. Stewart and J. P. Wright, eds., *Hume and Hume's Connexions* (Edinburgh, 2004), pp. 1–22.
[20] Hume, *An Abstract of a Book Lately Published, Entitled, A Treatise of Human Nature, &c* (1740), in *T*, p. 407.
[21] *HL*, I, p. 33. Hume's relationship to Hutcheson has generated much scholarly disagreement from the publication of Norman Kemp Smith's *The Philosophy of David Hume* (London, 1941) to the present day. For a judicious critical discussion of the contours of that debate, see Luigi Turco,

Hume returned to the issue of the indebtedness of modern moral philosophy to the ancients in the *Enquiry Concerning the Principles of Morals* (1751). Moral philosophers continued to focus on 'solving ... Questions' that were as 'endless' as they were 'merely verbal', with the result that little progress had been made in moral science:

> In this kingdom, such continued ostentation, of late years, has prevailed among men in *active* life with regard to *public spirit*, and among those in *speculative* with regard to *benevolence*; and so many false pretensions to each have been, no doubt, detected, that men of the world are apt, without any bad intention, to discover a sullen incredulity on the head of those moral endowments, and even sometimes absolutely to deny their existence and reality. In like manner, I find, that, of old, the perpetual cant of the STOICS and CYNICS concerning *virtue*, their magnificent professions and slender performances, bred a disgust in mankind; and LUCIAN, who, though licentious with regard to pleasure, is yet, in other respects, a very moral writer, cannot, sometimes, talk of virtue, so much boasted, without betraying symptoms of spleen and irony.[22]

In '*speculative*' matters, none had emphasised '*benevolence*' more strongly than Hutcheson, who initially professed himself the disciple of both Shaftesbury and the 'Antient Moralists'. (Indeed, it is worth remarking that Hutcheson professed to establish '*the Ideas of Moral Good and Evil*' in accordance with the '*Sentiments of the Antient Moralists*' – 'sentiments' on which Hume would focus his attention in his essays.)[23] Small wonder, then, that a modern day Lucian had appeared – Mandeville, from whose attacks Hutcheson sought to defend Shaftesbury and his Stoic guides – who declared, with scarcely concealed 'spleen and irony', that 'moral distinctions' were merely the 'inventions of politicians'.[24]

Mandeville's treatment of morality was heavily indebted to Pierre Bayle;[25] and it was to Bayle and perhaps Mandeville himself whom

---

'Hutcheson and Hume in a Recent Polemic', in Emilio Mazza and Emanuele Ronchetti, eds., *New Essays on David Hume* (Milan, 2007), pp. 171–98.

[22] *EPM*, p. 53.

[23] As indicated by the original subtitle of *An Inquiry into the Original of Our Ideas of Beauty and Virtue. In which the Principles of the late Earl of Shaftesbury are Explain'd and Defended, against the Author of the Fable of the Bees: and the Ideas of Moral Good and Evil are Establish'd, According to the Sentiments of the Antient Moralists* (London, 1725). For Hutcheson's subsequent attempts to distance himself from both Shaftesbury and, with greater qualification, from the ancients – partly, perhaps, on account of Hume's provocations – see Thomas Ahnert, *The Moral Culture of the Scottish Enlightenment, 1690–1805* (New Haven, CT, 2014), pp. 51–65.

[24] *E* (LF), p. 280, *E* (C), p. 216.

[25] John Robertson, *The Case for the Enlightenment: Scotland and Naples, 1680–1760* (Cambridge, 2005), pp. 261–80.

Hume turned for 'Diversion & Improvement' after his attempts to follow the austere moral teachings of Stoic authors induced a prolonged depressive episode from the late 1720s.[26] As an undergraduate at the University of Edinburgh, Hume would have 'absorbed' what Hutcheson, recalling his own experience as a student at Glasgow, described as 'the first elements of the search for truth, where I tasted to the full the immortal sublimities of Vergil and Homer, the delights, tasteful charm, elegant wit, the jest and humour in Xenophon, Horace, Aristophanes and Terence, and likewise the abundant elegance and scope of Cicero's writings in all branches of philosophy'.[27] After university, the allure of this literature retained its appeal for Hume: even as his family intended him for the law, 'while they fancied I was poring upon Voet and Vinnius, Cicero and Virgil were the authors which I was secretly devouring'.[28] In 1726, Hume also acquired a copy of Shaftesbury's *Characteristicks*, which reformulated Stoic moral teaching for a modern audience, as did Hutcheson's *Inquiry into the Original of Our Ideas of Beauty and Virtue*, published the previous year.[29] Yet Hume's attempts to follow the regimen of self-cultivation and self-discipline recommended by the Stoic philosophers and their modern admirers as the only path to virtue and happiness precipitated a profound mental crisis:

> There was another particular, which contributed more than any thing, to waste my Spirits & bring on me this Distemper, which was, that having read many Books of Morality, such as Cicero, Seneca & Plutarch, & being smit with their beautiful Representations of Virtue & Philosophy, I undertook the Improvement of my Temper & Will, along with my Reason & Understanding. I was continually fortifying myself with Reflections against Death, & Poverty, & Shame, & Pain, & all the other Calamities of Life.[30]

Hume's hard-won personal experience of the vacuity of Stoic moral teaching would have made him eminently receptive to Mandeville's 'spleen and irony' in the *Fable of the Bees* (1714, 1723), which offered a savage

---

[26] *HL*, I, p. 12.

[27] Francis Hutcheson, *Inaugural Lecture on the Social Nature of Man* [1730], in *Francis Hutcheson: Two Texts on Human Nature*, ed. Thomas Mautner (Cambridge, 1993), p. 125.

[28] 'My Own Life' [1776], in *HL*, I, p. 1. This claim is corroborated by Hume's description of his reading in *HL*, I, pp. 9–10.

[29] For Hutcheson and Stoicism, see M. A. Stewart, 'The Stoic Legacy in the Early Scottish Enlightenment', in M. J. Osler, ed., *Atoms, Pneuma, and Tranquility: Epicurean and Stoic Themes in European Thought* (Cambridge, 1991), pp. 273–96.

[30] *HL*, I, pp. 32–33.

critique of Shaftesbury – and, in *Part II* (1728), of 'that curious Metaphysician' Hutcheson. As Mandeville noted in his inimitable style:

> I could swagger about Fortitude and the Contempt of Riches as much as *Seneca* himself, and would undertake to write twice as much in behalf of Poverty as ever he did, for the tenth Part of his Estate: I could teach the way to the *Summum bonum* as exactly as I know my way home: I could tell People that to extricate themselves from all worldly Engagements, and to purify the Mind, they must divest themselves of the Passions, as Men take out the Furniture when they would clean a Room thoroughly; and I am clearly of the Opinion, that the Malice and most severe Strokes of Fortune can do no more Injury to a Mind thus stript of all Fears, Wishes and Inclinations, than a blind Horse can do in an empty Barn. In the Theory of all this I am very perfect, but the Practice is very difficult; and if you went about picking my Pocket, offer'd to take the Victuals from before me when I am hungry, or made but the least Motion of spitting in my Face, I dare not promise how Philosophically I should behave myself.[31]

As Mandeville's critics were quick to observe, his vitriolic attack on Stoic moral philosophy was decidedly unoriginal: 'the *Fable of the Bees*', William Warburton quipped, 'is but the *Tap-droppings* of *Hobbes* and *Rochefoucault's* unnatural *Beverage*'.[32] Hobbes had similarly dismissed the quest for the *summum bonum*; like Mandeville, he considered it 'not much better than a Wild-Goose-Chace':[33]

> the Felicity of this life, consisteth not in the repose of a mind satisfied. For there is no such *Finus ultimus*, (utmost ayme,) nor *Summum Bonum*, (greatest Good,) as is spoken of in the Books of the old Morall Philosophers. Nor can a man any more live, whose Desires are at an end, than he, whose Senses and Imaginations are at a stand. Felicity is the continuall progresse of the desire, from one object to another; the attaining of the former, being still but the way to the later.[34]

Shaftesbury's own writings were animated by a concern to confront the 'revivers' of a vulgar form of Epicureanism 'in latter days' – notably in England (with Hobbes and Locke), France (with La Rochefoucauld and Jacques Abbadie) and the Low Countries (Bayle) – who used 'the play of words' to reduce all the springs of human action to self-interest and

---

[31] Bernard Mandeville, *The Fable of the Bees*, ed. F. B. Kaye (2 vols., Oxford, 1924), I, 'Remark O' [1714], p. 152. For the reference to Hutcheson, see Mandeville *The Fable of the Bees*, II, p. 345.
[32] William Warburton, *A Critical and Philosophical Enquiry into the Causes of Prodigies and Miracles, as Related by Historians: With an Essay towards Restoring Method and Purity in History* (London, 1727), p. 31.
[33] Mandeville, 'A Search into the Origin of Society' [1723], in *Fable*, I, p. 332.
[34] Thomas Hobbes, *Leviathan*, ed. Noel Malcolm (3 vols., Oxford, 2012 [1651]), II, 1.11, p. 150.

self-love.[35] Shaftesbury declared that these modern Lucians 'set themselves against all these Good men as Socrates Cato & c.' and their modern admirers, and appeared to have 'abandon'd vertue' altogether – by, as Hume put it, denying its very 'existence and reality'.[36]

As the foregoing suggests, Hume's observation in 1751 that debates within modern moral philosophy represented a rather tiresome restaging of the exchanges in the late Hellenistic period between the rival philosophical sects was, by this time, old hat. Hume's perspective was, however, distinctive: it was for this very reason, he argued, that the science of man had remained in its infancy. Hume grasped that, because modern moral philosophers identified themselves – or, more commonly, their antagonists – with one or other of the ancient sects, by critiquing those sects an author could comment indirectly (but intelligibly) on the errors of their modern disciples: for example, Shaftesbury and Hutcheson (via Stoicism) or Mandeville (Epicureanism).[37] Hume's withering verdict on the pre-Copernican state of contemporary moral philosophy indicated that modern philosophers, adopting the experimental approach, had to emancipate themselves from this captivity to the ancients. This, however, need not imply that Hume was contemptuous of the achievements of the ancient moralists *tout court*, as some scholars have argued.[38] Their treatment of moral subjects was, in certain respects, infinitely superior to that of their modern admirers, not excluding the pioneers of the 'Science of Man'.[39] Nor did it mean that the educated modern *reader*, who made no claim to the title of philosopher, would not find a rich source of stimulation, entertainment, and instruction in their works. To such a reader,

---

[35] For this turn against Stoicism from the seventeenth century, see Christopher Brooke, *Philosophic Pride: Stoicism and Political Thought from Lipsius to Rousseau* (Princeton, NJ, 2012). For the British debate on these issues, see Christian Maurer, *Self-Love, Egoism and the Selfish Hypothesis: Key Debates from Eighteenth-Century British Moral Philosophy* (Edinburgh, 2019).

[36] Shaftesbury, *Sensus Communis* [1709], in *Characteristicks of Men, Manners, Opinions, Times*, ed. Douglas Den Uyl (3 vols., Indianapolis, IN, 2001), I, pp. 54–55; The National Archives, Kew, Shaftesbury Papers, PRO 30/24/27/14 (draft of the 'Socratick History'), p. 100. For a further discussion of Shaftesbury's classicism, see Stuart-Buttle, *From Moral Theology*, ch. 2.

[37] Aaron Garrett, 'The Lives of the Philosophers', *Jahrbuch für Recht und Ethik*, 12 (2004), pp. 41–56, at p. 44.

[38] Peter Loptson, 'Hume and Ancient Philosophy', *British Journal for the History of Philosophy*, 20 (2012), pp. 741–72.

[39] See, for example, Hume's remarks on the merits of 'the philosophers of antiquity who treated of human nature' in the *Abstract* in *T*, p. 407; the claim in his early memoranda (no. 257) that the 'Moderns have not treated Morals so well as the Antients': David Hume, 'Hume's Early Memoranda, 1729–1740: The Complete Text', ed. Ernest Campbell Mosser, *Journal of the History of Ideas*, 9 (1948), pp. 492–518, at p. 517; and the assertion of Hume's first-person spokesman in 'A Dialogue', in the second *Enquiry*, that moral science is 'the only one, in my opinion, in which [the ancients] are not surpassed by the moderns': *EPM*, p. 114.

'the ancients were familiar voices'; their works, 'preserved, published, translated, and frequently reprinted, ... shared bookshelves with authors contemporary to the readers' and 'were seventeenth- and eighteenth-century authors, in that sense'.[40] Indeed, and notwithstanding any scars left by his personal experience of doing so in the 1720s, Hume declared that even the Stoic sages could serve as models for imitation by moderns who turned (as they ought) to moral philosophy and ancient history for practical guidance in how to lead good and happy lives.[41]

Hume's four essays, I now want to argue, advance both of these claims. Moral *philosophers* must recognize that the 'search for truth' (as Hutcheson termed it) was impeded rather than advanced by a reverence for the ancient moralists; but educated *readers* could and should turn to their writings in their quest for happiness and self-knowledge. Here Hume's choice of the monologue, rather than dialogue form is significant.

5.2 Philosophical Monologue: Against the Authority of the Sage

As Hume's various cautions to his reader indicate, the form adopted in the four essays was highly distinctive. In a recent article, Colin Heydt declares that they represent 'the *only* set of philosophical monologues of which I am aware in the history of Western philosophy'.[42] Why, then, did Hume not follow his model, Cicero's *De finibus*, in adopting the dialogue form? A clue is provided by Hume in the essay that immediately preceded 'The Epicurean' in the 1742 volume – 'Of the Rise and Progress of the Arts and Sciences'. There, Hume offers *De oratore* as modelling the 'Spirit of Dialogue', on account of Cicero's declared commitment to

> writing a conversation [his interlocutors] once had on the subject, my purpose being, in the first place, to dispel that notion, which had always prevailed, that one of them had no great learning and the other none at all;

---

[40] Alan Charles Kors, *Naturalism and Unbelief in France, 1650–1729* (Cambridge, 2016), p. 49.

[41] As Hume's presentation of Cleanthes as the model of the virtuous man in the conclusion to the second *Enquiry* indicates: *EPM*, pp. 72–73. That Cleanthes was able to live virtuously need not imply that he (or the ancient sages more generally) understood the true *principles* of morals, or indeed the capital point that moral motivation owes nothing whatsoever to religious belief. It is not accidental that Hume, in a work (the *Dialogues*) written in the same period as the second *Enquiry*, took Cleanthes as the representative of Stoic philosophical theism (and religious moralism), the untenable philosophical foundations of which the sceptic, Philo exposes with relish. As regards the study of ancient history, see Hume's remark in 'Of the Study of History' (1741) that 'I must think it an unpardonable ignorance in persons of whatever sex and condition, not to be acquainted with the history of their own country, together with the histories of ancient GREECE and ROME': *E* (LF), p. 566, *E* (C), pp. 27–28.

[42] Heydt, 'Relations of Literary Form', p. 7 n.19; italics mine.

secondly, to preserve in literary form the sentiments concerning eloquence which to my thinking were expressed to perfection by those consummate orators, if in any way I should have succeeded in recapturing and representing their pronouncements; and lastly, I protest, to rescue, as far as possible, from disuse and from silence, the reputation of these men which was already beginning to wane. [...] I thought that it was a tribute due from me to those great intellects, that while all still held them in living memory, I should render that memory immortal, if I could.[43]

In his dialogues on moral questions, however – that is, on 'different ideas of human life and of happiness' – Hume declared that Cicero had violated his own rules when it came to the dialogue form. Cicero represented his Epicurean speaker in *Tusculanae Disputationes* (Atticus) in 'a pitiful light', and similarly treated his Stoic interlocutor in *De finibus* (Cato) 'in somewhat of a cavalier manner'. This is because, on moral questions, Cicero took his own philosophy to be (uniquely) capable of identifying truths that representatives of the other sects fail to grasp; he intervenes directly in the dialogue, and the other characters are portrayed as 'humble admirer[s] of the orator' who are to receive 'his instructions, with all the deference which a scholar owes to his master'.[44] Conversely, a more 'tolerable Equality [is] maintain'd among the speakers' in *De natura deorum*: '*Cicero*, being a great Sceptic in Matters of Religion, and unwilling to determine any Thing on that Head among the different Sects of Philosophy, introduces his Friends disputing concerning the Being and Nature of the Gods, while he is only a Hearer; ... and he recounts the Conference as only from Hearsay.'[45]

Hume, like Hume's Cicero, was *not* a 'great Sceptic' in matters of morality: the science of man can, and must, be laid on a 'solid foundation', and be made to yield true conclusions.[46] It follows that a dialogue on moral questions would necessarily violate 'the Spirit of Dialogue' as Cicero understood it in *De oratore*, with the author (or his spokesperson) instructing the other speakers, who defer to his authority. This is precisely what we find when Hume did turn his hand to such a dialogue, which served as the conclusion to the second *Enquiry*; and one might surmise that it was because it violated the rules of the form (as Hume understood them) that he expressed some reservations about it: 'I have scarcely wrote any thing more whimsical, or whose Merit I am more diffident of.'[47] By the end of

---

[43] Marcus Tullius Cicero, *De oratore*, trans. H. Rackham and E. W. Sutton (Cambridge, MA, 1942), 2.2.7–8.

[44] *E* (LF), p. 129, *E* (C), pp. 112–13.

[45] This passage was removed in 1768: *E* (LF), p. 623, *E* (C), pp. 587–88.   [46] *T*, p. 4.

[47] *HL*, I, p. 145.

'A Dialogue', the other speaker, Palamedes, has been silenced completely, and Hume's 'I' is permitted to engage in monologue, without interruption or challenge.[48] By this means, Hume establishes (seemingly to Palamedes's satisfaction) that the 'principles of morals' he has uncovered in the work as a whole – 'principles' that build upon 'a foundation almost entirely new',[49] one quite different from that upon which the ancient moralists constructed their ethical theories – are unchallengeable. This is the kind of dialogue effected by Shaftesbury in *The Moralists* (1709), where the Epicurean-Sceptic is converted utterly to the Stoic's vision of 'human life and of happiness'; and by Mandeville in *Part II* of the *Fable*, which reconstructs the debate between an admirer of Shaftesbury (Horatio) and a disciple of Mandeville's (Cleomenes), so as to reverse the outcome.[50]

Berkeley's *Alciphron, or the Minute Philosopher* (1732), meanwhile, allowed the Christian moralist (the author's spokesman, Euphranor) to triumph decisively over the free-thinking assailants of religion (loosely representing Shaftesbury and Mandeville), who failed to grasp that the true end of life, and the only stable source of happiness, is to be found in loving God and following His will in all things. There is no room for uncertainty in matters of such importance as religion; and as Berkeley's subtitle declares, the work offers *An Apology for the Christian Religion, against those who are called Free-Thinkers.*[51] Conversely, Hume – as, on his reading, had Cicero – considered religion to be the ideal 'Matter' on which the 'Spirit of Dialogue' could be indulged, precisely because 'Doubt, uncertainty, suspence of judgement appear the only result of our most accurate scrutiny, concerning this subject.'[52] The subject was, furthermore, of no practical consequence for human life and conduct: 'What Danger can ever come from ingenious Reasoning & Enquiry? The worst *speculative* Sceptic ever I knew, was a much better Man than the best superstitious Devotee & Bigot.' It was for this reason that, in the *Dialogues*, Hume was committed in earnest to making the arguments of his interlocutors – irrespective of his own personal views – as strong as possible, and to not intervening in their discussion. Here, Hume paraphrases *De oratore*: 'By this Means, that vulgar Error would be avoided, of putting nothing but Nonsense into the Mouth of the Adversary.'[53]

---

[48] See *EPM*, p. 116 to the end (p. 123), where from Palamedes's 'You need go no further ...' Hume's spokesman dominates what has long since ceased to be a conversation.
[49] *T*, p. 4.   [50] Stuart-Buttle, *From Moral Theology*, pp. 242–56.
[51] George Berkeley, *Alciphron: or, the Minute Philosopher. In Seven Dialogues. Containing an Apology for the Christian Religion, against those who are called Free-Thinkers* (2 vols., London, 1732).
[52] *NHR*, p. 87.   [53] *HL*, I, p. 154.

Unlike in 'Metaphysics & Theology', however, in morals no less than 'in Politics & natural Philosophy, whatever Conclusion is contrary to certain Matter of Fact must certainly be *wrong*, and there *must* be some *Error* lie somewhere in the Argument'.[54]

Thus understood, Hume's four philosophical monologues indicate both the merits (relative to modern philosophy) and the demerits (in comparison to Hume's own science of man) of ancient moral philosophy. In its favour is that the ancients did not take the 'Reasoning turn' that had 'carry'd' the moderns 'away from Sentiment'.[55] To its grievous disadvantage was that the ancients – and their modern admirers, whether neo-Stoics such as Hutcheson or neo-Epicureans such as Hobbes and Mandeville – lacked self-knowledge. They failed to grasp that the sentiments that gave rise to their 'ideas of human life and of happiness' were subjective, and mistook a part (of human nature and its multiplicity of desires and needs) for the whole. Here the short descriptors of each philosopher's position are indicative: the Epicurean is '*The man of elegance and pleasure*'; the Stoic, 'the man of action and virtue'; and the Platonist, 'the man of contemplation, and *philosophical* devotion'.[56] The Sceptic lacks any such descriptor, for the simple reason that he is able to grasp that all of these things – pleasure, action, contemplation and even devotion – are 'goods', the pursuit of which might conduce to the individual's happiness (and to virtue) in their particular case. This is why Hume can claim that the 'sentiments' of these 'sects' will 'naturally form themselves in the world', and give rise to contrasting visions of happiness and virtue. The case is quite different when it comes to the 'ideas of human life and of happiness' entertained in a Christian age by enthusiasts such as Blaise Pascal, because the 'sentiments' that inform those ideas are (unlike those of the ancients) inherently *unnatural*. They lead their advocates to attempt (vainly) to lead entirely '*artificial* lives' by denying the 'natural' desires and needs that animate human beings in society (hence their subscription to the 'monkish virtues of mortification, penance, humility, and passive suffering').[57] Such 'sentiments' – unlike those of the ancient moralists – will be abhorrent to all sane individuals at all times and places, except those whose minds and hearts have, from their earliest infancy, been subject to the priest's 'chissel and the hammer'.[58]

---

[54] *HL*, I, p. 151; italics mine. The claim that Hume considered religion, but not morality to be an appropriate subject matter for dialogue is further explored in Michel Malherbe, 'Hume and the Art of Dialogue', in *Hume and Hume's Connexions*, pp. 201–23.

[55] Hume, 'Hume's Early Memoranda', ed. Mossner, p. 517.

[56] *E* (LF), pp. 138, 146, 155, *E* (C), pp. 119, 125, 132.   [57] *NHR*, p. 63.   [58] Ibid., p. 72.

All of Hume's ancient philosophers recognise happiness and virtue to be inseparable; none – even the Platonist – so much as entertains the possibility that a necessary condition of true happiness (i.e. in a world to come) might be suffering and misery in this life.[59] Yet all define virtue according to their predominant inclinations: whether in friendship, indolence and the enjoyment of nature's bounty (the Epicurean); in activity and labour, creating through art and industry goods that nature has not furnished fully formed, including a good character (the Stoic); or in the repose that is to be found in contemplation of, and the expression of fervent devotion towards, the only being truly capable of such exquisite artistry, and of the Stoic's desired self-sufficiency that comes from an immunity to the slings and arrows of outrageous fortune, that is, God (the Platonist). As the Sceptic observes, all the philosophers 'are led astray, not only by the narrowness of their understandings, but by that also of their passions'. Indeed, their philosophies represent nothing more than an attempt to rationalise their own preferences, given to them by a 'predominant inclination' that does not depend on 'our choice' but rather on one's education, 'natural propensities, ... constitution and temper'.[60] This attempt to understand, and to justify, one's own moral and aesthetic sentiments *to oneself* is far from deplorable, as it allows for self-knowledge and a deliberate pursuit of what one takes (on closer inspection) to be 'good' or desirable. What is deplorable, however, is the attempt to lay claim to authority in determining what *others* ought to pursue, and thereby to declare that there is but one road – one's own – to happiness. The attempt to convince others that what they take to be indifferent is not merely a good that 'ought' to be pursued, but even the highest of all goods (the *summum bonum*), is futile. 'Good and ill, both natural and moral, are entirely relative to human sentiment and affection', and the Stoic's attempt to persuade the Epicurean of the error of his ways is bound to fail (and vice versa), because no one can 'alter his feelings, PROTEAS-like', at will.[61] It is also dangerous, because the philosopher who sets himself up as a sage, claiming authority over others, feels constrained to ignore the 'change[s] of inclination' within oneself that every individual experiences periodically over the course of their lives. At one time, an individual might broadly share the sentiments expressed by the Stoic; at another, they might find

---

[59] For an illuminating discussion of eighteenth-century conceptions of happiness and its relation to virtue, see Darrin M. McMahon, 'From the Happiness of Virtue to the Virtue of Happiness: 400 B.C.–A.D. 1780', *Daedalus*, 133 (2004), pp. 5–17.
[60] *E* (LF), pp. 160, 167–68, *E* (C), pp. 135, 141–42.   [61] *E* (LF), p. 168, *E* (C), p. 141.

themselves in sympathy with the Epicurean.[62] Yet their claim that one must choose one road, and one road only, to happiness compels them to pursue goods that now appear 'indifferent or disagreeable' to them, thereby rendering them hypocritical and (it follows) unhappy.[63]

In Hume's essays, the Stoic offers criticisms of the Epicurean, the Platonist of the Stoic and Epicurean, and the Sceptic of all three that there is good reason to think Hume shared. All, in this sense, speak for Hume. Yet no one philosophy displaces the other, and this is to some extent true even when it comes to the Sceptic. This is because the Sceptic himself accepts that there is something uniquely valuable in each philosophy, which speaks to sentiments that different people (or, indeed, the same person at different times in their life) will 'naturally' experience: 'each of these kinds of life is agreeable in its turn, and ... their variety or their judicious mixture chiefly contributes to the rendering all of them agreeable'.[64]

5.3 Conclusion: Beyond Circularity

It follows that the claim that Hume's objective, in the essays, is to deny that moral philosophy can (as all of the ancient schools claimed) offer 'medicine for the mind', supporting individuals in the ways of virtue, needs qualification.[65] Here the intervention of Hume's voice, as author, in the form of a footnote added to 'The Sceptic' in 1768 is significant. In denying the therapeutic function of moral philosophy, 'The Sceptic, perhaps, carries the matter too far', because so long as the individual's 'temper be antecedently disposed after the same manner as that to which' the philosophers they read 'pretend to form it', then such reading 'may, at least, fortify that temper, and furnish it with views, by which it may entertain and nourish itself'. At times of trial, when 'passion is awakened, [and] fancy agitated...the philosopher is lost in the man', who no longer knows what he wants, or why he (and whether he ought to) want(s) it. What has been lost is self-knowledge: a clear sense of one's settled

---

[62] An example of an ancient philosopher whose movement between these philosophical positions attracted considerable comment from eighteenth-century moralists was Horace: see Frank Stack, *Pope and Horace: Studies in Imitation* (Cambridge, 1985).

[63] *E* (LF), p. 160, *E* (C), p. 135.   [64] *E* (LF), p. 160, *E* (C), p. 136.

[65] A claim advanced in M. A. Stewart, 'Two Species of Philosophy: The Historical Significance of the First *Enquiry*', in Peter Millican, ed., *Reading Hume on Human Understanding* (Oxford, 2002), pp. 67–95; and more forcefully still in James A. Harris, 'Hume's Four Essays on Happiness and Their Place in the Move from Morals to Politics', in Mazza and Ronchetti eds., *New Essays*, pp. 223–35.

character, and one's 'predominant inclination'. Hume's advice here is not
to turn, as he did in his youth, to one sect only – the Stoics – to secure the
tranquility and assurance that he so craved. Insofar as the Stoics express
ideas of life and happiness that do not correspond to one's own inclinations, the attempt to model oneself according to their precepts is bound
to be an exercise in futility and self-torment. Rather, such an individual
should sample the works of representatives of *all* the philosophical schools,
because doing so will lead to self-knowledge.[66] One's aversion to the more
austere of Stoic precepts will be as revelatory as one's sympathy with
sentiments expressed by the representative of another sect. But as human
nature is complex, so one's sympathy with any one school is unlikely to be
total; and here, one must not look to any particular philosopher (or school)
as possessing the truth, the whole truth, and nothing but the truth:

> Assist yourself by a frequent perusal of the entertaining moralists: Have
> recourse to the learning of PLUTARCH, the imagination of LUCIAN, the
> eloquence of CICERO, the wit of SENECA, the gaiety of MONTAIGNE,
> the sublimity of SHAFTESBURY. Moral precepts, so couched, strike deep,
> and fortify the mind against the illusions of passion … Despise not these
> helps; but confide not too much in them neither; unless nature has been
> favourable in the temper, with which she has endowed you.[67]

All of the ancient philosophers had been 'endowed' with a favourable
temper; they possessed a firmness of character, and a degree of constancy
in their predominant inclinations, that ensured a tolerable consistency
between their moral practice and their moral precepts. This was why, 'If
a Man made Profession of Philosophy, whatever his Sect was, [the
Antients] always expected to find more Regularity in his Life and
Manners, than in those of the ignorant & illiterate.'[68] In the ancient
world, deluded and hypocritical religious fanatics such as Pascal, whose
'ideas' about happiness and virtue could not but diverge from their real
(and secret) 'sentiments', were entirely unknown. The ancient philosophers' teachings worked for *them*; what they failed to understand was that
they would not work for *all*.

   Hume's intervention, as author, in 'The Sceptic' – the final of the four
essays – thus serves to emphasise the point made by Hume in his letter to

---

[66] Here, what Malherbe ('Hume and the Art of Dialogue', p. 215) says about philosophical dialogue
  also applies to Hume's philosophical monologues: 'the reader should not search for the supposedly
  concealed purpose of the author, because what he has to discover is not the author, but himself; and
  he can find himself only in the dialogue of the moral world', a dialogue between moral philosophies
  that Hume is here inviting his readers to construct for themselves.
[67] *E* (LF), p. 177n17, *E* (C), p. 147n6.   [68] *HL*, I, p. 154.

Hutcheson of 1739. The disagreements between the ancient philosophical sects were 'endless', because their attempt to identify one *end* for human-kind (the *summum bonum*) was misconceived. To the extent that modern moral philosophers, who professed to offer a science of man, continued to ask the same question – 'what is the End of Man? Is he created for Happiness or for Virtue? For this Life or the next? For himself or his Maker?' – they remained trapped in the endless circularity depicted in Hume's four essays.[69] Lucian's splenetic, ironical rejoinder to the ancient Stoics' 'magnificent pretensions' was rewritten, predictably in cruder form (as 'insipid raillery'),[70] in Mandeville's response to Shaftesbury; Mandeville's denial of the reality of virtue was exposed as an absurd overreaction by Hutcheson, whose claims for benevolence were again excessive; and so the carousel turns. So long as one accepts the legitimacy of the questions set for moral philosophy by the ancients, the discussion must end in 'doubt, uncertainty [and] suspense of judgment'.[71] Morality would, then, be a fitting subject for interrogation by the true 'Spirit of Dialogue'. Yet the moral scientist, who builds upon the foundation of experience and applies the experimental method to moral subjects, recognises that such questions are 'quite wide of my purpose'.[72] 'The Sceptic' can see that his philosophical rivals are asking the wrong questions; he identifies what the right questions are for the scientist of man; but he does not, and cannot address them. That task is left to Hume, and to other moderns, whose love of truth is *their* 'predominant inclination'.

[69] *HL*, I, p. 33.   [70] *E* (LF), p. 538, *E* (C), p. 7.   [71] *NHR*, p. 87.   [72] *HL*, I, p. 33.

CHAPTER 6

Aesthetics and the Arts in Hume's Essays

Timothy M. Costelloe

The terms 'art', 'arts', and 'the arts' occur often in the *Essays*. In a wider
sense, and sometimes with the addition of 'science', Hume uses them to
denote skills, modes of behaviour, or ways of doing things, virtuous and
otherwise, typical of human beings as they conduct themselves in the
activities that constitute *inter alia* government, politics, religion, commerce, industry, and law. For arts that reflect physical labour aimed at
securing the necessities of life, Hume attaches 'low', 'popular', 'useful' or
'vulgar', and for others related to the economy of production and trade,
'manual', 'mechanical' or 'of manufacture' and 'of commerce'. In a
narrower sense, he also employs them in connection with a specific set
of practices now gathered under 'the fine arts', a phrase he never employs
himself, unsurprising given that it was a category still under construction
in the early decades of the eighteenth century. Even in Hume's hands,
however, the grouping was sufficiently formed to include not only the
now-familiar members of architecture, literature, music, painting, sculp-
ture, and theatre but eloquence and gardening as well.[1] Hume mentions all
of these by name, and treats them collectively as 'arts' with a variety of
interchangeable qualifiers, each indicative of the connection to leisure,
pleasure, and entertainment: 'agreeable', 'civilised', 'cultivated', 'elegant',
'finer', 'liberal', 'noble', 'polite', 'refined', and 'sublime'. It is primarily in
connection with his discussion of the arts in this narrower sense that
Hume's contribution to 'aesthetics' and 'philosophy of art' is to be found,

---

[1] For Hume's use of 'finer' and 'refined' to describe the arts, see *E* (LF), pp. 90, 223, 241, 256, *E* (C),
pp. 87, 178, 191, 201, and *E* (LF), pp. 114, 119, 125, 271, *E* (C), pp. 102, 106, 110, 211,
respectively. Even this narrower sense can be very broad: at one point, Hume includes under it not
only eloquence, painting, poetry, philosophy, and ethics but also politics, generalship, and
astronomy (*E* (LF), pp. 270 and 276, *E* (C), pp. 210 and 214. The now-standard and widely
accepted history of 'the fine arts' as an identifiable 'system' is P. O. Kristeller, 'The Modern System
of the Arts: A Study in the History of Aesthetics Part I' and 'Part II', *Journal of the History of Ideas*, 12
(1951), pp. 496–527, and 13 (1952), pp. 17–46.

though there are aspects of the wider sense that, as we shall see, deserve consideration as well.

Unlike some other contributors to the then nascent discipline, however, Hume never undertook a systematic presentation of his views, and readers have been obliged to construct them from pieces scattered across his corpus more generally. That Hume had such a work in mind is likely given his declaration in the Advertisement to the *Treatise* that, should the first two books – 'Of the Understanding' and 'Of the Passions' – please the *'taste of the public'*, he would *'proceed to the examination of* Morals, Politics, *and* Criticism'.[2] In various ways – in Book 3 of the *Treatise*, the second *Enquiry*, the *History*, and numerous essays – Hume kept his word about the first two, but the third never materialised in any obvious or straight-forward way. When he does address aesthetics and the arts in his major writings, it is while pursuing other matters. In Book 2 of the *Treatise*, for example, he marshals beauty and deformity in support of his claims for the double relation of impressions and ideas,[3] in the second *Enquiry* he connects aesthetic value to its moral counterpart,[4] and in the *Dialogues* he appeals to aesthetic affect to elucidate the phenomenology of religious belief.[5] Hume also comments on the arts (primarily literature) at various junctures in the *History*, in the course of his reflections on the development of English society, learning and manners.[6] The only place where the proposed 'examination' of 'criticism' comes anywhere close to fruition, however, is in the *Essays*, where he dedicates a series of essays to a variety of pertinent topics: 'Of the Delicacy of Taste and Passion', 'Of Eloquence', 'Of Simplicity and Refinement in Writing', 'Of Tragedy', and 'Of the Standard of Taste'.

While the gravitational pull of these 'aesthetic essays', as we might call them collectively, is unavoidable, it has tended to distort the topography of 'Hume's aesthetics' in at least two, not altogether positive, ways. First, among the essays themselves, two in particular – 'Of Tragedy' and 'Of the Standard of Taste' – have stolen the limelight and pushed others into relative obscurity; the latter essay, in particular, has generated a literature possibly larger than on the rest of the *Essays* combined, and achieved a status quite disproportionate to its modest length (thirty-five paragraphs), a fate not without irony given that Hume composed it in some haste as a

---

[2] *T*, p. 2.   [3] Ibid., pp. 195–98.   [4] *EPM*, pp. 80, 105–6, 131, and 161–62.
[5] David Hume, *Dialogues Concerning Natural Religion and Other Writings*, ed. Dorothy Coleman (Cambridge, 2012), pp. 31–32 and 89–91.
[6] *HE*, IV, p. 386, V, pp. 149–55, and VI, pp. 542–45.

replacement for two other, controversial essays – 'Of Suicide' and 'Of the Immortality of the Soul' – that were withdrawn after their first publication; under different circumstances, the essay might not have been written at all.[7] Hume's essays on tragedy and the standard of taste certainly have intrinsic merit – 'Of the Standard of Taste' inspired responses almost from the moment it appeared in 1757 – but the attention they have received in modern scholarship has left the impression that he was alone (or among a highly select company) in paying attention to these subjects, when they were the focus of debates engaged in by many writers. A complete picture of Hume's contribution, moreover, requires consideration of other essays as well, those where he treats the arts historically ('Of the Rise and Progress of the Arts and Sciences') and in the context of political economy 'Of Commerce' and 'Of Refinement in the Arts').

Second, taking his essays as *locus primus* for elucidating Hume's aesthetics encourages the belief that they stand alone and can be read independently of the work that preceded them, as if Hume's well-known (declared) disappointment with the reception of the *Treatise* inspired such a radical change of mind as to constitute a new beginning.[8] In actuality, while they represent treatments of issues that Hume does not address in such detail anywhere else, the aesthetic essays are best understood as extensions or specific applications of more general principles that Hume had framed already; to claim otherwise risks wilfully misreading his wider corpus, attention to which can actually ease interpretive worries that might otherwise arise. A defence of the first observation falls beyond the parameters of the current chapter, but part of my aim in what follows is to recognise the second, that is, to present Hume's discussions of art and aesthetics in the *Essays* as important treatments of issues that are at once examples of how he brings his established principles to bear upon specific topics that compose his contribution to the field. I shall discuss these, consecutively, under the headings of 'Taste and Its Standard', 'Literary Style and Artistic Representation', 'The Paradox of Tragedy', and, finally, in Section 6.4, 'A History and Political Economy of the Arts'.

[7] For the circumstances of its composition, see *HL*, II, pp. 252–54; Ernest Campbell Mossner, *The Life of David Hume*, 2nd ed. (Oxford, 1980 [1954]), pp. 319–35; and James A. Harris, *Hume: An Intellectual Biography* (Cambridge, 2015), pp. 361–62. An overview of the modern literature (up to 2004 at least) is found in Timothy M. Costelloe, 'Hume's Aesthetics: The Literature and Directions for Future Research', *Hume Studies*, 30 (2004), pp. 87–126, though there have been additions in the interim. A selection of relevant contributions is also collected in Babette Babich, ed., *Reading David Hume's 'Of the Standard of Taste'* (Berlin, 2019).
[8] This line of interpretation figures prominently in Harris's *Hume*. Harris defends the view that, after the *Treatise*, the essays 'mostly … broke new intellectual ground' (p. 145).

6.1   Taste and Its Standard

The concept of 'taste' has its distant origins in Aristotle and, more immediately for Hume and his contemporaries, in mid-seventeenth-century Spain (*gusto*), from where it found its way, with linguistic equivalents (*goût, Geschmack*), into the general lexicon of European thought; by the beginning of the eighteenth century, it was already a ubiquitous term of art and became, subsequently, an increasingly conventional way of explaining the origin of moral and aesthetic value.[9] Different writers parsed 'taste' variously as a faculty, capacity, or internal sense, but each manifestation shared the common denominator of explaining how some objective feature of the world might impact subjects so as to raise in them 'ideas' (as the dominant terminology of Lockean epistemology had it) that constitute right and wrong, in the moral sphere, and, in the aesthetic, good and bad judgement associated with the triad, first established by Joseph Addison, of novelty, beauty, and the grand or sublime.[10] Hume is influenced by writers in the British tradition (Anthony Ashley Cooper, the Third Earl of Shaftesbury and Francis Hutcheson) who drew the analogy between the external senses and their internal counterpart, but his sympathies lie closer to the French (Jean-Baptiste, the abbé Dubos, in particular), with its emphasis on *sentiments* and states of pain or pleasure, which, as Hume says, constitute the 'very essence' of beauty and deformity.[11] Beauty, moreover, is a specific *kind* of sentiment, a 'calm passion', a secondary or reflective impression – as Hume explains his distinctions in Book 2 of the *Treatise* – that arises from a bodily sensation or from the idea of that sensation in response to the 'form' of some object. For this reason, Hume can trace beauty and deformity 'of all kinds' to that same origin,[12] and predicate the 'sense of beauty and deformity' equally of 'action, composition, and external objects';[13] he thus moves easily, amid the calculus of qualities agreeable and useful to a possessor or others, between the virtues and vices that constitute the beauty and deformity of moral character, and

---

[9] For a wide-ranging discussion of taste in the eighteenth century, see James Noggle, *The Temporality of Taste in Eighteenth-Century British Writing* (Oxford, 2012), and on the immediate background for Hume, Dabney Townsend, *Hume's Aesthetic Theory: Taste and Sentiment* (New York, 2001), ch. 2.

[10] See Joseph Addison, 'The Pleasures of the Imagination', in *The Spectator*, ed. Donald F. Bond (5 vols., Oxford, 1965), I, pp. 535–82. For consideration of Addison and the other views aired by writers of the period, see Timothy M. Costelloe, *The British Aesthetic Tradition: From Shaftesbury to Wittgenstein* (Cambridge, 2013), Part 1, and Paul Guyer, *A History of Modern Aesthetics, Volume 1: The Eighteenth Century* (Cambridge, 2014).

[11] *T*, p. 195.   [12] Ibid.   [13] Ibid., p. 181.

objects of nature or art that produce analogous sentiments because they are useful or promote pleasure and approbation.[14]

'Taste', whether aesthetic or moral, is an ambiguous concept, however, denoting as it does an atemporal capacity that at once requires time and activity to actualise and perfect; this tension is inherited from its original gustatory home where the relevant organs are taken to respond instantly and untutored to the presence of sweet and bitter but require education to detect the finer details of their intentional objects. Like many writers of the period, Hume reflects this tension, treating taste as both a potentiality and an accomplishment (and sometimes, echoing its bodily origins, a 'sensation' as well), which he manages by drawing on the language of 'cultivation' and its cognates: individuals 'susceptible to those finer sensations', as he writes in the first *Enquiry*, with 'temper and judgment' and a 'fine ear', as he expresses the same through a musical metaphor in the *Treatise*, are in a position to 'give praise to what deserves it'.[15] In the *Essays*, Hume extends and refines this point by way of 'delicacy', the subject of the opening essay, 'Of the Delicacy of Taste and Passion', where, as its title indicates, Hume expands the concept from taste (or what he sometimes calls 'imagination') to include passion or emotion as well (terms Hume tends to use interchangeably).

These are really branches of the same stock, however, both a 'disposition' or 'talent', which, when cultivated, marks a person of greater sensibility and thus increased susceptibility to 'lively enjoyments' and 'pungent sorrows', in the case of passion, and, in the case of taste, to the perfection and faults of art;[16] the same brings, in addition, a heightened capability of finding satisfaction and enjoyment in places others cannot penetrate. Hume captures both in his reflections on the art of essay-writing itself ('Of Essay-Writing'), its great benefit being to connect the labour and solitude of the 'learned' world to that of the 'conversible', the latter involving a 'social Disposition, ... a Taste of Pleasure ... and the Observation of the Blemishes or Perfections of the particular Objects' that surround 'reflections on human Affairs, and the Duties of common life'.[17] Elsewhere, in 'Of the Standard of Taste', Hume identifies delicacy of taste with a state where the 'organs are so fine, as to allow nothing to escape them; and at the same time so exact as to perceive every ingredient in the composition',[18] an achievement reflected paradigmatically in the episode he borrows from *Don Quixote* in the shape of Sancho's kinsmen, ridiculed

[14] *T*, pp. 195–96 and *EPM*, p. 80.   [15] *T*, pp. 303–4.   [16] *E* (LF), p. 4, *E* (C), p. 35.
[17] *E* (LF), pp. 533–34, *E* (C), p. 3.   [18] *E* (LF), p. 235, *E* (C), p. 187.

at first for detecting the one leather and the other iron in the hogshead of
wine, but having their oenological finesse vindicated ultimately, when a
key with a leather thong is found at the bottom.[19]

Hume also takes the opportunity to play taste *against* passion, giving the
nod to the former for its ability to temper the excesses to which the latter
makes one liable: delicate taste improves the judgement because it requires
knowledge, strong sense, and the expanded view born of taking different
perspectives, all of which subdue the 'rougher and boisterous' passions and
encourage the 'tender and agreeable'.[20] Here, in rudimentary form, is a
sketch of the much-discussed 'true judge in the finer arts', in whom, as
Hume supplies details in the fuller picture, delicacy and strong sense are
supplemented by practice, comparison, and freedom from prejudice,[21] an
ideal figure and analogue in the aesthetic sphere to Cleanthes – that 'model
of perfect virtue' – in the moral.[22] Hume's true judge also forms part of his
answer to a question that occupied many writers in his century – from
Addison at the beginning to Dugald Stewart at its end – of how to square
the claims of connoisseurship with the fact that taste varies through time
and across place and even among individuals who otherwise share a
common life. This means, as Walter Hipple observes of the period
generally, identifying '*true* taste', a goal writers pursued 'by analyzing the
natural effect of the qualities of objects on the faculties of mind'.[23]
Following this course, and like others before and after him, Hume
acknowledges both the sheer 'variety of taste' and just how 'obvious' it is
even to the 'most careless enquirer'.[24] To the philosophical mind, however, it is 'natural' – almost an imperative – to go further and 'seek a
Standard of Taste', which means finding a 'rule, by which the various
sentiments of men may be reconciled; at least, a decision, afforded,
confirming one sentiment, and condemning another'.[25]

Hume's formulation of the issue is important, since it contains and
adumbrates two distinct theses around which 'Of the Standard of Taste' is
constructed: one a response to the call for 'reconciliation', the other to
find criteria for deciding among 'competing' sentiments. The first is less
a solution to the problem than a dissolution of it, since 'reconciling'
sentiments involves articulating two contradictory principles of 'common
sense', both of which, in the spirit of Immanuel Kant's later 'Antimony of

---

[19] *E* (LF), pp. 234–35, *E* (C), p. 186.   [20] *E* (LF), p. 6, *E* (C), p. 36.
[21] *E* (LF), p. 241, *E* (C), p. 191.   [22] *EPM*, pp. 145–46
[23] Walter J. Hipple, *The Beautiful, the Sublime, and the Picturesque in Eighteenth-Century British
Aesthetic Theory* (Carbondale, IL, 1957), p. 81.
[24] *E* (LF), p. 227, *E* (C), p. 181.   [25] *E* (LF), p. 229, *E* (C), p. 183.

Taste', Hume shows to be true or at least intelligible as manifestations of
the two elements that compose a judgement of taste: subjectively, it is
aesthetic, involving a sentiment in the form of a calm passion that arises in
an individual, but, objectively, it is governed by criteria to which reasonable people should and do assent.[26] Born of these two elements, the first
principle recognises that 'each mind perceives a different beauty', and finds
proverbial expression in *de gustibus non est disputandum*, that in matters of
taste there is no dispute,[27] while the second reflects the fact that people
recognise and acknowledge some works of art and their creators to be
better than others, so that for a person to place Ogilby over Milton or
Bunyan over Addison – Hume's own examples – is a sort of madness,
comparable to maintaining a 'mole-hill to be as high as TENERIFE, or a
pond as extensive as the ocean'.[28] Reconciling one judgement with its
opposite involves showing that both have merit insofar as they speak to
different aspects of taste: everyone does have their own taste and there is no
dispute when it comes to personal preferences, but one can quarrel when
claims demand universal assent because they presuppose a standard
to exist.

The second thesis – confirming or condemning 'competing' sentiments – then involves recognising and emphasising the objective side of
this antinomy, and there is nothing obscure about the rules governing such
judgements: they are not speculative or metaphysical, 'fixed by reasonings
a priori', but empirically derived 'general observations, concerning what
has been universally found to please in all countries and in all ages'.[29]
As the general principles of morals are discoverable by analysing 'that
complication of moral qualities' that constitute 'PERSONAL MERIT',[30]
so principles of taste can be ascertained by analysing qualities of objects
that constitute *aesthetic* merit, and this is achieved methodologically by
cataloguing works that excite 'durable admiration'; such is the case of
Homer, for example, 'who pleased at ATHENS and ROME two thousand
years ago, [and] is still admired at PARIS and at LONDON'. The
contingencies of changing circumstances – 'climate, government, religion,
and language' – do not touch the qualities that give Homer's writings their
value and 'have not been able to obscure his glory'.[31] Hume recognises that
not all sentiments are actually or always 'conformable to these rules',[32] and

---

[26] Immanuel Kant, *Kritik der Urteilskraft*, ed. Prussian Academy of Sciences, Immanuel Kant,
Gesammelte Schriften (29 vols., Berlin, 1900–), V, §§55–57.
[27] *E* (LF), p. 230, *E* (C), p. 183.   [28] *E* (LF), pp. 230–31, *E* (C), pp. 183–84.
[29] *E* (LF), p. 231, *E* (C), p. 184.   [30] *EPM*, p. 76.   [31] *E* (LF), p. 233, *E* (C), p. 185.
[32] *E* (LF), p. 232, *E* (C), p. 185.

the task then becomes – with Addison, Shaftesbury, and Hutcheson as precedents and guides – a matter of discovering the various factors that explain why people equipped by nature with the potential to give praise to what deserves it ('taste' as a faculty) have failed to actualise and use it as they might ('taste' as an accomplishment): the different 'humours', 'dispositions', and variation in individual passions; 'manners and opinions' of a time and place; one's age; the 'defect or perversion' of one's faculties;[33] and being drawn to objects that resemble in some manner the culture with which one is familiar.[34] It is *pari passu* in the 'joint verdict' of those who avoid such imperfections, the true judges – 'rare' because the criteria are so demanding, 'valuable' for the singular insights they offer – that the 'true standard of taste and beauty' is to be found.[35]

6.2 Literary Style and Artistic Representation

The question one might press on Hume, however, is precisely *what* about a work of art qualifies it as being durably admirable. *Which* qualities in Homer's writing inspire (or should inspire) sentiments that make an object universally pleasing through time and across place? If Hume is silent in response, he is open to the criticism that his aesthetics (and the paradigm of 'taste' *ut totum*) represents merely the particulars ('tastes') of one class, gender, race, and political or cultural perspective generalised and elevated hegemonically to the level of the universal ('Taste').[36] Hume does not raise the question directly, though he suggests at one point that a general answer might not be possible anyway given that individual arts have their own 'end or purpose': the 'object of eloquence is to persuade, of history to instruct, of poetry to please by means of the passions and the imagination', suggesting that different criteria for successful execution govern in each case.[37] In two essays, however – 'Of Eloquence' and 'Of Simplicity and Refinement in Writing' – he examines what constitutes good oratory and fine literary style, identifying features that the person of delicate taste detects, and thus explaining *why* some works deserve universal approbation

---

[33] *E* (LF), p. 243, *E* (C), p. 193.   [34] *E* (LF), p. 245, *E* (C), p. 194.
[35] *E* (LF), p. 241, *E* (C), p. 911. See also *E* (LF), pp. 113–14, *E* (C), p. 102.
[36] For a statement of this view in the Hume literature, see Richard Shusterman, 'The Scandal of Taste: Social Privilege as Nature in the Aesthetic Theories of Hume and Kant', *Philosophical Forum*, 20 (1989), pp. 211–29. Compare Rochelle Gurstein, 'Taste and "the Conversible World" in the Eighteenth Century', *Journal of the History of Ideas*, 61 (2000), pp. 203–21, who emphasises the anti-elitist strain in the genre.
[37] *E* (LF), p. 240, *E* (C), p. 190.

even if, for the reasons specified earlier, they do not always receive it. It is worth noting that the message Hume conveys in these essays recalls his later (1748) discussion (some fifteen paragraphs) in the first *Enquiry* concerning the 'effects' of association 'on the passions and imagination' (the paragraphs appeared in every edition except the final posthumous one of 1777, from which they were omitted).[38] Hume there considers different literary forms, ostensibly for purposes of proving that his three principles (resemblance, contiguity, and cause and effect) capture exhaustively the ways in which ideas are connected, but in the process he frames rules for literary creativity based not on what he or anybody else prefers, but on the demands dictated by certain aspects of human nature. Hume makes room for variation, including the associating principle particular writers choose (Ovid resemblance, for example, Homer cause and effect), but observes that if authors are to elicit an 'enlivened imagination and enflamed passion' as well as offer 'lasting entertainment' to readers,[39] they must have a plan and give 'unity' to their productions by connecting characters, actions, and events in a coherent way; the alternative will be the disjointed 'ravings of a madman'.[40]

In 'Of Eloquence',[41] Hume engages the same themes in explaining the superiority of ancient eloquence over its modern counterpart. It is not simply historical contingencies that explain why people flocked from all corners of Greece when Demosthenes pleaded at Athens, while modern Londoners barely register important debates in the Houses of Parliament. The difference lies in the inherent superiority of the 'sublime' and 'pathetic' style, which appeals to the passions, over the 'calm, elegant, and subtle' one that educates reason. The Greeks, Hume notes, who experienced both, 'upon comparison, gave the preference to that kind, of which they have left us such applauded models', with Demosthenes – a sort of true judge in the sphere of eloquence – approaching the 'nearest to perfection'.[42] Human beings take pleasure in being persuaded, and the mechanism of excitation is the same everywhere: the 'principles of every passion, and of every sentiment, is in every man; and when touched properly, they rise to life, and warm the heart, and convey that satisfaction, by which a work of genius is distinguished from the adulterate beauties of a capricious wit and fancy'.[43] Were the moderns exposed to a present-day Demosthenes, they too would flock to hear him speak.

---

[38] *EHU*, pp. 102–7.   [39] Ibid., pp. 103–4.   [40] Ibid., p. 102.
[41] On this, see also Chapter 10 by Ross Carroll in this volume.
[42] *E* (LF), pp. 106, 108, *E* (C), pp. 97–98.   [43] *E* (LF), p. 107, *E* (C), p. 98.

In 'Of Simplicity and Refinement in Writing', Hume makes similar observations with respect to literature. Oratory and writing are distinct arts, and, given the different 'end or purpose' to which each aims – persuasion and pleasure, respectively – the criteria for success will be different. At the same time, they share a common aim of eliciting strong sentiments of beauty, and in both cases the artists in question first inflame their own passions before communicating them to and rousing the same in the audience.[44] Hume also faults Cicero, his acknowledged greatness notwithstanding, for being 'too florid and rhetorical: His figures too striking and palpable: ... And his wit disdains not always the artifice of a pun, rhyme, or jingle of words',[45] all features that contradict the character of fine writing, which Hume identifies as a 'just mixture of simplicity and refinement'.[46] 'Refinement', like its close ally 'taste', can denote an achievement – a state attained, a status won – but here Hume is more interested in writing as such, the formal qualities that constitute style and render a composition worthy of praise or blame. He thus broaches the subject (raised explicitly by Addison and Hutcheson before him) of 'artistic representation', how to balance the demands of verisimilitude with the need to depart from reality for purposes of pleasing and moving an audience. The beauty of art, it transpires, is never a matter of the mere copying of objects – presenting them – but of *re*-presenting them, rendering them in such a way as to bring about an intended effect. 'Nothing can please persons of taste, but nature drawn with her graces and ornaments, *la belle nature*',[47] as Hume writes, objects of ordinary experience transformed into a 'reality that could be', as Charles Batteux had elucidated the idea, 'the truly beautiful, which is represented as if it actually existed, with all the perfections it could have'.[48]

Hume thus recognises that writing involves a delicate balancing act between two competing tendencies. On the one hand, the genius of authors lies in their creative ability to move the passions and pleasure an audience by arousing the correct sentiments, not ones that are 'merely natural',[49] which 'affect not the mind with any pleasure, and seem not worthy of our attention', but offspring of 'a species of painting'[50] that portray the world in such 'strong and remarkable' strokes as to 'convey a lively image to the mind'.[51] Subjects from 'low life' – the 'pleasantries of a

---

[44] See *EHU*, pp. 103–4 and *E* (LF), p. 104, *E* (C), p. 196.   [45] *E* (LF), p. 105, *E* (C), p. 97.
[46] *E* (LF), p. 193, *E* (C), p. 158.   [47] *E* (LF), p. 192, *E* (C), p. 157.
[48] Charles Batteux, *The Fine Arts Reduced to a Single Principle*, trans. James O. Young (Oxford, 2015 [1746]), p. 13.
[49] *E* (LF), p. 191, *E* (C), p. 157.   [50] *EHU*, p. 104.   [51] *E* (LF), p. 192, *E* (C), p. 157.

waterman, the observations of a peasant, the ribaldry of a porter or hackney coachman' – being, though natural, inherently 'disagreeable', are to be avoided as much as direct reproductions of the world: 'What an insipid comedy should we make of the chit-chat of the tea-table, copied faithfully and at full length?'[52] On the other hand, while embellishments are indispensable, literary representation is by necessity 'founded on false-hood and fiction, on hyperboles, metaphor, and an abuse and perversion of terms from their natural meaning'.[53] Poets, moreover, are 'liars by profession ... always endeavour[ing] to give an air of truth to their fictions';[54] they are possessed of a 'native enthusiasm',[55] and thus masters at sweeping themselves and others away into a kind of madness.[56]

Translating these opposite forces into the language of 'qualities' or 'style' for 'fine writing' leaves Hume treading warily between 'simplicity', which reflects and captures nature, and 'refinement' that embellishes and distorts it, criteria he marshals elsewhere to distinguish modern 'politeness' from its ancient counterpart.[57] The former demand means that they preserve some 'just representation' of or 'resemblance' to the original, which is lost when embellishment becomes ornamentation, excess of which is a 'fault in every kind of production'.[58] The noblest works of art, in fact, are 'beholden for their chief beauty to the force and happy influence of nature',[59] and refinement too easily becomes 'uncommon expressions, strong flashes of wit, pointed similes, and epigrammatic turns', all of which are a 'disfigure-ment, rather than an embellishment of discourse'.[60] In the final analysis, Hume recommends an 'excess' of simplicity over that of refinement: it does not, like its counterpart, celebrate mere novelty that corrupts taste, and, more importantly, it is more beautiful because it appeals, again, to the passions rather than 'reflections and observations'.[61] These criteria draw Hume inevitably to the literature of antiquity for models of excellence,[62] the Greeks being distinguished, as he writes in the *History*, by their 'correctness and delicacy' and 'an amiable simplicity, which ... is so fitted to express the genuine movements of nature and passions'.[63] From 'the simple purity of Athens', he traces a natural history of degenerating taste, however, over-refinement manifest through love of novelty, and a gradual departure from the simple depiction of nature to increasing artifice and

[52] *E* (LF), pp. 191–92, *E* (C), p. 157.   [53] *E* (LF), p. 231, *E* (C), p. 184.   [54] *T*, p. 83.
[55] *E* (LF), p. 139, *E* (C), p. 118.   [56] See *T*, p. 85.   [57] *E* (LF), pp. 130–31, *E* (C), pp. 112–13.
[58] *E* (LF), p. 192, *E* (C), pp. 113–14.   [59] *E* (LF), p. 139, *E* (C), p. 119.
[60] *E* (LF), p. 192, *E* (C), p. 157.   [61] *E* (LF), p. 195, *E* (C), p. 159.
[62] *E* (LF), p. 196, *E* (C), p. 160.   [63] *HE*, VI, p. 543 and V, p. 149.

adornment; hardly a major writer (John Milton included) escapes the lash of Hume's critical pen for their traitorous involvement.[64]

6.3   The Paradox of Tragedy

In 'Of Tragedy', Hume addresses the puzzling fact that scenes, which would induce pain, disgust, or horror when witnessed in real life, bring pleasure when confronted in artistic works and, specifically, in tragedy where the emotions aroused are markedly intense. This 'paradox of tragedy' is of ancient origin, with its stirrings in the pre-Socratic conception of poetry, reflected in Plato's discussion of the human 'hunger for tears', and receiving its best-known formulation in Aristotle's remarks on the 'tragic pleasure of pity and fear' that the poet aims to 'produce by a work'.[65] Addison had raised the issue (in 1711), and appealed to the 'Sense of our own Safety' as a solution, suggesting that the appearance of harm is accompanied by a pleasure of freedom from danger. Addison's name is absent from 'Of Tragedy', his view perhaps too close to Hume's for the latter to draw a satisfactory contrast with his own. Addison also emphasises the importance of literary depiction ('Description') and includes a strong element of emotional transformation that is reminiscent of Hume's own appeal to 'conversion'.[66] Hume looks instead to the French and finds his foil in Dubos and Bernard de Fontenelle: the former had traced tragic pleasure to the avoidance of boredom, the latter to the audience's awareness that no real suffering is involved.[67] Whatever the reason for Hume's choice of interlocutors, his characterisation of the problem sits comfortably with his expressed views on literature and the passions discussed earlier – the 'whole art of the poet is employed, in rouzing and supporting the compassion and indignation, the anxiety and resentment of his audience' – from which he moves quickly to highlight the puzzling effect in question, namely, that people are 'pleased in proportion as they are afflicted, and never are so happy as when they employ tears,

[64] See, for example, *HE*, V, pp. 149–45 and VI, pp. 542–43, and Costelloe, *The British Aesthetic Tradition*, pp. 61–63.

[65] Plato, *Republic*, trans. G. M. A. Grube, 2nd ed. (Indianapolis, IN, 1992), 605c–606b, and Aristotle, *Poetics*, in *The Complete Works of Aristotle*, ed. Jonathan Barnes (2 vols., Princeton, NJ, 1984), II, 1453b12–13.

[66] See Addison, 'The Pleasures of the Imagination', pp. 567–68, and for the modern scholarly literature, see Costelloe, 'Hume's Aesthetics', pp. 107–9.

[67] See Jean-Baptiste Dubos, *Réflexions Critiques sur la Poésie et sur la Peinture*, 6th ed. (3 vols., Paris, 1765 [1719]), I, pt. 1, ch. 7, and Bernard le Bovier de Fontenelle, '*Réflexions sur la Po*étique' [1724], in Fontenelle, *Oeuvres Complètes*, ed. Alain Niderst (8 vols., Paris, 1989), III, pp. 111–59.

sobs, and cries to give vent to their sorrow'.[68] It appears that the 'same object of distress, which pleases in a tragedy, were it really set before us, would give the most unfeigned uneasiness'[69] and it thus becomes 'an unaccountable pleasure, which the spectators of a well-written tragedy receive from sorrow, terror, anxiety, and other passions, that are in them- selves disagreeable and uneasy'.[70]

Having considered and rejected the solutions of Dubos and Fontenelle – the former ignores the fact that the same passions are disagreeable when experienced outside a literary depiction, the latter leaves unexplained the assumed reality of the scene required if one is to be moved by it – Hume offers his solution: that 'from that very eloquence, with which the melancholy scene is represented ... the whole impulse of those [melancholy] passions is converted into pleasure, and swells the delight which the eloquence raises in us'.[71] The first part is straightforward, being an appeal to the effect of writing and speech on the passions of an audience. The problematic part concerns Hume's so-called 'Principle of Conversion', the mechanism whereby the impulse or vehemence arising from sorrow, compassion, or indignation, is redirected by the sentiments of beauty inspired by the artistic representation. For the latter, as Hume describes it, 'being the predominant emotion, seize the whole mind, and convert the former into themselves, at least tincture them so strongly as totally to alter their nature'. In tragedy, the effect is even more pronounced because the genre is fundamentally imitative, which being 'always itself agreeable', aids the process whereby the 'whole feeling' is converted 'into one uniform and strong enjoyment'.[72]

The appearance of the conversion principle in 'Of Tragedy' must be set against Hume's earlier discussions of the 'violent passions' in Book 2 of the *Treatise* where he makes two claims relevant to the later essay. He suggests, first, that when two passions are 'both present in the mind, they readily mingle and unite' and the 'predominant passion readily swallows up the inferior, and converts it into itself', and second, that opposite passions can increase the 'violence' of the predominant one to a pitch higher than it would otherwise possess.[73] Both apply to the case of tragedy, though the latter seems most relevant, there being no better example of the conflict between the painful sorrow excited by the scenes depicted and the

---

[68] *E* (LF), p. 217, *E* (C), p. 174.   [69] *E* (LF), p. 218, *E* (C), p. 175.
[70] *E* (LF), p. 216, *E* (C), p. 174.   [71] *E* (LF), pp. 219–20, *E* (C), p. 176.
[72] *E* (LF), p. 220, *E* (C), p. 176.   [73] *T*, pp. 269 and 270.

sentiments of beauty inspired by the mode of presentation.[74] The latter are more pleasurable precisely *because* they are opposed by pain and that feeling increases, as Hume says, 'in proportion' to the depth of affliction.

These passages certainly provide a context for 'Of Tragedy' and enrich Hume's phenomenology of what an audience might experience at a performance, but they do not settle questions about the mechanism of conversion itself. One answer lies in claiming that Hume must be predicating 'conversion' not of the passion as such, but of the *movements or agitations* it causes: the original passions are not then changed so much as their motions redirected ('converted'). This explains a good deal, but it involves assuming that Hume means something that he does not say.[75] An alternative option is to look at another use to which Hume puts 'conversion' in the *Treatise*, namely, to explain how an idea becomes so enlivened as to approach the force and vivacity of (is 'converted' into) an impression. When one recalls or imagines an occasion that produced or could produce an impression of sorrow, say (an appropriately tragic passion), we come to *feel* sorrow by 'converting' the idea into an impression. A similar process takes place when one forms an idea of *somebody else's* passion as well, which is then converted, through sympathy, to a passion one feels oneself: 'When I see the *effects* of passion in the voice and gesture of any person', Hume writes, 'my mind immediately passes from these effects to their causes, and forms such a lively idea of the passions, as is presently converted into the passion itself'.[76] This is an apt description of what occurs in a literary tragedy, where an idea of the passion represented is formed by readers or members of the audience in whom it becomes enlivened and is 'converted' into and appears as a new impression. The fact that this is felt as pleasure rather than pain is then due to the beauty of the poetic representation and the sentiments of beauty it inspires; the latter, then 'being the predominant emotion', as Hume writes, 'seize the whole mind, and convert the former into themselves, at least tincture them so strongly as totally to alter their nature'.[77] Through tragic literature, one does not take pleasure in another's pain, then, but pleasure in the beauty of its representation.

---

[74] See Margaret Watkins, *The Philosophical Progress of Hume's Essays* (Cambridge, 2020), pp. 148–49.

[75] See Alex Neil, '"An Unaccountable Pleasure": Hume on Tragedy and the Passions', *British Journal of Aesthetics* 39 (1999), pp. 12–25. Neil's interpretation is defended by Watkins, *The Philosophical Progress*, pp. 149–51, though it involves assuming that Hume's 'language can be looser than is ideal for purposes of analysis' (p. 149). The observations that follow draw on Costelloe, *The British Aesthetic Tradition*, pp. 56–57. For a more recent discussion, see Amyas Merivale, *Hume on Art, Emotion, and Superstition: A Critical Study of the Four Dissertations* (New York, 2019), ch. 10.

[76] *T*, p. 368.   [77] *E* (LF), p. 220, *E* (C), p. 176.

6.4   Conclusion: A History and Political Economy of the Arts

While the essays considered thus far provide the principal material for collating the parts that compose Hume's philosophical aesthetics, the picture would be incomplete without looking further afield to three other essays. The first, 'Of the Rise and Progress of the Arts and Sciences', is notable for being, as Hume describes it, a 'history',[78] which aims to trace the 'causes' that explain why one 'nation is more polite and learned, at a particular time, than any of its neighbours'.[79] In the aesthetic essays, Hume is concerned primarily with the atemporality of taste and how principles of human nature might be interrogated for the qualities that constitute great art; Homer is durably admirable because he *transcends* changing circumstances. In this essay, by contrast, 'the arts' refers to a historical object, a set of practices subject to the contingencies of time and change, and, given its specific focus, those connected to the form of government that prevails. Hume retains the basic premise that the 'natural genius of mankind' is the 'same in all ages' and affirms the corollary that the capacity of taste will actualise itself in regular and predictable ways; hence the great benefit to a culture – echoing the 'true judge' – of being 'possessed of patterns in every art' to 'regulate the taste, and fix the objects of imitation'.[80] At the same time, he shows that being founded on principles of human nature does not entail either that the arts will inevitably rise and flourish or that their progress will be uniform and smooth. As factors intervene to frustrate the development of individual taste, so the arts might be denied the fertile soil and nourishment they require to take root and grow, factors Hume identifies as free government and cooperative international trade. Whether the 'useful' or 'agreeable' arts predominate depends, in turn, on the prevalence of republican or monarchical governments and the social structure of each; the former encourages a 'strong genius' characteristic of the sciences and the latter a 'refined taste' typical of the liberal arts.[81]

   In 'Of Commerce' and 'Of Refinement in the Arts', Hume shifts from a historian's perspective to take the view of a political economist, and moves correspondingly from the narrow to the wider senses of 'the arts' to unite them all as commodities in a system of production and trade. Hume's language is admittedly ambiguous: on occasion he distinguishes the 'mechanical' arts of 'commerce' and 'manufacture' from those that are

---

[78] *E* (LF), p. 113, *E* (C), p. 102.   [79] *E* (LF), p. 115, *E* (C), p. 103.
[80] *E* (LF), p. 135, *E* (C), p. 116.   [81] *E* (LF), p. 126, *E* (C), p. 111.

'liberal',[82] and more often than not leaves readers to infer the referent from the context. Terminological ambiguity notwithstanding, Hume still collects the arts into a single category of 'finer arts' – be they liberal *or* mechanical – and identifies them as the outcome of two factors. First, they only arise when there are 'superfluous hands' to form them, which occurs when a society has secured the necessities of life and moved beyond agriculture or 'husbandry'. As such, the finer arts are all 'arts of luxury' because they presuppose both leisure and prosperity and augment the satisfaction of basic needs with entertainment and higher pleasures.[83] There are examples of strong states impoverished in the arts (Sparta being a case in point), but these are due to singular conditions that obtain (a small province with a martial spirit, inclined to defence due to the presence of aggressive neighbours), and are 'contrary to the more natural and usual course of things',[84] the 'common bent of mankind'[85] being that industry and the arts increase the power of the sovereign and the overall happiness of the state.

Second, the arts thus understood arise in response to the human passions, not, however, as in the aesthetic essays, in terms of identifying the qualities picked out by a cultivated taste, but as *commodities* the use and ownership of which 'gratify the senses and appetites'.[86] In the *Treatise*, Hume had already identified riches and the pleasure they bring with the power of acquisition or, more fundamentally, the '*supposition* of power, independent of its actual exercise', since there is 'joy' in anticipation alone even if the desire goes unsatisfied.[87] 'Of Commerce' presupposes and adds another dimension to Hume's earlier observations by identifying pleasure with 'luxury', which is nothing but 'great refinement in the gratification of the senses'.[88] Taste and consumption go hand in hand as two aspects of the same phenomenon: the true judge is but the perfect consumer by another name.

Hume emphasises, moreover, the extraordinary power of the passions in this regard. Foreign trade, he observes, generally precedes domestic luxury since it provides commodities both novel and 'ready for use' – not to mention a source of great profit – but once people have been thus 'acquainted with the *pleasures* of luxury and the *profits* of commerce, their *delicacy* and *industry*, being once awakened, carry them on to farther

---

[82] *E* (LF), p. 261, *E* (C), p. 204.   [83] *E* (LF), p. 256, *E* (C), pp. 200–1.
[84] *E* (LF), p. 259, *E* (C), p. 202.   [85] *E* (LF), p. 260, *E* (C), p. 203.
[86] *E* (LF), p. 263, *E* (C), p. 206.   [87] *T* pp. 203–4; italics mine.
[88] *E* (LF), p. 268, *E* (C), p. 209.

improvements', and they aspire to a 'more splendid way of life than their ancestors enjoyed'.[89] Luxury grows 'vicious' when it 'engrosses all a man's expence',[90] Hume admits, though the causes of the condition are the vices that underlie it rather than refinement itself. Luxury is neither virtuous nor vicious outside circumstances that provide a context for such valuations, though, in general, its effects on private and public life are overwhelmingly positive: where industry and arts flourish the mind acquires new vigour, people are more sociable and mutual regard increases, indulgence to excess is reduced where pleasures are refined and people discriminating, government grows more moderate, and the threat of factions is reduced. Taste, one might say, whether conceived aesthetically or economically, diffuses its good offices throughout the body politic, and, in Hume's view of it at least, holds the promise of progress on both an individual and a social level.

[89] *E* (LF), p. 264, *E* (C), p. 206.   [90] *E* (LF), p. 279, *E* (C), p. 216.

CHAPTER 7

Religion, Anticlericalism and the Worldly Paths to Happiness in Hume's Essays

R. J. W. Mills

In 'Of Public Credit' (1752) Hume opined that 'mankind are, in all ages, caught by the same baits'.[1] One such trick used to 'trepan' mankind was the priest's demand that we act for the 'glory of god', when what really is served is the 'temporal interest of the clergy'.[2] Similarly, in 'Of the Populousness of Ancient Nations' (1752), Hume observed that in all modern European languages, but not in ancient languages, 'clergy' and 'laity' are viewed as opposing terms, which he took as linguistic evidence of how the Christian priesthood has 'overbalanced the whole state'.[3] These two passages are characteristics of the anticlericalism found in the *Essays*, present as much in footnotes and passing asides as in the one essay dedicated to religion, 'Of Superstition and Enthusiasm' (1741).

Two themes emerge from surveying this commentary. First, Hume encouraged his reader to view priests as objects of social scientific observation, rather than as a sacrosanct body of individuals of superior piety. Key here was the interplay between human nature, the demands of ascetic religion and the social and political power of the priest. The impossibility of constant adherence to their religious duties turned priests into malicious and vengeful dissemblers, a fact of considerable importance given their power over the rest of humankind.

Second, Hume argued that something had gone terribly wrong with the establishment of Christianity. In contrast to benign pagan civil religion, the new church–state relationship subordinated civil to ecclesiastical authority, leading to a millennium of religious violence and persecution. Just as important to Hume was the disastrous colonisation of philosophy by early Christian apologists, which led to the former practice being corrupted into theology. Priesthoods emerged as parties of interest masquerading as parties of unquestionable principle. Both developments would have wholly negative effects on Europe for more than 1,700 years.

---

[1] *E* (LF), p. 363, *E* (C), p. 271.   [2] Ibid.   [3] *E* (LF), p. 389n. 21, *E* (C), p. 286n 17.

The themes are the progeny of a marriage between two different authorial stances towards religion. The first is Hume's belief that the relationship between human nature, society and religion could be studied by applying the methods of experiential reasoning as characterised by recent successes in natural philosophy, leading to identification of the general principles governing that relationship.[4] The second is Hume's strong anticlericalism that occasionally reached *philosophe*-levels of partiality, and which his contemporaries believed hindered his scientific study of human nature.

The marriage of anticlericalism and the 'science of man' was already present in Hume's *Essays Moral and Political* (1741–42), especially in the essays on parties. The riotously disdainful treatment of priests in the footnote included in 'Of National Characters' (1748) marks a difference in tone rather than a change in approach to religious matters. To stress the continued presence of anticlerical themes across the various iterations of Hume's *Essays*, moreover, means we must distinguish between Hume's approach to religion and his deliberate attempt to discuss politics in an impartial fashion. In the *Essays*, Hume's dislike of institutional religion was clear.

7.1   Parties of Religion and 'Of Superstition and Enthusiasm' (1741)

The one essay dedicated solely to religious topics in Hume's *Essays* was 'Of Superstition and Enthusiasm' (1741), which appeared in volume one of the *Essays Moral and Political*. It builds on the two preceding essays: 'Of Parties in general' and 'Of the Parties of Great Britain'. Read together, they encourage us to think of religious sects as parties of interest, emerging and changing in interaction with a variety of societal factors and the inherent propensities of human nature. Hume thus pulls back the curtain of priestly pretension to higher motivations to expose the common human underpinnings of their profession and claims to religious and political power.

In 'Of Parties in General', Hume holds that all party conflict, including that between religious sects, has its origins in our inherent tendency to disputatiousness when our strongly held beliefs are challenged. The human mind possesses a tendency to lay 'hold on every mind that approaches it': we assume others think and feel the same way we do.[5] We are happy when this assumption is correct, but we are 'shocked and disturbed by any

---

[4] See Chapter 4 by Margaret Watkins in this volume.   [5] *E* (LF), p. 60, *E* (C), p. 68.

contrariety' to our beliefs, regardless of whether the difference of opinion has any real-world consequence.[6] Our feeling of mental disquiet informs our 'eagerness' and 'impatience' in dispute, and helps explain why we become polarised on matters of principle.

The social danger of our natural argumentativeness was minimal in pre-Christian antiquity where religion was mythological, philosophy the preserve of powerless sects and priests were subordinate to politicians. The threat reached new heights, however, due to the unprecedented concentration of power in the Christian priesthood. The 'origin of all religious wars and divisions' that mired Christendom was the new 'authority of the priests, and the separation of the ecclesiastical and civil powers'.[7] These developments resulted from the 'accidental causes' behind the emergence of Christianity.[8] The new religion was initially ignored by Roman civil officials as they viewed it as just another sect within the established, and despised, Jewish population. Not subject to civil surveillance, Christian priests were able to 'engross all authority in the new sect' and snuff out dissent.[9] When Christianity became the established religion of Rome, the priesthood became a rival to political authority and, likewise, 'engendered a spirit of persecution' at the heart of Christendom.[10]

The takeover of the practice of philosophy by the early Christian apologists also rendered Europe a 'scene of religious wars and divisions'.[11] This was an unprecedented development in the history of civilisation. The religions of 'ignorant and barbarous' ages had taken the form of 'traditional tales and fictions', not mandated propositions.[12] As they were mythologies, not theologies, early religions rarely exacerbated humanity's natural disputatiousness. Things changed as philosophy, a practice in which rival sects dispute truth claims, spread across the ancient world. Christianity first emerged, as a proselytising, monotheistic religion, in a polytheist Roman Empire in which the practice of philosophy was well-established, even if only small circles participated in debate, however zealous. Seeking to convert Roman elites who were familiar with philosophy, the votaries of Christianity were 'obliged to form a system of speculative opinions' and to 'explain, comment, confute, and defend' their new faith against pagan philosophers.[13] In the process, Christianity was transformed into a system of theology, infused with the zealotry of philosophy. And the realm of

---

[6] *E* (LF), p. 61, *E* (C), p. 68.   [7] *E* (LF), p. 62, *E* (C), p. 69.   [8] *E* (LF), p. 60, *E* (C), p. 68.
[9] *E* (LF), p. 61, *E* (C), p. 69.   [10] *E* (LF), p. 62, *E* (C), p. 69.   [11] Ibid.   [12] Ibid.
[13] Ibid.

religion, heretofore one of storytelling, was transformed into a battle-ground over beliefs.

Despite the institutional victory over paganism, Hume argued, conflict continued within Christendom with the appearance of 'new divisions and heresies', a consequence of rivalrous priests and the absurdity of the nonsensical claims of theology.[14] In terms of clerical authority, the inherent disputatiousness of human nature was utilised by sectarians within Christianity as part of a strategy of 'begetting mutual hatred and antipathy among their deluded followers'.[15] The admixture of priestly interest with firmly held religious principle created 'cruel factions' more violent than any arising from mere 'interest and ambition'.[16] In 'modern times', the desire to destroy one's enemies is found 'amongst religious parties alone'.[17] Conflict over religious principle was especially combustible because it involved vexation over meaningless words. He wrote sardonically of how the wars of religion 'in this polite and knowing part of the world' revolved around disputes over 'utterly absurd and unintelligible articles of faith' that neither faction understood.[18]

Hume also made it clear that differences in religious principle bore no relation to morals. The theological issues that prompted vicious controversy were 'attended with no contrariety of action' in common life, such that everyone could be left to 'follow his own way, without interfering with his neighbour'.[19] He went further: the 'severest injunctions of religion' had no effect on 'general virtue and good morals'.[20] Here he was echoing Pierre Bayle's dissolution of the assumed link between religious belief and good morals, by holding that even the threat of damnation had little effect on our quotidian actions. The fury whipped up by priests over the social danger of heresy, by which fury they justified and extended their power, should be viewed as baseless.

Here we have the outlines, in 1741, of Hume's well-known argument in the 'Natural History of Religion' (1757) that the traditional paganism of antiquity was more tolerant and socially beneficial than Christianity, a philosophical monotheism. Less familiar is Hume's discussion of how religious persecution was present in the ancient world, though in the form of political and not priestly action. In a footnote to 'Of Parties in General', Hume claimed the ancient Romans were not 'great friends to toleration', as indicated by the Twelve Tables of Roman Law (451–450 BCE), even if

---

[14] *E* (LF), p. 63, *E* (C), p. 70.   [15] Ibid.   [16] Ibid.   [17] *E* (LF), p. 407, *E* (C), pp. 296–97.
[18] *E* (LF), p. 59, *E* (C), p. 67.   [19] *E* (LF), p. 60, *E* (C), p. 68.   [20] *E* (LF), p. 55, *E* (C), p. 65.

those persecutory laws were 'not rigorously executed'.[21] Hume actually wrote admiringly of Roman persecution because it involved a superior civilisation (the Roman) forcibly converting a more primitive one (the druidic Gauls), culminating in the eventual abolishment of druidism under Emperor Claudius (AD 41–54). Hume praised Roman religious persecution for proceeding with 'caution and moderation' and for having the benign goal of spreading 'ROMAN manners'.[22] The policy was conducted by political leaders to strengthen the Empire as a whole. This contrasted with the 'furious persecutions of Christianity' that resulted from the zealotry of its rulers and their favoured religious faction.[23]

In the following 'Of the Parties of Great Britain', Hume explained that the attitudes of priests and princes towards church–state relations stemmed from a desire to attain or maintain power. It was a general rule that current possession of institutional religious power led to heightened support of monarchy. Throughout history, 'ecclesiastical parties' have been 'enemies to liberty', a result of 'fixed reasons of interest and ambition'.[24] Freedom of thought and expression are inimitable to 'priestly power' and its 'pious frauds', and these liberties only exist in a 'free government' where religion is subordinated to government.[25] Sects of enthusiasts tend not to support monarchy, not because of any underlying religious principle but because they rarely establish the priesthoods and rituals needed to transform into powerful institutional religions. If they did, they too would support monarchy. Princes will always support episcopal over Presbyterian forms of ecclesiastical governance, because of the 'greater affinity between monarchy and episcopacy' and because the prince will be able to rule over the clergy through their 'ecclesiastical superiors'.[26]

In the case of Britain, the established clergy will always be members of the Court party, or the supporters of monarchy, whereas religious dissenters will always be supporters of the Country party, or supporters of parliament's power against the monarchy. During the British Civil Wars, the established clergy in England 'concurred with the king's arbitrary designs' because 'in return' they were allowed to persecute their theological 'adversaries'.[27] The established clergy were episcopal, the nonconformists were Presbyterian; the former supported the monarch, the latter, parliament. Follow the interests, and you will understand the stance of the party of religion on political power.

---

[21] *E* (LF), p. 61n. 9, *E* (C), p. 69n 3.   [22] *E* (LF), p. 62n. 9, *E* (C), p. 69n. 3.   [23] Ibid.
[24] *E* (LF), p. 65, *E* (C), p. 72.   [25] *E* (LF), pp. 65–66, *E* (C), p. 72.
[26] *E* (LF), p. 67, *E* (C), p. 72.   [27] *E* (LF), p. 69, *E* (C), p. 73.

'Of Superstition and Enthusiasm' (1741) built on the analysis of the preceding two essays by discussing the aetiology of the two eponymous 'corruptions of true religion' in human nature and their relationship to institutional power.[28] The essay applies the methods of the 'science of man' to identify the 'true sources' of religious corruption in terms of the usual workings of the 'mind of man'.[29] Hume used 'experience', that is, historical evidence and personal observation, and 'reason', that is, inductions from that experience, to support his claims about the qualities of human nature.[30] In both cases, the individual succumbing to the religious error experiences strong, yet inexplicable, feelings for which they seek, guided by their imagination, an object outside of themselves that corresponds to those feelings. If we are scared, we think there must be something to be scared about. In framing superstition and enthusiasm as religious errors, Hume implies that the believer in true religion possesses a sound mind, moderated passions and rational arguments. The essay also implies, however, that in the real world nearly all prominent religious belief is caused by the interplay between the passions, the imagination and the vicissitudes of life.

Superstition involves belief in the existence of powerful, malevolent agents of unintelligible motivation who are still appeased by worship and sacrifice. The imagination of an individual experiencing 'unaccountable terrors and apprehension' seeks an object for their fears.[31] The original causes of their terrors are actually challenging private or public circumstances, ill health or an inherent 'gloomy and melancholy disposition'.[32] There is no real object of superstitious fear: the threats that the imagination creates are 'entirely invisible and unknown' and the means of appeasing them are 'equally unaccountable'.[33] Empty of cognitive content, what these fears are caused by, really, is the individual's state of mind: a 'blind and terrified credulity'.[34]

The 'true sources' of enthusiasm are the inverse of those of superstition, though the faculty of the imagination plays the same role.[35] Enthusiasm is belief in direct divine inspiration, emerging from feelings of 'elevation and presumption'.[36] As with superstition, the origin of this belief is 'unaccountable' to the one experiencing it, but the Humean scientist of man observes it arise from worldly success, good health, 'strong spirits' and a 'bold and confident disposition'.[37] The feeling of elevation gives 'full range' to the mind to imagine whatever it wants, leading to the 'raptures,

---

[28] *E* (LF), p. 73, *E* (C), p. 77.   [29] *E* (LF), p. 74, *E* (C), p. 77.   [30] Ibid.
[31] *E* (LF), p. 73, *E* (C), p. 77.   [32] Ibid.   [33] *E* (LF), p. 74, *E* (C), p. 77.   [34] Ibid.
[35] Ibid.   [36] Ibid.   [37] Ibid.

transports, and surprising flights of fancy' of religious fanaticism.[38] The enthusiast is detached from the 'mortal and perishable' world and looks only to the 'world of spirits'.[39] Seeking an explanation for their raptures, they hit upon the 'immediate inspiration of the Divine Being'.[40] Their self-diagnosed status as chosen by God justifies all their beliefs and behaviours, regardless of their distance from common reason and morality.

These aetiologies of religious error inform three observations about the influence of superstition and enthusiasm 'on government and society'.[41] First, superstition is exploited by priests to further their own power, but enthusiasm counteracts priestcraft to an equal or greater extent than 'sound reason and philosophy'.[42] The superstitious individual thinks themselves unworthy of 'approaching the divine presence'.[43] Here steps in the priest who, through studied 'sanctity' and 'impudence and cunning', positions themselves as the intermediary of God, and whose services the superstitious individual gladly accepts.[44] Priests first emerged in early societies, Hume conjectures, because of 'timorous and abject' people seeking ways to approach their gods.[45] Nearly all religions have a component of superstition, and all religions have members who seek to exploit this fact. And the more superstition in a religion, the more powerful are its clerical authorities. Hume points to modern Judaism, Catholicism and Anglicanism as examples of religions in which the priesthood is powerful due to the preponderance of superstition. (Many of Hume's English readers might have baulked at the inclusion of the Church of England in this triptych.)

If superstition supports priestly power, enthusiasm breaks free from the 'yoke of ecclesiastics'.[46] Fanatical sects demonstrate greater independence in their forms of devotion. The more enthusiasm within a sect, the less power priests have in that sect – to the point that the Quakers have no priests at all. (Many of Hume's Scottish readers might have baulked at his description of Presbyterians as ungovernable fanatics.) The 'presumptuous pride' of the enthusiast makes them believe that they 'actually ... approach' God through their personal 'way of contemplation and inward converse'.[47] The 'fanatic consecrates himself' and therefore priests are not needed, and shared public rituals are not important.[48]

Building on arguments found in the two preceding essays on parties, Hume's second reflection is that religious enthusiasm burns brightly but weakens, whereas superstition endures. New fanatical sects consolidate in

[38] Ibid. [39] Ibid. [40] Ibid. [41] *E* (LF), p. 75, *E* (C), p. 78. [42] Ibid. [43] Ibid.
[44] Ibid. [45] Ibid. [46] Ibid. [47] *E* (LF), p. 76, *E* (C), pp. 78–79.
[48] *E* (LF), p. 76, *E* (C), p. 79.

response to the controversy caused by their opinions. Vehement debate means that the new sect 'always spreads faster, and multiplies its partizans with greater rapidity' than any established opinion.[49] The new sect benefits as much from the 'violence of enemies' as they do from their own zeal.[50] The hostility of established religions against challengers has the unintended consequence of strengthening the resolve of those challengers.

When they first emerge, fanatical sects threaten the status quo. They do not, however, possess the means of replication. Sects of enthusiasts are initially 'furious and violent', but with a 'little time become more gentle and moderate'.[51] Animated by a sense of their novelty and the vehement opposition they provoke, enthusiasts are at first extreme in belief and behaviour, and demonstrate 'contempt for the common rules of reason, morality, and prudence'.[52] These animating influences inevitably decline, and with them so does the sect's fanaticism. Eventually a complete alteration occurs: the once fanatical 'sink into the greatest remissness and coolness in sacred matters'.[53] Partly this is because furious passions do not persist. Partly it is because priesthoods within fanatical sects lack power. Due to the independence of spirit fanaticism encourages, no 'body of men' exists within the sect whose 'interest' it is to maintain the 'religious spirit', that is, maintain the fanatic at the same level of psychological intensity, through rites and rituals.[54]

Hume's suggestion in 'Of Superstition and Enthusiasm', that many enthusiasts who were formerly 'such dangerous Bigots' were now some of Britain's 'Greatest free-thinkers', affords us an opportunity to assess a possible contradiction with an observation made in 'Of the Independency of Parliament' (1741). In the latter essay, Hume noted that 'in all controversies' those who defended the 'established and popular opinions' are more 'dogmatic and imperious', whereas their challengers affect 'gentleness and moderation' as the best means of getting their new ideas a fair hearing.[55] As an example, Hume points to the recent controversies in Britain over the truth and role of biblical revelation and over ecclesiastical power between 'free-thinkers of all denominations', who Hume described admiringly as arguing with 'moderation and good manners', and the defenders of religious orthodoxy, who argued with 'furious zeal and scurrility'.[56] Hume viewed the freethinkers not as a party of religion, though they controverted politely on politico-religious topics, but a

---

[49] E (LF), p. 50, E (C), p. 63.   [50] E (LF), p. 51, E (C), p. 63.   [51] E (LF), p. 76, E (C), p. 79.
[52] E (LF), p. 77, E (C), p. 79.   [53] Ibid.   [54] E (LF), pp. 77–78, E (C), p. 79.
[55] E (LF), p. 608, E (C), p. 550.   [56] Ibid.

disparate group of philosophers united only by the principle of the freedom of philosophising. The implication of Hume's arguments is that insurgent political parties utilise moderation, whereas fanatical sects, *qua* enthusiasts, are always extreme at first blast.

The lack of durability of fanatical religion differs greatly to its superstitious counterpart. The latter grows in strength over time and supports the consolidation of priestly power. Superstition renders men 'tame and submissive', allowing the priest to become the 'tyrant and disturber of society'.[57] The long-term tendency of enthusiasm is towards peace: the fanatic ceases to be a fanatic and there are no powerful priests to bully anyone. Superstition, by contrast, enables 'endless contentions, persecutions, and religious wars' by letting priests hoard power over their terrified and credulous flocks.[58] The Catholic Church took control of Europe and threw the continent into 'dismal convulsions', whereas the bigots of the Reformation have been succeeded by 'very free reasoners' in favour of religious liberty.[59]

Hume's third observation extends the analysis of the realm of politics. Superstition is an 'enemy to civil liberty' and fits people to 'slavery', whereas enthusiasm encourages a 'spirit of liberty'.[60] Hume uses examples from recent British and French history to bolster this claim. Enthusiasts believe in religious toleration and political liberty. In Britain, this has meant they have always fallen in with the Whigs. Hume describes the latter party as a composite of 'deists and profest latitudinarians', enthusiasts and, increasingly, oppressed Catholics seeking religious toleration.[61] The superstitious High Church party in the Church of England, by contrast, supported the monarchy and, as Hume noted in 'Of the Protestant Succession' (1752), provided the ideological undergirding of a 'regular and avowed system of arbitrary power.'[62]

Hinting at the purely instrumental quality of clerical support for monarchy, Hume notes an exception to his rule: during the 'early Times of the *English* Government' the clergy were the 'principal Opposers of the Crown', because during that age of weak royal authority, the Church and monarchy were direct rivals for power.[63] In terms of France, whatever the disputants themselves might claim, the conflict between the Molinists and Jansenists was not the result of a 'thousand unintelligible disputes'

---

[57] *E* (LF), p. 78, *E* (C), p. 79.   [58] Ibid.   [59] Ibid.
[60] *E* (LF), p. 78, *E* (C), p. 80. For more on the influence of religion on recent British party politics, see Chapter 9 by Max Skjönsberg in this collection.
[61] *E* (LF), p. 79, *E* (C), p. 80.   [62] *E* (LF), p. 505, *E* (C), p. 358.
[63] *E* (LF), p. 611, *E* (C), p. 561.

over theological principle, but the opposition of the superstitious against the fanatical.[64]

Hume's implied reader, the 'man of sense', is taught to view theological disputes as epiphenomena of the underlying causes of conflict: the differences between two common but antagonistic 'state[s] of mind' and the relations of political and religious power they support.[65] The religious disputes of Christian history were variants of party conflicts to be understood in terms of rival power groups, animated as much by self-interest as by principle and, ultimately, from nonrational motivations guiding the faculty of the imagination. Epitomising his application of the 'science of man' to religion, Hume secularised religious psychology and conflict, taking the issues out of the realm of theological controversy, and into the social scientific explanatory framework of moral and accidental causes.

7.2   The 1748 Footnote on Clergymen

The mask of the neutral scientist of man slipped somewhat with the publication of Hume's 'Of National Characters', which first appeared in a slim volume entitled *Three Essays, Moral and Political* (1748). It defended the argument that 'moral' rather than 'physical' causes account for differences of manners between nations. Moral causes included 'all circumstances which are fitted to work on the mind as motives or reasons', whereas physical causes were 'qualities of air and climate' that altered 'the temper, by altering the tone and habit of the body'.[66] To explain moral causes, Hume used the example of how the duties of a particular profession affect the manners of those working in that profession. To this point he added the footnote on clergymen as a corporate body. Elsewhere in the *Essays*, Hume sought to exemplify moderate conversation of highly charged subjects. The footnote, however, is laden with rancour, though under the guise of scientific language.

The object of Hume's attack needs to be addressed, briefly. In the third edition of the *Essays Moral and Political*, published in the same year as the *Three Essays*, Hume added a short footnote to 'Of Superstition and Enthusiasm' that explicitly distinguished between priests and clergymen. The priest is wicked, power-hungry and entirely self-interested, whereas the clergyman is respectable, law-abiding and seeks to minister their flocks well. While Hume is sometimes read as distinguishing between *Catholic*

[64] *E* (LF), p. 79, *E* (C), p. 80.   [65] *E* (LF), p. 73, p. 79, *E* (C), p. 80, p. 77.
[66] *E* (LF), p. 198, *E* (C), p. 161.

priests and *Protestant* clergymen, the criterion deployed here clearly relates to character and not confession. The footnote to 'Of Superstition and Enthusiasm', however, clashes with the footnote in 'Of National Characters', where Hume uses 'priest' and 'clergyman' synonymously. As we possess merely circumstantial contextual evidence, we can only conjecture as to the significance of the contradiction. Hume's analysis in 'Of National Characters', however, clearly explains the psychological and social consequences of any corporate body holding institutional power but subject to religious duties beyond the ken of human nature.

In pursuing his goal in the main body of the essay of explaining how moral causes fix the 'character of different professions', Hume proclaimed the fact that, quoting a line from John Dryden's *Absalom and Achitophel* (1681), 'priests of all religions are the same'.[67] All clergymen are 'elevated above humanity' and develop a 'uniform character' peculiar to their profession.[68] He expanded in the footnote that due to the demands of their job, priests are, necessarily, hypocrites. Human nature does possess a 'strong propensity to religion', but this is only effective at 'certain times and in certain dispositions'.[69] The job of the priest, however, requires them to be devout with an inhuman 'constancy'.[70] We cannot perpetually hold in mind our religious beliefs and act with unwavering devotion. The rest of life – other passions, bodily needs, social interactions – gets in the way. By the demands of their profession, priests are regularly put into situations where they must 'feign' devotion.[71]

There is a peculiarly bodily element to Hume's account of the perverted behaviour of the priest, an inversion of established early modern tropes of atheists as monsters. The constant dissembling of religious 'fervor and seriousness' destroys the character of the individual priest, as it demands they suppress their 'natural movements and sentiments'.[72] The priest lives a perverted existence, detached from the normal workings of human nature. Obliged to appear to the multitude as keeping a 'remarkable reserve', they pay constant attention to their 'looks and words and actions', meaning they undertake their duties with a 'continued grimace and hypocrisy'.[73] Naturally devout priests do exist, Hume acknowledges, but their superior piety leads them to arrogantly believe, like a fanatic who believes in direct inspiration, that their 'zeal for religious observances ... compensate[s] for many vices and enormities'.[74]

---

[67] *E* (LF), p. 199, *E* (C), p. 162.   [68] Ibid.   [69] *E* (LF), p. 199n. 3, *E* (C), p. 162n. 2.
[70] Ibid.   [71] Ibid.   [72] *E* (LF), p. 200n. 3, *E* (C), p. 162n. 2.   [73] Ibid.   [74] Ibid.

Perversion of character combines with corporate interest to make priests cruel and malicious. The clergy 'pretend to a divine and supernatural authority' and become accustomed to being treated differently, especially by the 'ignorant multitude'.[75] All priests jealously protect the 'veneration' paid to the priesthood and are particularly vulnerable to the human propensity to be angered by challenges to their opinions.[76] They respond with a proverbial 'degree of fury', the *odium theologicum* or 'Theological Hatred', and suppress all dissent.[77] Priestly vengefulness was also a form of sublimation. The obligation of priests to dissemble meekness made them feel despicable, and they find relief from this unpleasant sentiment about themselves by vindictively pursuing their critics.

The conclusion of Hume's footnote on priests is that 'many of the vices of human nature are, by fixed moral causes, inflamed in that profession'.[78] Priests will always act as a corporate body motivated by 'ambition, pride, revenge, and a persecuting spirit'.[79] Exceptional individuals exist, who display the 'noble virtues of humanity, meekness, and moderation', but they do so because the strength of their character outweighs the influence of their profession.[80] (Emphasis on the importance of character in sur-mounting the vices of the profession is one shared element of the footnotes in 'Of Superstition and Enthusiasm' and 'Of National Characters'.) The very nature of priestly authority, however, means that most priests not only do not serve the common weal but also actively war against it. Moreover, while other professionals can promote the interests of society when they seek personal success at their chosen employment, clergymen can only satisfy their ambition by 'promoting ignorance and superstition and impli-cit faith and pious frauds'.[81]

The explanatory apparatus of the 'science of man', developed in the *Treatise* and expanded to include more social elements in the *Essays*, gave Hume an incisive tool for examining the motivations and actions of those in positions of religious authority. The footnote in 'Of National Characters', as elsewhere in the *Essays*, involved a demystification of a purportedly sacred profession usually treated with reverence, as well as the abandonment of ecclesiastical history and theology as the lenses through which to understand religious conflict. That said, the language of empirical investigation and the 'fixed' principles of human nature provided rhetorical cover for Hume's vituperative attack on the clergy. Whatever insight into human nature the footnote was based on, Hume's discussion was framed

---

[75] *E* (LF), p. 201n. 3, *E* (C), p. 163n. 2.   [76] Ibid.   [77] Ibid.   [78] Ibid.   [79] Ibid.
[80] Ibid.   [81] *E* (LF), p. 200n. 3, *E* (C), p. 163n. 2.

in the most damaging way. Priests are hypocrites and thin-skinned bullies, with no redeeming features *qua* priests.

Hume's discussion of clergymen in the *Essays* was qualitatively different from much of the early Enlightenment discourse on priestcraft. The freethinkers of the preceding decades viewed priests as a dangerous group within society who corrupted true religion in pursuit of their own temporal power and wealth. The focus was on priestly deformations of religion, such as when Protestants decried the Catholic destruction of primitive Christianity or when deists criticised priestly corruption of pristine natural religion. The various strands of priestcraft discourse shared an aim of liberating religion from the grip of clerical imposture and returning to the practice of true religion. Hume did not share this goal: he instead wanted to inform his readers of better ways to think about the social and political standing of institutional religion. He did so by analysing religion through the prism of the interrelationship between human nature, corporate interest and political and ecclesiastical power.

7.3   Religion and the Essays on Happiness

Our discussion so far has focused on Hume's guidance on how we should think about erroneous belief, religious faction and priestly authority. We turn now to Hume's four 'essays on happiness' that ended volume 2 of the *Essays, Moral and Political* (1742), in which each monologist representing a school of ancient philosophy had something to say about the role of religion in our pursuit of happiness. The Epicurean, Stoic and Sceptic all viewed concerns about the nature of God and the afterlife as insignificant to worldly happiness. It is only the Platonist who valued reverential study of God's creation as the *summum bonum*. As Tim Stuart-Buttle has argued in Chapter 5 of this *Guide*, the four 'essays on happiness' exposed the endless circularity of debates over what constitute the good life when built on reviving the arguments of ancient philosophy.[82] The Stoic criticised the Epicurean for their narrow focus on the private world of love and friendship, at the expense of the pursuit of virtue in the public world. The Platonist criticised the Stoic for their narrow focus on worldly virtue, at the expense of worship of their creator. The Sceptic held that there are many paths to happiness, but suggested that the Platonic approach was not narrow, so much as impossible to

---

[82] See Chapter 5.

consistently achieve. The distinction, I suggest, between narrowness and impossibility is important.

The close reader of the *Essays*, as well as Hume's other writings on religion, would notice that the three monologists aside from the Platonist made claims that elsewhere Hume articulated as findings of the new scientific study of human nature. Both the Epicurean and the Stoic suggested we should not concern ourselves with the unknowable unknowns of life: the origin of the universe, the nature of God, the character of divine providence and immortality of the soul. These topics are, according to the Stoic, the preserve of 'speculative reasoners', and not the rest of us, while the Epicurean viewed them as the cause of 'vain anxieties'.[83] The reader of Hume's *Treatise*, *EHU*, 'Natural History of Religion' or *Dialogues* would know that these concerns were 'vain' and 'speculative' because they were nonsensical: they were matters beyond our experience, are thus without any real foundation and therefore not a sound basis for one's sense of how to be happy.

Ending the happiness quartet was the Sceptic's monologue, which maintained that the path to happiness differed for every individual according to their own passions and inclinations. This was not relativism, however. Some paths to happiness are more likely to succeed than others, depending on whether they rely on 'steady or constant' passions.[84] The Platonist's focus on philosophical devotion was a case in point: because contemplation of the deity did not have a constant object in view, Platonic piety was doomed to failure. Such devotion could only be the 'transitory effect of high spirits, great leisure, a fine genius, and a habit of study and contemplation'.[85] The 'abstract, invisible object' of Platonic '*natural religion* ... cannot long actuate the mind, or be of any moment in life'.[86] Given we have no direct experience of God, any idea we think we possess is empty of cognitive content and is the creation of a philosophical enthusiasm akin to that Hume described in 1741.

To raise up more constant feelings of religious devotion required arousal of the 'senses and imagination', such as was provided by mythologies and the 'superstitions and observances' of most popular religions.[87] (Here Hume used 'superstition' to mean religious rites and ceremonies, rather than the psychological error identified in 'Of Superstition and Enthusiasm' [1741].) The Sceptic suggested, with some playfulness, that if we wished to consistently experience the passion of religious devotion, we should

---

[83] *E* (LF), p. 145, 154, *E* (C), p. 123–24, 130.   [84] *E* (LF), p. 167, *E* (C), p. 140.   [85] Ibid.
[86] Ibid.   [87] Ibid.

abandon the abstractions of natural theology and return to traditionary religion. Bringing this together with Hume's discussion on parties of religion in the first volume of the *Essays, Moral and Political*, we might suggest a life of religious happiness required moving into a postcolonial era in which Christianity relinquished its grip on philosophy, parties of religious principle were treated as parties of interest and we returned to the practice of religion as pure storytelling.

7.4   Forwarding Thinking Conclusions

The *Essays* detailed how the relationship between human nature, religious belief, and religious and political power had predictable patterns. Alongside being an anatomist of this relationship, Hume also gestured at acting as a reformer. Certainly, the space for manoeuvre was severely curtailed: it is, after all, human nature to fall for the bait that you serve God by serving priests, or to succumb to the errors of superstition and enthusiasm. Hume's starting point is a general scepticism that does not take at face value claims of religious truth and authority. We should understand priesthoods as parties of religion with distinct interests. Similarly, we can view the religious claims of laity and priesthood alike in terms of states of mind and social and political circumstances. The enthusiast does not have a direct link to God and neither does the priest threatening you with damnation. The discussion of religion in the *Essays* is part of Hume's attempt across many of his writings to unveil the human quality of religion.

Hume noted some reasons to be cheerful: the 'progress of learning and of liberty' in Britain since the Glorious Revolution had lessened religious fanaticism and clerical power.[88] At least, this is the view of the mouthpiece Hume uses in 'Whether the British Government Inclines More to Absolute Monarchy, or to a Republic' (1741). The dominant opinion in Britain was now ridicule of the clergy's 'pretension and doctrines' to the extent that 'religion can scarcely support itself in the world'.[89] The fact that belief in principles once taken as fixed and sacred verities could undergo such 'sudden and sensible change' indicates that religious principles, like their political counterparts, were based ultimately on the foundations of mutual consent.[90] The claims of priestly power could, plausibly, be weakened further as knowledge progressed and liberty expanded. A similar note was struck in 'Of the Protestant Succession'

---

[88] *E* (LF), p. 51, *E* (C), p. 63.   [89] Ibid.   [90] Ibid.

(1752): the post-Glorious Revolution settlement, during which the balance of power was weighted towards parliament over monarchy, had ensured that Britain's warring 'religious parties have been necessitated to lay aside their mutual rancour'.[91]

The *Essays* also contained the occasional comment reflecting Hume's own ironical brand of Erastianism. Ecclesiastical institutions have to be subordinate to civil authority for 'free governments' to have any 'security or stability', as Hume put it in 'Idea of a Perfect Commonwealth' (1752).[92] One piecemeal suggestion to limit clerical zealotry was to imitate the Roman Empire's 'expedient' of limiting entry to sacerdotal office to those over fifty years old, on the grounds that someone of advanced age would have had time to shake off the hotheadedness of youth and 'fix the[ir] character'.[93]

In his early essays, Hume saw no positive role for the clergy, who he viewed as subversive to civic peace and a fetter on individual freedom. He may have mellowed in his final years. In a late essay, 'Of the Origin of Government', published posthumously in 1777, Hume acknowledged that the clergy could have the 'useful object' of 'inculcat[ing] morality' and thus aid the 'distribution of justice'.[94] This desacralised vision of the clergy positioned them as handmaidens to civil authority and morality, and suggested the possibility of a benign role for institutional religion when severely subordinated to the needs of society. The essay also included the Montesquieu-inflected claim that religion served as a countervailing force that checked government authority from being 'entire and uncontroulable'.[95] In 'most countries', religion is a 'very intractable principle' that prevents the establishment of a complete absolutism.[96] This late essay indicates Hume's continued interest, as exhibited in the *Essays* and throughout his oeuvre, in how religions interact with political authority and how his contemporaries could think in new and empirical ways to curb the influence of priestcraft given the limits of human nature.

---

[91] *E* (LF), p. 508, *E* (C), p. 359.   [92] *E* (LF), p. 525, *E* (C), p. 371.
[93] *E* (LF), p. 201n. 3, *E* (C), p. 163n. 2.   [94] *E* (LF), pp. 37–38, *E* (C), p. 54.
[95] *E* (LF), p. 40, *E* (C), p. 56.   [96] Ibid.

PART III

Politics

CHAPTER 8

Reconstructing Oceana
Hume's 'Idea of a Perfect Commonwealth'
Danielle Charette

The *Political Discourses* (1752) end with a puzzle. Hume devoted most essays in the collection to practical subjects of political economy, such as taxes, the money supply, and the public debt. Yet the volume closes with 'Idea of a Perfect Commonwealth', a speculative piece in which Hume proposed to revive the question of what form of government constitutes 'the most perfect of all'.[1] His solution took the form of a large representative state – modelled explicitly after *The Commonwealth of Oceana* (1656) by James Harrington – in which provincial assemblies elect a national senate. The plan circulated widely in the late eighteenth century and became a common source in debates over the future of representative government. Hume's blueprint for an extensive federal commonwealth found a reception among the drafters of the U.S. Constitution, as well as early defenders of the French Revolution, who compared his plan with the National Assembly and Constitution of 1791.[2] But unlike James Madison, the abbé Sieyès or Harrington himself, Hume was not writing in the midst of a revolution and did not urge readers to replace their current government with his ideal constitution.

Hume was careful to say that forms of government are not like 'other artificial contrivances' that can be replaced with each new technological advancement. Only after warning the 'wise magistrate' against tampering with too many political 'experiments' did Hume provide the outline for his plan.[3] He divided this perfect government – which covers roughly the extent of Great Britain and Ireland – into 100 equally sized counties,

---

[1] *E* (LF), p. 513, *E* (C), p. 363.
[2] Mark Spencer, *David Hume and Eighteenth-Century America* (Rochester, 2006), pp. 154–97; Ryu Susato, 'Hume as an *Ami de la Liberté*: The Reception of His "Idea of a Perfect Commonwealth"', *Modern Intellectual History*, 13 (2016), pp. 569–96; Danielle Charette, 'Hume's "Idea of a Perfect Commonwealth" and Scottish Political Thought of the 1790s', *History of European Ideas*, 48 (2022), pp. 78–96.
[3] *E* (LF), p. 512, *E* (C), p. 363.

subdivided into 10,000 parishes. Elections occur in two tiers and create two distinct powers: (1) a large but decentralized legislature and (2) an executive senate. Male citizens who satisfy the property qualification meet annually at their local parish to choose a county representative by ballot. Elected representatives then participate in a second round of voting to select ten magistrates and one senator for their county. As a result of this staggered process, all senators are also magistrates, and all magistrates are also county representatives. A total of 10,000 representatives (one per parish) remain dispersed across their respective county assemblies and exercise the legislative power. Meanwhile, the 100 senators (one per county) convene in the capital city ('London') and are endowed with the executive power.[4]

What are we to make of this proposal? Some scholars regard it as a mere '*jeu d'esprit*' or 'trivial pastime'.[5] However, others argue that the essay reflects Hume's genuine engagement with the republican tradition and institutional reform.[6] This chapter seeks to clarify Hume's position towards British republicanism by tracing the ways in which his perfect constitution responds not only to Harrington's *Oceana* (1656) but also to Montesquieu's *Spirit of the Laws* (1748). The 'commonwealth' Hume proposed turns out to have as much in common with Montesquieu's understanding of modern monarchy as it does with Harrington's vision for an equal republic. Indeed, there is reason to suspect that Montesquieu's criticism of *Oceana* in his chapter 'On the English constitution' prompted Hume to devise his alternative version of Harrington's commonwealth.

Harrington maintained that English monarchy was unsustainable because it violated the principle that the balance of power must follow the balance of property.[7] In *Oceana*, he envisioned England transformed into an 'equal commonwealth' of freehold soldiers. Oceana's Agrarian law strictly limits the size of citizens' estates, while its system of 'equal rotation'

[4] *E* (LF), pp. 516–17, 521, *E* (C), pp. 364–65, 368.
[5] Frederick Whelan, *Order and Artifice in Hume's Political Philosophy* (Princeton, NJ, 1985), p. 342; Judith Shklar, 'Ideology Hunting: The Case of James Harrington', *American Political Science Review*, 53 (1959), pp. 662–92, at p. 664.
[6] John Robertson, 'The Scottish Enlightenment at the Limits of the Civic Tradition', in Istvan Hont and Michael Ignatieff, eds., *Wealth and Virtue: The Shaping of the Political Economy in the Scottish Enlightenment* (Cambridge, 1983), pp. 137–78; John B. Stewart, *Opinion and Reform in Hume's Political Philosophy* (Princeton, NJ, 1992), pp. 281–90; Ryu Susato, *Hume's Sceptical Enlightenment* (Edinburgh, 2015), pp. 177–213; Gilles Robel, '"Idea of a Perfect Commonwealth" ou le réalisme utopique de David Hume', *Études écossaises*, 11 (2009), pp. 9–29.
[7] James Harrington, *The Commonwealth of Oceana* [1656], in James Harrington, *The Political Works of James Harrington*, ed. J. G. A. Pocock (Cambridge, 1977), esp. pp. 163–64, 179–81, 191–99.

ensures the continuous distribution of civic offices.[8] Harrington asserted that a government ordered according to these principles would eliminate the internal causes of corruption, leaving Oceana 'as immortal, or long-lived as the world'.[9] Hume was notoriously sceptical of claims for immortality, whether they concerned political constitutions or the human soul.[10] Nevertheless, he distinguished *Oceana* as 'the only valuable model of a commonwealth, that has yet been offered to the public'. Unlike the 'plainly imaginary' republics of Plato or Thomas More, Harrington's model did not suppose any 'great reformation in the manners of mankind'.[11] Harrington had taken an institutional rather than a moral approach to political science, and Hume took the liberty of revising Harrington's institutions.

8.1 Encountering Montesquieu

This institutional approach has not stopped some readers from dismissing Hume's commonwealth as a satire. The abbé Jean-Bernard Le Blanc was quick to highlight the essay's 'contradictions' in footnotes to his French translation of the *Political Discourses* in 1754.[12] Le Blanc questioned the purpose of such 'chimerical perfections' and pointed readers to Hume's earlier essay, 'Whether the British Government Inclines More to Absolute Monarchy, or to a Republic' (1741), in which Hume expressed impatience with the sort of politician who invents a 'fine imaginary republic' in his closet.[13] Hume had censured Harrington in 'British Government' for assuming that the country's balance of property was incompatible with the reestablishment of monarchy, given that Harrington's work was 'scarcely published' before Charles II was restored to power.[14] As far as Le Blanc was concerned, Hume favoured monarchy, and 'Perfect Commonwealth' was simply proof that 'one neither says all that one thinks, nor thinks all that one says'.[15] Yet Hume's thoughts on Harrington

---

[8] Ibid., pp. 180–81.   [9] Ibid., pp. 320–21.
[10] E.g. *E* (LF), pp. 51–53, *E* (C), p. 64; and 'Of the Immortality of the Soul', *E* (LF), pp. 590–98.
[11] *E* (LF), p. 514, *E* (C), p. 364.
[12] *Discours politiques de Monsieur Hume*, trans. abbé Jean-Bernard Le Blanc (2 vols., Amsterdam, 1754), II, p. 374n. For more recent charges of satire, see James Conniff, 'Hume's Political Methodology: A Reconsideration of "That Politics May Be Reduced to a Science"', *The Review of Politics*, 38 (1976), pp. 88–108, at p. 101; and David Miller, *Philosophy and Ideology in Hume's Political Thought* (Oxford, 1981), pp. 158–59.
[13] Le Blanc in *Discours politiques de Monsieur Hume*, II, pp. 327n, 356–57n, 369–71n.
[14] *E* (LF), pp. 47–48, *E* (C) p. 60.
[15] 'D'ordinaire ni on ne dit tout ce qu'on pense, ni on ne pense, tout ce qu'on dit' (Le Blanc, *Discours politiques*, p. II, p.374n). On Le Blanc's rather 'esoteric' interpretation of Hume's republican

appear less contradictory if we pay attention to how Hume chose to reconstruct *Oceana*. This is where his study of Montesquieu becomes significant. Hume acquired a first edition of the *Spirit of the Laws* in the autumn of 1748. He wrote to Montesquieu in April 1749 to convey his admiration for the work, and the two scholars corresponded that summer about potentially printing an edition of the *Spirit of the Laws* in Scotland.[16] By September 1751, 'Perfect Commonwealth' was in press.[17]

Hume would have noticed that Montesquieu concluded his account of the English constitution with a biting criticism of Harrington's project:

> Harrington, in his *Oceana*, has also examined the furthest point of liberty to which the constitution of a state can be carried. But of him it can be said that he sought this liberty only after misunderstanding it, and that he built Chalcedon with the coast of Byzantium before his eyes.[18]

Montesquieu implied that Harrington built his English commonwealth on the wrong foundation – when a more moderate path to liberty was in view. Although Montesquieu shared Harrington's fascination with ancient republics and their agrarian laws, he never suggested that a state like England should emulate these regimes.

Hume began his alternative vision for a British commonwealth by praising Harrington's 'valuable model'. But he briskly proceeded to name Oceana's 'chief defects' – each of which his own model would eliminate. First, Hume removed Oceana's 'rotation' system because it disregarded officeholders' skill and experience. Second, he dispensed with Harrington's 'impracticable' Agrarian law. If even the Romans failed to prevent citizens from concealing their wealth under false titles, Hume assumed that a commercial society would struggle to enforce an equal division of lands.[19] His third objection was to the doctrine of 'dividing and choosing'. Harrington compared Oceana's bicameral legislature to two girls sharing a cake: if one girl slices and the other chooses, each will receive an equal

passages, see Paul Cheney, 'Constitution and Economy in David Hume's Enlightenment', in Margaret Schabas and Carl Wennerlind, eds., *David Hume's Political Economy* (New York, 2008), pp. 236–40.

[16] *HL*, I, pp. 133–38; John Hill Burton, *The Life and Correspondence of David Hume* (2 vols., Edinburgh, 1846), I, p. 457.

[17] *NHL*, p. 30.

[18] Montesquieu, *Spirit of the Laws*, trans. and eds. Anne M. Cohler, Basia C. Miller, and Harold Samuel Stone (Cambridge, 1989 [1748]), p. 166. Herodotus claimed in *The Persian Wars* (IV.144) that the Hellespontians failed to see Byzantium, the superior site just across the Bosporus Strait.

[19] *E* (LF), p. 515, *E* (C), p. 364. Montesquieu comments on the manipulation of Roman inheritances in the *Spirit of the Laws*, pp. 521–23, 525.

slice. By analogy, Oceana's senate would propose and discuss new laws, while its popular assembly would approve or reject the senate's legislation. Hume protested that this scheme handed too much power to the upper house, effectively allowing the senate to wield an absolute 'negative' over the popular assembly.[20]

These were not minor objections. Without any one of these three elements, Oceana's architecture collapses. Harrington defined an 'equal commonwealth' as a government 'established upon an equal Agrarian, arising into the superstructures or three orders, the senate debating and proposing, the people resolving, and the magistracy executing by an equal rotation through the suffrage of the people given by the ballot'.[21] Hume thus attacked Harrington's definition of a commonwealth at both its 'foundation' (i.e. the Agrarian law) and its 'superstructure' (i.e. equal rotation). Hume justified these revisions by invoking a classic republican maxim: 'A government, says MACHIAVEL, must often be brought back to its original principles.'[22] Harrington had misunderstood the nature of British government. It was up to Hume to rebuild *Oceana* according to different principles.

We know Montesquieu's analogy between Harrington and the blind men of Chalcedon left an impression on Hume because he quoted it years later, in a letter he sent his nephew in December 1775.[23] David Hume the Younger (later the advocate Baron Hume) was then a student at the University of Glasgow, where he would have encountered Montesquieu's ideas in the lectures of his professor John Millar. Hume's nephew apparently wrote to solicit his uncle's thoughts on what he was learning about republican constitutions because Hume answered, 'I cannot but agree with Mr Millar, that the Republican Form of [Government] is by far the best.' Yet Hume clarified that his agreement only applied to what was 'best' for ancient governments and small states. 'Modern manners' made the difference between European republics and monarchies less significant. Indeed 'one is at a Loss to which we shoud give Preference'.[24] Both republics and monarchies could protect civil liberty, though it was crucial to respect the established order and to remember that republicanism 'is only fitted for a small State'. Hume cautioned his nephew that any attempt to replace Britain's mixed monarchy with a republic would pave the way

---

[20] Harrington, *Oceana*, pp. 172–74. Compare *E* (LF), p. 515, *E* (C), p. 364.
[21] Harrington, *Oceana*, p. 181.   [22] *E* (LF), p. 516, *E* (C), p. 364.
[23] *HL*, II, p. 307. This paragraph borrows from my article 'Hume's "Idea of a Perfect Commonwealth" and Scottish Political Thought of the 1790s', p. 80.
[24] *HL*, II, p. 306.

for 'Anarchy, which is the immediate Forerunner of Despotism'. He elaborated:

> [Ha]rrington is an Author of Genius; but chimerical. No Laws, however rigorous [woud ma]ke his Agrarian practicable. And as the People have only a Negative, the Senate woud perpetually gain Ground upon them. You remember, that Montesquieu says, that Harrington establishing his Oceana in opposition to the English Constitution is like the blind Men who build Chalcedon on the opposite Shore to the Seat of Byzantium.[25]

Not only did Hume highlight the same 'defects' in Harrington's model that he addressed in 'Perfect Commonwealth', he also directed his nephew back to Montesquieu, whose judgement of Harrington he appears to endorse.

This agreement with Montesquieu complicates the conventional assumption that Hume wrote 'Perfect Commonwealth' with the aim of undermining Montesquieu's position that republican states must be small. Douglass Adair, for instance, influentially argued that Hume's essay 'demolished the Montesquieu small-republic theory'. Adair credited Hume with directly inspiring Madison's defence of an 'extended republic' in *Federalist* 10.[26] However, it is important to notice that the large commonwealth Hume devised (and that Madison adapted) rejects other core features that Montesquieu attributed to classical republics. More was at issue than size. Hume's optimal regime does not forbid luxury goods. Nor are there any educational programs for instilling self-sacrifice and civic patriotism. Conspicuously, the word 'virtue' never appears in the essay.[27] Although Hume does refer to his commonwealth as a 'republic' on several occasions, it is a republic that acknowledges the 'natural ambition of mankind'. As Montesquieu put it, 'Ambition is pernicious in a republic. It has good effects in monarchy.'[28] One reason Hume thought his commonwealth could represent a state as large as France or Great Britain was that a greater territory makes space for the distinctions and honours that Montesquieu associated with moderate monarchy and aristocracy. Yes,

---

[25] *HL*, II, pp. 306–7.

[26] Douglass Adair, '"That Politics May Be Reduced to a Science": David Hume, James Madison, and the Tenth Federalist', *Huntington Library Quarterly*, 20 (1957), pp. 343–60, at p. 349. On Adair and his critics, see Spencer, *Hume and Eighteenth-Century America*, pp. 154–97.

[27] Compare Montesquieu, *Spirit of the Laws*, esp. pp. 22–23, 35–36, 43–48, 96–98.

[28] For example, *E* (LF), pp. 522, 529, *E* (C), pp. 369, 373. Montesquieu, *Spirit of the Laws*, p. 27; compare p. 22. For the argument that England does not meet Montesquieu's definition of a republic, see Robin Douglass, 'Montesquieu and Modern Republicanism', *Political Studies*, 60 (2012), pp. 703–19.

representatives.[39] Stewart explained that Hume addressed this error of the ancients by extending the principle of representation across a large state: Hume built on the insight that even under absolute princes, 'the subordinate government of cities is commonly republican; while that of counties and provinces is monarchical'. By arranging his state into smaller assemblies, Hume integrated republican as well as monarchical features into a representative commonwealth where the manner of government would be 'steady and uniform' across the entire territory.[40]

This arrangement prioritised electoral uniformity over republican participation. Echoing Montesquieu, Hume claimed that citizens in local parishes would probably know enough to 'choose the best, or nearly the best representative'. But the role of parish electors is simply to choose the choosers.[41] Parishes vote for their county representatives in the first stage of balloting, and representatives go on to select magistrates and senators in the second stage. Hume asserted that most voters were 'wholly unfit for county-meetings', where a difference in rank would encourage 'grandees' to deceive them. Indeed, he regarded it as a positive feature of his plan that indirect elections would separate 'the lower sort of people' from 'the higher offices of the republic'.[42]

Hume reserved these higher offices for the senate, which effectively replicates the executive powers of the king and his privy council, excluding the royal veto. Senators also replicate the 'judicative authority' of the House of Lords by appointing higher judges and hearing appeals. Elected senators use the Venetian ballot to choose a series of annual officers from their own body. Officers include two secretaries of state, commissioners of the treasury, seats on different departmental councils, and 'a protector' who presides over the senate and 'represents the dignity of the commonwealth'. In 'extraordinary emergencies', the protector sits on a special council of at least ten senators, who together may hold 'dictatorial power' for six months.[43] The title of 'protector' (as opposed to a doge) calls to mind the Instrument of Government that installed Cromwell as Lord Protector in December 1653. But unlike Cromwell, Hume's protector

[39] Stewart, 'Lectures on Political Economy', p. 374. See Montesquieu, *Spirit of the Laws*, pp. 159–60.
[40] Quoted in Stewart, 'Lectures on Political Economy', pp. 374–75. See *E* (LF), pp. 527–28, *E* (C), pp. 372–73.
[41] *E* (LF), p. 522, *E* (C), p. 369. Bernard Manin has noted that eighteenth-century authors such as Montesquieu associated elections for the 'best' representative with aristocracy, rather than democracy (Bernard Manin, *The Principles of Representative Government* (Cambridge, 1997)).
[42] *E* (LF), pp. 522, 528, *E* (C), pp. 369, 373.   [43] *E* (LF), pp. 518–21, *E* (C), pp. 366–68.

serves only for a single year, and no one can serve as protector more than once.[44]

Most routine administration in the individual counties falls upon the magistrates, who manage tax collection, oversee criminal trials, and appoint local officials – including ministers in every parish. It may come as a surprise that Hume establishes an official church and council of religion.[45] Yet Hume was never the sort of atheist who thought Enlightenment politics could eliminate Christianity. He emphasized the need to prevent religious factionalism from endangering the political order, as it had during the Interregnum when '[e]very man had framed the model of a republic' for himself and was eager to impose his 'fantastical' vision on others.[46] Hume seems to have chosen 'Presbyterian government' as a compromise between Anglican royalism on the one hand and radical antinomianism on the other. Presbyters from every county make up the commonwealth's 'highest ecclesiastical court', but this court holds no final authority. Magistrates may remove 'any cause' from the court and decide it for themselves.[47]

Although the government is federal – with every county operating as 'a kind of republic within itself' – the counties are not autonomous. Magistrates work under the supervision of the executive departments (e.g. the councils of trade, laws, war, religion), and Hume grants the senate or 'any single county' the authority to annul bye-laws passed in another county – in essence, allowing a national veto on local legislation.[48] John Adams complained that Hume's plan amounted to 'a complicated aristocracy', intended to distract the people away from their representatives in the legislature.[49] Adams particularly disapproved of Hume's provision for sending bills to magistrates, rather than the full assembly of county representatives. This was 'an ingenious device ... to get rid of the people and their representative through a series of endless delays'.[50] One might

---

[44] E (LF), p. 524, E (C), p. 370.
[45] E (LF), p. 520, E (C), p. 367. Leslie Stephen complained that Hume's 'Utopia' made the church 'a department of State', in *History of English Thought in the Eighteenth Century* (2 vols., London, 1876), II, p. 185. However, Hume's example was clearly *Oceana*, where a council of religion both protects 'liberty of conscience' and supervises university instruction of theology (Harrington, *Oceana*, p. 251).
[46] *HE*, VI, p. 3. On Hume's Erastianism, see Susato, *Hume's Sceptical Enlightenment*, pp. 131–76.
[47] E (LF), p. 520, E (C), p. 367.   [48] E (LF), pp. 519–20, E (C), pp. 366–67.
[49] John Adams, *A Defence of the Constitutions of Government of the United States of America* (3 vols., Philadelphia, 1787), I, pp. 370–71.
[50] Ibid., I, p. 371.

begin to wonder whether Hume's ideal legislature is one that hardly meets at all.

But Hume insisted that his senate was still dependent on the legislative power.[51] He incorporated several provisions for keeping senators accountable, the most novel of which is an official oppositional body called 'the court of competitors'. County representatives who lose a senate election – but who earn at least a third of their county's vote – must take a seat among the 'competitors'. Members of this court give up eligibility for all political offices for one year. Yet competitors gain investigative access to public accounts and can initiate political accusations before the senate. Should the senate vote to acquit, competitors may 'appeal' to the county magistrates or representatives for a trial. Anyone successfully convicted must take a seat on the court – where he can then launch accusations of his own.[52] In addition to performing a judicative role, the court helps regulate the electoral process. If every senate election is competitive, the court may have as many as 100 members (one competitor per county). Or it may sit completely vacant. Hume does not say which outcome he thinks is more likely, though on the whole the court seems to encourage consensus candidates who can command a supermajority of their county's vote. In any case, Hume anticipated that the threat of the competitors would act as a check on the executive power. Senators would perceive the competitors as 'their rivals, next to them in interest, and uneasy in their present situation . . . sure to take all advantages against them'.[53]

Hume also believed that standardizing the franchise would regulate the relationship between the senate and county assemblies. A uniform property qualification for voting in parish elections would ensure that county representatives were 'men of fortune and education', not 'an undistinguishing rabble, like the ENGLISH electors'. Hume intimated that senators would be less likely to enter a 'combination' against the legislature because representatives and senators emerge from a similar social class in the county assemblies.[54] The assumption of commercial development that runs throughout the *Political Discourses* leaves open the possibility that every male subject in Hume's commonwealth will one day attain the economic autonomy necessary for citizenship.[55] But a universal franchise was not Hume's immediate priority, since he raised the property qualification in subsequent revisions to the essay.

---

[51] *E* (LF), pp. 523–24, *E* (C), pp. 369–70.   [52] *E* (LF), pp. 519–20, *E* (C), p. 367.
[53] *E* (LF), p. 524, *E* (C), p. 370.   [54] *E* (LF), pp. 523–24, *E* (C), p. 369.
[55] See Robertson, 'The Scottish Enlightenment', pp. 157–60.

In the initial 1752 edition, Hume extended the right to vote in parish elections to all 'freeholders' in the county and all 'householders' who pay 'scot and lot' taxes in town.[56] This requirement was effectively the same as Harrington's. The first order of Oceana grants 'freedom or participation in government' to all freemen who 'live of themselves', excluding servants.[57] But Hume became more specific about his definition of economic independence, eventually limiting the franchise to county freeholders earning £20 per year or householders worth £500 in stock.[58] He later recorded in the *History of England* that a £20 freehold was – adjusting for inflation – nearly equivalent to the 'forty shillings a-year in land' franchise that parliament adopted in 1430. Hume approvingly noted that the purpose of this statute was to curb the 'great disorder' caused by 'such a multitude of electors', and 'it were to be wished, that the spirit, as well as letter of this law, had been maintained'.[59] Given the variety of suffrages that preceded the 1832 Reform Act, even Hume's more conservative franchise recommendations would have expanded the electorate in many districts – not least in Scotland, where a narrow group of landlords and town councillors monopolized the royal burghs.[60] Yet his primary concern was electoral consistency, not necessarily inclusivity. Hume wanted to apply the same property standards in every parish to preserve the economic independence requisite for promoting the 'best' representatives across county government.

8.3 A More Perfect Monarchy?

In his initial letter to Montesquieu, Hume shared his thoughts on several specific passages from the *Spirit of the Laws*, the first of which was Montesquieu's observation:

> In order to favor liberty, the English have removed all the intermediate powers that formed their monarchy. They are quite right to preserve their liberty; if they were to lose it, they would be one of the most enslaved peoples on earth.[61]

Montesquieu claimed that nobility was the 'most natural' basis of intermediary power in monarchical government. But he also observed that the English had abolished their intermediary powers during the civil wars. Hume found this remark 'new and striking'. He predicted that 'the

---

[56] *E* (LF), p. 647, note b, *E* (C), pp. 1142–43.   [57] Harrington, *Oceana*, p. 212.
[58] *E* (LF), p. 516, *E* (C), p. 365.   [59] *HE*, II, pp. 452–53.
[60] Stewart, *Opinion and Reform*, pp. 285–86n.   [61] Montesquieu, *Spirit of the Laws*, pp. 18–19.

consequences' of Montesquieu's observation would 'certainly arrive in the event of a revolution in our government'.[62] Hume hoped to avert these consequences by strengthening an alternative intermediary power. In the place of a hereditary nobility, he looked to a growing population of tradesmen and merchants, whose elected representatives supply his commonwealth with an intermediary source of authority throughout the counties.[63]

Earlier in the *Political Discourses*, Hume attributed Europe's expanding social ranks to a rise in luxury exchange. He argued in 'Of Refinement in the Arts' that feudalism had separated society into just two classes: landowners and vassals, or, in effect, freemen and slaves. Commerce and industry upended this feudal property structure. Thanks to a superior cultivation of land, peasant farmers escaped their dependence on Gothic barons. Merchants and tradesmen in turn acquired a greater share of property, 'draw[ing] authority and consideration to that middling rank of men, who are the best and firmest basis of public liberty'.[64] By 'public liberty', Hume meant the liberty of parliament. He recounted that the middle ranks 'covet[ed] equal laws' to secure their property from the aristocratic barons on the one hand and an overbearing monarch on the other. This legal security encouraged further commercial activity and eventually 'threw such a balance of property into the hands of the commons'.[65] Hume accepted Harrington's basic thesis that an historical shift in the balance of property had empowered parliament and transformed England into a government of laws. But he did not conclude that this shift necessitated a return to either the 'equal agrarian' or 'equal rotation' of offices on which Harrington founded Oceana. Hume considered Harrington's main innovation to be his system for organizing multiple tiers of representation across an extensive government. In 'Perfect Commonwealth', Hume adapted Harrington's electoral framework to the spirit of commerce and competition that he and Montesquieu associated with modern Britain.[66]

This adaption built upon another revision to *Oceana* that Hume suggested in his earlier essay 'Of Civil Liberty'. Hume argued in 1741 that advancements in trade gave Europe's 'civilized monarchies' a powerful incentive to uphold the rule of law:

---

[62] *HL*, I, p. 134.
[63] On Hume and the culture of the 'middle ranks', see Margaret Schabas and Carl Wennerlind, *A Philosopher's Economist: Hume and the Rise of Capitalism* (Chicago, 2020), pp. 113–41.
[64] *E* (LF), pp. 277–78, *E* (C), pp. 214–15.   [65] Ibid.
[66] See especially, Montesquieu, *Spirit of the Laws*, pp. 325–36, 342–43.

But though all kinds of government be improved in modern times, yet monarchical government seems to have made the greatest advances towards perfection. It may now be affirmed of civilized monarchies, what was formerly said in praise of republics alone, *that they are a government of Laws, not of Men.* They are found susceptible of order, method, and constancy to a surprising degree. Property is there secure; industry encouraged; the arts flourish; and the prince lives secure among his subjects, like a father among his children.[67]

Harrington held that only a republican commonwealth, founded on the common interest of 'antient prudence', could govern itself as an 'empire of laws, and not of men'.[68] But Hume implied that Harrington's distinction between ancient prudence and modern corruption was obsolete. Modern monarchy had made 'the greatest advances toward perfection' because considerations of trade motivated rulers to respect their subjects' industry and property. Rulers and subjects now shared a common interest. This was why Hume could tell his nephew that 'Modern Manners' had diminished the practical difference between Europe's republics and monarchies – save for the fact that republics needed to be small.[69] Hume framed his ideas of both 'civilized monarchy' and a 'perfect commonwealth' in reply to Harrington. Both regimes defy the geographic and material conditions that have historically restricted republican government. Both are commercial states that realize order and security across a large territory.

However, Hume's plan for a perfect commonwealth reflects a more positive conception of constitutional liberty. While the civilized monarch can uphold civil liberty by securing his subjects' persons and property, Hume's commonwealth unites personal *and* public liberty. John Robertson refers to Hume's proposal as 'a projection into the future'. Its constitution anticipates a society in which the same economic security that bestows honour and consideration on the middle ranks will diffuse 'the capacity for citizenship ever wider', enabling a growing population of citizens to seek a voice in their own political representation.[70] Hume did not expect to see this outcome in the near term, and even his perfect constitution separates most citizens from direct legislative debate. Nevertheless, the *Political Discourses* identify the middle ranks as the 'firmest basis of public liberty', and Hume designed his perfect commonwealth to fortify this base.

---

[67] *E* (LF), p. 94, *E* (C), p. 90.   [68] Harrington, *Oceana*, pp. 161–64, 171.   [69] *HL*, II, p. 307.
[70] Robertson, 'The Scottish Enlightenment', p. 175.

Hume made clear that the current British government could use his plan to bring itself in line with 'the most perfect model of limited monarchy', if not the best overall regime.[71] For one thing, the British monarchy should restore 'the plan of CROMWELL's parliament'. Hume approved of the Instrument of Government insofar as it made the geographic distribution of representation consistent and required county electors to possess at least £200. This was a 'republican' regulation that actually made elections more exclusive.[72] As a second reform, Hume recommended *expanding* the House of Lords from 300 to 400 members, but with the stipulation that seats in the upper house should no longer be hereditary.[73] Lifetime peers should instead select their members from the House of Commons, and no member of the lower house may turn down an invitation to join the Lords. Hume assumed that this provision would remove 'turbulent' politicians from the commons, while at the same time forging a natural 'aristocracy' in the upper house. Such a peerage would act as 'an excellent barrier both to the monarchy and against it'. Together, these 'chief alterations' to the British monarchy would make it both more meritocratic and more republican, building up intermediary authorities between the people and the crown.[74]

8.4 Common Defence

Yet Hume conceded that even the most perfect limited monarchy would fall short of his perfect commonwealth in several respects. The most serious liability for monarchy remained the fact that 'the sword is in the hands of a single person, who will always neglect to discipline the militia, in order to have a pretence for keeping up a standing army'.[75] His commonwealth provides a template for how a modern state might avoid the need for a standing force by preserving an active militia and navy. The proposal calls for a Swiss-style militia, supplemented by an army of 20,000 conscripts, who are drawn out of an annual rotation and who undergo paid camp-training during the summer. In peacetime, magistrates appoint all

---

[71] *E* (LF), p. 526, *E* (C), p. 372.

[72] Until 1770, this phrase read, 'The plan of the republican parliament' (*E* (LF), p. 647, note g, *E* (C), p. 1146). For Hume's approval of the electoral system that created Cromwell's parliament in 1654, see *HE*, VI, p. 69.

[73] *E* (LF), p. 527, *E* (C), p. 372. Many Whigs called for representative reform in the Commons, but it was quite unusual for an eighteenth-century author to suggest a lifetime peerage. See James Moore, 'Hume's Political Science and the Classical Republican Tradition', *Canadian Journal of Political Science / Revue Canadienne de science Politique*, 10 (1977), pp. 809–39, at p. 819.

[74] *E* (LF), p. 527, *E* (C), p. 372.   [75] Ibid.

ranks up to colonel in their county's regiment, while the senate appoints the highest officers and naval captains. A national general appoints all army ranks when the commonwealth is at war. But the general's commission from the senate expires after twelve months, at which point his appointments require confirmation from the county magistrates. No officer can hold civil office in wartime.[76]

As Hume would recount in the *History of England*, the country's island geography kept its monarchs from investing in the large land forces that enabled continental monarchies to rule with 'unlimited authority'.[77] England's first standing army was, ironically, the New Model that overturned the Stuart monarchy in the name of a republic.[78] Parliament reconstituted the militia when it restored the monarchy, yet the crown's preference for a reliable standing force – free from the local gentry who still managed the militia – would remain a source of controversy for the next century of British politics.[79] In basing his commonwealth on *Oceana*, Hume knew he was drawing on a key source for the 'Country' opposition. Critics of the royal army routinely invoked Harrington to protest that no constitution could be free unless its people were armed.[80] Hume agreed that 'without a militia, it is vain to think that any free government will ever have security or stability'.[81] However, he differed from the typical 'neo-Harringtonian' opposition in that he did not blame modern commercial economies for weakening national defence.

Hume argued in 'Of Commerce' – the opening essay of the *Political Discourses* – that constant military service in Sparta and early Rome effectively amounted to 'a heavy tax' because war diverted citizens from more productive employments in trade and manufactures. '[C]ivilized governments', in contrast, were prudent to allow labourers to exchange their agricultural surpluses for luxury goods. Hume noted that the modern sovereign can always impose a tax on surplus goods in times of emergency, obliging subjects to retrench from their private pursuits for the purposes of raising a defensive force. But without the extra resources generated by commercial industry, ancient republics had to either disband their armies or engage in violent conquest to sustain their troops.[82] Harrington conceded as much in *Oceana*. To maintain its Agrarian law, Oceana follows Rome's example as a 'commonwealth for increase', planting colonies

[76] *E* (LF), pp. 520–21, *E* (C), p. 368.   [77] *HE*, V, p. 18.   [78] *HE*, VI, pp. 46, 65, 147.
[79] See John Robertson, *The Scottish Enlightenment and the Militia Issue* (Edinburgh, 1985), pp. 13–15.
[80] On this 'neo-Harringtonian' discourse, see J. G. A. Pocock, *The Machiavellian Moment: Florentine Political Thought and the Atlantic Republican Tradition* (Princeton, NJ, 1975), pp. 401–505.
[81] *E* (LF), p. 525, *E* (C), p. 371.   [82] *E* (LF), 257–62, *E* (C), pp. 201–5.

abroad and redistributing the enemy's spoils among its soldiers.[83] Hume objected that this imperial policy was self-defeating: '[e]xtensive conquests, when pursued, must be the ruin of every free government; and of the more perfect governments sooner than of the imperfect; because of the very advantages which the former possess above the latter'.[84] He closed his plan for a perfect commonwealth by observing that conquest was incompatible with the careful balance between executive and legislative power on which 'free government' depended.

Another passage from the *Spirit of the Laws* that Hume cited in his letter was Montesquieu's suggestion that England was 'a nation where the republic hides under the form of monarchy'.[85] Montesquieu had drawn an explicit analogy between England and Rome: before the 'loss of the republic' Rome's soldiers were also citizens. Yet under the empire, Augustus and his successors separated civil magistracies from military ones. Montesquieu noted that England's civil and military employments still came from a common estate of free citizens. But his comparison with Rome warned of a future in which executive and legislative power could easily collapse into a single despotic body, or what Montesquieu termed 'military government'.[86] 'Perfect Commonwealth' can be read as Hume's attempt to construct a more stable version of a republic that hides under a monarchy. To avoid military government, the commonwealth's army answers to the command of the executive senate, rather than the legislature, even as the militia's dispersal throughout the counties keeps its regiments under the eye of local representatives.[87] An active militia keeps arms in the hands of citizens and minimizes the need for either a large standing force or foreign mercenaries.

Hume expected readers to see a resemblance between his commonwealth and that of the United Provinces.[88] Montesquieu regarded the Dutch Republic as a prime example of a defensive confederation, in which allied provinces enjoy 'all the internal advantages of the republican government and all the external force of monarchy'. Montesquieu said it was against the nature of a confederate republic to engage in conquest, though such confederacies could replicate the size and security of a monarchy by

[83] Harrington, *Oceana*, pp. 320–25.   [84] *E* (LF), p. 529, *E* (C), p. 373.

[85] Montesquieu, *Spirit of the Laws*, p. 70; *HL*, I, p. 134.

[86] Montesquieu, *Spirit of the Laws*, pp. 69–70. On Montesquieu's analysis of unfree republics, see Iain McDaniel, *Adam Ferguson in the Scottish Enlightenment: The Roman Past and Europe's Future* (Cambridge, MA, 2013), pp. 12–38.

[87] *E* (LF), p. 521, *E* (C), p. 368. Compare with Montesquieu, *Spirit of the Laws*, p. 165.

[88] *E* (LF), p. 526, *E* (C), p. 371.

joining forces with neighbouring provinces.[89] Hume's commonwealth combines Montesquieu's understanding of an external federation with Harrington's system for internal representation. Yet Hume noted that his example of a monarchical-republic was better prepared to defend itself than the United Provinces because no one county has veto power over alliances.[90] The executive senate decides all matters of peace and war.

'Perfect Commonwealth' appeared as part of Hume's larger commentary on challenges to the British balance of power. He composed the *Political Discourses* just after the War of Austrian Succession and would continue to republish his *Essays* through the outbreak of the American Revolution. Hume worried that mercantilist warfare and an escalating national debt jeopardized not only external security but also the internal balance between London and the provinces. Britain's financial establishment concentrated on the capital city, even as the taxes levied to pay interest on war debts fell disproportionately on landowners in the county. Hume feared that 'connexions' between creditors and members of parliament would induce politicians to prioritize short-term confidence in the government's creditworthiness, at the expense of long-term preparedness against 'foreign enemies'.[91] His plan for a commonwealth works to forestall this security crisis by recentring the relationship between the capital and the counties. Dispersing representatives across the county assemblies would prevent urban creditors from co-opting the legislature. And making citizens responsible for their own defence would diminish the government's reliance on public credit. Hume designed his commonwealth's legislative and executive institutions to impede any 'single person' from seizing power.

8.5   Conclusion

Hume recognized that even his perfect commonwealth would not last forever. A free government like his 'ought to establish a fundamental law against conquests; yet republics have ambition as well as individuals, and present interest makes men forgetful of their posterity'.[92] Montesquieu had been similarly realistic about the fate of the English constitution: 'Since all human things have an end ... it will perish.' Montesquieu

[89] Montesquieu, *Spirit of the Laws*, pp. 131, 143.
[90] *E* (LF), p. 526, *E* (C), pp. 371–72. Compare *Spirit of the Laws*, p. 133.
[91] *E* (LF), pp. 357–65, *E* (C), pp. 264–72. See Istvan Hont, *Jealousy of Trade: International Competition and the Nation State in Historical Perspective* (Cambridge, MA, 2005), pp. 325–53.
[92] *E* (C), p. 373, *E* (LF), p. 529.

predicted that the English state would lose its liberty 'when legislative power is more corrupt than executive power'.[93] England would cease to be a free state when the distinction between the legislature and the army disappeared.

In echoing Montesquieu, Hume also challenged Harrington's conceit that the orders of Oceana would make it 'as immortal, or long-lived as the world'. Instead, Hume decided, 'It is needless to enquire, whether such a government would be immortal … The world itself probably is not immortal.'[94] Even in his most speculative essay, Hume insisted on the worldly limitations of political science. It was enough for Hume that 'such a government would flourish for many ages; without pretending to bestow, on any work of man, that immortality, which the Almighty seems to have refused to his own productions'.[95] He repeated this challenge to Harrington in the *History of England*:

> HARRINGTON's Oceana was well adapted to that age, when the plans of imaginary Republics were the daily subjects of debate and conversation; and even in our time it is justly admired as a work of genius and invention. The *idea, however, of a perfect and immortal Commonwealth will always be found as chimerical as that of a perfect and immortal man.* The style of this author wants ease and fluency; but the good matter, which his work contains, makes compensation.[96]

Where Harrington pursued the idea of a perfect *and* immortal commonwealth, Hume was content simply to focus on a perfect one.

The abbé Le Blanc was right to notice Hume's distaste for plans of imaginary republics. But he erred in classifying Hume's perfect commonwealth as a similarly 'chimerical' regime'.[97] Rather, Hume took 'the good matter' he found in *Oceana*'s electoral framework and reworked it into a constitution that was responsive to many of Montesquieu's observations in the *Spirit of the Laws*. The result was a government with 'all the advantages of both a great and little commonwealth'.[98] Hume concluded the *Political Discourses* with a model for how a free state like Britain might preserve itself for as long as humanly possible.

---

[93] Montesquieu, *Spirit of the Laws*, p. 166.
[94] Compare Harrington, *Oceana*, p. 321; *E* (LF), p. 528, *E* (C), p. 373.
[95] *E* (LF), pp. 528–29, *E* (C), p. 373.   [96] Hume, *HE*, VI, p. 153; italics mine.
[97] *Discours politiques*, trans. Le Blanc, II, p. 327n. Ironically, Le Blanc told Hume that he expected 'vos discours Politiques seroient parmi nous le même effet que *L'Esprit des Loix*' (Burton, *Life and Correspondence of David Hume*, I, p. 460).
[98] *E* (LF), p. 525, *E* (C), p. 371.

CHAPTER 9

'One of the Most Difficult Problems, That Can Be Met With'
Hume on Political Parties

Max Skjönsberg

> To determine the nature of [the British] parties is, perhaps, one of the most difficult problems, that can be met with, and is a proof that history may contain questions, as uncertain as any to be found in the most abstract sciences.
>
> Hume, 'Of the Parties of Great Britain' (1741)

Few, if any, political thinkers of the eighteenth century dealt as thoroughly and extensively with party as David Hume.[1] This chapter considers Hume's many essays devoted to the subject that were published between 1741 and 1758. Hume was in London between August 1737 and February 1739, and on his return to Ninewells, Scotland, he began drafting essays in the summer of 1739 at the latest.[2] Many around this time, especially those in opposition to Sir Robert Walpole's Whig administration, denied the continued relevance of the party distinction of Whig and Tory. Notably, Bolingbroke promoted the alternative division of Court and Country parties, as he sought to unite Tories and discontented Whigs in opposition to Walpole's Court Whigs.[3] By contrast, Walpole and his paid scribblers held that Whig and Tory were as relevant as ever, and that only a Whig administration could be trusted to protect the legacy of the Glorious Revolution.[4] For Hume, Whig–Tory as well as Court–Country alignments

---

[1] See Max Skjönsberg, *The Persistence of Party: Ideas of Harmonious Discord in Eighteenth-Century Britain* (Cambridge, 2021), esp. chs. 4, 6 and 8; Paul Sagar, 'Between Virtue and Knavery: Hume and the Politics of Moderation', *Journal of Politics*, 83 (2021), pp. 1097–1113; Joel E. Landis, 'Whither Parties? Hume on Partisanship and Political Legitimacy', *American Political Science Review*, 112 (2018), pp. 219–30; Mark G. Spencer, *David Hume and Eighteenth-Century America* (Rochester, NY, 2005), ch. 6.

[2] *NHL*, pp. 5–7.

[3] For the Country party tradition, see Max Skjönsberg, 'Patriots and the Country Party Tradition in the Eighteenth Century: The Critics of Britain's Fiscal-Military State from Robert Harley to Catharine Macaulay', *Intellectual History Review*, 33 (2023), pp. 83–100.

[4] Skjönsberg, *The Persistence of Party*, ch. 3.

were integral to British politics, with the former dividing the political nation along religious and, at least to an extent, dynastic lines, and the latter reflecting parliamentary conflict and the workings of the mixed and balanced constitution. His analysis can thus be read as a middle way between Bolingbroke and Walpole. Adopting the essay format from Addison and Steele's polite essays in the *Tatler* (1709) and *Spectator* (1711–12),[5] Hume's idea was to write about politics in a polite manner, but with a more philosophical and non-partisan bent than Bolingbroke's political writings.[6] He publicised this intention in the advertisement for the first edition of the first volume of *Essays, Moral and Political* (1741): 'the READER may condemn my Abilities, but must approve of my Moderation and Impartiality in my Method of handling POLITICAL SUBJECTS'.[7] What the Whig Addison and eclectic Tory Bolingbroke had in common was that they in their respective contexts called for all honest men to unite into what Addison called a 'neutral body' and Bolingbroke the 'Country party'.[8] Hume took a more realistic and characteristically sceptical view. For him, party was both an intrinsic part of the British constitution and a reflection of the fact that people were naturally inclined to conflict as well as gregarious sentiments.[9] The goal of the philosophically minded writer was simply to promote moderation[10] – a highly controversial message if considered in context.

9.1   'Of Parties in General'

Hume opened the essay 'Of Parties in General' (1741) with a curious tribute to lawgivers, who otherwise play no role in his political thought. He then proceeded to castigate parties, or factions,[11] in a well-known passage:

> As much as legislators and founders of states ought to be honoured and respected among men, as much ought the founders of sects and factions to be detested and hated . . . Factions subvert government, render laws impotent, and beget the fiercest animosities among men of the same nation, who ought to give mutual assistance and protection to each other . . . And what

---

[5] For the impact of Addison and Steele on Hume, see Nicholas Phillipson, *David Hume* (London, 2011 [1989]), pp. 24–27. See also James A. Harris, *Hume: An Intellectual Biography* (Cambridge, 2015), esp. pp. 154–66.

[6] *E* (C), p. 529.   [7] Ibid.   [8] *The Spectator*, No. 126, 25 July 1711.

[9] *EPM*, pp. 41, 76–77.   [10] See esp. Sagar, 'Between Virtue and Knavery'.

[11] In contrast with Bolingbroke, Hume used the two terms interchangeably. As Duncan Forbes pointed out, he frequently changed 'factions' into 'parties' and *vice versa* when editing his essays; see Forbes, *Hume's Philosophical Politics* (Cambridge, 1975), p. 202.

should render the founders of parties more odious is, the difficulty of extirpating these weeds, when once they have taken root in any state.[12]

His first more balanced observation was that parties 'rise more easily, and propagate themselves faster in free governments, where they always infect the legislature itself, which alone could be able, by the steady application of rewards and punishments, to eradicate them'.[13] After this opening, many readers may expect an explanation for how the legislature could eradicate parties. Instead, Hume stayed true to the title of the essay and proceeded to analyse the phenomenon of party supported by examples from history. He divided parties into *personal* and *real*, adding that most parties were a mixture of both. Personal factions were most common in small republics, where every domestic quarrel became an affair of state. Hume believed that people had 'such a propensity to divide into personal factions, that the smallest appearance of real difference will produce them', and like Jonathan Swift he referred to the Prasini and Veneti factions, which had begun as different teams wearing different colours, green and blue, in chariot racing, but culminated in what we call the Nika riots.[14] Hume commented that '[n]othing is more usual than to see parties, which have begun upon a real difference, continue even after that difference is lost', the reason being that after a division has occurred, people 'contract an affection to the persons with whom they are united, and an animosity against their antagonists', sentiments that are often transmitted to posterity.[15] That is why such parties are categorised as *personal*, even if they differed in opinion at the outset.

Hume's main interest, however, was parties he classified as *real*, meaning those representing a more tangible difference. In this category, he made a tripartite classification into parties from *interest, principle* and *affection*. Those based on interest he called 'the most reasonable, and the most excusable' of all factions.[16] This was bold; as Pocock has reminded us, '[p]arty was for most men tolerable only when it embodied principle and so was capable of virtue', whereas parties representing interests were seen as perpetuating 'the reign of corruption'.[17] Why, then, were parties from interest the most excusable? For one thing, they were inevitable. When parties represented different orders in the state, for example, nobles and people, 'they naturally follow a distinct

---

[12] *E* (LF), p. 55, *E* (C), p. 65.   [13] *E* (LF), pp. 55–56, *E* (C), p. 66.
[14] *E* (LF), pp. 56–57, *E* (C), p. 66.   [15] *E* (LF), p. 58, *E* (C), p. 67.   [16] Ibid.
[17] J. G. A. Pocock, *The Machiavellian Moment: Florentine Political Thought and the Atlantic Republican Tradition* (Princeton, NJ, 2003 [1975]), pp. 483–84.

interest'.[18] Such parties based on interest exist even in despotic governments, Hume argued, in a similar vein to Montesquieu in *Considérations sur les causes de la grandeur des Romains et de leur décadence* (1734).

In contrast with parties from interest, parties from principle, 'especially speculative principle, are known only to modern times, and are, perhaps, the most extraordinary and unaccountable *phænomenon*, that has yet appeared in human affairs'.[19] Divisions based on principles gave rise to madness and fury, and Hume explicitly linked ideological differences to 'religious controversies'. The reason was that such partisans, like religious fanatics, sought to make everyone a convert to their beliefs. Most people were eager to debate, even those with the most speculative opinions, because the human mind was 'wonderfully fortified by an unanimity of sentiments' and 'shocked by any contrariety'.[20] That is why two people of opposite principles of religion could not pass each other when travelling in different directions on a highway without arguing, although Hume believed that the road was 'sufficiently broad' for them to pass without disruption.[21]

While it may appear frivolous, Hume was convinced that the tendency in human nature to dispute and seek to convert others 'seems to have been the origin of all religious wars and divisions'.[22] He had earlier in the same essay broached the questions of both civil and religious wars, two concepts inescapably and fatally linked to party division in the most extreme form as he understood it. The rise of Christianity explained why parties from principle were known only in modern times, whereas the ancients had parties from interest such as nobles versus people, and personal factions such as those of Caesar and Pompey, although the latter were not discussed by Hume in this particular essay . In antiquity, '[t]he magistrate embraced the religion of the people . . . and united ecclesiastical with the civil power'.[23] By contrast, Christianity arose in opposition to the established religion and government, and priests could thus monopolise power within this new sect. The fact that priestly government continued after it had become the established religion led to a spirit of persecution at the heart of this religion. Hume emphasised that 'parties of religion' were 'more furious and enraged than the most cruel factions that ever arose from interest and ambition'.[24]

Hume concluded the essay with a paragraph on the third kind of real party: parties from affection, by which Hume meant dynastic parties.

---

[18] *E* (LF), p. 59, *E* (C), p. 67.   [19] *E* (LF), p. 60, *E* (C), p. 68.
[20] *E* (LF), pp. 60–61, *E* (C), p. 68.   [21] *E* (LF), p. 60, *E* (C), p. 68.
[22] *E* (LF), p. 61, *E* (C), p. 68.   [23] *E* (LF), p. 61, *E* (C), p. 69.   [24] *E* (LF), p. 63, *E* (C), p. 70.

It may seem difficult to distinguish this category of *real* party from the *personal* factions that Hume referred to earlier in the essay, but from the example he gives it is clear that he had different kinds of parties in mind. The key example of a real party from affection at the time was the Jacobite faction with its attachment to the Stuarts. The question of Jacobitism was often prominent in Hume's thinking, even if this essay was written four years before the Jacobite rebellion in 1745, and Hume was eager to downplay the significance of Jacobitism in his native Scotland. He had little sympathy with this type of party as it was often 'very violent'. Activated by the splendour of majesty and power, it could be based on an imaginary interest that makes people attached to a single person and gives them the impression that they have an intimate relationship with him or her. But it could also arise 'from spite and opposition to persons whose sentiments are different from [their] own'. In general, this inclination was often found in people with 'no great generosity of spirit' who are not 'easily transported by friendship beyond their own interest'.[25] The allusion to Jacobitism is an appropriate segue into Hume's second major essay on party.

9.2 'Of the Parties of Great Britain'

'Of the Parties of Great Britain' (1741) is one of the most heavily edited of Hume's essays, which is not strange considering how much the state of parties changed between the first edition of the *Essays* (1741) and *Essays and Treatises on Several Subjects* (1777). Crucially, he never withdrew the essay, but instead amended it. Hume began the essay by arguing that party division was inevitable in mixed governments such as the British, delicately balanced between its monarchical and republican elements. In addition to this uncertain balance, people's passions and prejudices would necessarily generate different opinions concerning the government, even among people of the best understanding. While all reasonable people would agree to maintain the mixed government, they would disagree about specifics. Those with mild temperaments would be inclined towards monarchy and entrust greater powers to the crown than the passionate lovers of liberty. In short, 'there are parties of PRINCIPLE involved in the very nature of our constitution, which may properly enough be denominated those of COURT and COUNTRY'.[26] The Court and Country parties would always subsist as long as Britain remained a limited monarchy, that is, as long as it retained its parliament.

---

[25] Ibid.   [26] *E* (LF), p. 65, *E* (C), p. 71.

Arguing for a Court–Country division was just to say that there would always be parties of government and opposition. Since there was no alternative centre of government than the monarch there would always be a Court party, and a Country party platform naturally formed to oppose it. Hume believed that leaders of factions were mainly motivated by interest, because they were closer to power, whereas inferior members were more attached to principles. The crown would naturally give government positions to those most favourable to monarchical power, who at this time paradoxically were the Whigs because of Jacobitism and proscription of the Tories.[27]

Turning to the religious dimension of party politics, Hume highlighted that 'in all ages of the world, priests have been enemies to liberty', since freedom of thought always posed a threat to priestly power.[28] For this reason, 'the established clergy, while things are in their natural situation, will always be of the *Court*-party; as, on the contrary, dissenters of all kinds will be of the *Country*-party; since they can never hope for that toleration, which they stand in need of, but by means of our free government'.[29] The Swedish sixteenth-century king Gustavus Vasa may have been the only king who managed to supress both the established church and liberty at the same time. The natural order would be the opposite, as in the situation in the Dutch Republic. As we shall see, however, religion and dynastic conflict had interrupted the natural development of politics in Britain.

Having outlined his 'general theory', Hume turned to domestic history and went on to explain 'the first rise of parties in ENGLAND'. Much like the French Huguenot historian Paul de Rapin's *Dissertation on the Whigs and the Tories*, Hume related the rise of party to the division between Roundhead and Cavalier during the 'great rebellion'.[30] It was not strange that the civil war divided the people into 'parties', since even the impartial in his own day could still not make up their minds about the event. Both king and parliament threatened to break the balance of the constitution by their respective absolutist and republican aims. Since the contest was so equal, interest played no role. Hume did not describe Roundhead and Cavalier as extremists; instead, he argued that neither 'disowned either monarchy or liberty' but simply reflected inclinations. That is how they fitted into his 'general theory' of party: 'they may be considered as court

---

[27] See Skjönsberg, *The Persistence of Party*, esp. pp. 30–33, 75–76, 96–97.

[28] *E* (LF), pp. 65–66, *E* (C), p. 72.   [29] *E* (LF), p. 66, *E* (C), p. 72.

[30] *E* (LF), p. 67, *E* (C), p. 73. For Rapin, see Skjönsberg, *The Persistence of Party*, ch. 2; Miriam Franchina, *Paul Rapin Thoyras and the Art of Eighteenth-Century Historiography* (Oxford, 2021); Ben Dew, *Commerce, Finance and Statecraft: Histories of England, 1600–1780* (Manchester, 2018), ch. 5.

and country-party, enflamed into civil war, by an unhappy concurrence of circumstances, and by the turbulent spirit of the age'.[31] They also suited the religious dimension of his theory, as the established clergy joined the king's party, and the nonconformists were on parliament's side.

The civil war was fatal to the Cavaliers first, as the king was executed in 1649, and the Roundhead cause second, with the royal family being restored in 1660. According to Hume, however, 'Charles II was not made wiser by the example of his father; but prosecuted the same measures, though at first, with more secrecy and caution.' This seems to have been why new parties arose 'under the appellations of *Whig* and *Tory*, which have continued ever since to confound and distract our government'. It was at this stage that Hume's general theory of party became less applicable, and gave way to the study of historical contingency. As he acknowledged, '[t]o determine the nature of these parties is, perhaps one of the most difficult problems, that can be met with, and is a proof that history may contain questions, as uncertain as any to be found in the most abstract sciences'. Since Whig and Tory had been preceded by Roundhead and Cavalier, Hume began by comparing them. His first claim was that 'the principles of *passive obedience*, and *indefeasible right*, which were but little heard among the CAVALIERS . . . became the universal doctrine . . . of a TORY'. Pushed to its extremity, this would imply an absolute as opposed to a limited monarchy, and 'a formal renunciation of all our liberties', since a *limited* monarchy that cannot be resisted would be an absurdity.[32] Quoting Bolingbroke directly for the first time in the essay, Hume added that passive obedience was bizarre enough to disturb the common sense of comparatively uncivilised peoples such as the Samoyedes or the Hottentots.[33] Fortunately, the Tories never carried this doctrine into practice, for '[t]he TORIES, as men, were enemies to oppression; and also as ENGLISHMEN, they were enemies to arbitrary power'. They may not have been as zealous for liberty as their antagonists, but were sufficiently flexible to forget about passive obedience and indefeasible right 'when they saw themselves openly threatened with a subversion of the ancient government'.[34] Hume here referred to the active part played by the Tories in the Glorious Revolution.

---

[31] *E* (LF), p. 69, *E* (C), p. 73.   [32] *E* (LF), p. 69, *E* (C), p. 74.
[33] *E* (LF), p. 611, *E* (C), p. 563; Bolingbroke, *Political Writings*, ed. David Armitage (Cambridge, 1997), p. 15.
[34] *E* (LF), p. 70, *E* (C), p. 74.

From the Revolution, 'the firmest foundation of BRITISH liberty' as Hume described it, a great deal could be learned about the Tories. The Revolution showed that the Tories were 'a genuine *court-party*, such as might be expected in a BRITISH government'.[35] While attached to monarchy they were also attached to liberty. Hume acknowledged that neither the Revolution nor the Hanoverian Succession of 1714 were satisfactory to the Tories, since they were at odds with their principles of passive obedience and indefeasible hereditary right, as well as their affections for the Stuart family. They compromised because 'any other settlement ... must have been dangerous, if not fatal to liberty'. Against this backdrop, Hume arrived at a general definition of a Tory since the Glorious Revolution as '*a lover of monarchy, though without abandoning liberty; and a partizan of the family of* STUART'. He could also derive his definition of a Whig as '*a lover of liberty though without renouncing monarchy; and a friend to the settlement in the* PROTESTANT *line*'.[36] The parties were different in degree rather than kind.

At this stage, Hume signalled his disagreement with Bolingbroke, who had argued that the real difference between Whig and Tory had disappeared after the Revolution. If Bolingbroke were right, it 'would turn our whole history into an ænigma'.[37] A crucial piece of evidence for the continuing existence of the Tory party was their Jacobitism: '[h]ave not the TORIES always borne an avowed affection to the family of Stuart, and have not their adversaries always opposed with vigour the succession of that family?'[38] How could Hume be so confident that the Tories were, at heart, Jacobite? As Walpole, convinced of the reality of the Jacobite threat, put it, '[n]o man of common prudence will profess himself openly a Jacobite', as doing so was not only treasonous but would also harm the cause.[39] For Hume, however, only Jacobitism could explain why the Tories, whose principles were more favourable to monarchy, had been hostile to all monarchs since the Revolution with the exception of Anne, who was both a Stuart and a devout Anglican, and selected a Tory administration in 1710–14. In other words, during the reign of Anne, affection, principle and interest coalesced for the Tories. Hume recognised that 'the TORY party seem, of late, to have decayed much in their numbers; still more in their zeal; and I may venture to say, still more in

---

[35] *E* (LF), p. 71, *E* (C), p. 75. [36] Ibid. [37] *E* (LF), pp. 611–12, *E* (C), pp. 563–64.
[38] *E* (LF), p. 612, *E* (C), p. 564.
[39] Cited in *History of Parliament: The House of Commons, 1715–54*, ed. Romney Sedgwick (2 vols., London, 1970), I, pp. 68–69.

their credit and authority'.[40] Most educated people and at least most philosophers since the time of the great Whig John Locke would be ashamed to be associated with the Tory party, he argued. By contrast, 'in almost all companies the name of OLD WHIG is mentioned as an uncontestable appellation of honour and dignity'.[41] Hume was fully aware, however, that the Tories had a power base that was more consistent and reliable than Jacobitism: High-Church Anglicanism. He was by no means saying that Toryism had become irrelevant; indeed, he was clear that '[t]here are ... very considerable remains of that party in ENGLAND, with all their old prejudices'.[42]

While Hume believed that the Whig–Tory dichotomy was tangible in the 1740s, he was mindful that the fact that the Whigs had become a Court party and many Tories resorted to Country party politics caused problems for his general theory. "Tis monstrous to see an established episcopal clergy in declared opposition to the court, and a non-conformist presbyterian clergy in conjunction with it', he wrote. The only thing that could have produced 'such an unnatural conduct in both', was that 'the former espoused monarchical principles too high for the present settlement, which is founded on the principles of liberty: And the latter, being afraid of the prevalence of those high principles, adhered to that party from whom they had reason to expect liberty and toleration'.[43] The most important evidence for Hume showing that the British party division had not turned into Court and Country was that almost all Dissenters sided with the Court, that is, the Whigs, and all the lower clergy of the Church of England (and the nonjurors) with the oppositional Tories. 'This may convince us, that some biass [sic] still hangs upon our constitution, some extrinsic weight, which turns it from its natural course, and causes a confusion in our parties', he concluded.[44] The extrinsic weight was religion, which Hume would analyse in greater detail in 'Of Superstition and Enthusiasm' (1741) as well as his *History of England.*

At the end of the essay, Hume returned to the dynastic question, re-emphasising that this was the main dividing line between the parties. Importantly, however, the Whigs were attached to the Hanoverian Succession only as a means to support liberty. Probably alluding to measures such as the Septennial Act (1716), the increase in crown patronage and the national debt, Hume acknowledged that the Whig government may

---

[40] *E* (LF), p. 614, *E* (C), p. 566.   [41] *E* (LF), p. 614, *E* (C), p. 567.
[42] *E* (LF), p. 72, *E* (C), p. 75.   [43] *E* (LF), p. 612, *E* (C), p. 564.
[44] *E* (LF), p. 72, *E* (C), p. 76.

have taken steps inimical to liberty, but only in the belief that this would support the present royal family and thus liberty in the long run, since the Stuarts posed a threat to the Revolution Settlement. The Tories, meanwhile, had 'so long [been] obliged to talk in the republican stile [sic], that they seem to have been made converts of themselves by their hypocrisy'.[45] What did it mean to talk in the republican style? In its simplest form, it meant that the Tories had sided with the Country party against the Court Whigs. Yet Hume may have had a more specific political programme in mind. When Hume spent time in London between August 1737 and February 1739, Tory-Jacobites such as Watkin Williams-Wynn attacked Walpole's ministry in parliament for curtailing freedom of speech, allowing public debt to rise, and corrupting both parliament and the people. When the reduction of the standing army was debated on 3 February 1738, William Shippen, another leading Tory-Jacobite, said that the maintenance of the standing army 'produces but one single good, which is security of the [Whig] administration'.[46] By 'the republican stile', Hume meant that Wynn, Shippen and other Tories had adopted the Country party rhetoric. This rhetoric, which had been Whig at the time of the Exclusion Crisis and then viewed by Tories as quasi-republican, was recommended by Bolingbroke, and had been staple Tory rhetoric since the beginning of the eighteenth century.

In the conclusion to the various editions of the essay prior to 1770, Hume turned to his native Scotland, arguing that there were never any Tories in that country but only Whigs and Jacobites. An outright Jacobite differed from a Tory by having 'no regard to the constitution, but is either a zealous partizan of absolute monarchy, or at least willing to sacrifice our liberties to the obtaining the succession in that family to which he is attached'.[47] We have seen that the Tories were not prepared to push things to that extreme. The reason behind the difference was that the political and religious divisions corresponded to each other in Scotland unlike in England. All Presbyterians were Whigs and all Episcopalians were Jacobites in Scotland. Since the Presbyterian Church had been re-established at the Williamite Revolution, Scottish Anglicans had no motivation to swear oaths to William. The Jacobites had thus been more violent in Scotland than their Tory 'brethren' in England, wrote Hume, with reference to the rebellion of 1715.

---

[45] *E* (LF), p. 72, *E* (C), p. 75.   [46] See Skjönsberg, *The Persistence of Party*, p. 128.
[47] *E* (LF), p. 615, *E* (C), p. 567.

Writing in 1741, Hume suggested that the Jacobite party was almost entirely extinguished in Scotland.[48] But whatever reason Hume, who had been away from his native land for most of the 1730s, may have had in making this point, the truth was that Jacobitism remained prevalent in Scotland, even in the lowlands.[49] The 'unhappy troubles'[50] of the 'Forty-five' would prove his initial assessment on this score wrong, and his reflections about the decline of Jacobitism in Scotland did not remain in the third edition of the *Essays,* published in 1748. In the wake of this event, Hume resumed his analysis of the party structure, which he believed was at the heart of British politics.

9.3   'Of the Original Contract' and 'Of Passive Obedience'

For the 1748 edition of the *Essays,* Hume removed some essays he regarded as 'frivolous and finical', and inserted three new ones.[51] Of the new essays, one was '*against* the original Contract, the System of the Whigs, another *against* passive Obedience, the System of the Tories'.[52] In terms of the content of the essays, however, the separation is not as clean as their titles suggest, as he dealt with both parties' respective speculative systems in the first, longer essay 'Of the Original Contract', and then the practical consequences of these systems in 'Of Passive Obedience'. He had also completed a third essay on the Protestant Succession, in which he 'treat[ed] that subject as coolly and indifferently, as I would the dispute between Caesar and Pompey' , adding that '[t]he conclusion shows me a Whig, but a very sceptical one'.[53] Having discussed 'Of the Protestant Succession' with friends, most of whom thought that it would be 'extremely dangerous' to publish, it did not appear until the publication of his next essay collection: the *Political Discourses* (1752).[54]

The demolition of the 'original contract' is one of the interventions that Hume is most famous for in the history of political thought. The idea that government was founded on and received its legitimacy from a

[48] *E* (LF), p. 616, *E* (C), pp. 567–68.
[49] Max Skjönsberg, 'David Hume and the Jacobites', *Scottish Historical Review,* 252 (2021), pp. 25–56.
[50] *HL,* I, p. 63.
[51] The three new essays, 'Of the Original Contract', 'Of Passive Obedience' and 'Of National Characters' had already appeared as *Three Essays, Moral and Political,* published earlier in 1748.
[52] *HL,* I, p. 112; italics mine.
[53] *HL,* I, p. 111; Duncan Forbes, 'Sceptical Whiggism, Commerce and Liberty', in A. S. Skinner and Thomas Wilson, eds., *Essays on Adam Smith* (Oxford, 1975), pp. 179–201.
[54] *HL,* I, pp. 112–13.

conditional contract between governors and the governed had long been a shibboleth of the Whigs. The term 'original contract' later played a role in the prosecution of the High-Church Tory Henry Sacheverell, impeached in 1709–10 for preaching non-resistance, notably in the speeches of Nicholas Lechmere, one of the managers of the trial.[55] Few in Hume's lifetime would have struggled to recognise the original contract as a Whig doctrine, and passive obedience as a Tory doctrine, although it was often pointed out that practice rarely corresponded to theory. While Hume targeted the speculative systems of the two parties and not the precise articulations of any philosopher, he singled out Locke as the Whig contract theorist *par excellence.*

While the related doctrines of divine right, indefeasible hereditary right, non-resistance and passive obedience had been ridiculed by many in the 1730s and 1740s, Hume among others,[56] it is safe to assume that many still believed in such theories. Bolingbroke did not speak for all Tories when he renounced these ideas.[57] Divine right Toryism and its twin Jacobitism remained buoyant in church circles and at the University of Oxford, with the latter being a training ground for the former. The immediate reason why thinkers opposed to the divine right theory of monarchy in the second half of the 1740s felt that they had to treat it seriously was the Jacobite rising in 1745, which was initially successful, especially in Scotland. Scottish Whigs could no longer pretend that Jacobitism was not a serious 'party' north of the border. The Jacobite defeat at Culloden in April 1746 and the bloody clampdown on Jacobitism that followed did not immediately sound the death knell for Jacobitism, as popular riots in the years that followed attest.[58] In his first essays from 1741, Hume had treated Jacobitism seriously in the sense that he linked the Tories with the movement. In the Scottish context, however, he had downplayed the threat of Jacobitism in his early essays. But the 'Forty-five' proved that the theory of divine right continued to have more sway in Britain than he had previously thought.

Hume's starting point was that 'no party, in the present age, can well support itself, without a philosophical or speculative system of principles, annexed to its political or practical one'. Divine right theory and the original contract represented such religious and philosophical systems of principles for the Tories and the Whigs, respectively, with passive

---

[55] Geoffrey Holmes, *The Trial of Doctor Sacheverell* (London, 1973), pp. 132, 139–40.

[56] *E* (LF), p. 51, *E* (C), p. 63.   [57] Bolingbroke, *Political Writings*, pp. 5, 22.

[58] Paul Monod, *Jacobitism and the English People, 1688–1788* (Cambridge, 1989), pp. 195–232.

obedience being a practical consequence of the former theory and resistance of the latter. Hume here revised his earlier ridicule of the divine right theory, now simply stating that 'one party [the Tories], by tracing up government to the DEITY, endeavour to render it so sacred and inviolate, that it must be little less than sacrilege, however tyrannical it may become, to touch or invade it'. The Whigs, on their part, 'by founding government altogether on the consent of the PEOPLE, suppose that there is a kind of *original contract*, by which the subjects have tacitly reserved the power of resisting their sovereign, whenever they find themselves aggrieved by that authority'.[59]

Hume's main intention was as ever to promote moderation, as he explicitly set out at the start of the essay. In the first instance, he contended that both systems were just, but not in the ways interpreted by the parties. Second, both sets of practical consequences were prudent, but not to the extreme to which each party carried them. How could the divine right theory be described as just by someone who famously did away with God in his own philosophy? Hume distinguished between divine right *kingship* and divine right *government*. For the religious, it would be appropriate to regard the deity as the author of all governments, and since human beings depended on government for comfort and security, it made sense for believers to view this as intended by a beneficent being. Finally, as government existed in all countries and all ages, this could also be ascribed to the intention of an omniscient being, for those who believed in such a thing. But the key problem with this theory was the belief in providence, which Hume regarded as at odds with the importance attached to lineal succession, and he consequently exploded the anti-Hanoverian case of the Jacobite Tories. For those who believed in providence and the argument from design, 'the greatest and most lawful prince' must be incorporated in the same divine plan as usurpers, robbers and pirates.[60] Many divines had relied on providence when shifting their allegiance from James to William and Mary after the Glorious Revolution.[61] Another problem for the Tory system, as Hume saw it, was that if authority *per se* was regarded as divine, this would have to apply to 'every petty jurisdiction ... and every *limited* authority' within a state, and even a constable would thus act 'by a divine commission'.[62]

---

[59] *E* (LF), pp. 465–66, *E* (C), p. 332.   [60] *E* (LF), p. 467, *E* (C), p. 333.
[61] Gerald Straka, 'The Final Phase of Divine Right Theory in England, 1688–1702', *English Historical Review*, 77 (1962), pp. 646–47.
[62] *E* (LF), p. 467, *E* (C), p. 333.

Hume then moved on to the original contract, with which he had already dealt at length in the third book of the *Treatise*. There, Hume had referred to the original contract as 'the foundation of our fashionable system of politics' and 'the creed of a party amongst us, who value themselves, with reason, on the soundness of their philosophy, and their liberty of thought', that is, the Whigs.[63] In a similar vein to his earlier treatment, Hume argued that if the contract was interpreted in what we may call the Hobbesian sense, with the people originally giving rise to government by having 'voluntarily, for the sake of peace and order, abandoned their native liberty, and received laws from their equal and companion', then 'all government is, at first, founded on a contract'.[64] The mistake often made was to believe that government continued to rest on no other foundation than a contract. Hume wanted to expose the absurdity that people 'owe allegiance to no prince or government, unless bound by the obligation and sanction of a *promise*', a promise from which they may free themselves.[65] He had argued in the *Treatise* that civil duties of obedience 'soon detach themselves from our promises, and acquire a separate force and influence'.[66] We disapprove of rebellion because the execution of justice would be impossible without submission to government. Allegiance to government rested entirely on opinion, of right and of interest, and it was underpinned by habit.[67] In 1748, he appears to have been even more eager than in the *Treatise* to dispute the idea that the sovereign promised justice and protection, and that if the subject believed they failed to deliver on this promise, the sovereign 'has thereby freed his subject from all obligations to allegiance'.[68] If interpreted this way, contract theory implied a charter of rights that could be invaded and a *right* of resistance in such cases.

Hume's objection to the original contract interpreted in this Lockean fashion was twofold: it was an historical absurdity that did not exist and had never existed anywhere, and, moreover, it posed a threat to the stability of government by encouraging rebellion. Hume was clear that resistance would occur when real oppression took place, and no one could condemn it in such cases, but there was no reason to encourage this behaviour, as resistance would always take place when necessary. The contract was also mistaken in placing so much emphasis on consent.

---

[63] *T*, p. 347.   [64] *E* (LF), p. 468, *E* (C), p. 333.   [65] *E* (LF), p. 469, *E* (C), p. 334.
[66] *T*, p. 349.
[67] *E* (LF), pp. 33, 37, 39, *E* (C), pp. 51, 54–55. See also Paul Sagar, *The Opinion of Mankind: Sociability and the Theory of the State from Hobbes to Smith* (Princeton, NJ, 2018).
[68] *E* (LF), p. 469, *E* (C), p. 334.

Hume remarked that Henry IV and Henry VII were elected kings by parliament, but never acknowledged this because they believed that it would weaken rather than strengthen their authority.[69] This type of Whiggism further bred a form of nationalism based on the idea that the British post-revolutionary regime was unparalleled. Hume agreed that it was to some extent, but not in the sense commonly thought,[70] and he was always eager to put notions of English exceptionalism to the test. Here he reminded his readers that the Glorious Revolution was not founded on universal consent, but the majority of 700 members of the Convention Parliament who decided the fate of the entire nation.[71]

In the following essay, 'Of Passive Obedience', Hume repeated the argument that, 'as government binds us to obedience only on account of its tendency to public utility', obedience ceases when it would lead to public ruin.[72] Hume followed Hobbes and Locke in quoting from Cicero's *De Legibus* that *salus populi suprema lex esto*.[73] He then used the same examples as when covering similar ground in the *Treatise*: no one would condemn those who rebelled against Nero and Philip II, however 'infatuated with party-systems' they may be.[74] Accordingly, even 'our high monarchical party', that is, the Tories, agreed that in 'extraordinary emergencies', 'when the public is in the highest danger, from violence and tyranny', resistance would be permitted. This was mainstream Scottish Whiggism, or indeed British establishment Whiggism. Hume's larger point, however, was that 'obedience is our duty in the common course of things' and that 'it ought chiefly to be inculcated'.[75] His main intention was to show that the respective systems of both parties contained a grain of truth, but that both could be equally dangerous if carried to extreme lengths.

Nevertheless, Hume closed the essay on passive obedience with some arguments in favour of the Whigs. The first was that the Tories erroneously sought to exclude the exceptions to the general rule of obedience. It is likely that Hume here meant the fiction that no resistance had taken place in 1688–89 and that James II/VII had abdicated the throne. This enabled Tories to obey William as king *de facto*, while James remained

---

[69] *E* (LF), p. 473, *E* (C), p. 337.
[70] '[T]he English Government is certainly happy, though probably not calculated for Duration, by reason of its excessive Liberty' (*HL*, II, p. 261).
[71] *E* (LF), p. 472, *E* (C), p. 336.   [72] *E* (LF), p. 489, *E* (C), p. 347.
[73] As the examples of Hobbes of Locke show, *salus populi* arguments could be used by 'resistance' and 'non-resistance' advocates alike.
[74] *E* (LF), p. 490, *E* (C), p. 347; *T*, p. 353.   [75] *E* (LF), p. 490, *E* (C), pp. 347–48.

king *de jure,* a way of thinking that continued to be a prominent part of Tory discourse for a long time after the Revolution.[76] It was a potentially destabilising fiction, however, since James's 'abdication' did not apply to his offspring. Accordingly, after the death of Anne, the last Stuart monarch, Jacobites argued that James 'III' (the Old Pretender) was the rightful sovereign, despite the Act of Settlement of 1701. Hume concluded that the Whigs should be applauded for insisting on exceptions to the rule of obedience, because they consequently defended both truth (James II had been deposed) and liberty (the power of parliament).[77]

Finally, Hume believed that the nature of the British constitution was more favourable to the Whigs since the king was above the law only regarding his own person. The king's government, on the other hand, was subject to the full force of the law, and if the king attempted to usurp more legislative power than the mixed constitution allowed, as Charles I and James II had done in the seventeenth century, it would become 'necessary to oppose them with some vehemence'.[78] Hume thus concluded that resistance to monarchs was necessarily more common in mixed forms of government than in simple ones, where monarchs had little incentive to run into difficulties that would warrant resistance.[79] As has often been pointed out, this appears to contradict Hume's earlier statement that resistance was only justified as a last resort 'when the public is in the highest danger, from violence and tyranny'.[80] This apparent contradiction may have stemmed from Hume's ambition to give both parties their due. In Section 9.4, we investigate Hume's attempt to go beyond this inconsistency in 'Of the Protestant Succession'.

9.4   'Of the Protestant Succession'

As noted, the two essays discussed in Section 9.3 were meant to be accompanied by a third and related essay on the Protestant Succession, the publication of which he postponed until 1752. The succession to the throne was a party-political issue and Hume believed that he had to deal with it to achieve his aim of mollifying party animosity. The essay was

---

[76] J. P. Kenyon, *Revolutionary Principles: The Politics of Party 1689–1720* (Cambridge, 1977), pp. 32–33; Anon., *Whig and Tory Principles of Government Fairly Stated in a Dialogue between an Oxford Scholar and a Whig Parson* (n.p., 1716), pp. 33–35, 40–41.
[77] *E* (LF), p. 491, *E* (C), p. 348.   [78] *E* (LF), p. 492, *E* (C), p. 349.   [79] See also *T*, pp. 360–61.
[80] *E* (LF), p. 490, *E* (C), p. 348. Frank McLynn has called Hume's thinking on resistance 'muddled', and Forbes has called it 'ambivalent'; see Frank McLynn, 'Jacobitism and Hume', *Hume Studies*, 9 (1983), p. 194 and Forbes, *Hume's Philosophical Politics*, p. 101, respectively.

provocative because Hume, by his own admission, treated the subject 'coolly and indifferently' – a precarious enterprise in the aftermath of the 1745–46 Jacobite rising. Like the contract, Hume had already dealt with the topic in Book III of the *Treatise*. In his earlier treatment, he had been clear that a disputed succession presented a near-intractable problem. When the principles deciding who should govern (most importantly long possession, present possession, and positive law) pointed in different directions, that is, long possession for the Stuart family, and present possession and positive law (the Act of Settlement) for Hanover, 'an impartial enquirer, who adopts no party in political controversies' would never be satisfied by any answer.[81]

Hume made several concessions to the Jacobite case in his contentious essay, in which he imagined himself a member of parliament between 1689 and 1714, the period between the Revolution and the Hanoverian accession. A restoration of the Stuart family at this time would have had the advantage of 'preserv[ing] the succession clear and undisputed, free from a pretender'. Blood was the most straightforward indicator of legitimacy in the minds of the multitude and strong feelings for the 'true heir of their royal family' were precisely what rendered monarchical government stable. It was foolish to place kings on the same level as the meanest of mankind, even if 'an anatomist finds no more in the greatest monarch than in the lowest peasant or day-labourer; and a moralist may, perhaps, frequently find less'. Such reflections are largely pointless since 'all of us, still retain these prejudices in favour of birth and family', and everyone prefers to see plays about kings rather than sailors.[82]

By comparison with the Stuarts, the Hanoverian Succession 'violate[d] hereditary right; and place[d] on the throne a prince, to whom birth gave no title to that dignity'. In contrast to his essays of the early 1740s, Hume was now prepared to defend the actions of the Stuart kings in the seventeenth century. Anticipating his later historical writings, Hume argued that James I and Charles I viewed England as a simple monarchy, based on the precedent of the Tudors and comparisons with other monarchs in Europe at the time. These ideas were bolstered by the flattery of courtiers, 'and, above all, that of the clergy, who from several passages of *scripture* ... had erected a regular and avowed system of arbitrary power'.[83] On the other hand, he argued that a limited monarchy, which he saw as an important achievement, could never have been established within that royal line. The Stuart family was simply too closely associated with the

---

[81] *T*, p. 560.   [82] *E* (LF), pp. 503–4, *E* (C), p. 356.   [83] *E* (LF), p. 505, *E* (C), pp. 357–58.

doctrine of divine right. Indeed, the last Stuart monarch, Queen Anne, revived the practice of touching for the king's evil, whereby the monarch touched subjects to cure scrofula, which William had previously discontinued because he viewed it as 'Popery'.[84] While Hume unsurprisingly regarded the royal touch as an 'ancient superstition', many educated people still believed in the practice at the time, including the Jacobite historian Thomas Carte.[85] According to Hume, '[t]he only method of destroying, at once, all these high claims and pretensions, was to depart from the true hereditary line, and choose a prince, who [was] plainly a creature of the public'. This 'secured our constitutional limitations' and a peculiar, but in Hume's view salutary, situation whereby '[t]he people cherish monarchy, because protected by it, [and t]he monarch favours liberty [i.e. parliament, representing the people], because created by it'.[86] As in his essays from 1741, and *Treatise* book III, Hume thus came down firmly on the side of the Revolution Settlement.

Be that as it may, he went on to enumerate the Hanoverian monarchy's further disadvantages by focusing on foreign dominions, which had engaged Britain in wars on the continent. From George I's accession in 1714 up until the start of Queen Victoria's reign in 1837, Britain shared its monarch with the German state of Hanover. The first Hanoverian monarch to be born in Britain was George III, who ascended the throne in 1760. His two predecessors were Germans, who spent a significant amount of time in Hanover and were, according to their critics, more interested in their native land than their new kingdom. These were constant themes in Jacobite propaganda. Foreign influence had been a worry from the start of the reign of William, who had largely relied on Dutch advisers and fought wars on the continent. As a response, the Act of Settlement barred foreigners from becoming privy councillors and members of parliament. The Act also forbade the monarch from engaging the nation in a war in defence of foreign territories without the consent of parliament. Nevertheless, shortly after the Hanoverian Succession, disagreement over the influence of Hanover on British foreign policy brought about a split within the Whigs.[87] In 1715, Hanover became involved in the Great Northern War (1700–21) against Sweden, which Hume referred to in

[84] David Green, *Queen Anne* (London, 1970), p. 105.
[85] *HE*, V, p. 491; Thomas Carte, *A General History of England* (4 vols., London, 1747–55), I, pp. 291–92n4.
[86] *E* (LF), p. 505–6, *E* (C), p. 358.
[87] W. A. Speck, 'The Whig Schism under George I', *Huntington Library Quarterly*, 40 (1977), pp. 171–79.

the early versions of the essay.[88] The main reason why the small state of Hanover was accepted into the alliance with Russia and other big powers was that George I had the British navy at his disposal. Britain's naval engagement gave ammunition to oppositional attacks on the ministry.

Meanwhile, the main disadvantage of the House of Stuart was their Catholicism. The Act of Settlement declared that 'whosoever shall hereafter come to the possession of this crown, shall join in communion with the church of England, as by law established'.[89] The whole point behind the legislation was indeed to secure the *Protestant* Succession. The Hanoverian Succession was on the agenda only because Anne's last surviving child died in 1700. The importance of not having another Catholic on the throne was realised by both parties and the Act of Settlement had been supported by virtually all Tories.[90] Two of the more optimistic scholars of Jacobitism have argued that a Stuart restoration would have been fully possible in 1714 had the Old Pretender given up his religion.[91] In 1741, Hume had already contended that Catholicism was an enemy of civil liberty and he now argued that Catholicism 'affords no toleration, or peace, or security to any other communion'.[92]

Hume pointed out that almost all Jacobites regarded the Catholicism of the Stuarts as problematic, as much as Hanoverian loyalists admitted that foreign dominions presented a difficulty. He then picked up the gauntlet he himself had thrown down in the *Treatise,* saying that '[i]t belongs, therefore, to a philosopher alone, who is of neither party, to put all the circumstances in the scale, and assign to each of them its proper poise and influence'. Hume began by criticising the reign of the Stuarts as a period when 'the government was kept in a continual fever, by the contention between the privileges of the people and the prerogatives of the crown', a domestic quarrel that allowed France to erect itself as a European superpower 'without any opposition from us, and even sometimes with our assistance'.[93] In contrast, in the sixty-year period after the Glorious Revolution, Britain had enjoyed a longer period of harmony, glory and liberty than any other nation, according to Hume. This stood in sharp contrast with the turbulence of the seventeenth century.

On the other hand, because of the exiled royal family, the same period had seen 'two rebellions [the 'Fifteen' and 'Forty-five'] ... besides plots

[88] *E* (LF), p. 646, *E* (C), p. 680.
[89] E. N. Williams, ed., *The Eighteenth-Century Constitution* (Cambridge, 1960), p. 59.
[90] Tim Harris, *Politics under the Later Stuarts* (London, 1993), p. 157.
[91] Eveline Cruickshanks and Howard Erskine-Hill, *The Atterbury Plot* (Basingstoke, 2004), p. 7.
[92] *E* (LF), pp. 78, 506, *E* (C), pp. 79–80, 358.   [93] *E* (LF), p. 507, *E* (C), p. 359.

and conspiracies without number'.[94] As Hume had argued in the *Treatise,* 'a century is scarce sufficient to establish any new government, or remove all scruples in the minds of the subjects concerning it'.[95] For him, dynastic conflicts were even more dangerous than disputes between privilege and prerogative, because they could only be settled by war rather than debate and compromise. The situation of Hanover was precarious because even if Hume believed that a parliamentary title may be more advantageous to a hereditary one in theory, he was clear that most people would not see it that way, as bloodline was key in the eyes of the multitude. Why, then, had the Stuarts not been restored? The answer was that anti-Catholic sentiments in Britain were simply too strong. This was all for the better: in addition to being more expensive and less tolerant than Protestantism, the most important argument against Catholicism was that it not only separated the head of the church from the regal office but also bestowed the sacerdotal, or priestly, office on a foreigner, the Pope, who had a separate and sometimes opposite interest to that of the British state. Moreover, even if Catholicism had been advantageous to society, it would be a mistake to have a sovereign of that religion when the great majority of the people were Protestant, especially since the spirit of moderation had made such slow advances in Europe.[96]

Although anti-Catholicism was the decisive factor for most people, Hume gave one final reason why the balance tipped in favour of Hanover, namely, that they had attained longevity.[97] While it may have been difficult for an 'impartial patriot' to choose between Hanover and Stuart immediately after the Act of Settlement, the Hanoverian regime had now been more or less consolidated and it would be highly unwise to restore the Stuarts by way of civil war.[98] Time had given legitimacy to the settlement, even if no one could have known at the outset that it would turn out to be beneficial. For Hume, a government had to be judged on its present merit; its foundation was, to a large degree, irrelevant. As he had set out in the *Treatise,* few, if any, governments in history had a better foundation than present possession, and a sudden change would result in confusion and bloodshed.[99] In the final analysis, then, Hume's intention was to undermine the Jacobite case.

We must remember, however, that his intention was to refute the speculative systems of both parties, and his approval of the Hanoverians was a balance-sheet assessment that boiled down to the avoidance of a

---

[94] *E* (LF), p. 508, *E* (C), p. 360.   [95] *T*, p. 356.   [96] *E* (LF), p. 510, *E* (C), p. 361.
[97] *T*, p. 362.   [98] *E* (LF), pp. 510–11, *E* (C), pp. 361–62.   [99] *T*, pp. 356–57.

bloody counter-revolution. This is why he said that he 'very liberally abused both Whigs and Tories' in the essay.[100] In comparison with establishment discourse in the aftermath of the 'Forty-five', his treatment of Toryism and Jacobitism was fairly balanced and comparatively respectful. While there is no evidence or reason to believe that Hume was ever a Jacobite, he did have many Jacobite friends, and he sent the new essays discussed in this chapter to the known Jacobite Lord Elibank in January 1748, joking that 'I am afraid that your Lordship will differ from me with regard to the Protestant Succession, whose Advantages you will probably rate higher than I have done'.[101]

In the aftermath of the Jacobite rebellion, Hume was critical of the vindictive behaviour of many Whigs. In October 1747, Hume wrote a lesser-known pamphlet in which he defended his friend Archibald Stewart, former Lord Provost of Edinburgh, who surrendered the city to the Jacobite army. As part of a wider crackdown on Jacobitism after Culloden, Stewart found himself imprisoned. Hume argued that Stewart had done a noble deed by avoiding a bloodbath since Edinburgh was so poorly defended. As Stewart was acquitted before Hume had published the pamphlet at the start of 1748, Hume added a postscript in which he noted that the trial had become a party-political affair, and Stewart's acquittal had been bemoaned by certain Whigs while it had been celebrated by the Tory-Jacobites. In the postscript, Hume, echoing Rapin's *Dissertation*, made a distinction between political and religious Whigs: 'The Idea I form of a political *Whig*, is that of a Man of Sense and Moderation, a Lover of Laws and Liberty, whose chief Regard to particular Princes and Families, is founded on a Regard to the publick Good'.[102] By contrast, Hume believed that the characteristics of a religious Whig were 'Dissimulation, Hypocrisy, Violence, Calumny, [and] Selfishness'.[103] According to Hume, '[t]his Species of *Whigs* … form but the Fag-end of the Party, and are, at the Bottom, very heartily despised by their own Leaders'.[104] He compared such Whigs to leading 'Roundheads' and 'Covenanters' from the Wars of the Three Kingdoms and Commonwealth era, including Oliver Cromwell. These could presumably be regarded as Whigs *avant la lettre* for Hume because of their anti-Episcopalian bias. On this basis, he argued that the

---

[100] *HL*, I, p. 167.
[101] Ernest Campbell Mossner, 'New Hume Letters to Lord Elibank', *Texas Studies in Literature and Language*, 4 (1962), pp. 431–60, at p. 437. See also Skjönsberg, 'David Hume and the Jacobites'.
[102] [David Hume], *A True Account of the Behaviour and Conduct of Archibald Stewart, Esq: Late Lord Provost of Edinburgh* (London, 1748), p. 33.
[103] Ibid., pp. 33–34.   [104] Ibid., p. 34.

'religious *Whigs* ... are much worse than the religious *Tories*; as the political *Tories* are inferior to the political Whigs'.[105] Provocatively, Hume presented divine right Tories as superior to Whig extremists: '[A] Zeal for Bishops, and for the Books of Common-Prayer, tho' equally groundless, has never been able, when mixt up with Party Notions, to form so virulent and exalted a Poison in human Breasts, as the opposite Principles.'[106] He concluded that all *political* Whigs, unlike *religious* Whigs, were pleased with the acquittal of Stewart because he was innocent, adding 'I am charitable enough to suppose, that the Joy of many of the *Tories* flowed from the same Motive.'[107] The postscript thus offered a classic Humean paradox: the Whigs may have had the soundest politics, but some of their supporters, the fanatic Presbyterians, were more violent and zealous than even the High-Church followers of the Tory party.

9.5 'Of the Coalition of Parties'

Hume's essay 'Of the Coalition of Parties' (1758) has rightly been considered as an 'apologia' for the first volume of his *History*.[108] The essay opened by conceding that it 'may not be practicable, perhaps not desirable' to abolish all distinctions of parties in a free, or mixed, government. For Hume, '[t]he only dangerous parties are such as entertain opposite views with regard to the essentials of government', be it the succession to the crown, as in the case of the Jacobites, or 'the more considerable privileges belonging to the several members of the constitution', as with the great parties of the seventeenth century. On such questions there could be no compromise or accommodation, and there was no room for such parties, since that type of party strife could easily turn into armed conflict. Writing at a time when William Pitt the Elder, supported by many Tories in parliament, had formed a broad-based Whig coalition with the Duke of Newcastle, Hume said that recent tendencies to coalition government indicated that such fundamental conflicts had come to an end. To promote such an 'agreeable prospect', nothing could be better than to encourage moderation by 'persuad[ing] each that its antagonists may possibly be sometimes in the right, and to keep a balance in the praise and blame, which we bestow on either side'.[109] This had been Hume's intention in his essays on the original contract and passive obedience, and he now confirmed that he intended to promote the same political agenda in

---

[105] Ibid., p. 33.   [106] Ibid., p. 33.   [107] Ibid., p. 34.
[108] Forbes, *Hume's Philosophical Politics*, p. 265.   [109] *E* (LF), pp. 493–94, *E* (C), p. 350.

his history of the Stuarts. The rest of the essay was a summary of the argument in his *History of Great Britain*, and some anticipations of his Tudor volumes (particularly appendix III), which he was working on at this time. 'The rule of government is the present established practice of the age', not some 'ancient constitution', of which people had little or no understanding, he concluded.[110]

We have reason to think that Hume in his essay may have been thinking about a 'coalition' of Whigs and Tories rather than simply a coalition of various Whigs. 'Of the Coalition of Parties' was an attempt to defend the present establishment on moderate principles, ones which the Tories could accept. He was convinced that the 'spirit of civil liberty' had evolved from the religious fanaticism of the Puritans, who had been the enemies of what became the Tory party in the late seventeenth century. Liberty had now 'purge[d] itself from that pollution' of fanaticism.[111] It had instead come to embody a spirit of 'toleration' rather than 'persecution', with which Hume had on one occasion associated 'religious Whiggism' in the late 1740s.[112] The key essay is 'Superstition and Enthusiasm', in which Hume had contended that enthusiasm is more violent when it first arises, but becomes milder than superstition over time. Also, with the 'high claims of [royal] prerogative' reduced, and the constitution settled as described at the end of the second Stuart volume, 'a due respect to monarchy, to nobility, and to all ancient institutions' was still possible. Hume clinched the argument by saying that 'the very principle, which made the strength of their party [i.e. the monarchical principle and passive obedience], and from which it derived its chief authority, has now deserted them, and gone over to their antagonists'.[113] The constitution had been settled in favour of liberty, a liberty supported by the monarchy, and if the Tories threatened this settlement by seeking to restore the Stuarts, they would be the factious innovators. Across his essays on party, Hume thus described how the Tories had gone from being the party of order to the party of opposition and innovation, while clinging onto principles incompatible with their new situation, and how the Whigs had gone in the opposite direction. He consistently attempted to give a fair hearing to both parties, and if he was often much harder on the Whigs, it was because he wanted to convert Tories and Scottish Jacobites into supporters of the Revolution Settlement. The paradox was that this settlement could only be protected in his own

---

[110] *E* (LF), p. 498, *F* (C), p. 353.   [111] *E* (LF), p. 501, *E* (C), p. 355.
[112] [Hume], *A True Account*, pp. 33–34.   [113] *E* (LF), p. 501, *E* (C), p. 355.

time on the Tory principle of passive obedience, but in the past, in 1688–89, on the Whig principle of resistance.

9.6 Conclusion

Hume occasionally seemed to be as disapproving of parties as Addison had been in the *Spectator*. As he set out in the advertisement to the first edition of the *Essays,* he believed that public spirit meant 'bear[ing] an equal Affection to all our Country-Men; not to hate one Half of them, under the Pretext of loving the Whole'.[114] A critical danger was that honour as a check on behaviour was largely ignored 'when men act in faction';[115] to partisans, it only mattered to be of service to their own party and to promote the interests of that body. Hume realised, however, that party was an intrinsic part of the British parliamentary system. His intention was thus not to recommend the abolition of parties but simply to 'repress [party-rage] as far as possible' and he hoped that his approach would be 'acceptable to the moderate of both Parties; at the same Time, that, perhaps, it may displease the Bigots of both.'[116] Echoing Bernard Mandeville, Hume believed 'every man ought to be supposed a knave' in politics; the point of his science of politics was to make it in the interest of even bad people to act for the public good, hence his emphasis on political institutions and constitutional mechanisms.[117]

Fully aware that party passion was not going to disappear, Hume's intention was to sound a note of moderation amid division and pacify party animosity by revealing the strengths and weaknesses of the Tories' and Whigs' ideologies alike, both of which could be beneficial if not taken too far. Neither speculative system held water if philosophically and historically probed, which Hume was keen to demonstrate, being convinced that the political legitimacy of states and political systems must be divorced from their foundations. His way of discussing politics and comparing parties set him apart from virtually all his contemporaries, and he even sought to discuss the Protestant Succession in a detached manner.

---

[114] *E* (C), p. 529.   [115] *E* (LF), p. 33, *E* (C), p. 51.   [116] *E* (C), p. 529.
[117] *E* (LF), pp. 42, 16, *E* (C), pp. 57, 41–42; *T*, p. 344; *EHU*, p. 68. See also Richard Bourke, 'Theory and Practice: The Revolution in Political Judgement', in Richard Bourke and Raymond Geuss, eds., *Political Judgement: Essays for John Dunn* (Cambridge, 2009), pp. 73–109. It should be noted that Hume elsewhere stressed that 'the science of politics affords few rules, which will not admit of some exception, and which may not sometimes be controuled by fortune and accident' (*E* (LF), p. 477, *E* (C), pp. 339–40). For Mandeville, see John Robertson, *The Case for the Enlightenment: Scotland and Naples, 1680–1760* (Cambridge, 2005), p. 266. For Hume and Mandeville, see also Mikko Tolonen, *Mandeville and Hume: Anatomists of Civil Society* (Oxford, 2013).

The main reason he gave against a Jacobite restoration was the need to avoid a civil war, and he arrived at this conclusion only after he had given a fair consideration to the counter-arguments. It was clear to him that obedience was the general rule and that resistance to the established government was only permitted in cases of egregious tyranny like that of Nero, and the Hanoverian kings did not come close. Although Hume's exact arguments only come alive when considered in their specific contexts, he set a gold standard for all subsequent debaters aspiring to moderation amid tribal strife. While it may not be possible to label even a balance-sheet Hanoverian a non-partisan in an age when dynastic conflict continued to play a role, he may have approximated that ideal as far as was possible in a divided society.

CHAPTER 10

Hume on Eloquence and the Failings of English Political Oratory[*]

Ross Carroll

Hume lived just long enough to witness the start of a promising period in the history of English political oratory. Charles James Fox and Edmund Burke had already made their mark in the House of Commons before Hume's death in 1776. The commotions caused by Parliament's repeated refusal to seat the radical John Wilkes as member of parliament (MP) for Middlesex, and the crisis surrounding Britain's contested sovereignty over its American colonies, occasioned Parliamentary exchanges that gripped the public's attention. The end of the suppression of Parliamentary reports in 1771 (an outcome of the Wilkes crisis) made speeches in the House of Commons more accessible for public consumption, commentary, and criticism. Early anthologies of noteworthy Parliamentary speeches – such as William Hazlitt's *The Eloquence of the British Senate* and Thomas Browne's *The British Cicero* (both early 1800s) – featured examples from the final decades of Hume's life. By the early nineteenth century, critics were confident that English orators now rivalled the best speakers from the ancient world. It 'cannot be denied', Thomas Browne declared, 'that Britain, as well as Greece and Rome, has had her Demostheneses and her Ciceros'.[1]

When Hume published the essay 'Of Eloquence' in 1742, however, this golden age of English oratory still lay in the distant future. What puzzled Hume in this essay was not only that English parliamentarians had failed to emulate the great orators of classical antiquity but also that they had ceased to even try.[2] Despite enjoying a perfect venue in the House of

[*] I would like to thank the Exeter Political Theory Reading Group for discussing Hume's essay with me and helping me gather my thoughts on it. I would also like to thank Celeste McNamara for discussing and commenting on the final version.

[1] Thomas Browne, *The British Cicero: Or, A Selection of the Most Admired Speeches in the English Language* (Philadelphia, 1810), p. iii.

[2] Hume was not alone in despairing of the quality of British eloquence. Hazlitt warned that readers who expected to find only eloquent speeches in his collection would be disappointed: 'a very small

Commons – a chamber that Hume considered primed for oratorical contests on affairs of state – few MPs had delivered speeches worth taking 'pains to preserve', or even considered it worthwhile to study classical eloquence.[3] English speakers were instead workman-like in their approach, Hume complained, producing an eloquence of consistent 'mediocrity'.[4] In this they resembled London 'cabinet-makers' who dependably churned out serviceable furniture but who rarely raised their sights higher than that.[5] Small wonder, Hume remarked, that Parliamentary debates in the early 1740s attracted little public notice. The most 'celebrated' English speakers, he archly observed, were considered not worth skipping dinner to hear.[6] Not even the Prime Minister, Sir Robert Walpole, defending himself from 'removal or impeachment', could provide sufficient spectacle to compete with a new play by Colley Cibber, the comedic actor and playwright whose memoirs had recently been published.[7] It is hard to imagine a more damning verdict delivered in a more disparaging tone.

If Hume was confounded by the paltry state of English eloquence, Hume scholars have in turn been confounded by this essay.[8] The source of bafflement is twofold. First, it is unusual for Hume to overtly champion ancient examples of political practice, particularly given his sensitivity to the historical gulf separating ancient and modern societies, and his unease with the demagoguery he considered characteristic of ancient polities. Second, for many of its readers, 'Of Eloquence' risks incoherence because Hume seems to backtrack in the essay's final paragraphs on his initial recommendation that English orators emulate the ancients. What begins as a forceful call for an English Demosthenes to step up seems to end on a note of hesitation over whether reviving classical eloquence is really such a good idea after all.

---

volume indeed would contain all the recorded eloquence of both Houses of Parliament'. William Hazlitt, *The Eloquence of the British Senate: Being a Selection of the Best Speeches of the Most Distinguished Parliamentary Speakers, from the Beginning of the Reign of Charles I to the Present Time: With Notes, Biographical, Critical and Explanatory* (London, 1808), I, p. vii. Other observers offered a more upbeat assessment of the British oratory of this period. The 1739 Parliamentary debates over whether Britain should escalate its imperial trade disputes with Spain to the point of war gave rise to a few speeches that, according to Voltaire, came close to the 'spirit of Demosthenes and of Cicero.' See Voltaire, 'Eloquence', in *The Encyclopedia of Diderot & d'Alembert Collaborative Translation Project*, trans. Theodore E. D. Braun (Ann Arbor, MI, 2004).
[3] *E* (LF), p. 99, *E* (C), p. 93.   [4] Ibid.   [5] Ibid.   [6] *E* (LF), p. 100, *E* (C), p. 93.   [7] Ibid.
[8] As Catherine Packham notes, the 'contradictions and conscious ironies' of this essay have generated 'considerable interpretive difficulties'. Catherine Packham, 'Cicero's Ears, or Eloquence in the Age of Politeness: Oratory, Moderation, and the Sublime in Enlightenment Scotland', *Eighteenth-Century Studies*, 46 (2013), pp. 499–512, at p. 500.

In this chapter, I examine Hume's argument step-by-step and make the case for why there is less need for bafflement than might at first appear. In doing so, I will (mostly) heed Hume's 'Advertisement' to the first (1741) volume of the *Essays*, where he requested that each essay be read on its own terms as a 'work apart'.[9] Whatever the relationship between 'Of Eloquence' and the rest of Hume's thought, I maintain, the essay does possess an underlying coherence and offers a compelling account of both why English oratory had lagged behind that of other nations such as France and how it could yet be reformed. Crucial to Hume's argument, I contend, is that any viable explanation of the inferiority of English oratory had to go beyond generic comparisons between ancient and modern societies. Rather, for Hume, this was a specifically English problem with roots in the English national character. If the revival of classical eloquence that Hume desired looked like it was failing, I conclude, this was due less to the unsuitability of pathetic speech to a modern commercial society, than to the peculiar place of Parliament in Britain's mixed constitutional order.

10.1   Hume and the Case for Sublime Oratory

What was it that made English eloquence so deficient in Hume's estimation? The comparison between Walpole's speeches and Cibber's comedies might suggest that English orators had simply failed to entertain their audiences. For Hume, however, the problem was far deeper and more consequential than that. Along with many of his fellow travellers in the Scottish *literati*, Hume considered the power to persuade as vital to human sociability in general, and to the smooth functioning of commercial society in particular. As Hume's friend Adam Smith would observe, the 'naturall inclination everyone has to persuade' meant that, in effect, 'every one is practising oratory on others thro the whole of his life' (even the mundane economic activities of trucking and bartering, Smith joked, qualified as a kind of 'oratory').[10] In this respect, political oratory was only a more advanced version of an everyday skill that all members of a modern society should learn.

When it came to the goals of political speech making, Hume inherited from François Fénelon an understanding of the political orator's role as

---

[9] *E* (C), p. 529.
[10] Adam Smith, *Lectures on Jurisprudence*, eds. R. L. Meek, D. D. Raphael, and Peter Stein (Oxford, 1978), p. 352; Nicholas Phillipson, *Adam Smith: An Enlightened Life* (New Haven, CT, 2012), p. 101.

both instructor and improver of his audience.[11] A speaker who aimed only to provide frivolous amusement or gain temporary advantage in a debate was debasing their art, regardless of how pleased the audience might be with their performance. Rather, what was lacking in English political oratory, Hume insisted, were speeches that could seize the imagination of their hearers, inflame their emotions, and ultimately shape their collective will on matters of public importance.[12] The missing ingredient in English political oratory, in other words, was not argument or sound reasoning, but sublimity. In this respect, Hume urged English orators to emulate authors such as Lord Bolingbroke, who produced a 'force and energy' with the written word that few (presumably including Bolingbroke himself) had matched with the spoken.[13]

Lamenting the lack of sublimity in political speech was not typical in Hume's day. For many of his contemporaries, sublime speech that could stun, entrance, enrapture, and even terrify an audience was often better suited to churches than to the floor of the House of Commons. Addison and Steele's *Spectator* (an inspiration for Hume's *Essays*) had argued that the moderns enjoyed a critical advantage over the ancients when it came to the sublime because Christianity furnished modern speakers with ideas that were 'infinitely enlarged'.[14] Closer to home, Hume's friend and ally in the Scottish Kirk, Hugh Blair, found that a sublime eloquence by which listeners are 'not only convinced, but are interested, agitated, and carried along with the Speaker' could be found not only in the transactions of 'popular assemblies' such as Parliament but also in the 'pulpit'.[15] For Blair, if the moderns were to close the gap on the ancients it would be largely attributable to the clerical profession, which 'gives peculiar advantages to Oratory, and affords it the noblest field'.[16]

Central to Hume's argument in 'Of Eloquence', by contrast, was that fearful contemplation of sin, death, or the afterlife should not be necessary to generate sublimity; rather, the day-to-day business of politics in an imperial metropole such as London provided more than ample material for sublime utterance. A political orator addressing a matter of constitutional

---

[11] François Fénelon, *Oeuvres diverses de Fénelon: Dialogues sur l'éloquence* (Paris, 1824).
[12] As Hume had noted in *Treatise of Human Nature*, the power of eloquence was nearly limitless: 'Nothing is more capable of infusing any passion into the mind, than eloquence, by which objects are presented in their strongest and most lively colours' (*T*, p. 273).
[13] *E* (LF), p. 109, *E* (C), p. 99.
[14] Joseph Addison and Richard Steele, 'No. 633', in Joseph Addison and Richard Steele, *The Spectator*, ed. Donald F. Bond (5 vols., Oxford, 1965), V, p. 164.
[15] Hugh Blair, *Lectures on Rhetoric and Belles Lettres* (3 vols., Dublin, 1783), II, p. 171.
[16] Ibid., II, p. 211.

propriety or political right should be able to shock, instruct, and delight their listeners all at once. By limiting themselves to conveying reasonable arguments in an orderly manner, English orators had needlessly forsaken this awesome power.

Given what Hume says elsewhere about the dangers of demagoguery, we might have expected him to applaud the more sedate style that English orators had developed rather than criticise it. This is especially the case considering that Hume associated sublime orators with democracy and republicanism, forms of politics towards which he was generally ambivalent. And yet Hume regarded the failure of English orators to achieve sublimity as not only aesthetically disappointing but politically disastrous. The inability to persuade an audience would have mattered less in an absolute monarchy where political speech took the form of either flattery or command. The situation was quite different in a more 'popular government' such as Britain's, where 'numerous assemblies' of representatives decided affairs of state by deliberation, persuasion, and voting.[17] In that context, orators capable of activating the imaginations of an audience were not a luxury; they were indispensable.

To alleviate the poverty of English eloquence, Hume recommended imitation of two ancient orators in particular: Demosthenes and Cicero.[18] This pair was remarkable, Hume argued, not only for the composition of their speeches but also for the vocal delivery and physical gestures they used to move their listeners. When Demosthenes or Cicero rose to speak, they accompanied their words with a 'vehemence of action' that English orators considered embarrassingly out of place in a national legislature.[19] Later in the eighteenth century, MPs would engage in all sorts of sentimentalised theatrics, from fainting at the end of speeches (as Richard Brinsley Sheridan did at the impeachment trial of the Governor of Bengal, Warren Hastings) to tossing daggers onto the floor of the House (as Burke would do to illustrate the danger of failing to counter a regicidal French republic). For Hume in 1742, however, English speakers were as tepid in their movements as they were in their speech. There was little

---

[17] In 'Of the Rise and Progress of the Arts of Sciences', Hume considered it uncontroversial that eloquence 'springs up more naturally in popular governments' whereas despotism stifles it. *E* (LF), p. 119, *E* (C), p. 106. For the history of the argument that political liberty and eloquence were mutually supportive, see Jean Starobinski, 'Eloquence and Liberty', *Journal of the History of Ideas*, 38 (1977), pp. 195–210.

[18] Although Marc Hanvelt has argued, with good reason, that of these two it was Demosthenes rather than Cicero who was the model for Hume's ideal orator. See Hanvelt, *The Politics of Eloquence: David Hume's Polite Rhetoric* (Toronto, 2012), p. 11.

[19] *E* (LF), p. 101, *E* (C), p. 94.

gesticulation with the hands, and the ancient practice of *supplosio pedis* (stamping the foot for dramatic effect) had so offended English taste that it had been restricted to theatres where actors still used it to communicate the 'most violent passions'.[20]

It was typical of Hume's method as philosopher and essayist to identify a gulf separating the manners and practices of ancient societies from those of modern, commercial states. In most cases, Hume either regarded these differences as unbridgeable or welcomed the displacement of ancient rusticity by modern refinements.[21] What has intrigued readers of this essay, however, is Hume's insistence that a return to some form of ancient sublimity was *both* possible and desirable.[22] 'Shall we assert', he asked rhetorically, 'that the strains of ancient eloquence are unsuitable to our age, and ought not to be imitated by modern orators?'[23] Hume answered his own question emphatically in the negative. Anticipating that such an answer would be controversial, Hume next presented three counter-arguments that apologists for English oratory might raise, none of which, as we shall see, he saw as excusing the weakness of English speeches.

10.2   Three Weak Excuses: Law, Good Sense, and the Absence of Political Disorder

The first objection that Hume considered was that the arduous, compli-cated, and technical nature of modern legal learning had rendered orator-ical study impossible or not worth the effort. Ancient orators could master the laws of their states with relative ease, leaving them sufficient leisure to hone their speaking skills. The modern student of law had no such luck. Studying law was a full-time commitment in eighteenth-century Britain, 'requiring the drudgery of a whole life to finish it'.[24] Hume was very well placed to make such a judgement.[25] He had embarked on legal studies at

---

[20] *E* (LF), p. 102, *E* (C), p. 94.
[21] As Peter Jones puts it, Hume's 'admiration for recent political progress and material advance [. . .] aligned him with the moderns'. See Peter Jones, 'Hume on the Arts and "The Standard of Taste": Texts and Contexts', in David Fate Norton and Jacqueline Taylor, eds., *The Cambridge Companion to Hume* (Cambridge, 2008), pp. 424–25. According to his most recent biographer, Hume had no 'nostalgia for a lost past' when it came to comparisons between the ancients and moderns. See James A. Harris, *Hume: An Intellectual Biography* (Cambridge, 2015), p. 150.
[22] As Potkay puts it, it is surprising to see Hume 'conjuring an image of a more ardent age, and regretting its passing'. See Adam Potkay, *The Fate of Eloquence in the Age of Hume* (Ithaca, NY, 1994), p. 26.
[23] *E* (LF), p. 102, *E* (C), p. 95.   [24] Ibid.
[25] According to Mossner, Hume here speaks from 'bitter personal experience'. See Ernest Campbell Mossner, *The Life of David Hume*, 2nd ed. (Oxford, 1980), p. 55.

the University of Edinburgh in his teenage years, eventually abandoning law for philosophy (having been seduced by the work of Cicero, one of his ideal orators).[26] The issue here was not only that modern law was more 'toilsome' to study than the ancient but also that the *audience* for legal argument had changed fundamentally.[27] The ancient speaker had to appeal to the 'equity and common sense of his judges', and so could deploy a wide array of persuasive techniques and emotive ploys.[28] By contrast, modern lawyers found themselves constrained by a dense thicket of conventions regarding everything from standards of evidence to the range of permissible arguments. If a lawyer pleading before a judge launched into a harangue or worked themselves into a frenzy, they risked being laughed at or dismissed out of hand.

    Hume conceded these differences but minimised their importance to the question at hand. Changes in legal culture could only account for the lack of grand speeches in legal tribunals and not all modern speeches were juridical in nature. Alluding to a key Aristotelian distinction, Hume pleaded that even if the *forensic* oratory of the courts had sunk into a technical jargon, the *deliberative* oratory of Parliament should remain untouched. This portion of Hume's argument echoed earlier reflections on eloquence from within the tradition of English republicanism, a tradition with which Hume was on ambivalent terms.[29] In 'Of Eloquence Considered Politically', published in his *Cato's Letters* of 1722, the commonwealth man John Trenchard had similarly found English legal culture hostile to the orator's art. A 'Hurricane of Tropes and Impetuous words' would be a 'waste' at the bar, he observed, and it was unsurprising that 'many excellent pleaders have been bad orators'.[30] But this in no way detracted from the importance of eloquence to free states where 'men are dealt with using reason and persuasion'.[31] For Trenchard, the kinds of speech that had long been excluded from the courts should still find a home in popular assemblies. Hume agreed.[32] The 'intricacy' of modern

[26] On the significance of Cicero to Hume's overall philosophical trajectory see Tim Stuart-Buttle, *From Moral Theology to Moral Philosophy: Cicero and Visions of Humanity from Locke to Hume* (Oxford, 2019), ch. 5.

[27] *E* (LF), p. 102, *E* (C), p. 95.   [28] Ibid.

[29] James Moore, 'Hume's Political Science and the Classical Republican Tradition', *Canadian Journal of Political Science / Revue Canadienne de Science Politique*, 10 (1977), pp. 809–39.

[30] John Trenchard, *Cato's Letters: Or, Essays on Liberty, Civil and Religious, and Other Important Subjects* (4 vols., London, 1755), III, p. 319.

[31] Ibid., III, p. 313.

[32] Goodman points out that Hume here is, if anything, 'more ready to mourn' the decline of classical eloquence than Trenchard was. See Rob Goodman, *Words on Fire: Eloquence and Its Conditions* (Cambridge, 2021), p. 92.

law, he held, 'might banish oratory from Westminster Hall, but not from either house of Parliament'.[33] So long as Parliament remained a place of consequential decision-making – and Hume's overall assessment of British politics at the end of the Walpole era suggested that this was still very much the case – then it was incumbent upon English orators to produce the kind of performances appropriate to deliberations on affairs of public importance.

The second challenge to Hume's argument was less easily overcome. Even if English orators could successfully imitate the pathos of the ancients, would they have any effect on a people whose 'modern customs' and general sobriety rendered them immune to emotional stimulation and wise to rhetorical tricks?[34] Hume's initial response to this objection was uncharacteristically weak and amounted to little more than urging English orators to try harder. After all, ancient orators also had to overcome audiences suspicious of attempts to play on their emotions. The difference, Hume continued, was that ancient orators had enough skill to evade their audience's defences. Paraphrasing Longinus's *On the Sublime*, Hume admired how a Cicero or a Demosthenes could send a 'torrent of sublime and pathetic' gushing forth that would catch their audiences unawares and leave them no time to spot the 'artifice by which they were deceived'.[35] Besides, the moderns had no monopoly on good sense. Julius Caesar, Hume notes, had as much good sense as any modern, but even he was occasionally 'subdued by the charms of CICERO's eloquence'.[36]

Hume had so little patience with the notion that modern orators were limited by their audience's tastes and inclinations because he had a more exalted sense of the skills a political orator should possess. For him, a quality speaker should not only *account* for their audience's taste; they should also *shape* that taste to their advantage and to the public good. The point of persuasion would be lost if speakers confined themselves to a style and content that their audience already found agreeable. In the case of Athens, Hume declared in a footnote, the orators 'formed the taste' of the people, not the other way around.[37] When orators cited the 'taste of their hearers' as an excuse for their 'lame performances', this only exposed their lack of talent and ambition.[38] In any case, he concluded, even the most average parliamentarian should be able to listen to a sublime speech, be moved by it, and appreciate the craft it displayed. For modern orators to claim otherwise was needlessly self-deprecating: 'It would be a strange

---

[33] *E* (LF), p. 103, *E* (C), p. 95.   [34] *E* (LF), p. 104, *E* (C), p. 96.   [35] Ibid.
[36] *E* (LF), p. 105, *E* (C), p. 96.   [37] *E* (LF), p. 105n16, *E* (C), p. 97n6.   [38] Ibid.

prejudice in favour of antiquity, not to allow a British parliament to be naturally superior in judgment and delicacy to an ATHENIAN mob.'[39] If a raucous Athenian assembly was no obstacle to quality eloquence, then a chamber of MPs with pretensions to gentility should not be either.

It is clear from this part of the essay that Hume regarded oratorical persuasion as involving far more than emotional manipulation. An eloquence that was too 'florid and rhetorical' (as Hume thought Cicero's occasionally had been) was inferior to one that delivered a 'continued stream of argument', as Demosthenes' always did.[40] The 'reasoning' characteristic of Demosthenes's speeches may have been 'vehement', but this was reasoning, nonetheless.[41] A political culture supportive of eloquence thus had to nourish both sensibility and critical judgement all at once.

But what kind of political conditions could foster such a culture? The third criticism Hume anticipated centred on precisely this issue. According to this new objection, ancient eloquence was so sublime only because the 'disorders' characteristic of ancient republics, coupled with the 'enormous crimes' committed by their citizens, gave more 'ample matter for eloquence' than moderns had available to them.[42] The greater the degree of civil dispute in a state, so this argument went, the more propitious the climate for orators. The claim that disorders created a fertile climate for oratory had some pedigree in that both critics and supporters of republicanism had long maintained that the contentiousness of republican politics fuelled eloquence. In the *Dialogue on Orators*, Tacitus has Maternus disregard eloquence as the 'offspring of license, which fools call liberty', a form of speech that could only flourish so long as the Roman state 'weakened itself by partisan politics and dissension and discord'.[43] By contrast, Maternus concludes, Romans should be grateful that the rise of the *Principate* had created a stable political order in which the 'prestige of orators is less and their glory duller' among a people now ready to settle down and 'obey their ruler'.[44] Trenchard had revived that argument, though he looked kindlier towards republican freedom. Although eloquence could be abused for purposes of rabble-rousing or deception, he maintained, this was 'an evil growing out of much good; and nothing but the abolishing of all liberty and learning can absolutely cure it'.[45]

[39] Ibid.   [40] *E* (LF), pp. 105–6, *E* (C), p. 97.   [41] *E* (LF), p. 105, *E* (C), p. 97.
[42] *E* (LF), p. 106, *E* (C), p. 97.
[43] Tacitus, *Agricola, Germany and Dialogue on Orators*, trans. Herbert W. Benario (London, 1991), p. 129.
[44] Ibid., pp. 129–30.   [45] Trenchard, *Cato's Letters*, III, p. 321.

Hume largely agreed. For Hume, modern British politics had no shortage of great public villains ('it would be easy to find a PHILIP in modern times') and there was no reason to assume that the disorders that facilitated ancient eloquence were a thing of the past.[46] To prove his point, Hume might have reminded his readers of the Jacobite uprising that had shaken the Anglo-Scottish union in 1715. Instead, he reached further back to the mid seventeenth century. The Wars of the Three Kingdoms in the 1640s represented the moment when 'BRITISH CICEROS' could have emerged and secured the future of English oratory.[47] For it was during that tumultuous time that 'liberty began to be established', along with government by 'popular assemblies'.[48] Hume did not speculate as to why these promising conditions yielded so little, other than to chalk it up to historical contingency. The emergence of any art or science occurs at least partly by accident and, in this respect, eloquence was no different.[49] All the same, even if disorder and public crimes were necessary conditions for good oratory, these had not been confined to the past.

Having dispensed with this last possible excuse for the poverty of English eloquence, Hume repeated his earlier prompting for English speakers to aim higher. Even a 'few successful attempts' at eloquence could 'rouze the genius of the nation', set an example to the youth, and elicit a taste for sublime oratory among the English once again.[50] English eloquence could yet be set ablaze; all that was required was for someone to produce a few sparks.

10.3   Eloquence and the English National Character

Had Hume ended his essay there, then it would have been a mostly unremarkable addition to the long literature comparing the cultural achievements of the ancients and moderns. He did not, however. Instead, Hume turned to explain why English eloquence paled in comparison, not only to antiquity but also to that found in other European states. It was this new explanation, I now suggest, that set Hume's essay

---

[46] *E* (LF), p. 106, *E* (C), p. 97.   [47] *E* (LF), p. 107, *E* (C), p. 98.
[48] *E* (LF), p. 106, *E* (C), p. 98.
[49] Later, in his *History of England*, Hume would expand on what had gone wrong at this crucial juncture. Because civil wars were 'not unfavorable' to the 'arts of eloquence', he wrote, this period produced Parliamentary speeches 'much superior' to those in any other age. But the rise of Cromwell and his military dictatorship put an end to favourable conditions for oratory (*HE*, VI, p. 150).
[50] *E* (LF), p. 106, *E* (C), p. 97.

apart from the battle between ancients and moderns and brought it instead into the realm of comparative cultural inquiry. Rowing back a bit from his claim that the emergence of any art owes much to randomness and chance, Hume pondered whether something specific to the English national character might be to blame. After all, other 'learned and polite nations' such as France had achieved sublime eloquence under far less favourable political circumstances.[51] What the French example proved categorically was that a speaker with a genius for eloquence will manage to showcase their talents, even when deprived of a suitable setting or weighty subject matter.

Hume illustrated French oratorical superiority with two telling examples. First, the French had shown that a modern law court could be a refuge for eloquence, by contrast with the inhospitable environment provided by English courts. The lawyer Olivier Patru, Hume remarked, never had the opportunity to address an assembly on questions of peace and war. But this never stopped him from achieving sublimity in 'debates concerning the price of an old horse, or a gossiping story of a quarrel betwixt an abbess and her nuns'.[52] No subject was so lowly that French lawyers could not generate sublimity when addressing it. On the rare occasions when the Paris *parlement* preoccupied itself with state affairs, such as during the commotions caused by the Mazarin ministry, speakers such as the *avocat général* Omer Talon (renowned for his thundering speeches defending the *parlement's* prerogatives) provided glimpses of what French eloquence could attain in an atmosphere of greater public freedom.

Second, the French had shown that sublimity could be achieved in speeches that had no other object than flattery. In the tradition of Longinus and Tacitus, flattery was a corruption of eloquence and a form of speech whose popularity signalled the death of a republican politics premised on persuasion among equals. For Hume, however, the 'panegyric and flattery' of French men of letters could reach the sublime, particularly in the context of admission ceremonies to the *Académie Française*.[53] To gain admission to the *Académie*, candidates were obliged to deliver speeches in praise of a vacant seat's previous occupant. On the surface at least, these addresses seemed unlikely to produce the kind of sublimity Hume was advocating. But despite having only the 'most barren of all subjects' to work with, these speakers produced a sublime style that would only improve if applied to a more 'engaging' subject.[54] Again, French genius could prevail over any obstacle.

---

[51] *E* (LF), p. 621, *E* (C), p. 579.   [52] *E* (LF), p. 621, *E* (C), p. 580.
[53] *E* (LF), p. 622, *E* (C), p. 580.   [54] Ibid.

Such praise for French oratorical efforts only made Hume's indictment of English oratory appear even more damning. Wishing, perhaps, to soften the blow for English readers, Hume speculated that English oratorical failings could be attributable to national character traits that were otherwise commendable. Hume now declared '*good sense*' – which he had earlier associated with the moderns more generally – to be a peculiarly English characteristic that explained English repugnance towards emotive speech.[55] English modesty, he added, could also explain why the English rebuffed any speech that sounded too lofty or grand. Considered in light of Hume's overall analysis, however, this was not much of a compliment. As Hume had made clear earlier in the essay, a sullen determination to repel the effects of oratory was not a point of pride. On the contrary, a lack of openness to being moved could signal rigidity, stiffness, and dogmatism just as easily as sobriety. As Hume understood it, eloquence – and the free political life associated with it – was a collaborative venture, requiring both skilled speakers and a receptive audience working in tandem.

Hume rounded off this discussion of English national character on an almost apologetic note:

> I may perhaps be allow'd to add, that the [English] people in general are not remarkable for Delicacy of Taste, or for Sensibility to the Charms of the Muses. Their *musical Parts*, to use the Expression of a noble Author, are but indifferent. Hence their Comic Poets to move them, must have recourse to obscenity, their Tragic Poets to Blood and Slaughter: And hence their Orators, being depriv'd of any such Recourse, have abandoned altogether the Hopes of Moving them, and have confined themselves to plain Argument and Reasoning.[56]

This general dullness of taste, Hume continued, had delayed England's oratorical progress. But this dismal situation was not fated to last. Switching to prophetic mode, Hume imagined that a young man might yet appear in Parliament who would 'accustom our ears' to a more commanding eloquence and allow the English public to finally realise what they had been missing.[57]

Hume's attempt to explain the state of English oratory with reference to the English national character set an important precedent that other philosophers followed. Adam Smith would ascribe the English preference for a 'plain, distinct, and perspicuous Stile' to the 'particular turn of the people' rather than to modern refinement as such.[58] He also followed

---

[55] Ibid.   [56] *E* (LF), p. 622, *E* (C), p. 581.   [57] Ibid.
[58] Adam Smith, *Lectures on Rhetoric and Belles Lettres*, ed. J. C. Bryce (Oxford, 1983), p. 196.

Hume in contrasting England with France to place the specificities of English oratorical culture into sharper relief.[59] The Scottish Enlightenment's other great *belle-lettrist*, Hugh Blair, also followed Hume in emphasising English exceptionalism. In his *Lectures on Rhetoric and Belles Lettres*, Blair paraphrased whole swathes of Hume's essay, borrowing several of Hume's examples, from Patru to the *Académie Française*. But where Blair departed from Hume was in his confidence that the lack of sublimity in English oratory could actually be easily explained. Whereas 'Mr Hume, in his Essay on Eloquence, [. . .] supposes, that no satisfactory reasons can be given to account for the inferiority of modern to antient Eloquence', Blair declared in a footnote, 'In this, I differ from him.'[60] This was a slight misreading of Hume's objective in that Hume sought the proximate causes of English oratorical weaknesses rather than those of the moderns as such. Telling, however, is that Blair's attempt to improve on Hume's arguments remained firmly within the parameters that Hume's essay had set. English national character, for Blair, remained the decisive factor. The English court, English common sense, and 'our phlegm and natural coldness' had dampened demand for high oratory, much as Hume himself had acknowledged.[61]

Hume's national character explanation for the state of English oratory also reached south of the border. Joseph Priestley, in his *Course of Lectures on Oratory and Criticism* of 1777, defaulted to an argument based on national character, even as he differed from Hume on the desirability of reviving ancient eloquence. Imploring his readers to resist the temptation to follow the classical example, Priestley returned to the possibility that the English might be too well endowed with common sense to be swayed by orators:

> It is . . . proper that all Englishmen in particular should be informed, that a person of liberal education in this country can hardly ever be in such a situation, as will not render the imitation of some of the boldest, the most successful, and admired strokes of Roman, not to say Grecian eloquence, extremely improper and ridiculous. The English pulpit, the English bar, and the English senate, require an eloquence more addressed to the reason, and less directly to the passions, than the harangues of a Roman pleader, or the speech of a Roman senator. Our hearers have generally more good sense and just discernment [. . .].[62]

---

[59] Ibid., p. 198.   [60] Blair, *Lectures on Rhetoric and Belles Lettres*, II, p. 212.
[61] Ibid., II, p. 217.
[62] Joseph Priestley, *A Course of Lectures on Oratory and Criticism* (London, 1777), p. 113.

Note that Priestley's argument does not rely on the distinction between modern and ancient societies. It is the English national character that renders classical eloquence ridiculous in that particular country. For Priestley, not even the pulpit could provide a refuge for classical eloquence among a people numb to anything other than rational argument.

Hume removed the portion of the essay on English character (three large paragraphs in total) for the 1770 edition of the *Essays*. Quite why he did so is unclear, although one possibility concerns the changed political context. Hume had been appalled at the antics of Wilkes and his followers, which may have diminished his faith in English good sense.[63] He may also have reckoned that passages praising French genius at the expense of English rusticity would be less favourably received in 1770 than in 1742. In the interim, England had fought the Seven Years' War with France, and the commercial, cultural, and political rivalry between the two imperial powers showed no signs of abating. And whereas Blair had presented himself as a member of the culture he described (referring tellingly to '*our* natural coldness'), his fellow-Scot Hume had written as an outside observer of English cultural traits, a more vulnerable position for a philosopher keen to secure the favour of the English learned classes.

There is, however, a more banal explanation available for Hume's decision. By dwelling at length on the coarseness of English taste, Hume had distracted from one of his main polemical points, which was that great orators should be able to win over any audience, regardless of their sobriety or lack of refinement. Even the dullest of audiences should recognise good speaking when they hear it (Demosthenes was able to appeal to the 'lowest vulgar of ATHENS').[64] More than that, towards the end of the essay Hume suggested that when it comes to judging eloquence, refinement might even prove a *disadvantage*. Because the purpose of deliberative eloquence is to persuade large crowds, it is the one art where the common people are the best judges of success. A 'common audience', Hume insists, will offer a truer assessment of a speaker than one made up 'men of science and erudition'.[65] By removing the discussion of the peculiarity of English sensibilities, Hume democratised oratorical taste while at the same time highlighting the uniqueness of eloquence when compared to the other arts and sciences.

---

[63] Potkay, *The Fate of Eloquence in the Age of Hume*. Harris similarly argues that Hume 'presumably' removed this passage because of his 'contempt for the behaviour of John Wilkes and his supporters'. See Harris, *Hume: An Intellectual Biography*, p. 515.
[64] *E* (LF), p. 105, *E* (C), p. 97.   [65] *E* (LF), p. 107, *E* (C), p. 98.

10.4   Giving Up on Classical Eloquence?

For an essay that supposedly champions sublimity, 'Of Eloquence' ends on a drab, even defeatist note.[66] Having just exhorted the English to continue reaching for the sublime, Hume in the final part of the essay appears to accept that this quest is futile. As a sort of compensation prize, English speakers should strive instead to correct a 'material defect' found in most of their speeches, namely, a lack of 'order and method'.[67] At first glance this looks like an odd recommendation, not least because it sits awkwardly with Hume's earlier claim that English oratory relied almost exclusively on calm argument and appeals to reason. On Hume's earlier analysis, English orators had, if anything, privileged orderliness to the detriment of their speeches. Moreover, Hume neither elaborated on what a good method looks like, nor provided an example; he just summoned English speakers to adopt one.

As Hume made clear, however, his specific target here was an excessive fondness among English speakers for extemporising. Hume conceded that overpreparation (the reading out of '*set speeches*' in particular) could make a speaker look awkward and wooden.[68] After all, the rapidly shifting terms of debate in the House of Commons demanded that speakers think on their feet and take account of what had already been said before intervening. For Hume, however, the need to pay attention to the vagaries of a live debate did not negate the need for speakers to organise their thoughts before entering the chamber. Parliamentary procedure required that the questions under consideration be published in advance and even the most seemingly spontaneous speaker should know ahead of time what they plan to say. Hume allowed that a degree of 'invention' may be necessary in the heat of the moment, but the audience should not be able to distinguish between what has been composed and what has been thought up on the spot.[69] If an accomplished speaker has planned carefully, then they should be able to adjust for contingencies while still getting their main point across.

For some commentators, Hume's call for English orators to embrace a more methodical and orderly style represented a retreat from his earlier

---

[66] For Goodman, Hume's essay 'ends at an impasse, petering out in the modest suggestion that members of Parliament might at least spend more time preparing their speeches and less time extemporizing'. See Goodman, *Words on Fire*, p. 92. For Potkay, Hume's ending resembles a 'digression, an afterthought', with all consideration of the sublime now 'vanished'. See Potkay, *The Fate of Eloquence in the Age of Hume*, p. 28.
[67] *E* (LF), p. 109, *E* (C), pp. 99–100.   [68] *E* (LF), p. 109, *E* (C), p. 99.   [69] Ibid.

defence of the sublime, or at the very least an ambivalence about reviving classical eloquence.[70] The shift in Hume's message, however, is not as dramatic as might at first appear, for two reasons. First, Hume had made clear earlier in the essay that although sublime orators might disorder the passions of their audience, they themselves were extremely orderly and precise in their habits of composition. The disruptive effects of a well-crafted speech could mask the orderly method that produced them. Second, Hume insisted that the practice of composing speeches in advance was itself of ancient pedigree. It began, he alleged, with Pericles, a states-man he regarded as a paragon of good sense.[71] Hume's concluding call for order and method was thus consistent with his earlier proposal to emulate ancient practice. When Hume recommended greater order and method, he was not suddenly making peace with the drift of modern eloquence away from the sublime.[72]

If Hume cannot be faulted for incoherence, he might nonetheless be judged to have underestimated the political obstacles that lay in the way of reviving classical eloquence. It was critical to Hume's case that the House of Commons was already a suitable venue for a new Demosthenes to emerge because it was a place where deliberative oratory could exercise a determining influence on public affairs. But was this an accurate descrip-tion at the time? Blair, whose commentary on 'Of Eloquence' was other-wise complimentary, had his doubts on this score. As he pointed out, Hume had possibly overstated the similarity between the popular assem-blies of Athens or Rome and the eighteenth-century House of Commons. Too often, Blair noted, the independence of the House of Commons had been compromised either by the 'high hand of arbitrary power' (presum-ably a reference to the Tudors and Stuarts) or, more recently, by 'minis-terial influence'.[73] If the important business of Parliament was minutely managed by ministers of the Crown, then the prospects of reviving classical eloquence were slim. Parliamentarians more preoccupied with Court favour than the judgement of their peers were unlikely either to attempt sublime speeches themselves or pay much heed to anyone who did. Thus,

---

[70] Potkay, *The Fate of Eloquence in the Age of Hume*, p. 60. For Goodman, these passages show that Hume was nostalgic for classical eloquence but was 'unable or willing to imagine what its return might look like'. See Goodman, *Words on Fire*, p. 92.

[71] His source here is Suidas.

[72] In this respect, I disagree with Packham who finds that Hume, by recommending the 'banalities of proper order and method' set up a 'confrontation between styles, between mediocrity and transcendent excess'. The sublime has an order and method of its own. See Packham, 'Cicero's Ears, or Eloquence in the Age of Politeness', p. 501.

[73] Blair, *Lectures on Rhetoric and Belles Lettres*, II, p. 217.

in Blair's judgement, both the motivation for classical eloquence and the necessary receptive audience were equally lacking in England's political system.

Hume, of course, had plenty to say elsewhere in the *Essays* about the place of Parliament in Britain's constitutional order and its complex relationship to the Court. He was not only aware of the influence of the Court on the workings of Parliament but affirmed it as necessary to prevent Parliament from using its power of the purse to dominate the executive. The 'crown has so many offices at its disposal', he wrote in 'Of the Independency of Parliament', that 'when assisted by the honest, and disinterested part of the house, it will always command the resolutions of the whole'.[74] But where some saw corruption, Hume saw a necessary constitutional counterweight that was 'necessary to the preservation of our mixed government'.[75] What this means, in effect, was that Hume was making an even bigger ask of English parliamentarians in 'Of Eloquence' than at first appeared. To succeed, they had to overcome not only the distaste for sublimity inherent to the English national character but also the constraints imposed by England's peculiar constitutional order. For in that order, a popular assembly was never just a popular assembly, and deliberative oratory had always to compete for the attention of listeners with the distant directives and inducements of the Court.

[74] *E* (LF), p. 45, *E* (C), pp. 58–59. I would like to thank Iain Hampsher-Monk for alerting me to the relevance of this essay to Hume's discussion of eloquence.
[75] *E* (LF), p. 45, *E* (C), p. 59.

PART IV

Political Economy

CHAPTER 11

Hume and Population

Sylvana Tomaselli

'In 1751, I removed from the country to the town, the true scene of a man of letters', wrote Hume in 'My Own Life'.[1] The biographical sketch, the brevity of which was in character insofar as Hume, he insisted, did not wish to appear vain, places him as if on a tide: in and out of the country, in and out of towns, in and out of retreat, in and out of Scotland, and in and out of France. Of a different movement were Hume's wealth and his fame, both of which grew according to his account, the first steadily, almost exponentially, the other not so, but upwards overall, whilst his health, also following a line, but in the opposite direction, steadily declined, he tells us, from the spring of 1775 to his death in the summer of 1776. Hume made no secret of his 'love of literary fame', acknowledging it to have been his 'ruling passion'.[2] He did not say this of money, but the rather unexpected declarations of his exact affluence at any one stage of his life leave no doubt as to his desire for, and pride in, financial independence. Together with that of his standing in the public eye, the record of his worth makes up an Ariadne thread of his narrative. Hume does reveal more than this about himself; amongst other revelations from a man who wished to eschew vanity, he did seem to mind what was thought not only of his writings but also of his person. The latter is illustrated in these autobiographical pages by his observing in the concluding remarks that '[m]y company was not unacceptable to the young and careless, as well as to the studious and literary; and as I took a particular pleasure in the company of modest women, I had no reason to be displeased with the reception I met with them'.[3] This self-presentation may come to mind in reading his *Essays*.

Following his move to 'the true scene for a man of letters' in 1751, Hume tells us that '[i]n 1752, were published at Edinburgh, where I then lived, my Political Discourses, the only work of mine that was successful on the first publication'.[4] It was, he wrote, 'well received abroad and at

<hr>

[1] *HL*, I, p. 3.   [2] Ibid., p. 7.   [3] Ibid.   [4] Ibid., pp. 3–4.

207

home'. By 'abroad', Hume meant France.[5] He had reason also to be pleased by the reception he himself received in Paris. Indeed, he was taken aback by the extent to which he had been feted. It may have contributed to his thought of 'settling there for life'.[6] Whilst he did not do so physically, he remained intellectually.

'My Own Life' has little, if anything to say, about Hume's ideas or the content of those works the repute of which he so much cared. It would thus seem an unpropitious place to turn for selecting which of the plethora of topics his *Essays* discuss or indeed why Hume himself chose those topics. Naturally, most were of the time, and one might say they were chosen for him by ongoing conversations and the spirit of the age. Even so, it is not altogether arbitrary to pursue some of the leads Hume's end of life self-portrait offers as entry points into the *Essays*, the first of which he had initially written more than three decades earlier. Money and opinion resonate in both. And there is also the matter of France and the French, as 'My Own Life' tells us that 'had not the war been at the time breaking out between France and England, I had certainly retired to some provincial town of the former kingdom, have changed my name, and never more have returned to my native country'.[7] To have done so might have ended Hume's career or identity as a man of letters, since he thought towns to be their proper milieu, thereby linking urbanity with a specific form of intellectual modality. He might then have been only a philosopher or a historian. However, on accepting, having first declined, the Earl of Hertford's invitation in 1763 to act as Secretary to the British Embassy, his second visit to France was principally to its capital. It was there that he received an exceptional welcome 'from men and women of all ranks and stations'.[8] It was the wish to settle in Paris that he most enthusiastically recounted over a decade later. 'There is', he wrote, 'a real satisfaction in living in Paris, from the great number of sensible, knowing, and polite company with which that city abounds above all places in the universe'.[9] Numbers mattered as well as quality. Hume enjoyed conversational intellectual engagement in person and on paper, and that too needs to be remembered.

Hume's reception in Paris owed much to the popularity of the *Essays*.[10] But a bridge between him and France was already built some years earlier,

---

[5] See Chapter 3 by Laura Nicolì in the present volume.   [6] *HL*, I, p. 6.   [7] Ibid., p. 4.
[8] Ibid., p. 6.   [9] Ibid.
[10] On Hume's reception in Europe, see Alix Cohen, 'The Making of a Philosophical Classic: The Reception of David Hume in Europe', *Rivista di Storia della Filosofia*, 62 (2007), pp. 457–68.

if only by his correspondence from 1749 with Montesquieu.[11] The early popularity in France of the *Political Discourses*, which were translated in 1754 by the abbé Le Blanc and went to a number of early editions,[12] may be partly owed to 'President Montesquieu', as Hume addressed him, and Hume's engagement with some of the Frenchman's views as expressed in both *Lettres Persanes* (1721) and *L'Esprit de Lois* (1748). Most notable amongst these are Montesquieu's apparent demographic contentions and related comments on sexual behaviour, marriage, and divorce as well as political institutions. Not only did they spur Hume's longest essay, 'more than a third of the three hundred pages of the *Political Discourses*', as James Harris has noted,[13] and may explain several of the chosen topics for his *Essays*, but they helped kindle demographic controversy.[14] 'Of the Populousness of Ancient Nations' appeared first in the first edition of *Political Discourses*' in 1752, as well as its second, and the third in 1754. It is not Hume's most systematic essay. Indeed, it reads like Hume's part in a long-drawn-out conversation. Its title may account for the relatively little scholarly interest it appears to be attracting, but within layers of classical references extensively footnoted are to be found several of Hume's interesting views on history, human nature, and politics. Its engagement with the widely celebrated Montesquieu as well as the Dutch-born scholar, and later residential canon of St George's Chapel, Windsor, Isaac Vossius (1612–89) afforded Hume a pretext for a display of erudition, critical reading, and literary and analytical skills. Here, we might recall his admission of his ruling passion: literary fame.[15]

If Montesquieu helped bolster Hume's reputation, he also benefited from the Scot's writings. Nicos E. Develetoglou, following Oswald Spengler and Joseph A. Schumpeter, suggested that it was largely Montesquieu who 'spread the belief that the population of the world, Europe and France in particular, had diminished' between the sixteenth and mid eighteenth centuries.[16] Hume played a part in that diffusion. Establishing the degree to which Montesquieu's writings shaped eighteenth-century demographic perception is complicated, but his influence was significant. That the ancient

---

[11] *HL*, I, pp. 133–38.   [12] Ibid., pp. 206–9.

[13] James A. Harris, *Hume: An Intellectual Biography* (Cambridge, 2015), p. 284.

[14] Roger B. Oake, 'Montesquieu and Hume', *Modern Language Quarterly*, 2 (1941), pp. 225–48, at p. 234.

[15] Harris notes that the prominence given to ancient literature was to appeal to a readership who took pride in their classical learning (Harris, *Hume*, p. 283).

[16] Nicos E. Develetoglou, 'Montesquieu and the Wealth of Nations', in David Carrithers, ed., *Charles-Louis de Secondat, Baron de Montesquieu* (Farnham, 2009), pp. 497–521, at p. 515.

world was more populated than the modern was, however, a view already propagated, if only by Vossius, who was cited with Montesquieu at the beginning of Hume's essay. Famed for his extensive knowledge of antiquity, Vossius published in 1685 *De Antiquae Romae Magnitudine*, in which he asserted that, in the first century AD, Rome had eight million inhabitants in comparison to modern Europe's thirty million.[17] Montesquieu knew of the work, which together with other sources, such as Jean Chardin's writings on Iran, contributed to his awareness of the then prevalent claims about the populousness of antiquity.[18] Importantly, though unsurprisingly, given the capaciousness of his intellectual ambition, Montesquieu discussed the demographic question in what one might call broadly cultural terms, and thus not principally as a matter of subsistence.[19] It is worth bearing in mind the various considerations put forward in the *Lettres Persanes* (1721) in relation to this subject to see how Hume elected to wade into the debate and to appreciate that from the start the discussion was a complex mix of social and political issues. If what Hume deemed the well-known 'extravagancies of Vossius, about this subject' account for the ('studious and literary') wide-ranging cross-referencing and careful analysis of ancient Greek and Roman historians to be found in the Scot's challenge to the Dutch antiquarian, Montesquieu's interest in the causal relations between mores, social practices, and political institutions help explain the character of the remainder of Hume's essay, and what one might detect as the irony in it.

In the first of the eleven letters of the *Lettres Persanes* devoted to populousness, Montesquieu has one of his cast of correspondents, Rehdi, write to Usbek, a Persian courtier travelling in Europe, that reading ancient and modern histories brought him to this conclusion:

> After doing calculations as exact as is possible in matters of this kind, I have concluded that the earth supports barely a fiftieth of the population that it had in Caesar's day. What is astonishing is that the population continues to diminish daily, and if this trend persists, within ten centuries the earth will be nothing but an uninhabited desert.
>
> We see here, my dear Usbek, the most terrible catastrophe the world has ever experienced; but people have barely noticed it, because it has occurred

---

[17] Roger B. Oake, 'Polygamy in the *Lettres persanes*', *Romanic Review*, 33 (1941), pp. 56–62 and David B. Young, 'Libertarian Demography: Montesquieu's Essay on Depopulation in the *Lettres Persanes*', *Journal of the History of Ideas*, 36 (1975), pp. 669–82.

[18] Young, 'Libertarian Demography', p. 671.

[19] Devletoglou, 'Montesquieu and the Wealth of Nations', p. 515; Young, 'Libertarian Demography', pp. 669–82.

so gradually, and over the course of a great many centuries; this points to an internal defect, a secret, hidden poison, a decline afflicting the human race.[20]

Of the numerous causes that could afflict humanity, Usbek, in his first reply, began with venereal decease, presumably syphilis, but setting that aside since its devastation had been halted, he promised to explain the moral, rather than the physical, causes of depopulation. Christianity and Islam were singled out in the subsequent letter as pernicious to the population, the latter because the condition of women in polygamous unions and harems limited birth; moreover, harems required eunuchs and female servants condemned to a life of virginity. Christianity, by forbidding divorce, encouraged prostitution, and had its own variants of harems, eunuchs, and virginal servants in monastic institutions, priests, and nuns. Outside Europe, Usbek continued, Islamic Africa was less peopled than under the Romans, while the slave trade depleted its western coastal regions. But if some religions had baneful demographic consequences, others stimulated growth. Thus Usbek's next letter explains that the Jewish people, despite the persecutions they endured, were replenished as each family lived in the hope of seeing the birth of the Messiah. Zoroastrianism led to demographic growth because nothing pleased God more than to have a child, plough a field, and plant a tree. Ancestor worship in China accounted for its prodigious population, although Usbek's explanation for this defies comprehension perhaps more than any other. Closing the letter, Usbek returned to Europe briefly and blamed primogeniture for low birth rates. The lands of 'savages' were sparsely populated as they were averse to labour, Usbek wrote in the following letter, and hunting and gathering did not provide sufficient subsistence to maintain large populations, which would have lacked structures of mutual assistance in the absence of states. What is more, women in those communities had the 'cruel habit' of aborting so as not to be displeasing to their husbands by pregnancy. In his closing paragraph to the letter, Usbek alluded to Henri II's edict in 1556 imposing the death penalty for abortion.

The next letter spoke of the baneful effect of moving people to new territories, especially when displacing them to barren lands, but Usbek also noted that, for all its extent, the slave trade had not filled America with people. History showed how deporting peoples decreased populations and

---

[20] Montesquieu, *Persian Letters*, ed. Andrew Kahn, trans. Margaret Mauldon (Oxford, 2008), pp. 149–50.

attested to the failure of colonial enterprises and territorial conquests: 'It is the fate of heroes to ruin themselves conquering countries that they immediately lose, or to subdue nations that they themselves are then forced to destroy'.[21] From this warning about the futility of territorial conquest and colonial expansion, the final letter perhaps predictably opened with the claim that:

> Tolerance in government encourages, to an astonishing degree, the propagation of the species. All republics offer constant proof of this, above all Switzerland and Holland; judged by the nature of their terrain these two countries are the worst in Europe yet they have the largest populations.[22]

Liberty and the opulence that followed it attracted immigrants, whilst abundance fed children as well as fathers, and the equality amongst citizens normally also produced economic equality. The opposite was the case under arbitrary power, where the prince and his retinue possessed all the wealth. Miserable men did not marry, Usbek stated, and, excepting peasants, if they did, they had few children. People were like plants, they had to be well-nurtured, or they were lost or degenerated. At this point, Usbek turned to France, where the fear of being enrolled in wars led its subjects to marry too early and despite lack of means, for a final pronouncement on the topic: 'If, in such a beneficent climate, in a kingdom as well organised as France, such things can occur, what must be the situation in other countries?'[23]

There were rich pickings in the *Lettres Persanes* from which Hume might choose to converse with Montesquieu's Persian characters. In Book XXIII of *L'Esprit des Lois*, which Hume also read attentively, Montesquieu returned to demographic considerations, but whilst Hume wrote with comments on it in his introductory letter to Montesquieu, he did not raise the issue of population. His engagement on this subject was ignited by Montesquieu's earlier work. Importantly, Book XXIII of Montesquieu's magnum opus did not quite make the unambiguous case for ancient nations being more populous than modern ones. Its four short paragraphs making up chapter 19, 'Dépopulation de l'univers', consists mostly of quotations about ancient Greece from ancient historians and refers to its modern-day sparseness. Chapter 24 states that there were more people in most regions of Europe under Charlemagne than in Montesquieu's day, adding that he did not have time to treat the subject in depth and cited Pufendorf as saying 'that under Charles IX [hardly an

---

[21] Ibid., p. 164.   [22] Ibid., pp. 164–65.   [23] Ibid., p. 166.

ancient] there were twenty million men in France'.[24] However, context, a critique of centralisation, and the absorption of smaller states into large ones should be borne in mind, for Montesquieu attributes population decrease to this political process. Book XXIII did at most claim, in the one short paragraph that constitutes chapter 26, that Europe was at present in need of laws to encourage population increase and that contemporary political rulers were only concerned with the means to do so, just as their ancient Greek counterparts were worried about the large number of their citizens. The overwhelming impression Book XXIII makes on the reader is that many factors, of which religions, cultural practices, and slavery appear to be most important, determine numbers, and, significantly, that neither the ancient world, nor modern Europe should be treated as uniform entities in demographic assessments, a point Hume was also to note.

Whilst it may be easy to take Montesquieu to be speaking through Rhedi when, as we saw earlier, that fictional character concluded from his reading ancient and modern histories that the ancient world was more populated than the modern one, this assumption should be firmly resisted. Rhedi was not Montesquieu's mouthpiece and, in any event, the point was what could be garnered from histories.[25] The opening gambit of Rhedi's letter was just that, a stepping stone into a topic that opened unto others. What followed through Usbek's letters was a critical account of the institutions and mores that had a demographic impact, and how the treatment of women, polygamy, some religions, invasions, conquests, empires, and slavery depleted peoples, whereas liberty, prosperity, and general well-being increased their numbers. Care should thus be taken in refraining from imputing to Montesquieu more than we should.

And this is also true in interpreting Hume. Discussing 'Of the Populousness of Ancient Nations', Harris has rightly argued that Hume 'did not himself seek to reach a definite conclusion on the matter',[26] citing Hume's letter in April 1750 to Dr John Clephane in which Hume accounted for the way he spent his time:

> The last thing I took my hand from was a very learned, elaborate discourse, concerning the populousness of antiquity; not altogether in opposition to Vossius and Montesquieu, who exaggerate that affair infinitely; but, starting

---

[24] Montesquieu, *The Spirit of the Laws*, trans. and eds. Anne M. Cohler, Basia C. Miller, and Harold Samuel Stone (Cambridge, 1989 [1748]), p. 452.
[25] *Pace* Harris, *Hume*, p. 284.
[26] Harris, *Hume*, p. 285; Ernest Campbell Mossner, *The Life of David Hume* (Oxford, 1954), p. 263.

with some doubts, and scruples, and difficulties, sufficient to make us suspend our judgment on that head.[27]

Adding in another letter to Gilbert Elliot in February 1751:

> I have amus'd myself lately with an Essay or Dissertation on the Populousness of Antiquity, which led me into many Disquisitions concerning both the public & domestic Life of the Antients. Having read over almost all the Classics both Greek and Latin, since I form'd that Plan, I have extracted what serv'd most to my Purpose: But I have not a Strabo, & know not where to get one in this Neighbourhood.[28]

Hume's 'learned, and elaborate discourse' was in effect with Rhedi, in that the sceptical Scot questioned whether ancient histories provided the strength of evidence to support what the fictional Rhedi claimed. Hume's essay was an exercise in close readings of ancient Greek and Roman histories. Did the sources warrant the claim of the populousness of the ancient world? He weighed the evidence. Hume, the historian, was in this period researching what became his *History of England*, first published in 1754. That he was thinking about what can be taken as evidence and how its nature needs to be acknowledged is revealed by what follows the passage just cited:

> Amongst other topics, it fell in my way to consider the greatness of ancient *Rome*; and in looking over the discourse [Vossius' *De antiquae Romae magnitudine* (1685)], I find the following period. 'If we may judge by the younger Pliny's account of his house, and by the plans of ancient buildings in Dr. Mead's collection, the men of quality had very spacious palaces [. . .].' Pray, on what authority are those plans founded? If I remember right, I was told they were discovered on the walls of the baths, and other subterraneous buildings. Is this the proper method of citing them?[29]

Such considerations shed light on the nature and style of Hume's argumentation in his essay on populousness as well as on the extent of the difference of opinion, if there really be any, between him and Montesquieu on the subject or, more accurately, between him, Montesquieu, Rhedi, and Usbek.

Thus if one inverts the chronological order of their writings, one can venture to think that Montesquieu would not have taken exception to Hume's grand opening: 'There is very little ground, either from reason or

---

[27] *HL*, I, p. 140.   [28] Ibid., pp. 152–53.   [29] Ibid., p. 140.

observation, to conclude the world eternal or incorruptible.'[30] Nor would he have thought the loose comparison between the ages of an individual human being, that is, 'infancy, youth, manhood, and old age', and those of humanity as entirely out of place, although he would not have taken the analogy any more seriously than Hume did. Still less would he have desisted from the view that

> if the general system of things, and human society of course, have any such gradual revolutions, they are too slow to be discernible in that short period which is comprehended by history and tradition. Stature and force of body, length of life, even courage and extent of genius, seem hitherto to have been naturally, in all ages, pretty much the same. The arts and sciences, indeed, have flourished in one period, and have decayed in another: But we may observe, that, at the time when they arose to greatest perfection among one people, they were perhaps totally unknown to all the neighbouring nations; and though they universally decayed in one age, yet in a succeeding generation they again revived, and diffused themselves over the world.[31]

Likewise, Montesquieu's works, not least his *Considérations sur les causes de la grandeur des Romains et de leur décadence* (1734) and *L'Esprit des lois*, leave no doubt as to his belief that societies differed from one another and their condition fluctuated over time, including as measured in the thriving of their arts and sciences. Again, Montesquieu would have been eager to follow Hume in noting that '[t]o prove, therefore, or account for that superior populousness of antiquity, which is commonly supposed by the imaginary youth or vigour of the world, will scarcely be admitted by any just reasoner'; he too would have thought that '[t]hese *general physical* causes ought entirely to be excluded from this question'.[32]

In examining the variables affecting numbers, Hume started, as Usbek had in his response to Rhedi's initial letter, with venereal diseases, to which he referred as a '*particular physical* cause of importance'.[33] 'Were it certain', Hume remarked, 'that ancient times were more populous than the present, and could not moral causes be assigned for so great a change; these physical causes alone, in the opinion of many, would be sufficient to give us satisfaction on that head.'[34] But was it certain, Hume then asked? And he went on to show it was not.

It is at this point that he turned to the 'extravagancies of VOSSIUS' and to 'an author of much greater genius and discernment [who] has ventured to affirm, that, according to the best computations which these subjects

---

[30] *E* (LF), p. 377, *E* (C), p. 279.   [31] *E* (LF), pp. 377–78, *E* (C), pp. 279–80.   [32] Ibid.
[33] Ibid.   [34] Ibid.

will admit of, there are now, on the face of the earth, the fiftieth part of mankind, which existed in the time of JULIUS CAESAR'.[35] The comparison, Hume continued, 'must be imperfect, even though we confine ourselves to the scene of ancient history; EUROPE, and the nations around the MEDITARRANEAN'. Here, it is important to remember that Montesquieu did not confine Usbek's and his own reflections in this way; he drew from worldwide travellers' accounts. Hume thought the comparison between ancient and modern populations was very problematic since the exact size of the population even in contemporary European nations and cities was unknown. The matter seemed so uncertain to him that, in the absence of secure data, he would 'intermingle the enquiry concerning *causes* with that concerning *facts*; which ought never to be admitted, where the facts can be ascertained with any tolerable assurance'.[36] The examination of causes was the part of his conversation with Montesquieu, whilst that of the facts was more directed at Vossius. Thus Hume intended to ask, firstly, whether the greater populousness of antiquity was probable, and, secondly, 'whether in reality it was so', adding that he would be satisfied with showing that the claim was 'not so certain as is pretended'.[37]

Much of the paragraph that followed might have been written by any number of eighteenth-century figures, including Montesquieu. Demographic questions mattered, Hume began, as they related to and were indicative of peoples' 'whole police, their manners, and the constitution of their government'.[38] All men and women shared the desire and power to procreate, a desire 'more active than is universally exerted'. What restrained it, he continued, 'must proceed from some difficulties in their situation, which it belongs to a wise legislature carefully to observe and remove'.[39] Thus within a few sentences of stating that he would be satisfied with demonstrating the uncertainty of the claim of the populousness of the ancient world, Hume implicitly positioned himself as having a rather grander aim in endeavouring to identify the constraints on demographic growth and, presumably, encouraging their removal. Were it not for constrictions, since 'every man who thinks he can maintain a family will have one, [. . .] the human species, at this rate of propagation, would more than double every generation'. In support of this claim, though not of the ratio itself, the statement of which is nonetheless noteworthy, Hume pointed to the rapidity with which 'mankind multiply in every colony or new settlement; where it is an easy matter to provide for a family; and where men are no wise straightened or confined, as in long-established

---

[35] Ibid.   [36] Ibid.   [37] *E* (LF), pp. 378–79, *E* (C), p. 281.   [38] Ibid.   [39] Ibid.

governments?'[40] Whilst Montesquieu did not think so well of colonies and settlements as we saw earlier, he would have acquiesced to the latter part of Hume's sentence. Indeed, whilst he might have weighted geographical and climatic factors somewhat differently, Hume's sentiments, as expressed in what follows, were very much his own:

> Every wise, just, and mild government, by rendering the condition of its subjects easy and secure, will always abound most in people, as well as in commodities and riches. A country, indeed, whose climate and soil are fitted for vines, will naturally be more populous than one which produces corn only, and that more populous than one which is only fitted for pasturage. In general, warm climates, as the necessities of the inhabitant are there fewer, and vegetation more powerful, are likely to be most populous. But if every thing else be equal, it seems natural to expect, that, wherever there are more happiness and virtue, and the wisest institution, there will also be most people.[41]

If the conception they had of happiness may have varied, that population growth was the index of a people's well-being was a view shared by many eighteenth-century theorists. Likewise, that it attested to good governance was a belief common to many of them on both sides of the Channel, although what constituted the latter and indeed also virtue was not uncontested.[42]

Given this, it followed for Hume that to establish whether the ancient world was more populated than the modern one, the domestic and political situation of both periods had to be investigated. 'The chief difference between the *domestic* oeconomy of the ancients and that of the moderns', Hume contended, 'consists in the practice of slavery, which prevailed among the former, and which has been abolished for some centuries throughout the greater part of Europe.'[43] This focus on slavery, which is notable in Ubesk's discussion, is striking. It does not feature in Thomas Robert Malthus's *An Essay on the Principle of Population* (1798), for instance, in which the only reference to 'slavery' is that of women amongst 'North American Indians', whose harsh treatment by men and exhausting labour led to high levels of miscarriage and infant mortality.[44]

---

[40] Ibid. [41] *E* (LF), p. 382, *E* (C), pp. 281–82.
[42] Sylvana Tomaselli, 'Moral Philosophy and Population Questions in Eighteenth-Century Europe', in M. S. Teitelbaum and J. M. Winter, eds., *Population and Development Review: Supplement*, 14 (1988), pp. 7–29.
[43] *E* (LF), p. 382, *E* (C), pp. 281–82.
[44] Thomas Robert Malthus, *An Essay on the Principle of Population as it Affects the Future Improvement of Society with Remarks on the Speculations of Mr. Godwin, M. Condorcet, and Other Writers* (London, 1798), pp. 12–13.

Whereas Malthus, whose father, Daniel Malthus, knew Hume, under-scored the contrasting nature of the mathematical incrementation of the potential exponential growth of population as compared to the arithmet-ical growth of food production, Hume, like Montesquieu and others in the eighteenth century, used the population debate to shine a light on social and political variables affecting decline and increase. In *An Essay on the Principle of Population* (1798), Malthus acknowledged Hume as well Adam Smith, whose *Wealth of Nations* he examined more particularly:

> The most important argument that I shall adduce is certainly not new. The principles on which it depends have been explained in part by Hume, and more at large by Dr Adam Smith. It has been advanced and applied to the present subject, though not with its proper weight, or in the most forcible point of view, by Mr Wallace, and it may probably have been stated by many writers that I have never met with. I should certainly therefore not think of advancing it again, though I mean to place it in a point of view in some degree different from any that I have hitherto seen, if it had ever been fairly and satisfactorily answered.[45]

Malthus pointed to what he thought to be the specific 'errors' of all three authors, although his principal targets, as the subtitle of his *Essay* made clear, were Condorcet and Godwin. While Malthus showed some reluc-tance in criticising Hume, he nonetheless claimed that:

> Hume, in his essay on the populousness of ancient and modern nations, when he intermingles, as he says, an inquiry concerning causes with that concerning facts, does not seem to see with his usual penetration how very little some of the causes he alludes to could enable him to form any judgement of the actual population of ancient nations. [...] If I find that at a certain period in ancient history, the encouragements to have a family were great, that early marriages were consequently very prevalent, and that few persons remained single, I should infer with certainty that population was rapidly increasing, but by no means that it was then actually very great, rather; indeed, the contrary, that it was then thin and that there was room and food for a much greater number. On the other hand, if I find that at this period the difficulties attending a family were very great, that, consequently, few early marriages took place, and that a great number of both sexes remained single, I infer with certainty that population was at a stand, and, probably, because the actual population was very great in proportion to the fertility of the land and that there was scarcely room and food for more.[46]

Malthus was, as he himself said, joining an ongoing exchange and there-fore looking at the issue from a different perspective.

[45] Ibid., p. 3.   [46] Ibid., p. 18.

Whilst he made the occasional comment about forms of government and debated the cause and consequences of early marriages as authors such as Mary Wollstonecraft did[47] and their effects on population,[48] Malthus's point of entry into the demographic discussion was not Hume's, who, whilst not ignoring the issue of subsistence, took the debate to the political stage. For him, the early eighteenth-century conversation on population level past and present afforded an opportunity to expose the blatant contradiction in the republican conception of liberty; having established within the first few pages of his essay that the difference between the '*domestic oeconomy*' of ancient and modern Europe consisted in the practice of slavery, he argued:

> Some passionate admirers of the ancients, and zealous partizans of civil liberty, (for these sentiments, as they are both of them, in the main, extremely just, are found to be almost inseparable) cannot forbear regretting the loss of this institution; and whilst they brand all submission to the government of a single person with the harsh denomination of slavery, they would gladly reduce the greater part of mankind to real slavery and subjection. But to one who considers coolly on the subject, it will appear, that human nature, in general enjoys more liberty at present, in the most arbitrary government of EUROPE, than it ever did during the most flourishing period of ancient times.[49]

Hume went on to decry '[t]he remains which are found of domestic slavery, in the AMERICAN colonies, and among some EUROPEAN nations', of which the dehumanising effects on slave owners would alone be found disgusting. He then proceeded to quote Columella, Demosthenes, and Seneca to illustrate that they were shameless in their brutal advice on how best to subjugate slaves in every way, before returning to the essay's overt topic.[50] But in doing so, Hume continued to provide further testimony to the cruelties recorded by ancient authors ranging from Plutarch to Xenophon, and in particular their accounts of the ways in which men and women were separated and their sexuality restricted. Hume did not wish to deny that there was some evidence that masters fathered children with their slaves, and that Columella advised

---

[47] Sylvana Tomaselli, *Wollstonecraft: Philosophy, Passion, and Politics* (Princeton, NJ, 2021), pp. 153–55, 170–71.

[48] Malthus, *Essay*, pp. 33, 35, 65, 92, 116.   [49] *E* (LF), p. 382, *E* (C), pp. 281–82.

[50] *E* (LF), pp. 382–83, *E* (C), p. 283. Later in the essay, Hume praises Dionysius Halicarnasseus: 'What pleases most, in that historian, is, that he seems to feel a proper resentment of these barbarous proceedings [in their civil wars], and talks not with that provoking coolness and indifference, which custom had produced in many of the GREEK historians' (*E* (LF), p. 414, *E* (C), p. 301).

them to reward and indeed free those that bore them more than three children. 'All I pretend to infer from these reasonings is', he explained, 'that slavery is in general disadvantageous both to the happiness and populousness of mankind, and that its place is much better supplied by the practice of hired servants'.[51] This was a point on which Malthus disagreed with Hume, arguing that there was good reason to doubt that servants were likely to leave the security and comfort of their employers' home to marry and raise families. Malthus read Hume as making a point only about fertility.[52] However, Hume was doing more than this. Indeed, given the first part of the essay in which he discussed the ancient '*domestic oeconomy*', one would be forgiven for thinking that the topic of Hume's essay was in fact the abomination of slavery, about which the lovers of antiquity and its liberty were oblivious.[53]

'Having considered the domestic life and manner of the ancients', compared to those of the moderns, where, 'in the main, we seem rather superior', Hume turned to the '*political* customs and institutions of both ages, and weigh[ed] their influence in retarding or forwarding the propagation of mankind'.[54] 'It must be owned', he admitted at this point in the discussion, 'that the situation of affairs in modern times, which regard to civil liberty, as well as equality of fortune, is not near so favourable, either to the propagation or happiness of mankind.'[55] Small states and equality of fortune favoured demographic growth – a view he was to qualify later in the essay. 'Enormous cities are', surprisingly given what we saw him write about Paris,[56] Hume remarked, 'destructive to society, beget vice and disorder of all kinds, starve the remoter provinces, and even starve themselves, by the prices to which they raise all provisions.'[57] Here the comparison favoured the ancients. 'SWITZERLAND alone and HOLLAND resemble the ancient republics', Hume remarked, 'and though the former is far from possessing any advantage either of soil, climate, or commerce, yet the numbers of people, with which it abounds, notwithstanding their enlisting themselves into every service in EUROPE prove sufficiently the advantages of their political institutions'.[58] As we saw earlier, a similar passage can be found in one of Usbek's letters.

---

[51] *E* (LF), p. 396, *E* (C), p. 290.   [52] Malthus, *Essay*, p. 21.
[53] *Pace* Mossner, *Life* (1954), p. 264, who calls it 'an incidental discussion of slavery'.
[54] *E* (LF), p. 400, *E* (C), p. 292.   [55] *E* (LF), p. 402, *E* (C), p. 294.
[56] He might have been thinking of large ancient cities, but what follows showed he had European states ruled by absolute princes and the monarch in mind.
[57] *E* (LF), p. 401, *E* (C), p. 292.   [58] *E* (LF), p. 402, *E* (C), p. 294.

It is only in 'the love of civil liberty and of equality, which is, [he] own [ed] of considerable importance' that Hume was happy to give the ancients the advantage.[59] Yet even that concession was qualified. The other side of the medal was factionalism. In ancient times, factions engendered slaughters with rare exceptions.[60] In peace, civil wars and in other forms of conflicts, the ancients were merciless, according to Hume. For all their love of liberty, the ancients 'seem not to have understood it very well'.[61] They enjoyed neither security of life nor of property, so little that it was best to impoverish oneself to be safe from the rapaciousness of the Athenian people.[62] Political instability was the norm rather than the exception. Returning to the domestic sphere, Hume, in contrast to Usbek in Letter 119 (admittedly in a different context), unexpectedly praised primogeniture: 'though it increases the inequality of fortunes, has, however, this good effect, that it accustoms men to the same idea in public succession, and cuts off all claim and pretension of the younger'.[63] The difficulty of establishing an aristocracy was a further cause of tumultuousness, in Hume's view, 'whenever even the meanest and more beggarly were excluded from the legislature and from public offices'.[64] The problem lay in the then prevailing conception of freedom:

> The very quality of freeman gave such a rank, being opposed to that of slave, that it seemed to entitle the possessor to every power and privilege of the commonwealth.[65]

Thus Hume's critique of republican notions of liberty found its way in the intersections and seams of his copious references to ancient Greek and Roman demographic sources, noting that whilst eighteenth-century Europe republics were remarkable for their rule of law and stability, '[a]lmost all of them are well-tempered Aristocracies', Hume contended.

Amongst other features of the modern world that made it superior to the ancient in terms of happiness and populousness were the flourishing of trade, manufactures, and industry.[66] Hume could not recall a passage in which urban growth was due to the establishment of a manufacture, and he believed that the 'barbarity of the ancient tyrants, together with the extreme love of liberty, which animated those ages, must have banished every merchant and manufacturer, and have quite depopulated the state,

---

[59] *E* (LF), p. 407, *E* (C), p. 297. [60] Ibid. [61] *E* (LF), p. 408, *E* (C), p. 298.
[62] *E* (LF), p. 413, *E* (C), p. 300. [63] Ibid. [64] *E* (LF), p. 415, *E* (C), p. 302.
[65] *E* (LF), p. 415, *E* (C), p. 303.
[66] Intermingled in these pages are details of individual fortune that might have inspired his own disclosures in 'My Own Life'.

had it subsisted upon industry and commerce'.[67] What commerce had taken place in that period consisted mostly in the exchange of commodities. Anticipating or reacting to the argument that agriculture was the determinant in demographic growth, he contended that agriculture could not flourish over extended periods of time without trade or manufacture. Expanding markets were required to stimulate agricultural production. And the political instability and devastation brought about by war undid whatever was achieved economically.

Here the Reverend Robert Wallace (1697–1771) might be considered as another potential contributor to the conversation. The two Scots knew and respected one another. Indeed, Wallace even supported Hume's failed candidacy for the chair of Ethics and Pneumatical Philosophy at Edinburgh University in 1745, and the two men exchanged views in correspondence and in print.[68] Wallace's *A Dissertation on the Numbers of Mankind in antient and modern Times* (1753) and *Various Prospects of Mankind, Nature and Providence* (1761) made his disagreement with Hume on progress and population clear. But, as Robert B. Luehrs has argued, rather focusing on the greater populousness of the ancient world, 'the fundamental issue in the Wallace–Hume debate was really the relative merits of an agrarian versus a commercial society in best fulfilling the needs and desires of its citizens'.[69] Wallace, like Montesquieu and Hume, believed that there were other factors than economics affecting populousness, but unlike them Wallace made agriculture central to his interventions in the debate. Whilst Ernest Campbell Mossner believes it probable that Hume entered the population debate independently of Wallace's impetus, Hume knew of Wallace's views, and encouraged him to publish what became *A Dissertation.* A copy, together with Hume's essay, was sent to Montesquieu, who sought translators for them both in 1753, and was believed to have been asked to adjudicate between the two authors. In answer to Hume's translator, the abbé Le Blanc's inquiry relating to this, Montesquieu wrote:

> They did not write to me in order to settle their dispute, as you were informed; I am not capable of that and, if I were arbiter, I should decide just as he did who judged the contest between the two shepherds in Virgil.[70]

---

[67] *E* (LF), p. 419, *E* (C), p. 304.
[68] Robert B. Luehrs, 'Population and Utopia in the Thought of Robert Wallace', *Eighteenth-Century Studies*, 20 (1987), pp. 313–35.
[69] Ibid., p. 320.   [70] Quoted in Mossner, *Life* (1954), p. 267. See also ibid., pp. 260–69.

As Hume's insistence on the importance of trade and manufacture to economic development is but one of the views underscored in his essay, the likely influence of Wallace on the shape of Hume's essay should not, *pace* Luehrs, be overstated, and certainly not to the exclusion of Montesquieu's. But whether with Wallace or anyone else, it was part of Hume's demographic conversation, one that he could just as easily have conducted with François Fénelon, whom he cited in other essays, such as 'On the Standard of Taste'.

Hume ended his layered essay with Montesquieu. If he had to imagine a period in which the world was more peopled than at present, Hume wrote, 'I should pitch upon the age of TRAJAN and the ANTONINES; the great extent of the ROMAN empire being then civilized and cultivated, settled almost in a profound peace both foreign and domestic, and living under the same regular police and government'.[71] But referring to Book XXIII, chapter 19 of *L'Esprit des Lois*, he added, 'we are told, that all extensive governments, especially absolute monarchies, are pernicious to population, and contain a secret vice and poison, which destroy the effect of all these promising appearances'.[72] Then returning to consider the historical evidence provided as he had for much of the essay, he studied the passage Montesquieu cited from Plutarch, which on examination Hume concluded to be self-contradictory. Although he had not followed Usbek on every point the latter made in the *Persian Letters*, on life in harems, for example, and although he did not use the opportunity that the Persian gave him to criticise religions (indeed, astonishingly, Hume had something relatively positive to say about monasteries in the essay),[73] Hume did, as we saw, speak of slavery in some depth, as had Usbek. What remains unclear is whether Hume took Montesquieu to be one of the 'passionate admirers of the ancients, and zealous partizans of civil liberty', thereby prompting his critique of republicanism and its obliviousness to a liberty contingent on slavery.

[71] *E* (LF), pp. 457–58, *E* (C), p. 328. [72] *E* (LF), p. 460, *E* (C), pp. 328–29.
[73] *E* (LF), p. 399, *E* (C), p. 291.

CHAPTER 12

Hume on Economic Inequality

Margaret Schabas

In his essay 'Of the Original Contract', David Hume observed 'how nearly equal all men are in their bodily force, and even in their mental powers and faculties, till cultivated by education'.[1] When it came to economic equality, however, Hume was more equivocal. There will always be rich and poor, he believed, and property rights should trump compassion for the less well-off.[2] Property and rank were by-products of our deeply rooted passions for pride and envy, and essential for sustaining the upward trajectory of commercial prosperity and political stability that Hume celebrated in his own kingdom. With a nod to ancient Sparta, he considered the prospect of an equal division of the necessities and comforts of life, and deemed it not only 'impracticable' but also 'pernicious'.[3] As he observed, 'perfect equality of possessions' would 'soon degenerate into tyranny'.[4]

There is an important difference between striving for a world of perfect equality, particularly in ancient times, and a modern world that seeks to lessen economic inequality, either of income or wealth, or both. As will be argued here, Hume firmly believed that greater equality of *income* tends to increase aggregate happiness for the nation as a whole, and he broached various policies for taxes and trade to achieve these ends. The received view is that Adam Smith was the first major economist to acknowledge the plight of the lower orders, with his famous tautology, that 'no society can surely be flourishing and happy, of which the far greater part of the

---

[1] *E* (LF), pp. 467–68, *E* (C), p. 333. I wish to thank the editors of this volume, my research assistant Zoe Zhiyu Luo, and Charles Goldhaber, Carl Wennerlind, Marc Hanvelt, and Calvin Normore for helpful revisions. This paper was presented at Padua (ESHET), at UCLA (Philosophy), at Duke University (CHOPE), and at the International Hume Society meetings in Oxford.
[2] See Annette Baier, *The Cautious Jealous Virtue: Hume on Justice* (Cambridge, MA, 2010), ch. 1, for a detailed account of Hume's preference to honour loan contracts regardless of the character or status of the debtor. By and large, Hume was a legal positivist.
[3] *EPM*, p. 20.   [4] Ibid., p. 21.

members are poor and miserable'.⁵ Hume, however, was of a similar mind if one takes the trouble to stitch together various passages in his texts, particularly his *Essays*, as well as his unpublished works and correspondence.⁶ He wished to see ordinary labourers enjoy higher wages and lift themselves out of poverty through the acquisition of skills. His eye was also directed to expanding those in the 'middle station', increasing the number of tradesmen, merchants, and manufacturers. Furthermore, while Britain was at the vanguard of this movement, Hume hoped that through international trade, a path of global enrichment would ensue.

As a young man, Hume left his ancestral home in southern Scotland to work for a merchant in Bristol. He stayed only four months, and then moved to France for three years. In 1737, Hume settled in London to oversee the publication of his first book, *A Treatise of Human Nature* (1739–40). Over the course of his life, he would return to London, living there on and off for about six years, but perhaps the most informative period for his economics came in 1748, when he toured the continent with General James St Clair. On the journey from Rotterdam to Vienna, Hume was struck by the prosperity of Western Europe, including the quality of the houses for the labourers. In the region of Frankfurt, everyone, including the farmers, lived in villages or towns, and the city itself displayed 'great Riches & Commerce'.⁷ Hume also remarked on the higher standard of living for ordinary people in Protestant Germany in contrast to what he observed in the Catholic regions, particularly on travelling through Bavaria, 'the first Poverty indeed we had seen in Germany'.⁸

As I have argued, Hume was a proto-Weberian, singling out the Protestant work ethic to explain, in part, the prosperity of London, Amsterdam, and Hamburg, as well as the relative poverty of Catholic Austria and Italy that he witnessed first hand.⁹ For Hume, labour was the motor engine of economic growth. As he observed, 'every thing in the

---

⁵ Adam Smith, *An Inquiry into the Nature and Causes of the Wealth of Nations*, eds. E. H. Campbell, A. S. Skinner, and W. B. Todd (2 vols., Oxford, 1976 [1776]), I, p. 96. For the received view, see Gertrude Himmelfarb, *The Idea of Poverty: England in the Early Industrial Age* (New York, 1984), pp. 42–63. However, Samuel Hollander, *The Economics of Adam Smith* (Toronto, 1973), p. 64 observed in passing that Hume was 'in favour of labour's well-being' and cites seminal work by A. W. Coats, which documents a similar shift among economists a few decades before Smith.

⁶ I have changed my mind since I wrote that Hume 'showed none of the admiration that Smith expressed for the oppressed, either for the lower orders of Europe or the enslaved and conquered in the Americas' (Margaret Schabas, 'Hume on Economic Well-Being', in Alan Bailey and Dan O'Brien, eds., *Bloomsbury Companion to Hume* (London, 2015), pp. 332–48, at p. 339).

⁷ *HL*, I, p. 122.　⁸ Ibid., pp. 124–25.

⁹ See Margaret Schabas, 'David Hume as a Proto-Weberian: Commerce, Protestantism, and Secular Culture', *Social Philosophy and Policy*, 37 (2020), pp. 190–212.

world is purchased by labour; and our passions are the only causes of labour'.[10] Moreover, 'there is no craving or demand of the human mind more constant and insatiable than that for exercise and employment'.[11] As Margaret Watkins has shown with her detailed canvas of Hume's *Essays*, he held a profound esteem for 'working' and industriousness, both individually and collectively.[12] His advice to the local magistrate was to let the money flow on its own accord, since this 'encreases the stock of labour, in which consists all real power and riches'.[13] Using a number of ingenious estimates, Hume's lengthy essay on demography demonstrated not only that the population of modern Europe exceeded that of ancient Rome but also that it was wealthier, due in part to a more skilled labouring class.[14] As a general rule, Hume declared that 'the greater number of people and their greater industry are serviceable in all cases; at home and abroad, in private, and in public'.[15]

In several of his essays, Hume celebrated 'the spirit of the age' and its imprint on both the minds and bodies of ordinary citizens who had collectively transformed Britain into a powerful commercial nation. The peasants of the past, he believed, lacked ambition and preferred to work about half the year, enjoying over a month of Saints' days.[16] When it came to contemporary skilled workers and tradesmen in British towns, however, the opposite held true. Hume appealed to their work ethic and capacity to be prudent and rational, and these dispositions became more pronounced as their incomes rose. 'In times when industry and the arts flourish, men are kept in perpetual occupation, and enjoy, as their reward, the occupation itself, as well as those pleasures which are the fruit of their labour. The mind acquires new vigour; enlarges its powers and faculties.'[17] Moreover, the rise of a manufacturing sector induced a more orderly and law-abiding citizenry. As Hume queried, 'can we expect, that a government will be well modelled by a people, who know not how to make a spinning-wheel, or to employ a loom to advantage?'.[18]

It is important to keep in mind that Hume devised his core ideas several decades before steam-powered textile factories transformed the cities of the

---

[10] *E* (LF), p. 261, *E* (C), p. 204.   [11] *E* (LF), p. 300, *E* (C), p. 231.
[12] See Margaret Watkins, *The Philosophical Progress of Hume's Essays* (Cambridge, 2019), pp. 104–8.
[13] *E* (LF), p. 288, *E* (C), p. 222.   [14] *E* (LF), pp. 377–464, *E* (C), pp. 279–331.
[15] *E* (LF), p. 283, *E* (C), pp. 218–19.
[16] In David Hume, 'Hume's Early Memoranda, 1729–1740: The Complete Text', ed. Ernest Campbell Mossner, *Journal of the History of Ideas*, 9 (1948), pp. 492–518, at p. 510n13, Hume cites Vauban's observation in 1698 that there were thirty-eight holy days per year in France and '180 Working days at a Medium'.
[17] *E* (LF), p. 270, *E* (C), p. 210.   [18] *E* (LF), p. 273, *E* (C), p. 212.

Midlands into sooty and squalid slums. Wool and linen cloth were the primary export goods and figured prominently in Hume's own economic analysis. Cloth production, with the exception of the silk industry of East London, was governed by the putting-out system, such that work was normally paid by the piece. According to Joel Mokyr, in the early 1700s, 'the majority of workers do not fall in the neat categorization of self-employed vs. wage-labor'; only about one-third were primarily wage-earners.[19] By the time Hume wrote his *Political Discourses* (1752), the number of waged-labourers had much increased, but employment before the Industrial Revolution took off was nonetheless highly seasonal, with many artisans returning to the farms at harvest time. In other words, the supply of labour was highly elastic and annual income, for the most part, was not fixed. As Hume observed in his essay 'Of Taxes', 'in years of scarcity, the *weaver* either consumes less or labours more, or employs both these expedients of frugality and industry'.[20]

The vagaries of the weather tended to induce considerable fluctuations in the price of basic food, both because of good and bad harvests and because, before the surge in canal construction in the 1760s, the movement of agricultural goods depended on the roads, which often became unpassable with heavy rainfall.[21] Before the eighteenth century, it was not readily apparent that a price was a direct function of the cost of production, a principle that would define classical political economy. Historically, prices for artisanal goods were negotiated in seasonal fairs or shops, oscillating around a well-understood customary price. Because artisans were mostly self-employed, they did not assign shadow wages or profits. It was only as capitalism expanded and wage-earners became more prevalent, that economists of the early eighteenth century, such as Charles Davenant, John Pollexfen, and Henry Martyn, discerned that the price of a domestically manufactured good was primarily a function of the wage.[22] Hume contributed to this analysis by articulating the law of

---

[19] See Joel Mokyr, *The Enlightened Economy: An Economic History of Britain: 1700–1815* (New Haven, CT, 2009), p. 24. He notes that England was at the vanguard of dismantling guilds and that labourers exhibited a life cycle whereby they worked mostly for wages in their youth but became more self-employed as they prospered.

[20] *E* (LF), p. 347, *E* (C), p. 261; italics mine.

[21] Hume noted the importance of the Turnpike Act of 1662, but 'the general and great improvement of highways took not place till the reign of George II' (*HE*, VI, p. 538). Lists of corn prices were readily available in newspapers or popular periodicals. As for the influence of the weather and seasons more generally, on harvests, transportation, and power sources (wind and watermills), see Mokyr, *Enlightened Economy*, p. 22.

[22] See Istvan Hont, *The Jealousy of Trade: International Competition and the Nation State in Historical Perspective* (Cambridge, MA, 2005), p. 245.

the falling rate of profit, due to the increasing spread and sophistication of banking and financial markets, and thus indicated more explicitly that the price was mostly governed by the return to labour.

Hume grasped the fact that there was considerable latitude for individual artisans when it came to the quality and quantity of their labour and that, if incentivised by higher returns, could result in significant economic growth. Higher wages, in principle, meant higher nominal prices, but because workers had become considerably more skilled and efficient, Hume argued that the real price of manufactured goods, adjusted for inflation, had fallen over the past fifty years and, as a result, labourers, on average, enjoyed a higher standard of living. The main drawback to higher nominal prices was the reduction in exports. 'No labour in any commodities, that are exported, can be very considerably raised in price, without losing the foreign market.'[23] As Hume argued in his paean for higher wages, however, 'as foreign trade is not the most material circumstance, it is not to be put in competition with the happiness of so many millions'.[24] In a different essay, he remarked that the relatively high nominal wages and prices in Britain are 'an inconvenience that is unavoidable, and the effect of that public wealth and prosperity which are the end of all our wishes'.[25]

These assertions are proof that Hume's gaze was firmly on the well-being of the lower orders and distinctly utilitarian in the sense of the greatest happiness for the greatest number. I wish, however, to make a stronger claim, namely, that Hume sought to reduce inequalities of income, to lift wage-earners out of extreme poverty and expand the middle rank. My case will be built upon three separate arguments, although some of the passages drawn from Hume's work will feed into more than one. First, for Hume, material prosperity and an improving moral stock went hand in hand, and both served utilitarian ends.[26] It was not only the increase in the standard of living per se that mattered but also the inculcation of certain virtues, honesty and industry, for example, that were more conducive to forging a happy and civil nation. The second unpacks Hume's belief that greater economic equality, in tandem with an ever-expanding skilled class of labourers, tends to increase political stability

---

[23] *E* (LF), p. 636, *E* (C), p. 639.   [24] *E* (LF), p. 265, *E* (C), p. 207.

[25] *E* (LF), p. 284, *E* (C), p. 219.

[26] Hume has been placed in the long trajectory of utilitarian thought since the classic study by Edward Albee, *A History of English Utilitarianism* (London, 1901), but more in the political than the moral sense. The classification of Hume's moral philosophy is much debated (see Jacqueline A. Taylor, *Reflecting Subjects: Passion, Sympathy, and Society in Hume's Philosophy* (Oxford, 2015)).

within a nation, and vice versa.[27] The relatively liberal regime of Britain had resulted in 'the superior ease and plenty of the common people', whereas the absolute monarchy in France had entrenched poverty among the lower orders.[28] The third attends to what Albert O. Hirschman aptly called 'the Montesquieu–Steuart vision', namely, that trading nations, by prospering, would be less likely to go to war with one another.[29] Trade was primarily fuelled by the expansion of manufactured goods, which in turn remunerated skilled and industrious workers and bolstered the 'middling sorts', many of whom were less inclined to fight for national honour. Hume developed this line of thinking, both by emphasising that the global flow of money and goods outweighed the actions of statesmen, and by exposing the inherent shortcomings of imperialism.

12.1   Utilitarian Appeals

In 'Of Commerce', the opening essay of his *Political Discourses*, Hume sounds for one fleeting moment like a socialist. Looking to Western Europe, with its advanced 'mechanical arts', Hume proclaimed that 'a too great disproportion among the citizens weakens any state. *Every person*, if possible, ought to enjoy the fruits of his labour, in full possession of all the necessaries, and many of the conveniences of life'.[30] Hume also sought to spread the fruits of labour more widely and prompt population growth. 'As the multitude of mechanical arts is advantageous, so is the *great number of persons to whose share* the productions of these arts fall.'[31] In the same passage, Hume broached an idea akin to the principle of diminishing marginal utility of income. 'No one can doubt, but such an *equality* [of income] is most suitable to human nature, and diminishes much less from the *happiness* of the rich than it adds to that of the poor.'[32] A similar observation is found in his *Enquiry concerning the Principles of Morals* (1751), namely, that 'whenever we depart from this equality [of necessities and conveniences], we *rob* the poor of more satisfaction than we add to the rich'.[33] Furthermore, excessive inequality empowers the rich to increase

---

[27] Knud Haakonssen, 'Introduction', to *David Hume: Political Essays*, ed. Knud Haakonssen (Cambridge, 1994), pp. xi–xxx underscored Hume's lifelong mission to increase political stability and reduce overseas conquests and colonisation.
[28] *E* (LF), p. 266, *E* (C), pp. 207–8.
[29] Albert O. Hirschman, *The Passions and the Interests: Political Arguments for Capitalism before Its Triumph* (Princeton, NJ, 1977), pp. 70–87.
[30] *E* (LF), p. 265, *E* (C), p. 207; italics mine.   [31] Ibid.   [32] Ibid.
[33] *EPM*, p. 20; italics mine.

the suffering of the poor. 'Where the riches are in few hands, these must enjoy all the power, and will readily conspire to lay the whole burthen [of taxes] on the poor, and *oppress* them still farther, to the discouragement of all industry.'[34]

Hume was not a socialist – the movement did not emerge as such until the early nineteenth century – but there are reasons to put him on the path towards liberal democracy, both economically and politically. Notwithstanding his general opposition to rebellion, he supported the cause of the Yankees, having forged a close friendship with Benjamin Franklin while living in London in the 1760s. Hume's political allegiances, liberal or conservative, are still much debated but unequivocally progressive.[35] In his brief sketch of the 'perfect commonwealth', he proposed to enlarge the franchise, decentralise the halls of power, and ground membership in the House of Lords in merit rather than birth.[36] In his economic analysis, Hume broached the critical idea that the payment of rent served no economic purpose, that it was a residual in the formation of a price, and that value was derived primarily from the labour embodied in the production of commodities. Hume's economics left a firm imprint on subsequent economists who considered themselves, rightly or wrongly, to be socialists.[37]

As a leading voice for the Enlightenment, Hume championed the expansion of rights and liberties, particularly freedom of the press and religious toleration, and sought to dismantle archaic laws and mores. His various texts on human sexuality and the nuclear family were particularly radical for his time and his attacks on established religion were legendary. Although he died over a decade before the French Revolution, his imprint on that rupture was profound and far-reaching, not least in the aftermath from which socialism emerged.[38] Hume believed that Britain had singular

---

[34] *E* (LF), p. 265, *E* (C), p. 207; italics mine.

[35] See, for example, Donald W. Livingston, 'On Hume's Conservatism', *Hume Studies*, 21 (1995), pp. 151–64 and Paul Sagar, 'On the Liberty of the English: Adam Smith's Reply to Montesquieu and Hume', *Political Theory*, 50 (2022), pp. 381–404.

[36] *E* (LF), pp. 512–29, *E* (C), pp. 363–73.

[37] Some of the leading economists of the nineteenth century – John Stuart Mill, Léon Walras, William Stanley Jevons, and Alfred Marshall – considered themselves to be socialists, although we might deflate that claim and classify them as liberal democrats. Helen McCabe, *John Stuart Mill, Socialist* (Montreal, 2021) has recently made a compelling case for classifying Mill as a socialist. David Ricardo, while not a socialist, exposed the parasitic nature of the landowning class and inspired Karl Marx as well as the so-called Ricardian socialists. On the appreciation of Hume's economics by subsequent economists, see Margaret Schabas and Carl Wennerlind, *A Philosopher's Economist: Hume and the Rise of Capitalism* (Chicago, 2020), ch. 7.

[38] See Laurence L. Bongie, *David Hume: Prophet of the Counter-Revolution*, 2nd ed. (Indianapolis, IN, 2000).

achievements in expanding rights and freedoms that empowered not just the middle class but also the lower orders. He celebrated the Magna Carta (1215) for extending 'very important liberties and privileges to *every order of men* in the kingdom; to the clergy, to the barons, and to the people'.[39] In his essay 'Of Taxes', Hume exposed the inherent problems with the poll tax and, in his *History of England*, wrote sympathetically about the 'hundred thousand men' led by Nat Tyler and Jack Straw in 1381 to see it abolished.[40] While critical of religious sects for their fanaticism, Hume believed that, in principal if not in practice, the egalitarian and emancipatory efforts of both the Levellers and the Quakers served the common good.[41]

The Enclosure Movement had caused initial suffering, Hume acknowledged, by displacing commoners from their ancestral lands, but it had the salutary effect of prompting economic growth. The consolidation of large parcels of arable land forced the labourers to 'shake off their former habits of indolence' and inspired the managers of each estate to transition from 'unskilful' farming methods to ones that were more productive.[42] Tudor England, Hume observed, had become a major exporter of both corn and woollen cloth due primarily to a more efficient workforce. Waged labour, Hume argued, is always more productive than the work of the indentured. 'The fear of punishment will never draw so much labour from a slave, as the dread of being turned off and not getting another service, will from a freeman.'[43] Waged labour was also more disciplined and reliable: 'a manufacturer reckons upon the labour of his servants, for the execution of any work, as much as upon the tools'.[44] Moreover, serious criminal activity had abated. Whereas two thousand persons per annum were executed in 1500, by the late Elizabethan era, the number had dropped to four hundred. To Hume, this meant that there 'has been a great improvement in morals since the reign of Henry VIII'.[45] It was the Glorious Revolution, however, by shifting the balance of power to the merchants and manufacturers, that brought widespread prosperity.[46] Since 1688, 'trade and manufactures, and agriculture, have encreased ... Nor is there another instance in the whole history of mankind, that so many *millions* of people have, during such a space of time, been held

---

[39] *HE*, I, pp. 442–43; italics mine.   [40] *E* (LF), p. 346, *E* (C), p. 260; *HE*, II, p. 291.
[41] *E* (LF), pp. 76–78, *E* (C), pp. 78–79.   [42] *HE*, III, pp. 369–70.
[43] *E* (LF), p. 390n, *E* (C), p. 286n19.   [44] *EHU*, p. 68.   [45] *HE*, III, p. 329.
[46] *E* (LF), p. 278, *E* (C), p. 215.

together, in a manner so free, so rational, and so suitable to the dignity of human nature'.[47]

Hume's praise for the rupture of 1688 is striking if one bears in mind that he was a gentleman descended from the Earl of Home (d. 1491), and that he mingled readily with the aristocracy throughout his life. In his *History of England*, however, Hume appreciated the transition during the Tudor era, whereby the wealth and 'influence' of the aristocracy had diminished, as 'the middle rank of men began to be rich and powerful'.[48] Hume made note of the considerable revenue the Crown earned by the sale of titles, thereby diluting the significance of ancestry. Even among 'the greats', the more admirable were the self-made geniuses, namely, poets (Milton) or philosophers (Newton) rising from humble means, rather than esteemed generals who were entitled from birth (John Churchill, first Duke of Marlborough).[49] Moreover, Hume did not ignore the achievements of the lower orders. 'The same age, which produces great philosophers and politicians, renowned generals and poets, usually abounds with skilful weavers, and ship-carpenters.'[50]

Hume's allegiance was strongest to those in the commercial 'middle station', a heterogeneous group that included merchants, bankers, and manufacturers. He remarked upon the ingenuity of merchants, for discovering hitherto unmet desires. '*Merchants* [are] one of the most useful races of men, who serve as agents between those parts of the state that are wholly unacquainted, and are ignorant of each other's necessities.'[51] Bankers were commended for devising new credit instruments such as bills of exchange, low-denomination bank notes, and daily credit accounts.[52] Above all, manufacturers were praised for discovering novel techniques, improving the quality of their wares, and thus expanding their market share overseas.[53]

While on balance, Hume's sympathies were with the middle station, he nonetheless showed an abiding concern for the lower orders and appreciated their contributions to economic expansion. Whereas 'poverty and hard labour debase the minds of the common people, and render them unfit for any science and ingenious profession', the higher domestic wages

---

[47] *E* (LF), p. 508, *E* (C), pp. 359–60; italics mine. For a recent assessment of the 1688 Revolution as the most critical watershed for Hume, see Sagar, 'Liberty of the English'. Given that Britain had about eight million people, Hume's remark about the benefit to millions necessarily included commoners (*E* (LF), p. 428, *E* (C), p. 311).

[48] *HE*, IV, p. 384.   [49] *E* (LF), pp. 549–50, *E* (C), pp. 13–14.
[50] *E* (LF), p. 270, *E* (C), p. 210.   [51] *E* (LF), p. 300, *E* (C), p. 231.
[52] *E* (LF), pp. 317–20, *E* (C), pp. 242–45.   [53] *E* (LF), pp. 328–30, *E* (C), pp. 249–50.

of his day have inspired workers to cultivate more skilled methods of production, 'to better their condition' and thus to lift themselves up from subsistence.[54] As standards of living rose, labourers inculcated a stronger work ethic, became more enterprising and, as a result, prospered. If a labourer has 'manufactures and commodities', that is, some conveniences and even luxuries, 'he will do it himself', that is, create a surplus, and become 'accustomed to industry'.[55] The advent of novel goods in the early modern period was a critical factor. 'Where luxury nourishes commerce and industry, the peasants, by a proper cultivation of the land, become rich and independent; while the tradesmen and merchants acquire a share of the property'.[56]

Conversely, poverty dampens productivity. Looking back to the feudal era, 'a violent method' was required to force 'the labourer to toil, in order to raise from the land more than what subsists himself and family'.[57] Hume also deplored the vicious patterns of consumption by the feudal barons, much like Smith's graphic example of the diamond buckles that diverted the annual labour of 1,000 men.[58] As Hume remarked, 'the same care and toil that raised a dish of peas [for the feudal baron] at Christmas, would give bread to a whole family during six months'.[59] In the modern era, 'where the labourers and artisans are accustomed to work for low wages, and to retain but a small part of the fruits of their labour, it is difficult for them, even in a free government, to better their conditions, or conspire among themselves to heighten their wages'.[60] Far better to reward good work with high wages and foster a more liberal polity. Hume also criticised the system of parish relief and 'giving alms to common beggars', because it perpetuated idleness and destitution, a view that would be echoed by the classical economists.[61]

Underemployment had not only typified the feudal era, Hume believed, but also hindered economic growth in many parts of eighteenth-century Europe, particularly Ireland. Hume had visited Cork briefly in 1746, and read Jonathan Swift's *Short View of the State of Ireland* (1727–28).[62]

---

[54] *E* (LF), pp. 198, 267, *E* (C), pp. 161, 208. See Schabas and Wennerlind, *Philosopher's Economist*, pp. 186–87.
[55] *E* (LF), p. 262, *E* (C), pp. 204–5.   [56] *E* (LF), p. 277, *E* (C), pp. 214–15.
[57] *E* (LF), p. 262, *E* (C), pp. 204–5.   [58] Smith, *Wealth of Nations*, p. 419.
[59] *E* (LF), p. 279, *E* (C), p. 216.   [60] *E* (LF), p. 266, *E* (C), pp. 207–8.
[61] *E* (LF), p. 457, *E* (C), p. 327; *EPM*, p. 11. This also suggests that Hume belongs to the socialist lineage of classical economists instantiated by John Stuart Mill; they voiced strong disapproval of poor relief as more than a temporary solution. See McCabe, *Mill*.
[62] *E* (LF), p. 310, *E* (C), p. 238. In 1765, Hume had planned to move from Paris to Dublin with British ambassador Lord Hertford, whom he had served in the Paris embassy as secretary. Because Hume was a reputed infidel, however, his appointment was blocked. While disappointed, Hume

As Istvan Hont documented, the plight of Ireland, particularly its dearth of manufacturing, figured prominently in the rich country–poor country debate of the period.[63] Low Irish wages engendered idleness and entrapped the people in poverty. In his essay 'Of Taxes', Hume quoted the observations of William Temple, who had drawn contrasts between the wealth of Holland and the poverty of Ireland, where 'the soil, and scarcity of people, all things necessary to life are so cheap, that an industrious man, by two days labour, may gain enough to feed him the rest of the week. Which I [Hume] take to be a very plain ground of the laziness attributed to the people'.[64] High wages, by contrast, created more demand for goods as well as strengthened the willingness to work well, and thus had a double effect on productivity.

Hume's monetary theory emphasised the neutrality of money, but he made an exception for the case of a sudden injection of money due to a trade surplus.[65] Solid Spanish coins coming to England from the sale of cloth created a temporary increase in purchasing power for the weavers as they settled their credit accounts with the local purveyors. The artisan 'carries his money to market, where he finds every thing at the same price as formerly, but returns with greater quantity and of *better kinds*'.[66] This prompted them to intensify their work per day and, as the new coins circulated, inspired others, such as the farmers, to work 'with greater alacrity and attention'.[67] All of this transpired before an increase in wages and prices. 'It is easy to trace the money in its progress through the whole commonwealth; where we shall find, that it must first quicken the diligence of every individual, before it encrease the price of labour [the wage].'[68] Hume clearly grasped that the quality of labour itself left much room for improvement, and that this would be best elicited when incentivised by an enlarged wage-basket of quality goods.

English goods, such as cloth and hardware, that were once crude and highly imperfect, had through skilled production become highly competitive in global markets. Some of this technical knowledge came from the shop floor, so to speak. As an example, Hume pointed to an unnamed

characterised the pending move as akin to 'Stepping out of Light into Darkness to exchange Paris for Dublin' (*HL*, I, p. 514).

[63] See Hont, *Jealousy of Trade*, pp. 250–53.   [64] *E* (LF), p. 344, *E* (C), p. 258.

[65] The insight that a sudden and unanticipated surge in the money supply could stimulate output was made famous by Milton Friedman, and he gave full recognition of his debt to Hume. See Schabas and Wennerlind, *Philosopher's Economist*, p. 208.

[66] *E* (LF), p. 287, *E* (C), p. 221; italics mine.   [67] *E* (LF), p. 286, *E* (C), p. 221.

[68] *E* (LF), p. 287, *E* (C), p. 221.

Dutch brewer who had brought the skills of dying woollen cloth to England during the Restoration, resulting in a surge in productivity.[69] In general, 'industry is much promoted by the knowledge inseparable from ages of art and refinement ... [and] by an application to the more vulgar arts, at least, of commerce and manufacture.'[70] With the right opportunities, 'low people, without education, will start up amongst us, and distinguish themselves in every profession'.[71] Later in life, Hume befriended Jean D'Alembert who had collaborated with Denis Diderot on the multi-volume *Encyclopédie,* renowned for its coverage of *les arts et métiers* and mission to elevate the self-realisation of artisans.[72]

Artisanal production prompted urbanisation, a feature of modern Europe that Hume much celebrated. As he estimated (correctly), 'in France, England, and indeed most parts of Europe, half of the inhabitants live in cities; and even of those who live in the country, a great number are artizans, perhaps a third'.[73] A metropolis such as London stimulated demand and thus accelerated the path to enrichment. Before the Industrial Revolution, London was the most concentrated site for manufacturing. As Hume noted in a letter to James Oswald in 1750, 'the manufactures of London, you know, are steel, lace, silk, books, coaches, watches, furniture, fashions'.[74] If one drew a circle with a radius of two hundred miles from the Dover–Calais corridor, Hume proposed, it would include an unprecedented concentration of people and wealth, not dissimilar to what at present is known as the European megalopolis of over 100 million persons stretching from Manchester to Milan.[75] The regions of western Germany, Hume reckoned, had twenty times more people than in the Roman era, and some of the best cultivated fields that he had ever witnessed.[76] Hume valued the half a million 'industrious' Huguenots who had left France after 1685, many of whom enriched English towns with their 'immense sums of money, those arts and manufactures'.[77]

Whereas in China, Hume noted, a labourer earned the equivalence of only three half-pence a day, in England the average per capita disposable

---

[69] *HE*, VI, p. 538.   [70] *E* (LF), p. 273, *E* (C), p. 212.   [71] *E* (LF), p. 208n, *E* (C), p. 168n.

[72] This mission is spelled out in Jean Le Rond d'Alembert, *Preliminary Discourse to the Encyclopedia of Diderot*, trans. Richard N. Schwab (Chicago, 1995 [1751]).

[73] *E* (LF), p. 256n, *E* (C), p. 200n1. Holland was half-urbanised by the mid seventeenth century. Hume made a record of the prospering middle classes of Reims and Rotterdam (*HL*, I, pp. 22, 115). Mokyr records that, for England, c. 1700, only 32 per cent worked primarily in agriculture – 'an astonishingly low figure for a "pre-industrial" economy' – and that 28 per cent of the households were 'shopkeepers, traders and artisans' (Mokyr, *Enlightened Economy*, p. 15).

[74] *HL*, I, pp. 143–44.   [75] *E* (LF), p. 448, *E* (C), p. 322.

[76] *E* (LF), p. 453, *E* (C), p. 325; *HL*, I, p. 122.   [77] *HE*, VI, p. 471.

income was six pence per day.[78] Yet at least in Hume's circles, one was
'esteemed but poor who has five times that sum [thirty pence per day, or
£45 per annum]'.[79] This was Hume's plight in his early twenties when he
tried to make ends meet on an annuity of about £50. It proved insufficient
to live in London or Paris where he stopped briefly, or even in Reims,
insofar as he found living there after one year too costly. Yet he estimated
in his essay on population that there were a million persons living in
London, and five thousand more arriving each year.[80] Glaswegian tradesmen, Hume observed, earned 10 shillings a week (£25 per annum). This
was below the poverty line for a gentleman such as himself, but clearly
considerably higher than the average of approximately £10 per annum
(six pence a day) for a commoner.[81]

  To capture Hume's picture using a normal distribution for income, he
had in mind a growing domestic product that would place a far greater
number of households within two standard deviations from the mean,
with a mean income that was gradually shifting to the right, and with ever-
diminishing numbers in the tails of the distribution of income (extreme
rich and poor income-earners). If one took Hume's divide between rich
and poor, say, £45 per annum as the mean (he and Smith each briefly
earned salaries of hundreds of pounds as tutors to wealthy aristocrats,
placing them in the top 1 per cent), and considered the range of, say,
£10 to £80 (plus or minus £35) as the region of two standard deviations,
this might form a better picture of what he had in mind in his efforts to see
the middle class swell and lift up the lower orders in tandem, ensuring that
no one working received an annual wage (£2.25) as low as was found in
China.[82]

  Hume was clear that our desire for luxuries is insatiable. Just as the
aristocrats covet their 'champagne and ortolans', the ordinary street porter
now relished his 'bacon and brandy'.[83] Domestic manufacturing might
persist 'till every person in the state, who possesses riches, enjoys as great

---

[78] *HL*, I, p. 144.   [79] *E* (LF), p. 429, *E* (C), p. 311.
[80] *E* (LF), pp. 388, 428, *E* (C), pp. 285, 311.   [81] *E* (LF), p. 320, *E* (C), pp. 244–45.
[82] The base salary for Adam Smith at the University of Glasgow was £50, but with various
    supplements (1 guinea from each student, revenue from lodgers, and other remunerations), he
    could earn up to £300 in a good year. He left the professorship because of a better offer, namely,
    £400 to become the tutor to the third Duke of Buccleuch. Hume had spent half a year or more
    trying to wrangle £70 from Lord Annandale, about half of his salary at the time. Hume was a proto-
    statistician and thought in terms of mean-reverting tendencies, variances, and distributions in his
    estimations of the leading indicators of the economy. See Schabas and Wennerlind, *Philosopher's
    Economist*, pp. 72–81.
[83] *E* (LF), p. 276, *E* (C), p. 214.

plenty of home commodities; and those in as great perfection, as he desires; *which can never possibly happen*'.[84] In other words, because human desires are unlimited, there is much potential for an increasing standard of living, and those better off bootstrap those beneath them. 'It is impossible but the domestic industry of every one must receive an increase from the improvements of the others.'[85] A nation with higher wages, one that uses skilled labour, and 'that has a large import and export [trade], must abound more with industry, and ... luxuries ... [and is] more powerful, as well as richer and happier'.[86] A nation with extensive manufacturing and international trade is one where 'a greater number of laborious men are maintained, without *robbing any one* of the necessaries, or even the chief conveniences of life'.[87] Hume thus envisioned a future with higher per capita levels of consumption, of a more diverse wage-basket, and the collective well-being of millions of labourers.

12.2 Political Stability

Hume argued that authoritative regimes that depend on the whims of kings or queens foster inequality. 'The poverty of the common people is a natural, if not an infallible effect of absolute monarchy.'[88] In the feudal era, 'all the labour is bestowed on the cultivation of the ground; and the whole society is divided into two classes, proprietors of land, and their vassals or tenants. The latter are necessarily dependent, and fitted for slavery and subjection ... [whereas] the former naturally erect themselves into petty tyrants ... and throw the whole society into such confusion'.[89] While Hume voiced much admiration for modern republics for eliminating such tyranny, when all was said and done, he came out in favour of constitutional monarchies such as his own, in part because they are more stable. 'Were England a republic, and were any private man possessed of a revenue, a third, or even a tenth part as large as that of the crown, he would very justly excite jealousy; because he would infallibly have great authority, in the government: And such an irregular authority, not avowed by the laws, is always more dangerous than a much greater authority, derived from them.'[90] In other words, republics were more vulnerable to the unbridled power of an excessively wealthy individual, whereas a

---

[84] *E* (LF), p. 264, *E* (C), p. 206.   [85] *E* (LF), p. 328, *E* (C), p. 249.
[86] *E* (LF), p. 263, *E* (C), pp. 205–6.   [87] Ibid.; italics mine.   [88] *E* (LF), p. 265, *E* (C), p. 207.
[89] *E* (LF), p. 277, *E* (C), pp. 214–15.   [90] *E* (LF), p. 50, *E* (C), p. 62.

constitutional monarchy thrived on a system of checks and balances between the Crown and the *nouveau riche.*

With the advent of modern commerce, political stability tended to move in tandem with a rising merchant class, or so Hume argued. It is the 'middling rank of men, who are the best and firmest basis of public liberty', if only because they do not 'submit to the tyranny of their sovereign'.[91] Moreover, 'any great blow given to trade … throws the whole system of government into confusion'.[92] Hume remarked that 'trade was never esteemed an affair of state till the last century', and he welcomed the many policies issued to expand unrestricted trade or prompt infant industries such as the production of Scottish linen.[93] Hume's *Essays* and *History of England* offers innumerable observations on trade policies that demonstrate the net gains for both the merchants and the public at large.[94]

Although as early as the sixteenth century, the wealth of some English merchants exceeded longstanding aristocrats, this also had trickle-down effects, for example, prompting higher incomes for other 'professionals' such as doctors or lawyers.[95] By 1750, Hume noted, British soldiers received double the wages of the French, in part because of the allure of other more remunerative careers, but also, he maintained, because they fought more effectively.[96] Furthermore, the incomes drawn by those in the middle class tended to be financial rather than landed, and that too depended on a stable polity to insure interest payments on Exchequer funds and government bonds. 'Land has many disadvantages in comparison of funds' and, 'were there no funds, great merchants would have no expedient for realizing or securing any part of their profit' … [Consequently, merchants] 'with large stocks and incomes, may naturally be supposed to continue in trade, where there are public debts [bonds]', since this gave them a place to park their liquid capital.[97]

Prosperity also enabled the sovereign to tax more effectively. Once everyone is above mere subsistence, it is far easier, particularly in times of war, for the Crown to bite into the surplus. 'They must be very heavy taxes, indeed, and very injudiciously levied, which the artisan will not, of

[91] *E* (LF), p. 278, *E* (C), p. 215.   [92] *E* (LF), p. 358, *E* (C), p. 267.
[93] *E* (LF), pp. 88, 324, *E* (C), pp. 86, 247.
[94] See John Berdell, 'Innovation and Trade: David Hume and the Case for Freer Trade', *History of Political Economy*, 28 (1996), pp. 107–26 and Jia Wei, 'Maritime Trade as the Pivot of Foreign Policy in Hume's History of Great Britain', *Hume Studies*, 40 (2014), pp. 169–203.
[95] *E* (LF), p. 329, *E* (C), p. 250.   [96] *E* (LF), p. 282, *E* (C), pp. 218–19.
[97] *E* (LF), p. 354, *E* (C), p. 265.

himself, be enabled to pay, by superior industry and frugality.'[98] Hume criticised Archibald Hutcheson, who had failed to notice in his treatise on taxes (1721) that 'the laborious poor pay a considerable part of the taxes by their annual consumptions'.[99] Instead, a tax on goods that are 'consumed by the common people' ought to be 'moderate' and 'laid on gradually' so as to be least discernable.[100] Hume advocated increasing excise taxes on luxuries, because 'such taxes are least felt by the people' and 'naturally produce sobriety and frugality'.[101] Moreover, Hume maintained that a tax on 'visible property in lands and houses would really at last answer for the whole', but he knew that this would be met with much resistance from the wealthier classes.[102] He emphatically opposed the poll tax because it had no inherent constraints and proved oppressive, unlike duties on imports that were limited by the elasticity of demand.[103] The fall of the Roman Empire was partly due to oppressive taxes and, as a result, Hume issued warnings to his readers not to follow suit.[104]

The public debt posed even greater threats to the stability of the polity. The interest on the debt alone was staggeringly high; Hume estimated that it was £45 million c.1740 and, by the Seven Years' War, had almost tripled.[105] In the case of an imminent collapse, Hume feared that the government might opt to rescue the '17,000 bondholders' and sacrifice 'the safety of millions'.[106] Far better, he argued, to declare a voluntary bankruptcy and harm the bondholders. Moreover, as the debt came due without sufficient funds in the Crown's coffers, members of the *rentier* class were less likely to honour their national ties and would emigrate, and the government possibly collapse that much the sooner.[107]

Hume knew full well that the public debt was in essence a mortgage on future generations. One method of reducing its burden was to impose new taxes, especially on the landowners. Because the debt was growing, however, this might, in the long term, induce a return to absolutism. Hume imagined a scenario with a property tax of 19 shillings on the pound. One could bid 'adieu to all ideas of nobility, gentry, and family', such that 'the several ranks of men, which form a kind of independent magistracy in a state', would be 'entirely lost'.[108] The nation would degenerate into 'a grievous despotism', devoid of a 'spirit, ambition, or enjoyment'.[109] Hume

---

[98] *E* (LF), p. 347, *E* (C), p. 261.   [99] *E* (LF), p. 361, *E* (C), p. 269.

[100] *E* (LF), p. 343, *E* (C), p. 258.   [101] *E* (LF), p. 345, *E* (C), p. 259.

[102] *E* (LF), p. 361, *E* (C), p. 269.   [103] *E* (LF), p. 346, *E* (C), p. 260.   [104] Ibid.

[105] Hume, 'Memoranda', p. 507.   [106] *E* (LF), p. 364, *E* (C), p. 271.

[107] *E* (LF), p. 357, *E* (C), p. 267.   [108] *E* (LF), pp. 357–58, *E* (C), p. 267.

[109] *E* (LF), p. 358, *E* (C), p. 267.

seems, with this remark, to wish to preserve the landowning aristocracy. Ranks are important, and in that respect, he did not wish to tamper with the distribution of wealth, nor abolish the private ownership of land. But he also envisioned an aristocracy that had evolved, contrasting the feuding barons of the Middle Ages with modern landowners, including his older brother who had inherited the family estate and, by studying 'agriculture as a science', achieved higher yields.[110] In sum, Hume welcomed aristocrats who were ambitious and not prone to vicious luxuries or idleness. A tax on property was effective because it was easier to collect, Hume noted, but it should not rise to the point where there was no incentive to improve the arable land.

Hume also suggested that excessive financial gains were unwarranted. In his *History of England*, he cited an observation by Josiah Child 'that in 1688 there were on the Change [Royal Exchange] more men worth 10,000 pounds than there were in 1650 worth a thousand' and that the number of coaches had 'augmented a hundred-fold'.[111] Yet Hume was challenged to see the value of trading equities. 'What possible advantage is there which the nation can reap by the easy transference of stock from hand to hand? ... What production we owe to Change-Alley, or even what consumption, except that of coffee, and pen, ink, and paper.'[112] Over time, he came to grasp that there was some value to the stock market and deleted that passage from the 1770 edition. Liquid capital – a share in the East India Company could be sold in fifteen minutes he noted – served to bring the profit rate in line with the interest rate, and hence lower the real price of goods.[113] Nevertheless, in the case of an excessive tax, 'property in money and stock in trade might easily be concealed or disguised' whereas land could not.[114] While Hume's thoughts on distributive justice using fiscal tools are half-baked, it is clear that he had an eye for unwarranted outcomes and inequalities and kept uppermost in mind the well-being of the nation as a whole.

12.3   Global Peace and Prosperity

Hume argued that 'enormous monarchies' are inherently unstable and that 'extensive conquests, when pursued, must be the ruin of every free

---

[110] *E* (LF), p. 261, *E* (C), p. 204. Hume had a number of friends in the Scottish aristocracy who were directly engaged in economic improvement, whether mining, shipping, or the linen trade. See Schabas and Wennerlind, *Philosopher's Economist*, p. 48.
[111] *HE*, VI, p. 538.   [112] *E* (LF), pp. 636–37, *E* (C), p. 639.   [113] *E* (LF), p. 353, *E* (C), p. 264.
[114] *E* (LF), p. 361, *E* (C), p. 269.

government'.[115] His argument for the inevitable collapse of empires appealed to human weaknesses. The 'ancient nobility' who spawned the most gifted military leaders would be disinclined to leave the capital city. Their 'affections attach them to their sovereign, [and hence they] live all at court; and never will accept of military employments, which would carry them to remote and barbarous frontiers, where they are distant both from their pleasures and their fortune'.[116] As a result, less dedicated officers were sent to the hinterlands and mercenaries were engaged. Because they had no relish for the homeland, they fought 'without zeal, without attachment, [and] without honour'.[117] As an example, Hume pointed to the collapse of the House of Bourbon because none of the brave and faithful elite 'would submit to languish in the garrisons of Hungary or Lithuania'.[118] A similar set of factors played a part in the 'melancholy fate' of the Roman Empire, albeit over a much longer stretch of time.[119] Tongue-in-cheek, Hume observed that, in his own day, Italian mercenaries were adept at fighting an entire day without shedding a single drop of blood.[120] More disconcerting, such mercenaries were 'ready on every occasion to turn them against the prince, and join each desperate malcontent, who offers pay and plunder'.[121]

Hume favoured global peace over conquest. His vision for the future was one of extensive international and unrestricted trade that put more and more people around the world on the path to economic prosperity and peace. It was fortunate, he declared, that 'the growth of trade and riches . . . [will never be] confined entirely to one people'.[122] This assuaged fears that a single nation would dominate because of its innate economic advantages. Indeed, and providentially, the opposite held true. If trade was limited or restricted altogether, it would 'deprive neighbouring nations of that free communication and exchange which the Author of the world had intended, by giving them soils, climates, and geniuses, so different from each other'.[123] Hume hoped statesmen would dismantle the 'numberless bars, obstructions, and imposts' they have imposed on trade, not to mention their foolish monetary policies that 'serve to no purpose but to check industry, and rob ourselves and our neighbours of the common benefits of art and nature'.[124] His specie flow mechanism demonstrated that money had a will of its own and would override specific policies to limit the export of bullion.

---

[115] *E* (LF), pp. 340–41, 529, *E* (C), pp. 256, 373.   [116] *E* (LF), p. 341, *E* (C), p. 257.
[117] Ibid.   [118] Ibid.   [119] Ibid.   [120] *E* (LF), p. 275, *E* (C), p. 213.
[121] *E* (LF), p. 341, *E* (C), p. 257.   [122] *E* (LF), p. 283, *E* (C), pp. 218–19.
[123] *E* (LF), p. 324, *E* (C), p. 247.   [124] Ibid.

One reason that global trade would ever expand was the mobility of
capital. Because the price of manufactured goods was mostly determined
by the wage bill, this self-regulating mechanism would serve to bootstrap
the poorer countries towards greater prosperity. 'Manufactures, therefore
gradually shift their places, leaving those countries and provinces which
they have already enriched, and flying to others, whither they are allured
by the cheapness of provisions and labour; till they have enriched these
also, and are again banished by the same causes.'[125] Poorer nations would
accumulate capital, acquire a more skilled workforce, and thereby achieve a
comparable standard of living, only to see the capital leave and enrich other
regions of the globe.

Remarkably, Hume grasped that this path of enrichment could transpire
not just in the manufacturing sector but also in the agrarian and service
sectors. He proposed that France should transfer its fields, acre by acre,
from corn to wine, and Britain do the opposite, and both become trading
partners. Hume yearned for the day when 'French wines [were] sold in
England so cheap and in such abundance as to supplant, in some measure,
all ale, and home-brewed liquors'.[126] The ideal of exclusive production of
French wine and British corn appealed to Hume, not only because it
increased output and lowered the cost (and Hume loved his French wine)
but also because the trade dependencies would promote peaceful relations.
As for the service sector, the Dutch, Hume believed, had saturated their
arable land by 1650, but had nonetheless prospered by 'being the brokers,
and factors, and carriers of others'; as a result, their possible decline might be
'warded off for many generations, if not wholly eluded'.[127] As other nations
prospered, their demand for Dutch services, already at an 'advantage' due to
'superior stocks and correspondence', would sustain the Dutch trade.[128]

Another economic force that would facilitate this global path to prosperity was technology transfer. Hume believed that 'every improvement,
which we [Britons] have since made [in the modern era], has arisen from
our imitation of foreigners'.[129] 'Imitation soon diffuses all those arts; while
domestic manufactures emulate the foreign in their improvements, and
work up every home commodity to the utmost perfection.'[130] This was
particularly true if workers were skilled and hard-working. 'If the spirit of
industry be preserved, it may easily be diverted from one branch to
another; and the manufacturers of wool, for instance, be employed in

---

[125] *E* (LF), pp. 283–84, *E* (C), pp. 218–19.   [126] *E* (LF), p. 315, *E* (C), p. 241.
[127] *E* (LF), pp. 330–31, *E* (C), pp. 250–51.   [128] *E* (LF), p. 331, *E* (C), p. 251.
[129] *E* (LF), p. 328, *E* (C), p. 249.   [130] *E* (LF), p. 264, *E* (C), p. 206.

linen, silk, iron, or any other commodities, for which there appears to be a demand.'[131] Hume pointed to the importance for a progressive nation to diversify and thus weather economic downturns, 'to which every particular branch of commerce will always be exposed'.[132] A healthy degree of competition prompts technical improvement and the expansion of manufacturing. 'The emulation among rival nations serves rather to keep industry alive in all of them: And any people is happier who possess a variety of manufactures, than if they enjoyed one single great manufacture, in which they are all employed.'[133] Again, Hume's gaze was firmly on the prosperity and happiness of the labouring class, protecting them from cyclical bouts of deprivation due to forces beyond their control.

Hume argued that a nation benefits best if its trading partners are also undergoing enrichment, and hence his celebrated prayer for the 'flourishing commerce' of Germany, Spain, Italy, and even France itself.[134] 'The more the arts increase in any state, the more will be its demands from its industrious neighbours.'[135] Jealousy has no place in international trade. There is, in fact, a type of global justice: 'Nature, by giving a diversity of geniuses, climates, and soils, to different nations, has secured their mutual intercourse and commerce, as long as they all remain industrious and civilized.'[136] The gains from trade are ubiquitous and, as trading nations become more interdependent, serve to shore up peace.

The greatest expenditure by the state was on warfare. Hume believed that as nations underwent enrichment, this would increase their chances of success if under siege. In his essay 'Of National Characters', Hume remarked that, of all the 'national qualities, [courage] is the most precarious'.[137] The means to preserve the stock of courage are 'discipline, example, and opinion', and these are best found in nations where 'industry, knowledge, civility, may be of constant and universal use, and for several ages, may become habitual to the whole people'.[138] Moreover, this had the salutary effect that wars were conducted more efficiently and humanely. 'Even foreign wars [between commercial nations] abate of their cruelty', because they are fought with more 'honour' and 'courage'.[139]

In his appeal to the innate uniformity of human beings, Hume may, alas, have had only men of European heritage in mind. His prejudicial remarks about people of colour or, for that matter, about the intelligence of women, suggest that he did not embrace one and all. Nevertheless, as

---

[131] *E* (LF), p. 330, *E* (C), pp. 250–51.   [132] Ibid.   [133] Ibid.
[134] *E* (LF), p. 331, *E* (C), p. 251.   [135] *E* (LF), p. 329, *E* (C), p. 250.   [136] Ibid.
[137] *E* (LF), p. 212, *E* (C), p. 170.   [138] Ibid.   [139] *E* (LF), p. 274, *E* (C), p. 213.

Jacqueline Taylor has argued, for Hume our identities by rank, gender, nation, or class, are for the most part socially constructed.[140] If circumstances evolved sufficiently – due to what Hume labelled 'moral causes' and 'physical causes' – so too would the social categories.[141] Hume was not an egalitarian when it came to race or sex, but he recognised that different social and economic arrangements could do much to diminish inequality.

As Hirschman has shown, Hume endorsed the idea of '*doux commerce*', of the harmless and innocent pursuit of wealth.[142] A person engaged in a profitable business acquires 'by degrees, a passion for it, and knows no such pleasure as that of seeing the daily increase of his fortune'.[143] This served to foster the virtues of industriousness, frugality, and enterprise, and thus the stock of happiness. For Hume, the man of business was engaged in quotidian interactions that tested his moral mettle and was thus in a position to strengthen his character. Not everyone, of course, is honest or honourable, but the tendencies to these ends are stronger than the converse. Even if an opportunity for fraud or theft presents itself, the honest person will tend to stay within the law, or so Hume believed. 'The antipathy to treachery and roguery is too strong to be counterbalanced by any views of profit or pecuniary advantage. Inward peace of mind, consciousness of integrity, a satisfactory review of our own conduct; these are circumstances very requisite to happiness, and will be cherished and cultivated by every honest man, who feels the importance of them.'[144]

Somewhat presciently – given what we now know from current empirical studies – Hume asserted that 'the difference of fortune makes less difference in happiness than is vulgarly imagined'.[145] Wealth in and of itself does not bring individual happiness, particularly for a person among the idle rich who has no means for distinction and who succumbs to 'the feverish, empty amusements of luxury and expense'.[146] He never asserted, as would Smith, that the allure of wealth is a beneficial deception; rather, Hume commits to the 'progress of reason' even for the lower orders.[147] There are important non-pecuniary goods for the happy life, however, such as friendship, peace of mind, and enjoyment of the liberal arts. Our love for our families and communities is testament to the human capacity to subordinate self-love and, in some instances, to find joy in the happiness of another even if there would be no gain for oneself.

---

[140] See Taylor, *Reflecting Subjects*, p. 180.   [141] *E* (LF), p. 198, *E* (C), p. 161.
[142] Hirschman, *Passions and Interests*, pp. 60–63.   [143] *E* (LF), p. 301, *E* (C), pp. 231–32.
[144] *EPM*, p. 82.   [145] Ibid., p. 57.   [146] Ibid., p. 82.
[147] See Schabas, 'Hume and the "Progress of Reason"'.

Happiness, for Hume, could only be sustained if grounded in a genuine accountability to one's self. In this respect, the virtuous person perceives what the less virtuous do not. Virtue requires constant attention to one's deservedness, and the shoring up of goodness; it is something one has to practice and keep readily in view; good deeds and good offices were critical to Hume's mission of social progress. Wisdom, for Hume, comes from grasping that there is a significant difference between wealth and happiness. 'Who admires not Socrates; his perpetual serenity and contentment, amidst the greatest poverty and domestic vexation; his resolute contempt of riches.'[148] The paradox of acquiring wealth is that one must be always fearful of its disappearance; these insecurities tend to prey upon the mind. Hume related the story of a recently deceased miser opting to swim the river Styx rather than pay Charon his fee. Possible punishments, chaining him to Prometheus or assisting Sisyphus, were ruled out as not severe enough. The only one sufficiently punitive was to return the miser back to earth, 'to see the use his heirs are making of his riches'.[149]

One could, however, be virtuous and wealthy at the same time. Hume's hypothetical son-in-law, Cleanthes, was described as 'a man of business and application', who 'preserves a perpetual serenity on his countenance, and tranquillity in his soul' and who was, in sum, a paragon of virtue.[150] Such equanimity was hard-earned, however, the product of attending to the needs and cares of those around him. Constant business keeps one's tendencies for splenetic dispositions in check, an insight that Adam Smith would also articulate. Moreover, as the fictitious father of Hume's grandchildren, Cleanthes could be relied upon to steward his accumulated assets for future generations.

In Book 3 of the *Treatise of Human Nature,* Hume devotes a section to 'Natural Abilities', and emphasises the fact that these could be enhanced or diminished under various circumstances. For example, 'good sense and genius beget esteem', while 'wit and humour excite love'.[151] In this same section, Hume explores the many factors that might not only forge the most virtuous character but also carry a person 'farthest in any of his undertakings'. The list is long but includes industry, application, frugality, and patience.[152] In sum, Hume thought long and hard about how we might transform sow's ears into silk purses. For the lower orders, he believed, prosperity and a liberal government had strengthened their moral character, and in no place more than in England. As he myopically claimed

---

[148] *EPM*, p. 63.   [149] *E* (LF), p. 572, *E* (C), pp. 31–32.   [150] *EPM*, p. 73.   [151] *T*, p. 388.
[152] Ibid., p. 389.

in his essay 'Of National Characters' (thereby undercutting much credibility), 'the English are the most remarkable of any people, that perhaps ever were in the world', due to their system of government and hence 'the great liberty and independency, which *every man* enjoys'.[153]

Hume's vision for the future was such that as each wealthy nation reached its apogee, as in the case of Holland, the wealth of the next hegemonic power would attain a greater height, as in the case of Britain. Looking to the future, Hume believed that America would next ascend and outstrip Britain, and that there was reason to believe that China might surpass both, if shipping costs were lowered and trade channels opened up.[154] The primary point, however, is that no 'one nation should be a monopolizer of wealth'.[155] This outcome was prevented by several deeply rooted features of our world, the global equilibration of specie in terms of the balance of trade, the transfer of technology, and the flight of capital to countries with lower wages. As populations grew and labourers prospered, extreme poverty would be eliminated. Because the middle class expanded and received higher incomes, in one nation and then the next, this would boost the incomes of the labourers as well; all boats would rise with the tide. There was, for Hume, a long-term distributive justice at the global level that also fostered a reduction in the economic inequality of income.

---

[153] *E* (LF), p. 207, *E* (C), p. 167; italics mine.
[154] *E* (LF), pp. 122, 313, *E* (C), pp. 108, 240; *HL*, I, p. 144.   [155] *HL*, I, pp. 271–72.

CHAPTER 13

Hume and the Politics of Money

Tom Hopkins

The publication of the *Political Discourses* in 1752 established Hume as a leading commentator on political economy.[1] Hume opens the collection with a warning that he will be leading us 'out of the common road' and down paths of thought more 'refined and subtile' than might be expected in discussion of *'commerce, luxury, money, interest, &c.'*. In the first essay, 'Of Commerce', however, we are invited to stray only a little before we are ushered back to the way marked out by received opinion, for Hume's purpose here is only to qualify, not to subvert, a maxim he holds to be 'true in general':

> The greatness of a state, and the happiness of its subjects, how independent soever they may be supposed in some respects, are commonly allowed to be inseparable with regard to commerce; and as private men receive greater security, in the possession of their trade and riches, from the power of the public, so the public becomes powerful in proportion to the opulence and extensive commerce of private men.[2]

He is, it is true, quick to concede to the critics of luxury that there may be circumstances in which the wealth of individuals could diminish the strength of the public. 'Man is', he notes, 'a very variable being'. But the examples of Sparta, or the early Roman Republic, would not serve to overthrow the general principle. Ancient policy, which purchased power in arms at the cost of general austerity, constituted a violent departure from the common course of human affairs. Wise sovereigns know to take mankind as they find them and will not seek to aggrandise the public by the poverty of individuals.[3] Luxury, born of the growth of manufacture

---

[1] With thanks to the editors for their advice, their encouragement, and, above all, their patience.

[2] *E* (LF), p. 255, *E* (C), p. 200; from 1760, the list read *'commerce, money, interest, balance of trade, &c.'*, reflecting the substitution of the title 'Of Refinement in the Arts' for 'Of Luxury' for the second essay in the sequence.

[3] *E* (LF), pp. 255–60, *E* (C), pp. 201–4. For the eighteenth-century luxury debate, Istvan Hont, 'The Early Enlightenment Debate on Commerce and Luxury' in Mark Goldie and Robert Wokler, eds.,

and the mechanical arts, stimulates industry. The 'stock of labour' available for the discretionary use of the public is increased without sensibly diminishing the prosperity of the nation at large. The power of sovereigns and the happiness of states go hand in hand.[4]

Conjoining power and plenty in this manner may have been, as Hume attests, a commonplace in discussions of the politics of commerce, but it provides a useful starting point for thinking about some of the thornier issues involved in interpreting Hume's 'economic' essays.[5] The eight essays that opened the *Political Discourses* – 'Of Commerce', 'Of Luxury/Of Refinement in the Arts', 'Of Money', 'Of Interest', 'Of the Balance of Trade', 'Of the Balance of Power', 'Of Taxes' and 'Of Public Credit', along with 'Of the Jealousy of Trade', inserted between the fifth and sixth essays after 1758 – formed an interconnected sequence concerned with the interplay between public and private interest in a political landscape reshaped by the growth of trade, both domestic and international. Insofar as 'men and commodities are the real strength of any community', the interests of the public and those of private individuals, taken singly or in aggregate, were, for Hume, best understood as broadly aligned.[6] 'Modern' policy started from the advantages to be drawn from the advance of industry and the refinements in taste, manners and knowledge with which it was attended. Hume's account of these advantages, it has often been noted, stands largely on ground first mapped out in Books 2 and 3 of

---

The Cambridge History of Eighteenth-Century Political Thought (Cambridge, 2006), pp. 379–418; and Christopher J. Berry, *The Idea of Luxury: A Conceptual and Historical Investigation* (Cambridge, 1994), ch. 6. On Hume's position, see Christopher J. Berry, 'Hume and Superfluous Value (or the Problem with Epictetus' Slippers)', in Carl Wennerlind and Margaret Schabas, eds., *David Hume's Political Economy* (New York, 2008), pp. 49–64.

[4] *E* (LF), pp. 261–62, *E* (C), pp. 204–5. On this conjunction, see, classically, Jacob Viner, 'Power versus Plenty as Objectives of Foreign Policy in the Seventeenth and Eighteenth Centuries', in Viner, *Essays on the Intellectual History of Economics*, ed. Douglas A. Irwin (Princeton, NJ, 1991), pp. 128–53; and Istvan Hont, *Jealousy of Trade: International Competition and the Nation-State in Historical Perspective* (Cambridge, MA, 2005), pp. 185–266. More broadly, see Lars Magnusson, *Mercantilism: The Shaping of an Economic Language* (Abingdon, 1994); Magnusson, *The Political Economy of Mercantilism* (Abingdon, 2015); and Philip J. Stern and Carl Wennerlind, eds., *Mercantilism Reimagined: Political Economy in Early Modern Britain and Its Empire* (New York, 2014).

[5] Hume nowhere refers to the subject matter of the essays as 'oeconomy', though the term is employed elsewhere in his writings to denote household management and, by extension, forms of organisation. The suggestion by Margaret Schabas and Carl Wennerlind, *A Philosopher's Economist: Hume and the Rise of Capitalism* (Chicago, 2020), pp. 17–18, that a passage in *EHU*, which speaks of 'our enquiries concerning the mental powers and oeconomy' (p. 11), should be understood as referring, even if obliquely, to a 'science of economics' appears doubtful; from the context, it is more likely to denote the 'oeconomy' of the mind. On the conceptual history of *oikonomia* and its cognates, see Keith Tribe, *The Economy of the Word: Language, History, and Economics* (Oxford, 2015), pp. 21–88.

[6] *E* (LF), p. 293, *E* (C), pp. 225–26.

the *Treatise of Human Nature.*[7] The happiness of individuals, we learn, in passages expanding on *T* 2.2.4, consists in the tempered admixture of three ingredients: action, pleasure and indolence. Industry, and the variety of occupations that it brings in its train, is a stimulant to the mind, imparting vigour, intellectual curiosity and a humane disposition.[8] In turn, industry, knowledge and humanity contribute to the greatness of states. When expedient, the industry of individuals could be turned to the service of the public; the cultivation of reason would serve in the perfection of the laws and of the arts of government; and the diffusion of humane maxims of conduct and habits of civility would moderate the rigour of the magistrates and the zeal of partisans alike.[9] This was to implicate the history of commerce and the arts in the natural history of justice and property that Hume had sketched in *T* 3.2, and which served as the basis for an extended critique of Locke's account of the origin of political society in contract.[10]

13.1   The Natural History of Property and Justice

Hume, like Locke, had no difficulty in motivating an account of the origins of *natural* society in 'that natural appetite betwixt the sexes'. Children were 'fashioned by degrees' for social life in a setting where the exercise of parental authority was governed by natural affection.[11] The

---

[7] James Bonar, *Philosophy and Political Economy*, 3rd ed. (London, 1922 [1893]), ch. 6, offered the first extended exploration of the connection between the 'ethical and psychological' elements of Hume's philosophy and the economic writings from a characteristically idealist standpoint. He was followed, to better effect, by Albert Schatz, *L'œuvre économique de David Hume* (Paris, 1902) and by Eugene Rotwein, 'Introduction', in David Hume, *David Hume: Writings on Economics*, ed. Eugene Rotwein, 2nd ed. (Madison, WI, 1970), pp. ix–cxi. More recently, see John Robertson, *The Case for the Enlightenment: Scotland and Naples, 1680–1760* (Cambridge, 2005), chs. 6–7; the essays by Richard Boyd and by Till Grüne-Yanoff and Edward F. McClennen in Wennerlind and Schabas, eds., *David Hume's Political Economy*; Willie Henderson, *The Origins of David Hume's Economics* (Abingdon, 2010), chs. 3–5; and Schabas and Wennerlind, *A Philosopher's Economist*, esp. ch. 4.
[8] *E* (LF), pp. 269–71, *E* (C), pp. 209–11.   [9] *E* (LF), pp. 273–74, *E* (C), pp. 212–13.
[10] On the natural history of justice, Annette C. Baier, *A Progress of Sentiments: Reflections on Hume's Treatise* (Cambridge, MA, 1991), ch. 10; Istvan Hont, *Politics in Commercial Society: Jean-Jacques Rousseau and Adam Smith*, eds. Béla Kapossy and Michael Sonenscher (Cambridge, MA, 2015), pp. 34–35, 42, 49, 51–52.
[11] *T*, p. 312; compare John Locke, *Two Treatises of Government*, ed. Peter Laslett (Cambridge, 1988 [1690]), bk. II, ch. VII, pp. 318–22 and, for the nature and limits of paternal power, bk II, ch. VI. For comparison, see Istvan Hont, 'Adam Smith's History of Law and Government as Political Theory', in Richard Bourke and Raymond Geuss, eds., *Political Judgement: Essays for John Dunn* (Cambridge, 2009), pp. 140–43. Compare Paul Sagar, *The Opinion of Mankind: Sociability and the Theory of the State from Hobbes to Smith* (Princeton, NJ, 2018), ch. 2, and, for the Lockean story, p. 112.

challenge was to explain how a sense of the advantages of society could subsist and develop outside the affective matrix of family life if one did not suppose, with Locke, an available, and divinely ordained, framework of natural rights and obligations. Hume dismissed the idea that the 'limited generosity' characteristic of human nature would suffice to motivate moral conduct on any large scale, at least under conditions of scarcity.[12] He appealed instead to the 'interested affection', the love of gain, schooled by experience in the value of restraint. The uninhibited pursuit of self-interest was destructive of lasting social bonds, but there was a remedy to be found. It turned on the distinction between short-term and long-term expectations. What was necessary was that the attention of individuals be directed towards the greater gains to be made over time in subordinating self-interest to mutually obliging rules of conduct. This required no 'contract' or 'promise', only the mutual expression, in deeds if not in words, of a common sense of the utility in abstaining from the possessions of others.[13] From this emergent 'convention' followed the elaboration of ideas of justice, property, right and obligation, seconded in their hold over the mind by the moral satisfaction to be derived from contemplation of the peaceful order they brought to society.[14] The argument was self-consciously framed to circumvent the theological premise of Locke's argument, dismissing both the existence and the need for a standard of justice independent of human judgement.[15]

Hume was under no illusion that this extended sense of self-interest, 'palpable' though it may be in even the most primitive of societies, would necessarily preclude injustice or disorder. He imagined that it could suffice 'where the possessions and the pleasures of life are few, and of little value, as they are in the infancy of society'.[16] Where more was at stake, the pull of short-term advantage would be rather stronger. The obscure light in which the precepts of justice must stand when compared with the objects of our own more immediate desires was sufficient explanation for defection from established principles of conduct. If the conventional foundations of society were not to give way to habitual iniquity, this 'infirmity of human

---

[12] *T*, pp. 317–18.   [13] Ibid., pp. 315–16.   [14] Ibid., p. 342.
[15] John Dunn, 'From Applied Theology to Social Analysis: The Break between John Locke and the Scottish Enlightenment', in Istvan Hont and Michael Ignatieff, eds., *Wealth and Virtue: The Shaping of Political Economy in the Scottish Enlightenment* (Cambridge, 1983), pp. 119–37; Istvan Hont, 'Commercial Society and Political Theory in the Eighteenth Century: The Problem of Authority in David Hume and Adam Smith', in Willem Melching and Wyger Velema, eds., *Main Trends in Cultural History: Ten Essays* (Amsterdam, 1994), pp. 54–94; Hont, 'Adam Smith's History of Law and Government as Political Theory'.
[16] *T*, p. 345.

nature' must be submitted to some external constraint, namely, the authority of civil government.[17] On the face of it, this was only to push the problem back a step, since there was no reason to suppose that the judgement of a magistrate should be any more secure against the solicitations of the passions than that of a private individual. Hume's answer was to argue once again that the passion of self-interest could be brought to check itself, if the general observation of the laws of justice could be made the immediate interest of a particular class within the state, the magistracy.[18] The origin of magistracy, Hume argued, picking up the thread of Locke's account of the early history of societies in chapter 8 of the *Second Treatise*, most likely lay in military rather than in civil government. Even a society without regular government would require captains in the event of foreign war. Once the advantages to be drawn from the government of a chief began to be felt in one sphere, it would require little for this authority to extend its reach to civil matters: 'Camps', Hume observed, 'are the true mother of cities.'[19] From the outset, the identification of the magistrate's interest with the interests of society thus extended beyond the execution and decision of laws. On Hume's account, they not only enforce existing conventions, but advance the creation of new ones, identifying their own advantage with that of their subjects. Government appears as a solution to the problem of coordinating collective action, bringing unity of design and purpose to projects of improvement, and foiling the efforts of those who would seek to lay the burden on others whilst enjoying the results: 'Thus bridges are built; harbours open'd; ramparts rais'd; canals form'd; fleets equip'd; and armies disciplin'd; every where [sic] by the care of government, which, tho' compos'd of men subject to all human infirmities, becomes, by one of the finest and most subtle inventions imaginable, a composition, that is, in some measure, exempted from all these infirmities.'[20]

As Annette Baier has archly noted, the words 'in some measure' carry more weight than may at first be evident.[21] Hume was developing a theory of legitimate government that would give authority its due without enjoining on subjects a duty of passive obedience. He was clear enough that the interest of magistrates in the preservation of order and the execution of justice did not extend to 'disputes betwixt themselves and their subjects'; nor, given the 'irregularity of human nature', should

[17] Ibid., p. 343. [18] Ibid., p. 344.
[19] Ibid., p. 346; compare Locke, *Two Treatises*, bk. II, ch. VIII, pp. 341–42. [20] Ibid., p. 345.
[21] Baier, *A Progress of Sentiments*, p. 261.

excesses of cruelty or ambition appear as anything other than a predictable political hazard. If duties of obedience were, ultimately, to be grounded on the interest of subjects in the maintenance of peace and justice, it was no stretch to conclude that where that interest ceased, so too must the obligation.[22] Where the line was to be drawn, however, was a matter of practical judgement hard to disentangle from estimates of narrow personal advantage on one hand, and the sentiments of loyalty and honour that habits of obedience tended to inculcate on the other. Locke's mistake, Hume charged, lay in the attempt to restrict the grounds on which this judgement must operate to the narrow question of right arising from the performance or non-performance of promises.[23]

13.2   Locke on Money and Civil Society

Locke, no more than Hume, had doubted that, in the infancy of society, the demands placed on government were slight and the potential for divergence between the interests of the people and their chosen chieftains limited.[24] So long as the measure of property remained bound to the equilibrium between the needs of a household and its capacity through labour to meet them, disputes over possession must have been rare and easily resolved. Locke never called into question the plenitude of God's creation; what explained the advent of sustained patterns of social conflict was not the exhaustion of natural resources, but the invention of money, and, as he emphasised, 'the tacit Agreement of Men to put a value on it'.[25] Not subject to spoilage, the coining of gold and silver permitted the accumulation and concentration of wealth; in using money, 'out of the bounds of Societie, and without compact', men have 'by a tacit and voluntary consent' established 'disproportionate and unequal Possession of the Earth'.[26] Locke found solace in the thought that however unequal the partition of land between territorial states, within political societies, 'the Laws regulate the right of property, and the possession of land is determined by positive constitutions'.[27] The problem, having once established an initial distribution of property by consent, and determined the laws of succession, delivery and accession that should govern its further development, was to show how the discretionary powers required to

---

[22] *T*, p. 353.   [23] *T*, pp. 352–64.   [24] Locke, *Two Treatises*, bk. II, ch. VIII, p. 342.
[25] Ibid., pp. 292–93. On the theodicical underpinnings of the argument, see John Dunn, *The Political Thought of John Locke* (Cambridge, 1969), pp. 90–91.
[26] Locke, *Two Treatises*, bk. II, ch. VIII, p. 302.   [27] Ibid.

uphold this legal order could be kept within their proper limits.[28] Ultimately, property owners had no other means of vindicating their legally established rights than by appeal to the executive power of the law of nature, and it was in these terms that Locke encouraged readers of the *Two Treatises of Government* to view the revolutionary crisis of 1688.[29] In the secular course of political life, however, the solution turned in no small measure on control of the fiscal apparatus of government, and this required thinking about the use of money not merely 'out of the bounds of Societie' but also in conjunction with the property order established within the civil state.[30]

Locke offered little more than a hint of what this entailed in the *Two Treatises*, but expanded on the subject in the 1691 *Some Considerations of the Consequences of the Lowering of Interest and Raising the Value of Money*, written in response to the campaign, orchestrated by Sir Josiah Child, for a statutory lowering of the rate of interest.[31] Locke took the partition of the earth and the unequal distribution of mineral resources as his analytical starting point:

> In a Country not furnished with Mines there are but two ways of growing Rich, either Conquest, or Commerce. By the first the *Romans* made themselves Masters of the Riches of the World; but I think that in our present circumstances, no Body is vain enough to entertain a Thought of our reaping the Profits of the World with our Swords, and making the Spoil and Tribute of Vanquished Nations, the Fund for the supply of the Charges of the Government, with an overplus for the wants, and equally craving Luxury, and fashionable vanity of the People.[32]

What remained was commerce, to which England was peculiarly well-suited by virtue of geography and national character. It was trade that had raised England to the rank of a European power, now on the defensive against rivals who would seize 'whatever parts of our Trade our Mismanagement, or want of Money, shall let slip out of our Hands'.[33] Locke, quite as much as Child, was clear that the money supply should be one of the principal cares of government: it was the circulation of money

---

[28] On property in civil society, James Tully, *A Discourse on Property: John Locke and His Adversaries* (Cambridge, 1980), ch. 7.

[29] Locke, *Two Treatises*, p. 137.   [30] Ibid., bk. II, ch. XI, pp. 360–62.

[31] On the textual and political background, see the editor's introduction to *Locke on Money*, ed. Patrick Hyde Kelly (2 vols., Oxford, 1991), I, pp. 3–39 and J. Keith Horsefield, *British Monetary Experiments, 1650–1710* (Cambridge, MA, 1960).

[32] John Locke, *Some Considerations of the Consequences of the Lowering of Interest and Raising the Value of Money in a Letter to a Member of Parliament*, in Locke, *Locke on Money*, ed. Kelly, I, pp. 222–23.

[33] Ibid., p. 223.

that turned 'the several Wheels of Trade'.[34] But to suppose that a reduction in the legal rate of interest would stimulate trade and agriculture was to mistake cause for effect. Increase of riches depended upon a favourable balance of trade and this could be secured only by industry and economy in consumption. Since a statutory reduction in the rate of interest could not compel foreign merchants and bankers to grant credit at anything other than the 'natural' rate, all that Child's measure would achieve would be redistribution of wealth from domestic creditors to domestic debtors.[35]

There was, Locke held, a necessary *Proportion of Money to Trade*, though he struggled to present the relationship in anything other than static terms.[36] In part, his strategy turned on distinguishing money's function as a 'counter', or unit of account, from its use as a 'pledge' in exchange.[37] In this second light, what mattered was the 'intrinsick value' of the coin, identified with its metallic content. But he further took a cue from Sir William Petty in insisting on the need to grapple with the 'quickness' or velocity of circulation of the coin. For this purpose, Locke's procedure was to treat the demand for money as a commodity – its 'Vent' – in approximate terms as a function of the standing monetary needs of three classes of consumer: landholders, labourers and 'brokers' or merchants, and to explain the natural rate of interest as determined by the relationship between this demand and 'the quantity of the then passing Money of the Kingdom'.[38] Maintained in its proper channels, money served to facilitate men's duty as stewards of creation to increase and to improve. Locke conceded, however, that in circulating 'some of it will unavoidably be dreined into standing pools'. His concern was chiefly with the problem of arbitrage in money markets overburdened with clipped coins circulating below their nominal value.[39] The resulting drainage of the coin abroad, and the distortions created in the lending markets, inflated borrowing costs, depressing both trade and land prices. When, in 1695, the issue of recoinage came before Parliament, Locke entered the

[34] Ibid., pp. 224, 233.
[35] For other critics of Child, see G. S. L. Tucker, *Progress and Profits in British Economic Thought, 1650–1850* (Cambridge, 1960), pp. 17–29.
[36] Locke, *Some Considerations*, in Locke, *Locke on Money*, ed. Kelly, I, p, 235. Compare Douglas Vickers, *Studies in the Theory of Money, 1690–1776* (Philadelphia, PA, 1959), pp. 45–61, and Kelly, 'Introduction', in Locke, *Locke on Money*, ed. Kelly, I, p. 84.
[37] Locke, *Some Considerations*, in Locke, *Locke on Money*, ed. Kelly, I, pp. 233–34.
[38] Ibid., pp. 235–42, 362. Compare Sir William Petty, *Political Arithmetick* (1690 [1676]), in Sir William Petty, *The Economic Writings of Sir William Petty*, ed. Charles H. Hull (2 vols., Cambridge, 1899), I, p. 310, for analysis in terms of circuits for wages, land rent and house rent.
[39] Locke, *Some Considerations*, in Locke, *Locke on Money*, ed. Kelly, I, p, 233; Vickers, *Studies in the Theory of Money*, pp. 48–49.

lists against William Lowndes's advocacy of 'raising' (i.e. devaluing) the coin by altering its nominal composition in silver. Locke's opposition was couched in terms sufficiently forceful to colour the government's own presentation of the case for restoration of the coin, even at the acknowledged cost of a contraction in supply.[40] At stake for Locke were the implications of deriving the origins of money from convention. On George Caffentzis's influential account, the devaluation of the coin, in breaking the link between denomination and 'intrinsick value' in silver exposed the status of money as what, in the *Essay Concerning Human Understanding*, Locke had termed a 'mixed mode': its physical referent could not exhaust the significance attached to it. The problem of semantic instability, central to Locke's philosophy of language, intruded into the discussion.[41] The use of a currency without a fixed metallic standard might be suitable to an 'Island separate from the Commerce of the rest of Mankind' and possessed of a fixed quantity of gold as silver; successive re-denominations of the coin would not in such a case disturb price stability.[42] It was otherwise when the quantity of metal available was in perpetual flux, as in any country open to trade. As Daniel Carey has emphasised, in this, as in his efforts to fix the signification of ethical terms, Locke's move was to appeal to an external standard of judgement, be it God or, as here, government.[43] What mattered was not the nominative standard first fixed, but that there was such a standard available and that it could meaningfully temper the instability that subjective judgements about the value of money threatened to introduce into the property order. For Hume, such a move was redundant.

13.3   Hume Contra Locke on Money

In the *Treatise*, Hume had given money conventional origins, likening the establishment of gold and silver as a 'common measure of exchange' to

<hr/>

[40] Locke's contributions to the debate, including the reply to Lowndes, *Further Considerations on Raising the Value of Money* (1695), are to be found in idem, *Locke on Money*, ed. Kelly, II.
[41] George Caffentzis, *Clipped Coins, Abused Words, and Civil Government: John Locke's Philosophy of Money*, new ed., ed. Paul Rekret (London, 2021); Daniel Carey, 'John Locke's Philosophy of Money', in Daniel Carey, ed., *Money and Political Economy in the Enlightenment* (Oxford, 2014), pp. 57–81. Compare Stefan Eich, *The Currency of Politics: The Political Theory of Money from Aristotle to Keynes* (Princeton, NJ, 2022), pp. 67–72. For 'mixed modes', John Locke, *An Essay Concerning Human Understanding*, ed. Peter Nidditch (Oxford, 1975), ch. XXII; on language, see Hannah Dawson, *Locke, Language and Early Modern Philosophy* (Cambridge, 2007).
[42] Locke, *Some Considerations*, in Locke, *Locke on Money*, ed. Kelly, I, 264.
[43] Carey, 'John Locke's Philosophy of Money', pp. 79–80; compare Dunn, *Political Thought of John Locke*, pp. 90–91.

the gradual emergence of language, and it was in this sense that, in 'Of Interest', he spoke of it as 'having chiefly a fictitious value'.[44] He opened the essay 'Of Money' by invoking one of Locke's favoured metaphors: money, he wrote, 'is none of the wheels of trade: It is the oil which renders the motion of the wheels more smooth and easy'. Taken in itself, the plenty or scarcity of money in a state should be a matter of indifference, 'since the prices of commodities are always proportioned to the plenty of money'.[45] Yet states did not exist in isolation: war, diplomacy and trade constituted the field of their mutual relations. Once the hypothetical case of a closed trading economy was set aside, fault lines would emerge. In war, a ready supply of money could pay for foreign mercenaries and for the equipage of fleets. But what might benefit the *public* might harm the *nation* by raising the price of labour and damaging foreign trade. Where labour costs were high, and not sufficiently compensated by industry, skill, or the retrenchment of mercantile profit made possible by the greater accumulation of stock in rich countries, manufacturing would decline: 'leaving those countries and provinces which they have already enriched, and flying to others, whither they are allured by the cheapness of provisions and labour; till they have enriched these also, and are again banished by the same causes'.[46] Locke had offered a static account of the relationship between price levels and the money supply. Hume rendered the relation dynamic with an account of the self-equilibrating nature of the in- and outflow of specie. Like water, he observed in 'Of the Balance of Trade', money allowed to communicate would find its level.[47]

As Istvan Hont has shown, Hume had his reasons for taking a more sanguine view of the wider consequences of this check on the concentration of wealth than some of his earliest readers. From Scotland, this 'happy concurrence of causes' took on quite different significance than when viewed from wealthy England; the politics of the Anglo-Scottish Union of 1707 looms large over what Hont has taught us to think of as

---

[44] *T*, p. 315. *Pace* Carl Wennerlind, 'An Artificial Virtue and the Oil of Commerce: A Synthetic View of Hume's Theory of Money', in Wennerlind and Schabas, eds., *David Hume's Political Economy*, pp. 105–27, Hume is at pains to distinguish such conventions from promises.

[45] *E* (LF), p. 281, *E* (C), pp. 218–19. The phrase 'wheels of trade' had been current since the 1660s.

[46] *E* (LF), pp. 283–84, *E* (C), pp. 219–20.

[47] *E* (LF), pp. 312–13, *E* (C), pp. 240–41. For background, see Jacob Viner, *Studies in the Theory of International Trade* (New York, 1937), esp. pp. 74–110 and 292–94. The question of whether Hume had seen Richard Cantillon's *Essai sur la nature du commerce en general*, circulating since the 1730s, but not printed until 1755, remains unresolved.

Hume's contribution to the 'rich country–poor country' debate.[48] Scotland's prosperity required leveraging the advantage of access to English markets by capitalising on low wage-rates in sectors with low barriers to market entry. From an English perspective, the scenario Hume sketched appeared in a rather different light: an admonition that commercial wealth was a fickle basis on which to rest the security of the nation, absent an ongoing, disciplined quest for productivity gains to offset wage differentials. One could think strategically about the interests of 'provinces' as well as those of states without losing sight of what distinguished the two. Through government, states enjoyed forms of agency available only derivatively, if at all, to politically subordinate provinces, including the power to tax, to borrow in the public name and to 'augment' (which is to say, to devalue) the coin. But the poor country's commercial advantages rested on none of these expedients, only on the absence of impediments to foreign trade.

The recoinage of 1696 had not closed the door on speculative monetary projects in the British kingdoms. The financial revolution of the 1690s set English public credit on a more stable long-term trajectory and, after the initial shock of the contraction in the money supply, credit began to recover.[49] In Scotland, however, the collapse of the Darien venture and the liquidity struggles of the Bank of Scotland had encouraged proposals for the expansion of the monetary supply through note issues backed by land or anticipated tax revenues.[50] The most notable was presented by the financier, John Law, who tied the concept to the encouragement of national fisheries and manufactures. Rejected by the Scottish Parliament, in 1714 the project nevertheless won the backing of the Duke of Orléans, Regent of France. The spectacular collapse of his Mississippi Scheme in 1720 set the terms for monetary and economic debate for much of the rest of the century, and deeply coloured Hume's writings.[51] In France, both defenders of Law's scheme, such as Jean-François Melon, and critics such as Charles Dutot, could agree that the kingdom had ample headroom for

---

[48] Hont, *Jealousy of Trade*, pp. 267–322; Hont, 'The "Rich Country–Poor Country" Debate Revisited: The Irish Origins and French Reception of the Hume Paradox', in Wennerlind and Schabas, eds., *David Hume's Political Economy*, pp. 243–323.

[49] On the 'financial revolution' of the 1690s, see P. G. M. Dickson, *The Financial Revolution in England: A Study in the Development of Public Credit, 1688–1756* (London, 1967); and John Brewer, *The Sinews of Power: War, Money and the English State, 1688–1783* (London, 1989).

[50] S. G. Checkland, *Scottish Banking: A History, 1695–1973* (Glasgow, 1975), pp. 23–53.

[51] [John Law], *Money and Trade Considered, with a Proposal for Supplying the Nation with Money* (Edinburgh, 1705); Antoin E. Murphy, *John Law: Economic Theorist and Policy-Maker* (Oxford, 1997).

monetary expansion. With a larger agrarian base than any of its rivals in trade, France had the potential to emerge as a self-sufficient manufacturing behemoth able to outcompete all-comers. Melon, whose *Essai politique sur le commerce* appeared in 1734, lacked the scepticism about Law that Dutot had acquired through more intimate knowledge of the inner workings of the *Compagnie des Indes*, and offered a robust defence of the use of a circulating public debt as a means to this end.[52] In 'Of Public Credit', Hume laid out a notably trenchant critique of the expansion of public borrowing in Britain driven by rivalry with France, and the argument acquired still greater urgency in the wake of the Seven Years' War.[53] But he was prepared to give ground to the idea that monetary expansion could provide at least a short-term stimulus to industry in the interval between the acquisition of money and the general rise in prices that he supposed would follow. Considering the case of the import of specie, the additional funds would at first be concentrated in a small number of hands who would, as a matter of course, put it to work. In employing labourers, they would set in train a circulation of money that 'must first quicken the diligence of every individual, before it encrease the price of labour'.[54] Yet money would sooner or later find its level, and the thought left Hume untroubled by the prospect of future revaluations of the coin. He recognised in the 'operations on money' that had perplexed Locke, not an outrage against natural justice, but a traditional expedient of government, more than bearable in a context where rising price levels owed more to the expansion of trade and industry offset by the influx of New World silver.[55]

More troubling was the recrudescence of adventitious schemes of paper credit, which enjoyed new favour in Scotland after the Jacobite Rebellion of 1745. The leading figures in Scottish Whig politics, Archibald Campbell, third Duke of Argyll and Andrew Fletcher, Lord Milton, looked with favour on the expansion of provincial banking beyond the

[52] Jean-François Melon, *Essai politique sur le commerce*, ed. Francine Markovits (Caen, 2014 [1734]), ch. xxiii; Charles Dutot, *Réflexions politiques sur les finances et le commerce*, ed. Paul Harsin (2 vols., Liège, 1935 [1738]); see Robertson, *The Case for the Enlightenment*, ch. 7 for a helpful discussion.
[53] Hont, *Jealousy of Trade*, pp. 325–53; J. G. A. Pocock, 'Hume and the American Revolution: The Dying Thoughts of a North Britain', in Pocock, *Virtue, Commerce and History: Essays on Political Thought and History* (Cambridge, 1985), pp. 125–41.
[54] *E* (LF), pp. 286–87, *E* (C), pp. 221–22. Margaret Schabas, 'Temporal Dimensions in Hume's Monetary Theory', in Wennerlind and Schabas, eds., *David Hume's Political Economy*, pp. 127–45; and Schabas and Wennerlind, *A Philosopher's Economist*, ch. 5.
[55] *E* (LF), pp. 287–88, *E* (C), pp. 222–23 citing Dutot's admittedly 'suspicious' figures on the effects of the devaluation of the reign of Louis XIV.

two Edinburgh banks. This was, as had been envisaged by the projectors of the 1700s, a scheme of government-sponsored industrial development, tailored now to the pressing demand for the integration of the Highlands into the British polity.[56] Hume announced his 'doubt' as to the wisdom of the policy in 'Of Money', but stated his objections in full in 'Of the Balance of Trade'.[57] On one level, his complaint about the expansion of paper credit beyond its ordinary use in mercantile transactions is the same as that directed by Locke against the conventional use of clipped coins at face value; paper money may circulate throughout the state, raising prices, but it is not received (at least without discount) abroad. There is a case to be made that Hume saw in paper credit a degree of moral hazard not present in the use of metal money, the conventional use of which might rest on a 'fiction', but one widely, if not universally, endorsed and tied to the real qualities of gold and silver as commodities in their own right.[58] But the burden of the essay's argument was directed elsewhere, to the manner in which artificial expansion of the money supply undercut the one real advantage Scotland enjoyed: low wages.

The question of wage discipline had troubled English writers since the Restoration, with high wages generally identified as an obstacle to foreign trade. There was broad agreement that the remedy was retrenchment in consumption, but the question of where this might fall was a matter of considerable controversy. Thomas Mun, writing in 1664, had argued that wage-rates were regulated by subsistence costs; labourers had no scope to economise and could not bear any share of taxation. Petty, on the other hand, supposed greater elasticity in wages; taxes on discretionary consumption goods would be borne by consumers in general, and would either excite labourers to greater industry or encourage thrift, an argument to which Hume gave qualified assent in 'Of Taxes'.[59] By contrast, Locke held

---

[56] Checkland, *Scottish Banking*, pp. 91–102; Charles W. Munn, *The Scottish Provincial Banking Companies, 1747–1864* (Edinburgh, 1981), pp. 10–39. On Campbell, Roger Emerson, *An Enlightened Duke: The Life of Archibald Campbell (1682–1761), Earl of Ilay, 3rd Duke of Argyll* (Kilkerran, 2013), esp. chs. 12–16. On Hume's relation to the debate on the Highlands, George Caffentzis, *Civilizing Money: Hume, His Monetary Project and the Scottish Enlightenment* (London, 2021), chs. 1–2; and on Scotland within the British fiscal state, Julian Hoppit, *The Dreadful Monster and Its Poor Relations: Taxation, Spending and the United Kingdom, 1707–2021* (London, 2021), ch. 2.

[57] *E* (LF), pp. 316–20, *E* (C), pp. 242–46.

[58] For suggestive exploration of these issues, Caffentzis, *Civilizing Money*, pp. 91–124, 147–72.

[59] *E* (LF), p. 343, *E* (C), p. 258; compare Thomas Mun, *England's Treasure by Forraign Trade, or, the Ballance of our Forraign Trade is the Rule of our Treasure* (London, 1664), ch. xvi; Petty, *Political Arithmetick*, ed. Hull, I, pp. 268–71; for subsequent developments; Edwin R. A. Seligman, *The Shifting and Incidence of Taxation*, 3rd ed. (New York, 1910), pp. 23–62; and for a recent discussion

that 'Taxes, however contriv'd, and out of whose Hand soever immediately taken, do in a Country, where their great Fund is in Land, for the most part terminate upon Land.'[60] The labourer, whose wage covered no more than what was necessary for subsistence, could not bear the charge, and merchants and brokers would not bear it, preferring to pass the burden on to the consumer.[61] Only the landowner, stymied by the inelasticity of rents, could find no means to shift taxes onto others. This gave landowners an immediate and pressing interest in public fiscal rectitude, as well as aligning the interests of government closely with those of fixed property. Locke was sensible of the fact that extravagant habits of consumption on the part of the 'Landed Man' could raise the cost of borrowing. His conception of property rights made of the need to balance expenditure against income as much a moral duty as a matter of prudence. But he preferred to explain the high cost of borrowing rather as the result of excessive intermediation in the credit markets, encouraged by an unstable currency. For his part, answering 'a celebrated writer' in 'Of Taxes', Hume confessed that he could see no reason why landowners should be any less adept at shifting the burden of taxes onto others than any other class, though he wryly conceded that it might be useful from the point of view of limiting public spending to convince them otherwise.[62] It was a point he would defend in correspondence with Turgot in 1766, by which time Locke's argument had become associated with the Physiocrats.[63]

What was at issue was more than the incidence of taxation. The question at hand was the relative standing of landed property in a trading economy. Locke was happy to grant an analogy between rental income and interest payments on money. Interest, like rent, represented the property owner's share of the advantage drawn from employment of their property, but whereas rent was proportioned to the market for a single commodity – for England the staple being wheat – the demand for money was proportioned to the 'Vent of all commodities, taken together'. Locke's argument implied that an increase in the money supply would

of Hume's views on taxation, Shane William Horwell, 'Taxation in British Political and Economic Thought, 1733–1816' (PhD dissertation, University College London, 2018), chs. 2–3.

[60] Locke, Some Considerations, in Locke, Locke on Money, ed. Kelly, I, p. 272.
[61] Ibid., pp. 274–75. For discussion, Seligman, Shifting and Incidence of Taxation, pp. 101–9; and for context, William Kennedy, English Taxation, 1640–1799 (London, 1913).
[62] E (LF), pp. 635–36, 346–47, E (C), pp. 257–61; the reference was broadened to encompass 'some political writers' in 1770, in the wake of discussion with Turgot.
[63] HL, II, 76, 93–94; and, for Turgot's side of the correspondence, Anne-Robert-Jacques Turgot, Œuvres de Turgot et documents le concernant, ed. Gustave Schelle, 2nd ed. (5 vols., Paris, 2018), II, pp. 438–46.

depress the rate of profit, and, with it prices, apparently on the assumption that this would translate into effective investment leading to an extended supply of commodities coming onto the market.[64] In this sense, a lowering of the *natural* rate of interest would indeed be a general boon to consumers. But it was not consumers, in general, but landowners in particular who bore the burden of public finance, and their overriding interest was in higher rents. Assuming stable levels of per capita consumption, no commodity exhibited greater price stability than wheat. The discovery of the Peruvian silver mines marked an epoch in monetary history; no such devaluation in the price of wheat could be observed, for its production remained always closely proportioned to consumption, and were it not for its perishable nature it might be regarded as a superior measure of value than silver or gold.[65] Absent decline in standards of husbandry or the fertility of the land, a rising price in wheat, and with it rising rents, could be chiefly attributed to increases in demand resulting from population growth, an index of prosperity. Conversely, falling rents were to be regarded as 'an infallible sign of the decay of your Wealth'. Locke commended the raising of rents as 'worth the Nations Care: For in that and not in the falling of *Interest* lies the true advantage of the Landed-man, and with him of the Publick'.[66]

Locke's treatment of interest rates as a function of the money supply had been attacked by Joseph Massie in 1750.[67] In 'Of Interest', Hume built on Massie's argument to the effect that a low rate of interest proceeded 'from the increase of industry and commerce, not of gold and silver'.[68] But he carried the argument on to more explicitly political terrain in contrasting the circumstances of a society lately emerged from the 'savage state' to one in which commerce has become well established. In the former, only two classes would be observed, a labouring peasantry and idle landowners. 'But as the spending of a settled revenue is a way of life entirely without occupation, men have so much need of somewhat to fix and engage them, that pleasures, such as they are, will be the pursuit of the greater part of the landholders, and the prodigals will always be more numerous than the misers.' Consumption habits, not the availability of

---

[64] Locke, *Some Considerations*, in Locke, *Locke on Money*, ed. Kelly, I, pp. 261–62; Tucker, *Progress and Profits in British Economic Thought*, p. 27.

[65] Locke, *Some Considerations*, in Locke, *Locke on Money*, ed. Kelly, I, pp. 262–63.

[66] Ibid., pp. 288–89.

[67] [Joseph Massie], *An Essay on the Governing Causes of the Natural Rate of Interest, Wherein the Sentiments of Sir William Petty and Mr. Locke on that Head, are Confounded* (London, 1750).

[68] *E* (LF), p. 297, *E* (C), p. 229.

money, were the ultimate determinants of the rate of interest.[69] What was necessary to facilitate lending was precisely the gathering of money into a few hands 'to compose a great monied interest'.[70] A commercial society, in widening the field of economic activity, created ever-more opportunities to meet the 'insatiable' craving of the human mind for employment, substituting for dissolute consumption pleasure in the fruits of industry. This, Hume explained, is 'why trade increases frugality, and why, among merchants, there is the same overplus of misers above prodigals, as among the possessors of land, there is the contrary'.[71] The extension of credit resources was the result not of an increased money supply, but of the industry and frugality of merchants. In this sense, as a proof of the increase of industry, 'interest is the barometer of the state, and its lowness is a sign almost infallible of the flourishing condition of a people'.[72]

For Locke, the instability of money as a standard of value provoked an anxious search for means by which it could be confined to its proper function of giving circulation to wealth without subverting the established property order and with it, civil society. Hume could see trouble enough in the intertwining of commerce and reason of state that he named 'jealousy of trade', and in the concomitant rise of a class of state creditors whose interests would, he feared, sooner or later confront the nation with a choice between debt repudiation and military catastrophe.[73] The dilemmas thrown up by the division of mankind into states hardly escaped his notice. But, as the *History of England* would demonstrate at length, he was rather more attentive than Locke to the transformation of state capacity and political culture entailed by the growth of industry and commerce.[74] There was no need to entrust the fortunes of commercial society to regulative principles that were both artificial and arbitrary, or to the supposed virtues of the idealised 'Landed Man'. What was required for nations to flourish was the patient application of an ever-more refined prudential judgement on the part of statesmen.

---

[69] *E* (LF), p. 298, *E* (C), p. 230.   [70] *E* (LF), p. 299, *E* (C), pp. 230–31.
[71] *E* (LF), pp. 301–2, *E* (C), pp. 232–33.   [72] *E* (LF), p. 303, *E* (C), p. 233.
[73] Hont, *Jealousy of Trade*, 'Introduction' and ch. 4.
[74] In this connection, see Jia Wei, *Commerce and Politics in Hume's History of England* (Woodbridge, 2017).

Bibliography

Manuscripts

Staatsarchiv Basel-Stadt, Basel, PA98a 5.
Bibliothèque nationale de France, Paris, MS Fr.15230.
Private archives of Marquis de Luppé, Beaurepaire, MS Fonds La Grange, [Geneviève de Malboissière], 'De l'origine, et des progrês des arts, et des sciences'.
The National Archives, Kew, PRO 30/24/27/14.

Primary Sources

Adams, John. *A Defence of the Constitution of the Government of the United States of America* (3 vols., Philadelphia, 1787).

Addison, Joseph and Steele, Richard. *The Spectator*, ed. Donald F. Bond (5 vols., Oxford, 1965).

Anon. *Whig and Tory Principles of Government Fairly Stated in a Dialogue between an Oxford Scholar and a Whig Parson* (n.p., 1716).

A General Treatise of Naval Trade and Commerce, As founded on the Laws and Statutes of this Realm, in which Those relating to his Majesty's Customs, Merchants, Masters of Ships, Mariners, Letters of Marque, Privateers, Prizes, Convoys, Cruizers, &c. are particularly considered and treated with due Care, under all the necessary Heads, from the earliest Time down to the present (2 vols., 1738–39 and 2 vols., London, 1753).

'Rev. of Hume, Vermischte Schriften über die Handlung', *Freye Urtheile und Nachrichten zum Aufnehmen der Wissenschaften und Historie Überhaupt*, 11 (Hamburg, 1754), pp. 773–76.

'Rev. of Hume, Vermischte Schriften über die Handlung', *Freymühige Nachrichten von Neuen Büchern, und Andern zur Gelehrtheit Gehörigen Sachen*, 12 (Zurich, 1755), pp. 275–77.

The Herald; or, Patriot Proclaimer (London, 1758).

'Rev. of Hume, Moralische und Politische Versuche', *Altonaische Gelehrte Anzeigen* (Altona, 1759), pp. 85–87.

'Rev. of Hume, Abriß des Gegenwärtigen Natürlichen und Politischen Zustandes von Großbritannien', *Allgemeine Deutsche Bibliothek*, 7 (1768), pp. 64–67.

The Beauties of English Prose: being a select collection of moral, critical, and entertaining passages, disposed in the manner of essays (4 vols., London, 1772).

The Beauties of the Magazines, and other Periodical Works, selected for a series of years: consisting of Essays, Moral Tales, Characters, and other Fugitive Pieces, in Prose (2 vols., Altenburgh, 1775).

Dedicated to The Queen: An Essay on the Immortality of the Soul; Shewing the Fallacy and Malignity of a Sceptical One, Lately Published, Together with Another on Suicide; and Both Ascribed, by the Editor, to the late David Hume, Esq. (London, 1784).

The Amicable Quixote; or, The Enthusiasm of Friendship (4 vols., London, 1788).

The Security of the Rights of the Citizens of the State of Connecticut Considered (Hartford, 1792).

For All Ranks of People, Political Instructions (London, 1795).

'Rev. of David Hume's Geist', *Neue Allgemeine Deutsche Bibliothek. Anhang zum Ersten bis Acht und Zwanzigsten Bande. Erste Abteilung* (Kiel, 1797), pp. 284–85.

'Rev. of Hume, Hume's Politische Versuche', *Leipziger Jahrbuch der Neuesten Literatur vom Jahre 1800. Zweyter Band Januar bis März 1801* (Leipzig, 1801), cols. 541–43.

'Rev. of David Hume's politische Zweifel', *Revision der Literatur für die Jahre 1785–1800 in Ergänzungsblätter zur Allg. Lit. Zeitung dieses Zeitraums. Zweyten Jahrgangs Erster Band* (Jena, 1802), cols. 140–42.

Aristotle. 'Poetics', in Aristotle, *The Complete Works of Aristotle*, ed. Jonathan Barnes (2 vols., Princeton, NJ, 1984).

Bascroft, Joseph. *A Help to Elocution and Eloquence* (London, 1770).

Batteux, Charles. *The Fine Arts Reduced to a Single Principle*, trans. James O. Young (Oxford, 2015 [1746]).

Baudeau, Nicolas. *Encyclopédie méthodique. Commerce* (3 vols., Paris, 1783–84).

Berkeley, George. *Alciphron: or, the Minute Philosopher* (2 vols., London, 1732).

Bibliothèque raisonnée des ouvrages des savants de l'Europe (Amsterdam, 1728–53).

Blair, Hugh. *Lectures on Rhetoric and Belles Lettres* (3 vols., Dublin, 1783).

Bolingbroke. *Political Writings*, ed. David Armitage (Cambridge, 1997),

Browne, Thomas. *The British Cicero: Or, A Selection of the Most Admired Speeches in the English Language* (Philadelphia, PA, 1810).

Burton, John Hill. *Life and Correspondence of David Hume* (2 vols., Edinburgh, 1846).

Carey, Matthew. *The School of Wisdom: or, American Monitor. Containing a Copious Collection of Sublime and Elegant Extracts, from the Most Eminent Writers, on Morals, Religion and Government* (Philadelphia, PA, 1800).

Carte, Thomas. *A General History of England* (4 vols., London, 1747–55).

Chastellux, François Jean. *De la félicité publique ou considérations sur le sort des hommes dans les différentes époques* (Amsterdam, 1772).

Cicero, Marcus Tullius. *De oratore*, trans. H. Rackham and E. W. Sutton (Cambridge, MA, 1942).

Coetlogon, Dennis de. *Diogenes's Rambles: or, Humorous Characters of the most noted people at present in the world: In Allusion to the Story Of the Cynic's searching Athens at Noon-Day with a Candle and Lanthorn to find out a Man* (London, 1743).

Cooper, Anthony Ashley, 3rd Earl of Shaftesbury. *Characteristicks of Men, Manners, Opinions, Times*, ed. Douglas Den Uyl (3 vols., Indianapolis, IN, 2001).

d'Alembert, Jean Le Rond. *Preliminary Discourse to the Encyclopedia of Diderot*, trans. Richard N. Schwab (Chicago, 1995 [1751]).

Diderot, Denis. *Pensées détachées ou Fragments politiques échappés du portefeuille d'un philosophe*, ed. Gianluigi Goggi (Paris, 2011 [1771]).

   Ceci n'est pas un conte, in Denis Diderot, *Les Deux amis de Bourbonne et autres contes*, ed. Michel Delon (Paris, 2002 [1773]).

   Lettres à Sophie Volland, 1759–1774, eds. Marc Buffat and Odile Richard-Pauchet (Paris, 2020).

Diderot, Denis and D'Alembert, Jean-Baptiste Le Rond, eds. *Encyclopédie ou Dictionnaire raisonné des sciences, des art et des métiers* (28 vols., Paris, 1751–72).

Dubos, Jean-Baptiste. *Réflexions critiques sur la poésie et sur la peinture*, 6th ed. (3 vols., Paris, 1765 [1719]).

Dutot, Charles. *Réflexions politiques sur les finances et le commerce*, ed. Paul Harsin (2 vols., Liège, 1935 [1738]).

Fénelon, François. *Oeuvres diverses de Fénelon: Dialogues sur l'éloquence* (Paris, 1824).

Fischer, Christian August. 'Rev of Hume, Hume's Politische Versuche', in *Neue Allgemeine Deutsche Bibliothek. Anhang zum Neun und Zwanzigsten bis Acht und Sechzigsten Bande, Zweyte Abtheilung* (Berlin, 1803), p. 617.

Fontenelle, Bernard le Bovier de. 'Réflexions sur la Poétique' [1724], in Bernard le Bovier de Fontenelle, *Oeuvres complètes*, ed. Alain Niderst (8 vols., Paris, 1989), III, pp. 111–59.

Forbonnais, François Véron Duverger de. *Elemens du commerce*, 2nd ed. (2 vols., Leyden, 1754).

Fréron, Elie-Catherine, ed. *L'Année littéraire* (Amsterdam, 1754–76).

Grimm, Friedrich Melchior et al., eds. *Correspondance littéraire, philosophique et critique* (1753–93), ed. Maurice Tourneux (16 vols., Paris, 1877–82).

   et al., eds. *Correspondance littéraire, philosophique et critique* (1753–62), eds. Ulla Kölving et al. (12 vols., Ferney-Voltaire, 2006–).

Guden, Philipp Peter. *Polizey der Industrie, oder Abhandlung von den Mitteln, den Fleiß der Einwohner zu Ermuntern* (Braunschweig, 1768).

Handbuch für den Staatsmann: Oder Analise der Vorzüglichsten Französischen und Ausländischen Werke Über Politik, Gesetzgebung, Finanzen, Polizei, Ackerbau, Handlung, Natur- und Staatsrecht (2 vols., Zurich, 1791).

Harrington, James. *The Commonwealth of Oceana* [1656] in James Harrington, *The Political Works of James Harrington*, ed. J. G. A. Pocock (Cambridge, 1977).

Hazlitt, William. *The Eloquence of the British Senate: Being a Selection of the Best Speeches of the Most Distinguished Parliamentary Speakers, from the Beginning of the Reign of Charles I to the Present Time: With Notes, Biographical, Critical and Explanatory* (2 vols., London, 1808).

Helvétius, Claude-Adrien. *De l'Esprit* (Paris, 1758).

Herder, Gottfried. 'Rev. of Hume's und Rousseau's Abhandlungen über den Urvertrag', *Nachrichten von Gelehrten Sachen Herausgegeben von der Akademie der Nützlichen Wissenschaften zu Erfurt* 55 (1797), reprinted in Johann Gottfried Herder, *Sämtliche Werke*, ed. Bernhard Suphan (Hildesheim, New York, and Anstalt, 1880), XX, pp. 288–90.

Herodotus. *The Persian Wars*, ed. and trans. A. D. Godley (4 vols., Cambridge, MA, rev. repr. 1925).

Hobbes, Thomas. *Leviathan*, ed. Noel Malcolm (3 vols., Oxford, 2012 [1651]).

[Holbach, Paul-Henri Thiry d']. *Système de la nature ou des lois du monde physique et du monde moral* (2 vols., London [Amsterdam], 1770).

Le Bon-Sens, ou Idées naturelles opposées aux idées surnaturelles (London [Amsterdam], 1772).

La Morale universelle, ou Les Devoirs de l'homme fondés sur sa nature (3 vols., Amsterdam, 1776).

Die gesamte erhaltene Korrespondenz. eds. Hermann Sauter and Erich Loos (Stuttgart, 1986).

Hume, David. *Essays, Moral and Political* (Edinburgh, 1741).

A True Account of the Behaviour and Conduct of Archibald Stewart, Esq: Late Lord Provost of Edinburgh (London, 1748).

'Von der Menge der Menschen bey den Alten Nationen', *Hamburgisches Magazin: Oder gesammelte Schriften, zum Unterricht und Vergnügen, aus der Naturforschung und den Angenehmen Wissenschaften Überhaupt*, 10 (Hamburg, 1753), pp. 451–502.

Discours politiques de Monsieur Hume, trans. abbé Jean-Bernard Le Blanc (2 vols., Amsterdam, 1754).

Vermischte Schriften über die Handlung, die Manufacturen und die Andern Quellen des Reichthums und der Macht eines Staats (Hamburg, 1754).

Philosophische Versuche über die Menschliche Erkenntniß von David Hume, Ritter: Als Dessen Vermischter Schriften Zweyter Theil, ed. Johann Georg Sulzer (Hamburg, 1755).

Moralische und Politische Versuche, als Dessen Vermischter Schriften Vierter und Letzter Theil (Hamburg, 1756).

Sittenlehre der Gesellschaft: Aus dessen Vermischter Schriften Dritter Theil (Hamburg, 1756).

'Aus Humes Versuch über die Eifersucht in Ansehung der Handlung', *Hannoverische Beyträge zum Nutzen und Vernügen, vom Jahre 1761*, 3 (Hannover, 1762), pp. 813–20.

Abriß des Gegenwärtigen Natürlichen und Politischen Zustandes von Großbritannien: Ein Vollständiges Handbuch für Reisende, Nebst einer Umständlichen Nachricht von der Handlung, den Staatsverhältnissen und dem Interesse dieses Reiches, aus dem Englischen des Herrn Hume, Verfassers der Geschichte von Großbritannien (Copenhagen, 1767).

Das Genie des Hrn. Hume: Oder Sammlung der Vorzüglichen Grundsätze dieses Philosophen, Welche Zugleich einen Genauen Begriff der Sitten, Gebräuche, Gewohnheiten, Gesetze und der Regierungsform der Englischen Nation wie Auch Einige Hauptzüge ihrer Geschichte und Einige Kurze Anekdoten Berühmter Männer Enthält, trans. Johann Gottfried Bremer (Leipzig, 1774).

'Hume's Versuch Über die Bürgerliche Freiheit', trans. Johann Georg Wiggers, in Valentin August Heinze, ed., *Kielisches Magazin vor die Geschichte, Statsklugheit und Statenkunde* 2 (Kiel, 1784), pp. 59–110.

'D. Hume's Versuch über die Nationalcharactere', trans. Carl Friedrich Pockels, *Beiträge zur Beförderung der Menschenkenntniss: Besonders in Rücksicht Unserer Moralischen Natur* 1 (Berlin, 1788), pp. 51–89.

'D. Hume's Versuch über Aberglauben und Schwärmerei', trans. Carl Friedrich Pockels, *Beiträge zur Beförderung der Menschenkenntniss: Besonders in Rücksicht unserer Moralischen Natur* 2 (Berlin, 1789), pp. 77–90.

David Hume's Geist: Erstes Bändchen Politik, trans. Christian August Fischer (Leipzig, 1795).

David Hume's Politische Zweifel: Allen Partheien Gewidmet, trans. Christian August Fischer (Leipzig, 1799).

David Hume's Politische Versuche. Von Neuem aus dem Englischen Übersetzt Nebst einer Zugabe von Christian Jacob Kraus, in Christian Jacob Kraus, *Vermischte Schriften über Staatswirthschaftliche, Philosophische und Andre Wissenschaftliche Gegenstände*, ed. Hans von Auerswald (Königsberg, 1813).

The Philosophical Works of David Hume, eds. T. H. Green and T. H. Grose (4 vols., London, 1886).

The Letters of David Hume, ed. J. Y. T. Greig (2 vols., Oxford, 1932).

'Hume's Early Memoranda, 1729–1740: The Complete Text', ed. Ernest C. Mossner, *Journal of the History of Ideas*, 9 (1948), pp. 492–518.

New Letters of David Hume, eds. Raymond Klibansky and Ernest C. Mossner (Oxford, 1954).

The History of England: From the Invasion of Julius Caesar to the Revolution in 1688, ed. William B. Todd. (6 vols., Indianapolis, IN, 1983).

Essays, Moral, Political, and Literary, ed. Eugene F. Miller (Indianapolis, IN, 1985).

An Enquiry Concerning the Principles of Morals, ed. Tom L. Beauchamp (Oxford, 1998).

An Enquiry Concerning Human Understanding, ed. Tom L. Beauchamp (Oxford, 2000).

A Dissertation on the Passions/The Natural History of Religion, ed. Tom L. Beauchamp (Oxford, 2007).

A Treatise of Human Nature, eds. David Fate Norton and Mary Norton (2 vols., Oxford, 2007).

Dialogues Concerning Natural Religion and Other Writings, ed. Dorothy Coleman (Cambridge, 2012).

Essays, Moral, Political, and Literary, eds. Tom L. Beauchamp and Mark A. Box (2 vols., Oxford, 2022).

Hume, David, Jean-Jaques Rousseau, and Garlieb Merkel, *Hume's und Rousseau's Abhandlungen Über den Urvertrag: Nebst einem Versuch Über die Leibeigenschaft den Liefländischen Erbherren Gewidmet* (2 vols., Leipzig, 1797).

Hutcheson, Francis. *Two Texts on Human Nature*, ed. Thomas Mautner (Cambridge, 1993).

An Inquiry into the Original of Our Ideas of Beauty and Virtue in Two Treatises, ed. Wolfgang Leidhold (Indianapolis, IN, 2004).

Intelligenzblatt der Neuen Allgemeinen Deutschen Bibliothek (Kiel, 1799).

Iselin, Isaak. *Schriften zur Ökonomie*, ed. Lina Weber in Isaak Iselin, *Gesammelte Schriften* (4 vols., Basel, 2014–).

Jones, William. *Memoirs of the Life, Studies, and Writings of the Right Reverend George Horne, D.D.* (London, 1795).

Journal économique ou Mémoires, notes et avis sur les arts, l'agriculture, le commerce, etc. (Paris, 1751–72).

Journal encyclopédique (Liège, 1756–93).

Journal étranger (Paris, 1754–62).

Kant, Immanuel. *Prolegomena zu einer Jeden Künftigen Metaphysik die als Wissenschaft Wird Auftreten Können* (Riga, 1783).

Kritik der Urteilskraft, ed. Prussian Academy of Sciences, Immanuel Kant, *Gesammelte Schriften* (29 vols., Berlin, 1900–).

Kant's Briefwechsel, I, 1747–1788, ed. Rudolf Reicke, Immanuel Kant, *Gesammelte Schriften* (29 vols., Berlin, 1900–).

Knox, Vicesimus. *The Spirit of Despotism* (London, 1795).

Kraus, Christian Jakob. 'Vorrede', in *David Hume's Politische Versuche. Von Neuem aus dem Englischen Übersetzt*, trans. Christian Jakob Kraus (Königsberg, 1800), pp. iii–viii.

Lackington, James. *Memoirs of the Forty-Five First Years of the Life of James Lackington* (London, 1793).

[Law, John]. *Money and Trade Considered, with a Proposal for Supplying the Nation with Money* (Edinburgh, 1705).

Logan, John. *Elements of the Philosophy of History, First Part* (Edinburgh, 1781).

Sermons by the late Reverend John Logan (Edinburgh, 1791).

Locke, John. *An Essay Concerning Human Understanding*, ed. P. H. Nidditch (Oxford, 1975 [1690]).

Two Treatises of Government, ed. Peter Laslett (Cambridge, 1988 [1690]).

Locke on Money, ed. Patrick Hyde Kelly (2 vols., Oxford, 1991).

Luppé, Albert de, ed. *Une jeune fille au XVIIIe siècle. Lettres de Geneviève de Malboissière à Adélaïde Méliand (1761–1766)* (Paris, 1925).

Malthus, Thomas Robert. *An Essay on the Principle of Population as it Affects the Future Improvement of Society with Remarks on the Speculations of Mr. Godwin, M. Condorcet, and Other Writers* (London, 1798).

Mandeville, Bernard. *The Fable of the Bees*, ed. F. B. Kaye (2 vols., Oxford, 1924).

[Massie, Joseph]. *An Essay on the Governing Causes of the Natural Rate of Interest, Wherein the Sentiments of Sir William Petty and Mr. Locke on that Head, are Confounded* (London, 1750).

Maty, Matthieu and Mauves, M. de. *Journal britannique* (The Hague, 1750–57).

Melon, Jean-François. *Essai politique sur le commerce*, ed. Francine Markovits (Caen, 2014 [1734]).

Mercure de France (Paris, 1724–91).

[Mirabeau, Victor Riquetti]. *L'Ami des hommes ou Traité de la population* (4 vols., Avignon, 1756–60).

Montesquieu. *De l'Esprit des lois*, in Montesquieu, *Œuvres complètes*, ed. Roger Caillois (2 vols., Paris, 1949–51).

The Spirit of the Laws, trans. and eds. Anne M. Cohler, Basia C. Miller, and Harold Samuel Stone (Cambridge, 1989 [1748]).

Persian Letters, ed. Andrew Kahn, trans. Margaret Mauldon (Oxford, 2008).

Mortimer, Thomas. *A New and Complete Dictionary of Trade and Commerce* (London, 1766).

The Elements of Commerce, Politics, and Finances (London, 1772).

Mossner, Ernest Campbell. 'New Hume Letters to Lord Elibank', *Texas Studies in Literature and Language*, 4 (1962), pp. 431–60.

Mun, Thomas. *England's Treasure by Forraign Trade, or, the Ballance of our Forraign Trade is the Rule of our Treasure* (London, 1664).

Naigeon, Jacques-André. *Encyclopédie méthodique. Philosophie ancienne et moderne* (3 vols., Paris, 1791–94).

Néaulme, Jean, ed. *Le Petit réservoir, contenant une variété de faits historiques et critiques, de morale et de poésie, etc.* (The Hague, 1750–51).

Nicolai, Friedrich. *Das Leben und die Meinungen des Herrn Magister Sebaldus Nothanker* (3 vols., Berlin, 1773).

Nouveau Cordial pour r'animer les esprits abbatus. Ou L'Inquisiteur Anglois où Se trouve un Mélange curieux et fort amusant de divers Essais d'esprit … Traduit de l'Anglois par James De La Cour (Frankfurt, 1755–56).

Perey, Lucien and Maugras, Gaston, eds. *Une femme du monde au XVIIIe siècle: dernières années de Mme d'Épinay* (Paris, 1883).

Petty, Sir William. *Political Arithmetick* (1690 [1676]), in Sir William Petty, *The Economic Writings of Sir William Petty*, ed. Charles H. Hull (2 vols., Cambridge, 1899).

Plato. *Republic*, trans. G. M. A. Grube, 2nd ed. (Indianapolis, IN, 1992).

Postlethwayt, Malachy. *The Universal Dictionary of Trade and Commerce, translated from the French of the celebrated Monsieur Savary* (2 vols., London, 1757).

Priestley, Joseph. *The Rudiments of English Grammar* (London, 1768).

A Course of Lectures on Oratory and Criticism (London, 1777).

Robinet, Jean-Baptiste. *Considérations sur l'état présent de la littérature en Europe* (London, 1762).

Sartorius, Georg Friedrich. 'Rev. of Kraus, Vermischte Schriften vol. vii', *Göttingische Gelehrte Anzeigen* (Göttingen, 1814), pp. 1105–12.

Smith, Adam. *An Inquiry into the Nature and Causes of the Wealth of Nations*, eds. E. H. Campbell, A. S. Skinner, and W. B. Todd (2 vols., Oxford, 1976 [1776]).

Lectures on Jurisprudence, eds. R. L. Meek, D. D. Raphael, and Peter Stein (Oxford, 1978).

Lectures on Rhetoric and Belles Lettres, ed. J. C. Bryce (Oxford, 1983).

Stewart, Dugald. 'Lectures on Political Economy', in Dugald Stewart, *The Collected Works of Dugald Stewart*, ed. William Hamilton (11 vols., Edinburgh, 1854–60).

Suard, Jean-Baptiste-Antoine. *Correspondance littéraire avec le margrave de Bayreuth (1773–1775)*, ed. Éric Francalanza (Paris, 2010).

Suard, Jean-Baptiste-Antoine and Arnaud, François, eds. *La Gazette littéraire de l'Europe* (Paris, 1764–66).

Sulzer, Johann Georg. 'Vorrede', in David Hume, *Philosophische Versuche über die Menschliche Erkenntniß von David Hume, Ritter: Als Dessen Vermischter Schriften Zweyter Theil*, ed. Johann Georg Sulzer (Hamburg, 1755), pp. [i–xx].

Swediauer, Franz Xaver. *The Philosophical Dictionary: or, The Opinions of Modern Philosophers on Metaphysical, Moral and Political Subjects* (4 vols., London, 1786).

Tacitus. *Agricola, Germany and Dialogue on Orators*, trans. Herbert W. Benario (London, 1991).

Trenchard, John and Gordon, Thomas. *Cato's Letters: Or, Essays on Liberty, Civil and Religious, and Other Important Subjects* (4 vols., London, 1755).

Turgot, Anne-Robert-Jacques. *Œuvres de Turgot et documents le concernant*, ed. Gustave Schelle, 2nd ed. (5 vols., Paris, 2018).

Voltaire. *Dictionnaire philosophique*, ed. Christiane Mervaud (2 vols., Oxford, 1994 [1764]).

'Eloquence', in *The Encyclopedia of Diderot & d'Alembert Collaborative Translation Project*, trans. Theodore E. D. Braun (Ann Arbor, MI, 2004).

Wallace, Robert. *A Dissertation on the Numbers of Mankind in Antient and Modern Times* (Edinburgh, 1753).

Dissertation historique et politique sur la population des anciens tems, comparée avec celle du nôtre (Amsterdam, 1769).

Warburton, William. *A Critical and Philosophical Enquiry into the Causes of Prodigies and Miracles, as Related by Historians: With an Essay towards Restoring Method and Purity in History* (London, 1727)

Williams, E. N., ed. *The Eighteenth-Century Constitution* (Cambridge, 1960).

Wilson, John. *Principles of Elocution, and Suitable Exercises* (Edinburgh, 1798).

Zeitung für die Elegante Welt, 3 (Leipzig, 1803).

Secondary Sources

Abramson, Kate. 'Happy to Unite, or Not?' *Philosophy Compass*, 1 (2006), pp. 290–302.

'Hume's Distinction between Philosophical Anatomy and Painting', *Philosophy Compass*, 2 (2007), pp. 680–98.

Adair, Douglass. '"That Politics May Be Reduced to a Science": David Hume, James Madison, and the Tenth Federalist', *Huntington Library Quarterly*, 20 (1957), pp. 343–60.

Adam, Ulrich. *The Political Economy of J. H. G. Justi* (Oxford, 2006).

Ahnert, Thomas. *The Moral Culture of the Scottish Enlightenment, 1690–1805* (New Haven, CT, 2014).

Albee, Ernest. *A History of English Utilitarianism* (London, 1901).

Alimento, Antonella. 'Translation, Reception and Enlightened Reform: The Case of Forbonnais in Eighteenth-Century Political Economy', *History of European Ideas*, 40 (2014), pp. 1011–25.

Babich, Babette, ed. *Reading David Hume's 'Of the Standard of Taste'* (Berlin, 2019).

Baier, Annette C. *A Progress of Sentiments: Reflections on Hume's Treatise* (Cambridge, MA, 1991).

The Cautious Jealous Virtue: Hume on Justice (Cambridge, MA, 2010).

Battersby, Christine. 'The *Dialogues* as Original Imitation: Cicero and the Nature of Hume's Skepticism', in Nicholas Capaldi et al., eds., *McGill Hume Studies* (San Diego, CA, 1976), pp. 239–52.

Benn, T. V. 'Les *Political discourses* de David Hume et un conte de Diderot', in T. V. Benn et al., eds., *Currents of Thought in French Literature: Essays in Memory of G. T. Clapton* (Oxford, 1965), pp. 253–76.

Berdell, John. 'Innovation and Trade: David Hume and the Case for Freer Trade', *History of Political Economy*, 28 (1996), pp. 107–26.

Berry, Christopher J. *The Idea of Luxury: A Conceptual and Historical Investigation* (Cambridge, 1994).

'Hume and Superfluous Value (or the Problem with Epictetus' Slippers)', in Carl Wennerlind and Margaret Schabas, eds., *David Hume's Political Economy* (New York, 2008), pp. 49–64.

Boguna, Julija. 'Nützt es dem Volke, Übersetzt zu Warden? Oder: Was Translation Über die (Livländische) Aufklärung Verraten Kann', in Silke Pasewalck and Matthias Weber, eds., *Bildungspraktiken der Aufklärung/Education practices of the Enlightenment* (Oldenbourg, 2020), pp. 51–72.

Bonar, James. *Philosophy and Political Economy*, 3rd ed. (London, 1922 [1893]).

Bongie, Laurence L. 'Hume en France au dix-huitième siècle' (PhD dissertation, Sorbonne University, 1952).

'David Hume and the Official Censorship of the "Ancien Régime"', *French Studies*, 12 (1958), pp. 234–46.

'Hume, *Philosophe* and Philosopher in Eighteenth-Century France', *French Studies*, 15 (1961), pp. 213–27.

David Hume: Prophet of the Counter-Revolution (Oxford, 1965).

'Retour à Mademoiselle de la Chaux', *Recherches sur Diderot et l'Encyclopédie*, 6 (1989), pp. 62–104.

David Hume: Prophet of the Counter-Revolution, 2nd ed. (Indianapolis, IN, 2000).

Bouchard, Gregory Ernest. 'The Philosophical Publishing Life of David Hume' (PhD dissertation, McGill University, 2013).

Bourke, Richard. 'Theory and Practice: The Revolution in Political Judgement', in Richard Bourke and Raymond Geuss, eds., *Political Judgement: Essays for John Dunn* (Cambridge, 2009), pp. 73–109.

Box, M. A. and Silverthorne, Michael. 'The "Most Curious & Important of All Questions of Erudition": Hume's Assessment of the Populousness of Ancient Nations', in Mark G. Spencer, ed., *David Hume: Historical Thinker, Historical Writer* (University Park, PA, 2013), pp. 225–54.

Brewer, John. *The Sinews of Power: War, Money and the English State, 1688–1783* (London, 1989).

Brooke, Christopher. *Philosophic Pride: Stoicism and Political Thought from Lipsius to Rousseau* (Princeton, NJ, 2012).

Caffentzis, George. *Civilizing Money: Hume, His Monetary Project and the Scottish Enlightenment* (London, 2021).

Clipped Coins, Abused Words, and Civil Government: John Locke's Philosophy of Money, ed. Paul Rekret, new ed. (London, 2021).

Capaldi, Nicholas and Livingston, Donald, eds. *Liberty in Hume's History of England* (Dordrecht, 1990).

Carey, Daniel. 'John Locke's Philosophy of Money', in Daniel Carey, ed., *Money and Political Economy in the Enlightenment* (Oxford, 2014), pp. 57–81.

Carpenter, Kenneth E. *Dialogue in Political Economy: Translation from and into German in the 18th Century* (Boston, MA, 1977).

Charette, Danielle. 'Hume's "Idea of a Perfect Commonwealth" and Scottish Political Thought of the 1790s', *History of European Ideas*, 48 (2022), pp. 78–96.

Charles, Loïc. 'French "New Politics" and the Dissemination of David Hume's *Political Discourses* on the Continent, 1750–70', in Carl Wennerlind and Margaret Schabas, eds., *David Hume's Political Economy* (London, 2008), pp. 181–202.

Checkland, S. G. *Scottish Banking: A History, 1695–1973* (Glasgow, 1975).

Cheney, Paul. 'Constitution and Economy in David Hume's Enlightenment', Margaret Schabas and Carl Wennerlind, eds., *David Hume's Political Economy* (New York, 2008), pp. 223–42.

Chisick, Harvey. 'The Representation of Adam Smith and David Hume in the *Année Littéraire* and the *Journal Encyclopédique*', in Deidre Dawson and

Pierre Morère, eds., *Scotland and France in the Enlightenment* (Lewisburg, 2004), pp. 240–63.

Cohen, Alix. 'The Making of a Philosophical Classic: The Reception of David Hume in Europe', *Rivista di Storia della Filosofia*, 62 (2007), pp. 457–68.

Conlon, Pierre M. *Le Siècle des Lumières: bibliographie chronologique* (23 vols., Geneva, 1983).

Conniff, James. 'Hume's Political Methodology: A Reconsideration of "That Politics May Be Reduced to a Science"', *The Review of Politics*, 38 (1976), pp. 88–108.

Conti, Gregory. 'Hume's Low Road to Toleration', *History of Political Thought*, 36 (2015), pp. 165–91.

Costelloe, Timothy M. 'Hume's Aesthetics: The Literature and Directions for Future Research', *Hume Studies*, 30 (2004), pp. 87–126.

The British Aesthetic Tradition: From Shaftesbury to Wittgenstein (Cambridge, 2013).

Coventry, Angela and Walls, Andrew, eds. *David Hume on Morals, Politics, and Society* (New Haven, CT, 2018).

Cruickshanks, Eveline and Erskine-Hill, Howard. *The Atterbury Plot* (Basingstoke, 2004).

Dawson, Hannah. *Locke, Language and Early Modern Philosophy* (Cambridge, 2007).

De Labriolle, Marie-Rose. 'Journal étranger I', in *Dictionnaire des journaux 1600–1789* (IHRIM / MSH-LES / Voltaire Foundation, 2015–2021), https://dictionnaire-journaux.gazettes18e.fr/journal/0732-journal-etranger-1.

Demeter, Tamás. *David Hume and the Culture of Scottish Newtonianism: Methodology and Ideology in Enlightenment Inquiry* (Leiden, 2017).

Devletoglou, Nicos E. 'Montesquieu and the Wealth of Nations', in David Carrithers, ed., *Charles-Louis de Secondat, Baron de Montesquieu* (Farnham, 2009), pp. 497–521.

Dew, Ben. *Commerce, Finance and Statecraft: Histories of England, 1600–1780* (Manchester, 2018).

Dickson, P. G. M. *The Financial Revolution in England: A Study in the Development of Public Credit, 1688–1756* (London, 1967).

Douglass, Robin. 'Montesquieu and Modern Republicanism', *Political Studies*, 60 (2012), pp. 703–19.

Dunn, John. *The Political Thought of John Locke* (Cambridge, 1969).

'From Applied Theology to Social Analysis: The Break between John Locke and the Scottish Enlightenment', in Istvan Hont and Michael Ignatieff, eds., *Wealth and Virtue: The Shaping of Political Economy in the Scottish Enlightenment* (Cambridge, 1983), pp. 119–37.

Eich, Stefan. *The Currency of Politics: The Political Theory of Money from Aristotle to Keynes* (Princeton, NJ, 2022), pp. 67–72.

Emerson, Roger L. 'The "Affair" at Edinburgh and the "Project" at Glasgow: The Politics of Hume's Attempts to Become a Professor', in M. A. Stewart and J. P. Wright, eds., *Hume and Hume's Connexions* (Edinburgh, 2004), pp. 1–22.

Emerson, Roger L. 'Hume and Ecclesiastical History: Aims and Contexts', in Mark G. Spencer, ed., *David Hume: Historical Thinker, Historical Writer* (University Park, PA, 2012), pp. 13–36.

    An Enlightened Duke: The Life of Archibald Campbell (1682–1761), Earl of Ilay, 3rd Duke of Argyll (Kilkerran, 2013).

Fairchild, Hoxie N. 'Hartley, Pistorius, and Coleridge', *PMLA*, 62 (1947), pp. 1010–21.

Fieser, James, ed. *Early Responses to Hume*, 2nd ed. (Bristol, 2005).

Fogelin, Robert J. *Hume's Scepticism in the Treatise of Human Nature* (London, 1985).

Forbes, Duncan. *Hume's Philosophical Politics* (Cambridge, 1975).

    'Sceptical Whiggism, Commerce and Liberty', in A. S. Skinner and Thomas Wilson, eds., *Essays on Adam Smith* (Oxford, 1975), pp. 179–201.

Franchina, Miriam. *Paul Rapin Thoyras and the Art of Eighteenth-Century Historiography* (Oxford, 2021).

Gargam, Adeline. *Les Femmes savantes, lettrées et cultivées dans la littérature française des Lumières ou la conquête d'une légitimité (1690–1804)* (2 vols., Paris, 2013).

Garrett, Aaron. 'The Lives of the Philosophers', *Jahrbuch für Recht und Ethik*, 12 (2004), pp. 41–56.

Gawlick, Günther and Lothar Kreimendahl. *Hume in der Deutschen Aufklärung. Umrisse einer Rezeptionsgeschichte* (Stuttgart-Bad Cannstatt, 1987).

Gesang, Bernward. *Kants Vergessener Rezensent: Die Kritik der Theoretischen und Praktischen Philosophie Kants in Fünf Rezensionen von Hermann Andreas Pistorius* (Hamburg, 2007).

    'Pistorius, Herman Andreas (1730–98)', in Heiner F. Klemme and Manfred Kuehn, eds., *The Bloomsbury Dictionary of Eighteenth-Century German Philosophers* (London, 2010), pp. 589–91.

Goodman, Rob. *Words on Fire: Eloquence and Its Conditions* (Cambridge, 2021).

Green, David. *Queen Anne* (London, 1970).

Gurstein, Rochelle. 'Taste and the "The Conversible World" in the Eighteenth Century', *Journal of the History of Ideas*, 61 (2000), pp. 203–21.

Guyer, Paul. *A History of Modern Aesthetics, Volume 1: The Eighteenth Century* (Cambridge, 2014).

Haakonssen, Knud. 'Introduction', in Knud Haakonssen, ed., *David Hume: Political Essays* (Cambridge, 1994), pp. xi–xxx.

Hanvelt, Marc. *The Politics of Eloquence: David Hume's Polite Rhetoric* (Toronto, 2012).

Hanvelt, Marc and Spencer, Mark G. 'David Hume's "A Character of Sir Robert Walpole": Humean Faction Fears, the "Rage against the Scots", and Future Historians', *Scottish Historical Review*, 98 (2019), pp. 361–89.

Harris, James A. 'Hume's Four Essays on Happiness and Their Place in the Move from Morals to Politics', in Emilio Mazza and Emanuele Ronchetti, eds., *New Essays on David Hume* (Milan, 2007), pp. 223–35.

    Hume: An Intellectual Biography (Cambridge, 2015).

Harris, Tim. *Politics under the Later Stuarts* (London, 1993).

Henderson, Willie. *The Origins of David Hume's Economics* (Abingdon, 2010).

Heydt, Colin. 'Relations of Literary Form and Philosophical Purpose in Hume's Four Essays on Happiness', *Hume Studies*, 33 (2007), pp. 3–19.

Himmelfarb, Gertrude. *The Idea of Poverty: England in the Early Industrial Age* (New York, 1984).

Hipple, Walter J. *The Beautiful, the Sublime, and the Picturesque in Eighteenth-Century British Aesthetic Theory* (Carbondale, IL, 1957).

Hirschman, Albert O., *The Passions and the Interests: Political Arguments for Capitalism before Its Triumph* (Princeton, NJ, 1977).

Hollander, Samuel. *The Economics of Adam Smith* (Toronto, 1973).

Holmes, Geoffrey. *The Trial of Doctor Sacheverell* (London, 1973).

Hont, Istvan. 'Commercial Society and Political Theory in the Eighteenth Century: The Problem of Authority in David Hume and Adam Smith', in Willem Melching and Wyger Velema, eds., *Main Trends in Cultural History: Ten Essays* (Amsterdam, 1994), pp. 54–94.

    Jealousy of Trade: International Competition and the Nation State in Historical Perspective (Cambridge, MA, 2005).

    'The Early Enlightenment Debate on Commerce and Luxury', in Mark Goldie and Robert Wokler, eds., *The Cambridge History of Eighteenth-Century Political Thought* (Cambridge, 2006), pp. 379–418.

    'The "Rich Country–Poor Country" Debate Revisited: The Irish Origins and French Reception of the Hume Paradox', in Carl Wennerlind and Margaret Schabas, eds., *David Hume's Political Economy* (London, 2008), pp. 243–323.

    'Adam Smith's History of Law and Government as Political Theory', in Richard Bourke and Raymond Geuss, eds., *Political Judgement: Essays for John Dunn* (Cambridge, 2009), pp. 131–71.

    Politics in Commercial Society: Jean-Jacques Rousseau and Adam Smith, eds. Béla Kapossy and Michael Sonenscher (Cambridge, MA, 2015).

Hoppit, Julian. *The Dreadful Monster and Its Poor Relations: Taxation, Spending and the United Kingdom, 1707–2021* (London, 2021).

Horsefield, J. Keith. *British Monetary Experiments, 1650–1710* (Cambridge, MA, 1960).

Horwell, Shane William. 'Taxation in British Political and Economic Thought, 1733–1816' (PhD dissertation, University College London, 2018).

Immerwahr, John. 'Hume's Essays on Happiness', *Hume Studies*, 15 (1989), pp. 307–24.

    'The Anatomist and the Painter: The Continuity of Hume's *Treatise* and *Essays*', *Hume Studies*, 17 (1991), pp. 1–14.

Jauss, Hans Robert. 'Literary History as a Challenge to Literary Theory', *New Literary History*, 2 (1970), pp. 7–37.

Jones, Peter, ed. *The Reception of Hume in Europe* (London, 2005).

    'Hume on the Arts and "The Standard of Taste": Texts and Contexts', in David Fate Norton and Jacqueline Taylor, eds., *The Cambridge Companion to Hume*, 2nd ed. (Cambridge, 2008), pp. 14–46.

Jordan, Mark D. 'A Preface to the Study of Philosophic Genres', *Philosophy and Rhetoric*, 14 (1981), pp. 199–211.

'The Terms of the Debate over "Christian Philosophy"', *Communio*, 12 (1985), pp. 293–311.

Kemp Smith, Norman. *The Philosophy of David Hume* (London, 1941).

Kennedy, William. *English Taxation, 1640–1799* (London, 1913).

Kenyon, J. P. *Revolutionary Principles: The Politics of Party 1689–1720* (Cambridge, 1977).

Knufmann, Helmut. 'Das Deutsche Übersetzungswesen des 18. Jahrhunderts im Spiegel von Übersetzer- und Herausgebervorreden', *Börsenblatt für den Deutschen Buchhandel – Frankfurter Ausgabe* 91 (1967), Anhang: *Archiv für Geschichte des Buchwesens* 61, pp. 2676–716.

Kontler, László. *Translations, Histories, Enlightenments: William Robertson in Germany, 1760–1795* (New York, 2014).

Kors, Alan C. *Naturalism and Unbelief in France, 1650–1729* (Cambridge, 2016).

Krake, Astrid. '"Translating to the Moment" – Marketing and Anglomania: The First German Translation of Richardson's *Clarissa* (1747/1748)', in Stefanie Stockhorst, ed., *Cultural Transfer through Translation: The Circulation of Enlightened Thought in Europe by Means of Translation*. Internationale Forschungen zur Allgemeinen und Vergleichenden Literaturwissenschaft, vol. 131 (Amsterdam, 2010), pp. 103–19.

Kraus, Hans-Christof. *Englische Verfassung und Politisches Denken im Ancien Régime. 1689 bis 1789*, Veröffentlichungen des Deutschen Historischen Instituts London (München, 2006).

Kristeller, P. O. 'The Modern System of the Arts: A Study in the History of Aesthetics Part I' and 'Part II', *Journal of the History of Ideas*, 12 (1951), pp. 496–527, and 13 (1952), pp. 17–46.

Kuehn, Manfred. 'The Reception of Hume in Germany', in Peter Jones, ed., *The Reception of Hume in Europe* (London, 2005), pp. 98–138.

'Kraus, Christian Jacob (1753–1826)', in Heiner F. Klemme and Manfred Kuehn, eds., *The Bloomsbury Dictionary of Eighteenth-Century German Philosophers* (London, 2010), pp. 438–40.

Kühn, Erich. *Der Staatswirtschaftslehrer Christian Jakob Kraus und seine Beziehungen zu Adam Smith* (Königsberg, 1902).

Lahti, Leo, Marjanen, Jani, Roivainen, Hege, and Tolonen, Mikko. 'Bibliographic Data Science and the History of the Book (c. 1500–1800)', *Cataloging & Classification Quarterly*, 57 (2019), pp. 5–23.

Landis, Joel E. 'Whither Parties? Hume on Partisanship and Political Legitimacy', *American Political Science Review*, 112 (2018), pp. 219–30.

Livingston, Donald W. 'On Hume's Conservatism', *Hume Studies*, 21 (1995), pp. 151–64.

Lloyd, Genevieve. *Enlightenment Shadows* (Oxford, 2013).

Lock, Alexander. 'The Influence of the Published Works of David Hume in Eighteenth-Century France and Germany', *History Studies*, 10 (2009), pp. 45–61.

Loptson, Peter. 'Hume and Ancient Philosophy', *British Journal for the History of Philosophy*, 20 (2012), pp. 741–72.

Loveland, Jeff. *An Alternative Encyclopedia? Dennis de Coetlogon's 'Universal History of Arts and Sciences' (1745)* (Oxford, 2010).

Luehrs, Robert B. 'Population and Utopia in the Thought of Robert Wallace', *Eighteenth-Century Studies*, 20 (1987), pp. 313–35.

Mackey, Louis H. 'On Philosophical Form: A Tear for Adonais', *Thought*, 42 (1967), pp. 238–60.

Magnusson, Lars. *Mercantilism: The Shaping of an Economic Language* (Abingdon, 1994).

    The Political Economy of Mercantilism (Abingdon, 2015).

Malherbe, Michel. 'Hume and the Art of Dialogue', in M. A. Stewart and John P. Wright, eds., *Hume and Hume's Connexions* (Edinburgh, 1994), pp. 201–23.

    'Hume's Reception in France', in Peter Jones, ed., *The Reception of David Hume in Europe* (London, 2005), pp. 43–97.

    'Hume en France: la traduction des *Political discourses*', in Ann Thomson, Simon Burrows, and Edmond Dziembowski, eds., *Cultural Transfers: France and Britain in the Long Eighteenth Century* (Oxford, 2010), pp. 243–56.

Manin, Bernard. *The Principles of Representative Government* (Cambridge, 1997).

Maurer, Christian. *Self-Love, Egoism and the Selfish Hypothesis: Key Debates from Eighteenth-Century British Moral Philosophy* (Edinburgh, 2019).

Maurer, Michael. *Aufklärung und Anglophilie in Deutschland*, Veröffentlichungen des Deutschen Historischen Instituts London, vol. 19 (Göttingen, 1987).

Mazza, Emilio. *La peste in fondo al pozzo: l'anatomia astrusa di David Hume* (Milan, 2012).

    'Exposing the Children: Montesquieu, Hume and Something "Pretty Unusual"', *I Castelli di Yale*, 6 (2018), pp. 45–77.

    'The Eloquent "Enquiry": Virtue or Merit in Its Proper Colours', in Jacqueline Taylor, ed., *Reading Hume on the Principles of Morals* (Oxford, 2020), pp. 300–23.

    'As "Men of Sense": Godwin, Baroja, Bateson and Hume's "Of National Characters"', in Peter J. E. Kail, Angela Coventry and Dejan Šimković, eds., *Hume's Legacy, Belgrade Philosophical Annual*, 34 (2021), pp. 159–82.

Mazza, Emilio and Mori, Gianluca. 'How Many Atheists at D'Holbach's Table?', in Laura Nicolì, ed., *The Great Protector of Wits: Baron D'Holbach and His Time* (Leiden, 2022), pp. 173–201.

Mazza, Emilio and Nacci, Michela. *Paese che vai: i caratteri nazionali fra teoria e senso comune* (Venice, 2021).

Mazza, Emilio and Piccoli, Edoardo. '"La grande variété du goût": David Hume à Paris', in Cristophe Henry and Daniel Rabreau, eds., *Le Public et la politique des arts au siècle des Lumières* (Bordeaux, 2011), pp. 21–44.

McCabe, Helen. *John Stuart Mill, Socialist* (Montreal, 2021).

McDaniel, Iain. *Adam Ferguson in the Scottish Enlightenment: The Roman Past and Europe's Future* (Cambridge, MA, 2013).

McLynn, Frank. 'Jacobitism and Hume', *Hume Studies*, 9 (1983), pp. 171–99.

McMahon, Darrin M. 'From the Happiness of Virtue to the Virtue of Happiness: 400 B.C.–A.D. 1780', *Daedalus*, 133 (2004), pp. 5–17.

Merivale, Amyas. *Hume on Art, Emotion, and Superstition: A Critical Study of the Four Dissertations* (New York, 2019).

Mertz, Rudolph. 'Les amitiés françaises de Hume et le mouvement des idées', *Revue de littérature comparée*, 9 (1929), pp. 644–713.

Meyer, Paul H. 'Hume in Eighteenth-Century France' (PhD dissertation, Columbia University, 1954).

Miller, David. *Philosophy and Ideology in Hume's Political Thought* (Oxford, 1981).

Miner, Robert C. 'Pascal on the Uses of Scepticism', *Logos*, 11 (2008), pp. 1–12.

Mokyr, Joel. *The Enlightened Economy: An Economic History of Britain: 1700–1815* (New Haven, CT, 2009).

Monod, Paul. *Jacobitism and the English People, 1688–1788* (Cambridge, 1989).

Moore, James. 'Hume's Political Science and the Classical Republican Tradition', *Canadian Journal of Political Science / Revue Canadienne de Science Politique*, 10 (1977), pp. 809–39.

Mossner, Ernest Campbell. 'Hume's *Four Dissertations*: An Essay in Biography and Bibliography', *Modern Philology*, 48 (1950), pp. 37–57.

'Hume and the French Men of Letters', *Revue internationale de philosophie*, 6 (1952), pp. 222–35.

The Life of David Hume (Oxford, 1954).

The Life of David Hume, 2nd ed. (Oxford, 1980).

Munn, Charles W. *The Scottish Provincial Banking Companies, 1747–1864* (Edinburgh, 1981).

Murphy, Antoin E. *John Law: Economic Theorist and Policy-Maker* (Oxford, 1997).

Neil, Alex. '"An Unaccountable Pleasure": Hume on Tragedy and the Passions', *British Journal of Aesthetics*, 39 (1999), pp. 12–25.

Nicolì, Laura. '"Mon Cool Warm Hearted Philosophe": Geneviève de Malboissière's Unpublished Translation of Hume's *Of the Rise and Progress of the Arts and Sciences*' (forthcoming).

'The French Story of David Hume's Two Essays' (forthcoming).

Noggle, James. *The Temporality of Taste in Eighteenth-Century British Writing* (Oxford, 2012).

Nokkala, Ere. *From Natural Law to Political Economy: J. H. G. Justi on State, Commerce and International Order* (Zurich, 2019).

Norton, David Fate and Popkin, Richard H., eds. *David Hume: Philosophical Historian* (Indianapolis, IN, 1965).

Oake, Roger B. 'Montesquieu and Hume', *Modern Language Quarterly*, 2 (1941), pp. 225–48.

'Polygamy in the *Lettres persanes*', *Romanic Review*, 33 (1941), pp. 56–62.

Oz-Salzberger, Fania. *Translating the Enlightenment: Scottish Civic Discourse in Eighteenth-Century Germany* (Oxford, 1995).

'The Enlightenment in Translation: Regional and European Aspects', *European Review of History / Revue européene d'Histoire* 13/3 (2006), pp. 385–409.

Packham, Catherine. 'Cicero's Ears, or Eloquence in the Age of Politeness: Oratory, Moderation, and the Sublime in Enlightenment Scotland', *Eighteenth-Century Studies*, 46 (2013), pp. 499–512.

Pasewalck, Silke and Matthias Weber. 'Einleitung', in Silke Pasewalck and Matthias Weber, eds., *Bildungspraktiken der Aufklärung/Education practices of the Enlightenment* (Oldenbourg, 2020), pp. 1–8.

Perinetti, Dario. 'Hume at La Flèche: Skepticism and the French Connection', *Journal of the History of Philosophy*, 56 (2018), pp. 45–74.

Phillipson, Nicholas. *David Hume* (London, 2011).

  Adam Smith: An Enlightened Life (New Haven, CT, 2012).

Pocock, J. G. A. 'Hume and the American Revolution: The Dying Thoughts of a North Britain', in J. G. A. Pocock, *Virtue, Commerce and History: Essays on Political Thought and History* (Cambridge, 1985), pp. 125–41.

  The Machiavellian Moment: Florentine Political Thought and the Atlantic Republican Tradition (Princeton, NJ, 2003 [1975]).

Potkay, Adam. *The Fate of Eloquence in the Age of Hume* (Ithaca, NY, 1994).

Prince, Michael B. *Philosophical Dialogue in the British Enlightenment: Theology, Aesthetics and the Novel* (Cambridge, 1996).

Reinert, Sophus A. *Translating Empire: Emulation and the Origins of Political Economy* (Cambridge, MA, 2011).

Richter, Susan. *Pflug und Steuerruder: Zur Verflechtung von Herrschaft und Landwirtschaft in der Aufklärung*, Beihefte zum Archiv für Kulturgeschichte, vol. 75 (Köln, Weimar & Wien, 2015).

Rivers, Isabel. *Reason, Grace and Sentiment: A Study in the Language of Religion and Ethics in England, 1660–1780* (2 vols., Cambridge, 1991–2000).

Robel, Gilles. 'Bibliographie sélective', in David Hume, *Essais moraux, politiques et littéraires et autres essais*, ed. Gilles Robel (Paris, 2001), pp. 811–38.

  '"Idea of a Perfect Commonwealth" ou le réalisme utopique de David Hume', *Études écossaises*, 11 (2009), pp. 9–29.

  'Hume's *Political Discourses* in France', in Stephen W. Brown and Warren McDougall, eds., *The Edinburgh History of the Book in Scotland. II: Enlightenment and Expansion 1707–1800* (Edinburgh, 2012), pp. 221–32.

Robertson, John. 'The Scottish Enlightenment at the Limits of the Civic Tradition', in Istvan Hont and Michael Ignatieff, eds., *Wealth and Virtue: The Shaping of the Political Economy in the Scottish Enlightenment* (Cambridge, 1983), pp. 137–78.

  The Scottish Enlightenment and the Militia Issue (Edinburgh, 1985).

  The Case for the Enlightenment: Scotland and Naples, 1680–1760 (Cambridge, 2005).

Rotwein, Eugene. 'Introduction', in David Hume, *David Hume: Writings on Economics*, ed. Eugene Rotwein, 2nd ed. (Madison, WI, 1970), pp. ix–cxi.

Ryan, Y., Mahadevan, A. and Tolonen, M. 'A Comparative Text Similarity Analysis of the Works of Bernard Mandeville', *Digital Enlightenment Studies*, 1(1) (2023), pp. 28–58. doi: https://doi.org/10.61147/des.6

Sagar, Paul. *The Opinion of Mankind: Sociability and the Theory of the State from Hobbes to Smith* (Princeton, NJ, 2018).

'Between Virtue and Knavery: Hume and the Politics of Moderation', *Journal of Politics*, 83 (2021), pp. 1097–1113.

'On the Liberty of the English: Adam Smith's Reply to Montesquieu and Hume', *Political Theory*, 50 (2022), pp. 381–404.

Sandrier, Alain. 'D'Holbach et Hume: scepticisme et propagande irréligieuse', in Geneviève Artigas-Menant et al., eds., *Les Relations franco-anglaises aux XVIIe et XVIIIe siècles: périodiques et manuscrits clandestins, La Lettre clandestine*, 15 (2007), pp. 221–39.

Santucci, Antonio. 'Hume e i *philosophes*', *Rivista di filosofia*, 56 (1965), pp. 150–77.

Schabas, Margaret. 'Temporal Dimensions in Hume's Monetary Theory', in Carl Wennerlind and Margaret Schabas, eds., *David Hume's Political Economy* (London, 2008), pp. 127–45.

'Hume on Economic Well-Being', in Alan Bailey and Dan O'Brien, eds., *Bloomsbury Companion to Hume* (London, 2015), pp. 332–48.

Schabas, Margaret and Carl Wennerlind. *A Philosopher's Economist: Hume and the Rise of Capitalism* (Chicago, 2020).

Schatz, Albert. *L'œuvre économique de David Hume* (Paris, 1902).

Sebastiani, Silvia. *The Scottish Enlightenment: Race, Gender and the Limits of Progress* (New York, 2013).

Sedgwick, Romney, ed. *History of Parliament: The House of Commons, 1715–54* (2 vols., London, 1970).

Seligman, Edwin R. A. *The Shifting and Incidence of Taxation*, 3rd ed. (New York, 1910).

Seth, James. 'A Scottish Philosopher in France', *Transactions of the Franco-Scottish Society*, 5 (1910), pp. 208–18.

Sher, Richard B. *The Enlightenment and the Book: Scottish Authors and Their Publishers in Eighteenth-Century Britain, Ireland, and America* (Chicago, 2006).

Shklar, Judith. 'Ideology Hunting: The Case of James Harrington', *American Political Science Review*, 53 (1959), pp. 662–92.

Shusterman, Richard. 'The Scandal of Taste: Social Privilege as Nature in the Aesthetic Theories of Hume and Kant', *Philosophical Forum*, 20 (1989), pp. 211–29.

Skinner, Quentin. 'The Limits of Historical Explanations', *Philosophy*, 41 (1966), pp. 199–215.

'Meaning and Understanding in the History of Ideas', *History and Theory*, 8 (1969), pp. 3–53.

Skjönsberg, Max. 'David Hume and the Jacobites', *Scottish Historical Review*, 252 (2021), pp. 25–56.

The Persistence of Party: Ideas of Harmonious Discord in Eighteenth-Century Britain (Cambridge, 2021).

'Patriots and the Country Party Tradition in the Eighteenth Century: The Critics of Britain's Fiscal-Military State from Robert Harley to Catharine Macaulay', *Intellectual History Review*, 33 (2023), pp. 83–100.

Speck, W. A. 'The Whig Schism under George I', *Huntington Library Quarterly*, 40 (1977), pp. 171–79.

Spencer, Mark G. *David Hume and Eighteenth-Century America* (Rochester, NY, 2005).

ed. *David Hume: Historical Thinker, Historical Writer* (University Park, PA, 2013).

ed. *Hume's Reception in Early America: Expanded Edition* (New York, 2017).

'Was David Hume, the Historian, a Plagiarist? A Submission from His *History of England*', *Clio*, 47 (2019), pp. 25–50.

Stack, Frank. *Pope and Horace: Studies in Imitation* (Cambridge, 1985).

Starobinski, Jean. 'Eloquence and Liberty', *Journal of the History of Ideas*, 38 (1977), pp. 195–210.

Stephen, Leslie. *History of English Thought in the Eighteenth Century* (2 vols., London, 1876).

Stern, Philip J. and Wennerlind, Carl, eds. *Mercantilism Reimagined: Political Economy in Early Modern Britain and Its Empire* (New York, 2014).

Stewart, John B. *Opinion and Reform in Hume's Political Philosophy* (Princeton, NJ, 1992).

Stewart, M. A. 'The Stoic Legacy in the Early Scottish Enlightenment', in Margaret J. Osler, ed., *Atoms, Pneuma, and Tranquility: Epicurean and Stoic Themes in European Thought* (Cambridge, 1991), pp. 273–96.

'Two Species of Philosophy: The Historical Significance of the First *Enquiry*', in Peter Millican, ed., *Reading Hume on Human Understanding* (Oxford, 2002), pp. 67–95.

Stockhorst, Stefanie. 'Introduction. Cultural Transfer through Translation: A Current Perspective in Enlightenment Studies', in Stefanie Stockhorst, ed., *Cultural Transfer through Translation: The Circulation of Enlightened Thought in Europe by Means of Translation* (Amsterdam, 2010), pp. 7–26.

Straka, Gerald. 'The Final Phase of Divine Right Theory in England, 1688–1702', *English Historical Review*, 77 (1962), pp. 638–58.

Stuart-Buttle, Tim. *From Moral Theology to Moral Philosophy: Cicero and Visions of Humanity from Locke to Hume* (Oxford, 2019).

'"An Authority from Which There Can Be No Appeal": The Place of Cicero in Hume's Science of Man', *Journal of Scottish Philosophy*, 18 (2020), pp. 289–309.

Susato, Ryu. *Hume's Sceptical Enlightenment* (Edinburgh, 2015).

'Hume as an *Ami de la Liberté*: The Reception of His "Idea of a Perfect Commonwealth"', *Modern Intellectual History*, 13 (2016), pp. 569–96.

Taylor, Jacqueline A. *Reflecting Subjects: Passion, Sympathy, and Society in Hume's Philosophy* (Oxford, 2015).

Thompson, Martyn P. 'Reception Theory and the Interpretation of Historical Meaning', *History and Theory*, 32 (1993), pp. 248–72.

Tolonen, Mikko. *Mandeville and Hume: Anatomists of Civil Society* (Oxford, 2013).

Tolonen, Mikko, Mäkelä, Eetu, Ijaz, Ali, and Lahti, Leo. 'Corpus Linguistics and Eighteenth Century Collections Online (ECCO)', *Research in Corpus Linguistics*, 9 (2021), pp. 19–34.

Tolonen, Mikko, Hill, Mark, Ijaz, Ali, Vaara, Ville, Lahti, Leo. 'Examining the Early Modern Canon: The English Short Title Catalogue and Large-Scale Patterns of Cultural Production', in Ileana Baird, ed., *Data Visualization in Enlightenment Literature and Culture* (London, 2021), pp. 63–119.

Tomaselli, Sylvana. 'Moral Philosophy and Population Questions in Eighteenth-Century Europe', in M. S. Teitelbaum and J. M. Winter, eds., *Population and Development Review: Supplement*, 14 (1988), pp. 7–29.

 Wollstonecraft: Philosophy, Passion, and Politics (Princeton, NJ, 2021).

Townsend, Dabney. *Hume's Aesthetic Theory: Taste and Sentiment* (New York, 2001).

Tribe, Keith. *Governing Economy. The Reformation of German Economic Discourse 1750–1840* (Cambridge, 1988).

 The Economy of the Word: Language, History, and Economics (Oxford, 2015).

Tucker, G. S. L. *Progress and Profits in British Economic Thought, 1650–1850* (Cambridge, 1960).

Tully, James. *A Discourse on Property: John Locke and His Adversaries* (Cambridge, 1980).

Turco, Luigi. 'Hutcheson and Hume in a Recent Polemic', in Emilio Mazza and Emanuele Ronchetti, eds., *New Essays on David Hume* (Milan, 2007), pp. 171–98.

Venturi, Franco 'Scottish Echoes in Eighteenth-Century Italy', in Istvan Hont and Michael Ignatieff, eds., *Wealth and Virtue: The Shaping of Political Economy in the Scottish Enlightenment* (Cambridge, 1986), pp. 345–62.

Vesanto, Aleksi. 'Detecting and Analyzing Text Reuse with BLAST' (MA dissertation, University of Turku, 2019).

Vesanto, Aleksi, Salakoski, Asko Nivala Tapio, Salmi, Hannu, and Ginter, Filip. 'A System for Identifying and Exploring Text Repetition in Large Historical Document Corpora', *Proceedings of the 21st Nordic Conference of Computational Linguistics*, Gothenburg, Sweden, May 23–24, 2017. Linköping Electronic Conference Proceedings, pp. 330–33.

Vickers, Douglas. *Studies in the Theory of Money, 1690–1776* (Philadelphia, PA, 1959).

Viner, Jacob. *Studies in the Theory of International Trade* (New York, 1937).

 'Power versus Plenty as Objectives of Foreign Policy in the Seventeenth and Eighteenth Centuries', in Jacob Viner, *Essays on the Intellectual History of Economics*, ed. Douglas A. Irwin (Princeton, NJ, 1991), pp. 128–53.

Waszek, Norbert. 'Bibliography of the Scottish Enlightenment in Germany', *Studies on Voltaire and the Eighteenth Century*, 230 (1985), pp. 283–303.

Watkins, Margaret. *The Philosophical Progress of Hume's Essays* (Cambridge, 2019).

Weber, Lina. 'Predicting the Bankruptcy of England: David Hume's *Political Discourses* and the Dutch Debate on National Debt in the Eighteenth Century', *Early Modern Low Countries* 1 (2017), pp. 135–55.

Wei, Jia. 'Maritime Trade as the Pivot of Foreign Policy in Hume's *History of Great Britain*', *Hume Studies*, 40 (2014), pp. 169–203.

Commerce and Politics in Hume's History of England (Woodbridge, 2017).

Wennerlind, Carl. 'An Artificial Virtue and the Oil of Commerce: A Synthetic View of Hume's Theory of Money', in Carl Wennerlind and Margaret Schabas, eds., *David Hume's Political Economy* (London, 2008), pp. 105–27.

Whelan, Frederick. *Order and Artifice in Hume's Political Philosophy* (Princeton, NJ, 1985).

Willenberg, Jennifer. *Distribution und Übersetzung Englischen Schrifttums im Deutschland des 18. Jahrhunderts* (Munich, 2008).

Young, David B. 'Libertarian Demography: Montesquieu's Essay on Depopulation in the *Lettres Persanes*', *Journal of the History of Ideas*, 36 (1975), pp. 669–82.

Index

Kant's *Groundwork of the Metaphysics of Morals*
EDITED BY JENS TIMMERMANN
Kant's *Idea for a Universal History with a Cosmopolitan Aim*
EDITED BY AMÉLIE OKSENBERG RORTY AND JAMES SCHMIDT
Mill's *On Liberty*
EDITED BY C. L. TEN
Hegel's *Phenomenology of Spirit*
EDITED BY DEAN MOYAR AND MICHAEL QUANTE